Frontispiece   Governor Thomas Hutchinson

THE LOYALISTS
OF MASSACHUSETTS
THEIR MEMORIALS, PETITIONS
AND CLAIMS

BY

E. ALFRED JONES, M.A., F.S.A.

Author of

"The Old Silver of the American Churches"
"American Members of the Inns of Court"
and of "The Loyalists of New Jersey"

*With 63 Portraits
in Photogravure*

CLEARFIELD

Originally published
London, 1930

Reprinted by
Genealogical Publishing Company
Baltimore, Maryland, 1969

Library of Congress Catalog Number 71-86810

Reprinted for Clearfield Company by
Genealogical Publishing Company
Baltimore, Maryland
1995, 2012

ISBN 978-0-8063-0196-9

Made in the United States of America

PREFACE

IN addition to those whose names are mentioned in the text, I desire to express my appreciation of help from the following : The Frick Art Reference Library, New York ; Mr. Henry W. Belknap, of the Essex Institute, Salem ; Mr. William T. A. Fitzgerald, Register of Deeds for Suffolk County ; Mr. Francis H. Bigelow ; Mr. Otis G. Hammond, of the New Hampshire Historical Society ; Mr. Henry Stoddart Ruggles, of Wakefield, Massachusetts ; Mrs. Austin Wadsworth ; Mr. C. K. Bolton, of the Boston Atheneum ; Mr. Julius H. Tuttle, Librarian of the Massachusetts Historical Society ; the Museum of Fine Arts, Boston ; and Mrs. Alfred Henry Tetlow.

To the owners of portraits, whose names are recorded in the List of Portraits and in the text, I am especially indebted for permission to illustrate them and for their generous gifts of photographs.

Since the printing of the text some few changes in the ownership of portraits have occurred, namely: The portrait of John Gray is on loan from Mrs. W. Arthur Dupee at the Museum of Fine Arts at Boston. Daniel Leonard's miniature belongs to the Taunton Historical Society. Joshua Loring's portrait is no longer in the possession of the British and Foreign Bible Society. The present owner of the three Oliver portraits is William H. P. Oliver, Esq. Mrs. Percy Stuart Maroney is the owner of the pastel of Dr. William Paine. The portrait of Benjamin Thompson (Count Rumford) is in the National Portrait Gallery in London, and that of Governor John Wentworth in the New York Public Library.

E. ALFRED JONES.

INTRODUCTION

THE genesis of this work is to be found in the bundles of original and unpublished Loyalist manuscripts in the Public Record Office in London. Many of these documents have, unfortunately, perished from neglect in the past, while others are unfit for perusal from damp and other natural causes.

In the bundles catalogued as Audit Office 13 are the original memorials and petitions, with letters, certificates to military service and loyal conduct, original commissions, great numbers of documents relating to real and personal property, conveyances of estates, copies of wills and other papers of interest.

Happily, the memorials and petitions would seem to have been copied in detail and recorded in large volumes, with the evidence of witnesses for or against the claimants and the comments of the Commissioners and the amounts of the rewards and pensions, and are described as Audit Office 12 (A.O. 12.)

Throughout these pages the loyalists have been allowed to declare their sentiments in their own words, as expressed in their petitions and memorials.

The Act of Parliament appointing Commissioners to enquire into the losses of the loyalists was passed in 1783, and the above-mentioned memorials and petitions, in the handwriting of the loyalists or, in the case of the illiterate, in that of their agents, were submitted to the first Commissioners appointed, who included John Eardley-Wilmot and Daniel Parker Coke, both members of the Bar and independent members of Parliament, and both generally opposed to the Government's American policy. These two eminent men had already been painfully familiar with the distress of the American loyalist refugees in London, having been appointed in July, 1782, by Lord Shelburne to enquire into the cases of those who were in receipt of temporary allowances from the Treasury, and of those who were claiming public assistance.

The Commissioners sat in the charming seventeenth-century house, called Newcastle House, still standing in Lincoln's Inn Fields, and here they listened in person to the sufferings and claims of the refugees then in London and to many others who fled from America immediately upon the conclusion of the war, while later the petitions of those exiles who sought refuge in Nova Scotia and New Brunswick were examined on the spot by other Commissioners.

Not without interest are the views of the loyalists as expressed by the two Commissioners. Coke, in a debate in the House of Commons on June 26, 1786, observed that " when he entered upon the execution of his duty as a Commissioner to investigate the cases of those unfortunate sufferers, he was far from having a predilection in their favour, but that in the course of his Enquiries, he had discovered such merit and sufferings, and such fidelity and attachmnt to this Governmt that he now entertained the warmest Sentiments in their favour, that he always considered the

House as pledged to grant the full amount of the Losses, as they were liquidated, and under that Idea, he had been intent to pass them down & reject them unless they were proved in the most satisfactory manner. That he was surprized after the House had been called upon to grant £700,000 for the purpose of erecting useless Fortifications, there could be any hesitation to comply with a demand so evidently founded in the principles of Justice and humanity."

"Mr. Wilmot began with observing that when he entered upon his duty as a Commissioner, the Conduct and the situation of the Loyalists had raised in his mind a predilection in their favour, which continually increased as he proceeded in the business. That for near four years past, his daily and almost his hourly labour had been employed in that service, and during the course of it he had received such proofs of fidelity & attachment and sufferings and distress, as in his opinion justly entitled them to every mark of favour and attention, which the Government could confer . . . . That it was his earnest wish the House could replace them in situations equal to what they had lost in America. But that was not possible, double the sum liquidated by the Commissions would not indemnify them, and besides most of them had to lament the loss of a Husband, Father, Son, or Brother, who fell in defence of the cause of this Country."

Wilmot in 1815 published his "Historical View of the Commission for enquiring into the Losses, Services, and Claims of the American Loyalists . . . . with an Account of the Compensation granted to them by Parliament in 1785 and 1788," in which he gives a short account of the result of the enquiry and of "the liberal compensation granted to that suffering and meritorious class of his Majesty's subjects, which redounds, and must for ever redound, so highly to the honor of the British nation."

He adds a note on the motives of the loyalists in these words :

There were "a considerable number in each province who, from various motives, took part at first with the Mother Country in this contest ; some from their native attachment ; and what they thought their duty to their Sovereign ; others from their official situations ; many from policy, the dread of Civil War, and of its issue ; and many more, perhaps, from an opinion that Great Britain would soon relax from the rigour of her demands, or at least would never abuse the power she claimed ; but on the contrary, confine it within such limits, and subject it to such restrictions, as would remove all just cause of dissatisfaction, and prevent all possibility of future abuse and oppression.

"This was the case in the years 1773 and 1774, prior to the declaration of the American Congress, setting forth 'the causes of their taking up arms,' and previously to their Declaration of Independence in July, 1776. But when these measures were adopted by the Congress, and by the Colonies at large, and when Great Britain had, in 1776, shewn a fixed determination to support her Authority by force of arms, accompanied with conciliatory propositions, and a disposition 'to revise the Laws by which the Americans might think themselves aggrieved' ; the friends of Great Britain, who now came to be all denominated Loyalists, encreased in number, and were joined, not only by many men of property and abilities who had hitherto taken no part, but also by many who had been adverse to her at the first, and even by some of the Members of Congress itself." (*Ib.*, pp. 4–5.)

The most powerful families in Massachusetts, whether in the law or commerce, are represented among the loyalists, and there is scarcely a name of distinction which is not found in these pages.

Sir Francis Bernard, the able Governor, finds a place here (although he never set foot in America after 1768) as the writer of letters on his position in the disturbed times of 1765 and 1766, when he expressed the hope that the unpopular Stamp Act might be abandoned.

At the head of the list stands his successor, Thomas Hutchinson, who declared that Bernard would have been regarded as one of the best of New England Governors if he had left America just after the gift to him of Mount Desert by the province in 1762 for his services in the war with France—an island soon (1779) to be confiscated by the State which had given it to him. Thomas Hutchinson was not only the last Royal Governor of Massachusetts, but also the chief member of a notable family. After a long and distinguished career of public service as statesman, jurist, and historian, always guided by a conscientious desire to be loyal both to his native province and to the Crown,* he died a refugee in London in 1780.

The Coffin family of Boston, notable for services to the Crown, is represented by John Coffin, who took a distinguished part in the defence of Quebec in the siege by the Americans under Montgomery. Another was Jonathan Perrie Coffin, whose brothers were William Coffin, General John Coffin and Admiral Sir Isaac Coffin.

John Chandler—the "Honest Tory," member of the Provincial Council, Colonel of militia, magistrate, a leading advocate of the "Worcester Protest," which he was compelled to renounce to save himself from death and subscribe to "a very treasonable league and covenant"—and several of his sons were active loyalists.

A man of many accomplishments was Samuel Curwen, of Salem, whose political differences with his wife caused him to write that on no account was her dust to be mingled with that of his own family, and that he would be "not a little deranged" to find her arising by his side on the Resurrection morning. Both their portraits hang together in the Essex Institute at Salem, whither he returned after the peace.

Timothy Dwight, of Northampton, was deprived of all his public offices for his zealous loyalty, and after suffering actual confinement from 1774, escaped and sailed in April 1776 to the Mississippi, where he attempted with members of his family to form a settlement, but died there just over a year later.

Then there is the stern and unbending George Erving, "Mandamus Councillor," who regarded the Boston Post Bill of 1774 as a punishment

---

* Memorial in the First Church, Boston, erected by the Colonial Society of Massachusetts in 1917.

to the innocent and a reward for the guilty. Tradesmen and other inferior persons, the chief agents in the outrages (he says) found themselves more at ease than they had ever been before. In a later memorial (1786) he expresses his mortification at the favour shown by the British Government to the " American rebels " in contrast with the neglect of the loyalists who had hazarded everything and lost all in maintaining their fidelity to the Crown. His brothers, John and William, were also loyalists.

Among the officials none were more prominent than Thomas Flucker, Secretary of Massachusetts and stern critic of the motives of some loyalists and of their claims for compensation.

One of the most distinguished was Dr. Sylvester Gardiner, who complains of the evasion in Massachusetts of the fifth and sixth articles of the provisional Treaty of Peace. Many loyalists (he says) had in consequence of the Treaty attempted to return to their former homes in America, but were either seized and imprisoned, or sent back whence they came with " usage of severity."

The Goldthwait family is represented by Colonel Thomas Goldthwait and his two sons, Henry and Thomas, and his nephew, Captain Philip Goldthwait. Other members of the same family were also loyal, namely, his brothers, Joseph and Ezekiel, and his three nephews, Joseph, Samuel and Michael B. Goldthwait.

None was more respected than Harrison Gray, the elder, Treasurer and Receiver General of Massachusetts. His two sons and brother were equally loyal.

Francis Green proudly claims descent from " ancestors emigrated from Great Britain at the settlement of New England, who (in an honorable succession in public stations in America) have transmitted to him the principles of loyalty to the Crown." He served as an officer in the 40th Foot at Louisburg, in Canada, and at Martinique and Havana. Not only was he a vigorous loyalist early in the Revolution, but in 1775 he was appointed Captain of the third company of the Associated Volunteers of Boston, and later equipped certain vessels for service in the war. After returning to Massachusetts in 1797, he devoted the remainder of his life to the education of deaf mutes, as an act of poignant remembrance of the affliction of his son, Charles, who was both deaf and dumb.

Next may be mentioned Benjamin Hallowell, Comptroller of the Customs, the writer of a letter in 1774, stating that the passing of the Quebec Act in 1774 [an important measure in the history of religious liberty] had had an amazing effect in Massachusetts in increasing the clamour and opposition to the mother country. His eldest son, Nicholas Ward Boylston, is numbered among the loyal, while another son attained high rank in the Royal Navy as Admiral Sir Benjamin Hallowell-Carew. His brother, Robert Hallowell, was Deputy Comptroller and afterwards Comptroller of the Customs at Boston.

The Hatch family provides Colonel Nathaniel Hatch, member of the Provincial Council, and his son Paxton, who, while a student at Philadelphia College, refused to forsake his loyalty, and consequently suffered insults and reproaches, and was denied the common necessaries of life.

Henry Hulton, Commissioner of Customs, was an educated and cultured man, as is revealed in the interesting letters of his spinster sister, Ann, published as *Letters of a Loyalist* (1927).

Colonel Elisha Jones, a member of the General Assembly, was an ardent loyalist and left eleven sons, eight of whom served in the British forces and the others in divers ways. Joshua Loring, the elder, is recorded as a fervent loyalist, and as the father of four sons in the British service. Equally loyal was the Murray family.

The Oliver families are represented by Lieutenant Governor Andrew Oliver and his two sons, Brinley Sylvester and Daniel ; Peter Oliver, last Chief Justice under the Crown, and his son, Peter ; and by Thomas Oliver, the last Lieutenant Governor under appointment from England.

Sir William Pepperell, with his brothers, is included, as is also his distinguished father-in-law, Isaac Royall, a man of moderate Whig views, who in 1774 had written to Lord Dartmouth assuring him of the loyalty of the people, though they were jealous of their constitutional rights, and expressing the opinion that if the Revenue Act were repealed harmony would be restored between America and England. The memory of Isaac Royall is cherished to this day at Harvard as a benefactor by his legacy founding the first Professorship of Law. Three members of Sir William Pepperell's family, the Sparhawks, are recorded here, but not John Sparhawk, the writer of a letter from Portsmouth, New Hampshire, to Pepperell saying that " when the Contest is between Lawless Mobs on the one side, and the three Estates of the British Empire on the other—the Laws of God and man, as well as the principles of honor and policy clearly point which side we ought to take." (A.O. 13/97.)

The distinguished part taken by Brigadier General Timothy Ruggles, with his sons, is mentioned later.

Nathaniel Ray Thomas was, as member of the Mandamus Council, leader of the loyalists of Marshfield, which had " through a ten years' political struggle and warfare, never deviated from, but had uniformly and invariably preserved and maintained its Integrity and Loyalty "—the only town in New England which had, " in spite of the threats and intimidations of surrounding Towns, counties, and Provinces, dared, publickly and collectively to own and acknowledge " the allegiance of the inhabitants, and the supremacy of the British legislature. At length he was obliged to leave his home, accompanied by nearly 200 loyalists.

Benjamin Thompson, the future Count Rumford, was the well-known commander of the King's American Dragoons.

John Vassall was a representative of a family as prominent in the West Indies as in Massachusetts, while Francis Waldo was the bearer of a name prominent in the early history of New England.

Not the least conspicuous was Abijah Willard who had served with the Massachusetts forces at Louisburg in 1745, was a " Mandamus Councillor," and became a member of the first Provincial Council of New Brunswick.

The honoured name of Winslow is enshrined in the history of loyalism through several members of the family. Edward, whose ancestor was Governor of the Plymouth Colony from 1620, served with great honour in several public stations in Plymouth County—a veteran loyalist who was for nine years the " butt of the licentious " and " the victim of every species of insult and abuse which the utmost rancour and malice could invent to a man at the age of 67." His son of the same name became a Judge of the Supreme Court of New Brunswick, and his *Winslow Papers* are a mine of information on the origins of that Canadian province.

The ministry of the predominant religious faith in New England, the Congregationalist, finds only one representative here, though other ministers of much influence in that body were loyalists, as is shown elsewhere.* This is the venerable Mather Byles, the elder, who, in 1775, was deprived of his pastorate at Hollis Street Church in Boston, where he had laboured with zeal and credit for 43 years, and maintained his loyalty to the last hour. For the remaining thirteen years of his life he subsisted on the daily charity of the loyal subjects in Boston. His son of the same name was a convert from Congregationalism to Episcopacy.

The leader of the Episcopal clergy was the aged Rev. Henry Caner, Rector of King's Chapel, Boston, a cultivated scholar and the proud owner of a large library of nearly 1,000 books, besides pamphlets and other works, who had been a warm advocate for a resident Bishop in the American Colonies. He was held in great respect by his flock and was suggested by men of influence as the first Bishop of the new Colony of Penobscot. Rather than allow the historic silver vessels, given to King's Chapel by William III, George II, and George III, to be desecrated by the " rebels " he carried them away to Nova Scotia. His curate, the Rev. John Troutbeck, likewise was a sufferer and an exile for his loyalty. After their flight from Boston the services of King's Chapel were conducted for a while by the Rev. Winwood Serjeant, of Christ Church, Cambridge, Massachusetts (detained at Boston by illness), whose devotion to the Crown was such that he refused to substitute prayers for the Congress for those for the King, and rather than omit the latter he closed King's Chapel and followed others into exile.

Another Boston clergyman, the Rev. William Walter, makes the assertion that he was the only clergyman in the town to condemn in public the unchristian acts of violence which the mob showed in 1767 to Andrew Oliver, Distributor of Stamps.

The name of the Rev. William McGilchrist, the beloved Rector of St. Peter's, Salem, finds no place here, for he had died in 1780, steadfast in loyalty and in determination not to read the Declaration of Independence or to abandon reading the prayers for the King and Royal family during Divine Service.

None suffered greater persecution for his loyalty than the Rev. William Clark, of Dedham.

* *The New England Clergy and the American Revolution,* by Alice M. Baldwin, 1928, p. 159.

Rather than swear allegiance to the United States and abjure his Sovereign, the Rev. Joshua Wingate Weeks suffered persecution for nearly four years, and finally fled from his home at Marblehead. In his original Journal,* a valuable commentary of the times, he complains with a tinge of bitterness of the neglect of the loyalists by the British, whereas the Americans " hang the turbulent, imprison the dangerous, fine the wealthy. They allure the ambitious with the hopes of preferment and distribute estates to those who have lost their property for the sake of joining them. And by such means as these, they have strengthened their cause amazingly whereas on the part of the King nothing has ever been done of this kind." Of his eight children four became officers in the British army.

The last name to be enrolled in these pages is that of the Rev. John Wiswall, an ardent loyalist.

Other faiths are those of the Sandemanians, represented here by three members of the Church at Boston—" that goodliest of all sights "—a church which was founded at Portsmouth, New Hampshire, by Robert Sandeman himself in 1765 and included some loyalists. The Quakers comprise the Bowers family, of Swansea, chief of whom was Jerathmel Bowers, and William Horton. There would, however, seem to have been loyalist Quakers at Dartmouth, among whom George Gay sought refuge early in the rebellion.

The list of loyalists includes a great number of lawyers or men with some legal training, twenty-eight of whom rank as Harvard men. Taking them, not in order of personal distinction, but in alphabetical arrangement, Robert Auchmuty comes first, as Advocate General and Judge of the Vice-Admiralty Court, counsel for Captain Preston in the so-called " Boston Massacre " case and a faithful servant of the Crown ; Daniel Bliss, brother of Jonathan Bliss (also a loyalist and afterwards Chief Justice of Nova Scotia) ; and Sampson Salter Blowers, attorney for Captain Preston and the soldiers of the 29th Regiment in the second case and for a short time during the occupation of New York by the British, Solicitor General of New York, afterwards Attorney General, Judge and Chief Justice successively in Nova Scotia.

A fourth was Judge William Brattle, lawyer, theologian, physician, and soldier. William Browne, a great territorial magnate, of Salem, had some legal training and was Judge of the Superior Court of Massachusetts in 1774 and claims to have been offered the dignified office of Governor of the Province as an inducement to forsake his loyalty ; he was compensated by the British Government as some token of appreciation of his steadfast support of the Crown by being appointed Governor of Bermuda, where two more loyalist lawyers, Andrew Cazneau, " a gentleman of character, talents and virtue " became Judge of the Vice-Admiralty Court and member of the Council ; and Daniel Leonard, mentioned later. Ward Chipman, pupil of the two eminent lawyers, Jonathan Sewall and Daniel Leonard, achieved prominence within a few years as Solicitor General and

* In the possession of the Marblehead Hist. Soc. and published in the Collections of the Essex Institute of Salem, 1916.

Judge of the Supreme Court of New Brunswick and as agent of Great Britain in the Treaty of Ghent.

Samuel Fitch was Advocate General of Massachusetts and one of the founders of a club of young lawyers in Boston. Benjamin Gridley was known as a spirited loyalist, as a writer in the Boston newspapers between 1765 and 1776 in defence and support of the British Government, and as a magistrate who had on one occasion put the Mutiny Act in force to suppress the attempts to bribe British soldiers to desert. As an exile in London he joined the Volunteer Force raised by Sir William Pepperell shortly after the sealing of the alliance between France and America. Martin Howard, the able Chief Justice of North Carolina, is included as the owner of pro- perty in Boston.

Distinguished as a lawyer and as author of the well-known letters under the *nom de guerre* of *Massachusettensis*, was Daniel Leonard, who was rewarded by the position of Attorney General and member of the Council of Bermuda, where his colleagues were the above-mentioned William Browne and Andrew Cazneau. His kinsman was George Leonard, of whom the Rev. Joshua Wingate Weeks says in his Journal that he was eagerly engaged in crushing the rebellion and that he took an active part at Lexington.

James Putnam, of Worcester (whose most notable legal pupil was John Adams, second President of the United States), aroused bitter enmity for his authorship of the " Worcester Protest," mentioned in the Appendix. His name is for ever recorded as last Attorney General of Massachusetts under the Crown—an office which he had previously declined in 1768. Samuel Quincy, last Solicitor General before the Revolution, shared with Daniel Leonard and Jonathan Sewall, the intimate and confidential and bosom friendship of John Adams.

A man of many parts was Timothy Ruggles, for he was Colonel and Commander-in-Chief of the Massachusetts troops through the long campaigns against the French in North America between 1755 and 1763, Speaker of the House of Representatives of Massachusetts, breeder and owner of a celebrated stud of horses, and a staunch supporter of what he called the " best government both in theory and administration that had ever blest the earth." At the age of 64 he volunteered to raise a regiment of 1,500 men to quell the rebellion* and in 1775 he warned the British Government against appointing smugglers to the vacancies in the Provin- cial Council, as most of the political troubles of the past (he says) had arisen from the power of such men. Three sons were loyalists.

Joshua Upham, active in the war, became one of the first Judges of the Supreme Court of New Brunswick, as well as member of the Executive

---

* A copy of his Association, dated December 22, 1774, contains this paragraph :—
" That we will, upon all occasions, with our lives and fortunes, stand by and assist each other in the defence of his life, liberty, and property, whenever the same shall be attacked or endangered by any bodies of men, riotously assembled upon any pre- tence, or under any authority not warranted by the laws of the land." (*American Archives, op. cit.* Ser. IV, vol. i, pp. 1057-8.)

and Legislative Council of that province, where so many loyalists had sought refuge.

Then there are other lawyers, as James Boutineau, descendant of French settlers in Boston ; Rufus Chandler ; Thomas Danforth ; David Ingersoll ; Samuel Porter, of Salem ; Jeremiah Dummer Rogers ; Seth Williams and Abel Willard.

Of the same number was Jonathan Sewall, Solicitor-General and Attorney-General of Massachusetts, regarded by friend and political foe alike as unsurpassed at the Bar in intellectual eminence as a lawyer and advocate, and in lively wit and brilliant imagination, though perhaps not the equal as a lawyer of Daniel Dulany, of Maryland, also a loyalist. He is one of many loyalists who have rendered noble service to Canada or have given sons to the service of that country, his two sons, Jonathan and Stephen, having risen to legal eminence—the first as Chief Justice, and the second as Solicitor-General in the province of Quebec.

Just as most of the lawyers were loyal to the Crown, so too were the leading physicians, surgeons and apothecaries. From Townshend, famed for the number of its Tories, came Dr. Joseph Adams, a most resolute loyalist. Dr. Thomas Boulton was active and unwearied in support of the British Government, having served at Lexington and Bunker Hill, and in defence of Quebec during the siege by the Americans. Before his flight from Boston he had delivered the humorous and satirical parody of Dr. Warren's " Treasonable Oration," which was afterwards printed. Dr. John Calef was also a sufferer for his loyalty. He had served his country in the naval and military forces in the Colonial wars, and as surgeon of the *Massachusetts* frigate at the siege of Louisburg, became a member of the House of Representatives and was active in promoting the scheme for the settlement of Penobscot as a haven of refuge for the persecuted loyalists. The names of John Jeffries and William Lee Perkins deserve permanent recognition in the medical history of Massachusetts, the first for his course of lectures on anatomy in Boston in 1765, which ante-dated by sixteen years those of Dr. John Warren, for long regarded as the first medical lecturer in the province, and the second for the first medical lectures in Massachusetts. Dr. Jeffries ranks as one of the earliest aeronauts as a passenger in Blanchard's balloon in the crossing of the Straits of Dover in 1785.

Dr. Nathaniel Perkins is described as the most eminent physician in Massachusetts, while Dr. James Lloyd was " most forward and open and determined in his opposition to the rebellion, to a degree of imprudence."

The name of one of the founders of the American Antiquarian Society, Dr. William Paine, is to be found here with that of Dr. Samuel Stearns, author of *Astronomical Observations,* and in 1786 of a moving pamphlet on the severe treatment accorded to him in attempting to remove his family from Massachusetts after the war. Dr. Stearns was imprisoned at Worcester for 35 months without trial, in violation of the Treaty of Peace.

But there are other medical men mentioned in this book as well as

some who are not included here as memorialists—namely, Dr. Samuel
Danforth, who was suffered to remain unmolested in Boston because of
the scarcity of qualified physicians and surgeons ; Dr. John Joy ; Michael
B. Goldthwait ; Dr. Miles Whitworth ; and Benjamin Loring.

Two teachers may be mentioned—namely, Richard Holland, acting
at Boston under the Society for the Propagation of the Gospel, and
during the war a Lieutenant in the Loyal New Englanders and in another
loyalist corps. The second, the Rev. Robert Boucher Nickolls, claims to
have been the only person in Massachusetts who had any share in the
instruction of youth in principles at all favourable to the union of the
colonies with the mother country, all the seminaries of learning in New
England having been solely calculated to form republicans and independents in Church matters. A man of no ordinary stamp, he was presented
some time after his flight to England with a living and was closely associated as a pamphleteer and preacher with Wilberforce and Granville
Sharp in the suppression of the slave traffic.

Greater than either of these (though his name does not appear as a
claimant, having died in 1778) was John Lovell, headmaster of the famous
Latin School at Boston, the nursery of many conspicuous men, two of
whose sons were loyalists, while a third, James, was as active on the other
side of the great conflict.

Another name not unworthy of notice is that of Isaac da Costa, who
would seem to have published in London in 1775, " A Plan of the Town
and Harbour of Boston and the Country Adjacent with the Road from
Boston to Concord . . . "—an interesting plan showing the " Place of
the late Engagement between the King's troops and the Provincials," and
Concord and Lexington.

Here also are the names of fifty heroic women who suffered exile
rather than abjure their Sovereign. Among them is the name of Anna
Borland, who fled from Boston to prevent her sons from joining the
" rebel army." Similarly, Jane Gordon bought commissions for three
sons in the British army, that they might be saved from serving with the
Americans, the eldest of whom attained the rank of Major-General.
Hannah Cordis, herself a fervent loyalist and landlady of the celebrated
British Coffee House in Boston, the scene of many stirring episodes, is
here, as is also Margaret Draper, who, after her husband's death in 1774,
continued to print her newspaper, *The Massachusetts Gazette, or Boston
Weekly News Letter*, and thwarted, in face of persecution, all attempts
to make it " subservient to the party of rebellion," until at last she too
was compelled to join other refugees in the flight from Boston. All ranks
in society are represented. Thus we find Rebecca Hallowell, whose
mansion house in Boston was let by the State of Massachusetts to
Samuel Adams* in 1776, and by him left in a ruinous condition in 1784,
when he was followed there by Joseph Coolidge by the indulgence of the

* A copy of the resolve granting him certain articles of furniture of absentee
loyalists, as compensation for his unpaid salary as Clerk of the House of Representatives, is in *A.O.* 12/82, f.8.

same authority. Another victim of the Revolution was Elizabeth Dumaresq, born and educated in the style of a gentlewoman, but obliged to engage herself as a servant. Recorded in these pages are the names of Elizabeth Loring, who figured in a romance with the Commander-in-Chief, Sir William Howe; Dorcas Griffith, the discarded mistress of John Hancock; and Mary Hutchinson, president of a club of eight loyalist ladies, who met at tea once or twice weekly at Boston, "in opposition to the Rebells."

In the same company is to be found Mary Dwight, of Northampton, who, after the flight of her husband Timothy to the Mississippi, "suffered every evil that misguided zeal, vulgar ignorance and virulence could dictate." Not only was she denied the common intercourse and civil offices of her friends, but as a loyalist she was compelled to pay heavy contributions and military mulcts, while her children and domestics were pressed into the American service, upon pain of imprisonment.

Among the names are some ninety graduates of Harvard, but these do not comprise all the loyalist members of that College, who numbered just over 200, counting those published in the *Harvard Graduates' Magazine* (Vol. 14, No. 54, pp. 358–360). One name is that of Daniel Leonard, the lawyer, who had been Captain of the "Harvard Fencibles," a military company formed in 1757; and another is George Inman, whose father, upon taking his degree, gave the "genteelest entertainment" ever seen in New England on any occasion. Two of the 400 guests at this dinner were Henry Hulton, one of the Commissioners of Customs, and his spinster sister, Ann, whose lively letters on events during the early part of the American Revolution have been published. Ann Hulton remarks that here is a college indeed, but the independence, liberty, and indulgence of the youths made too many of them proficient in vice.

Graduates of Yale comprise the venerable divine, the Rev. Henry Caner, and Timothy Dwight, who perished in the abortive attempt to form an asylum for the loyalists on the Mississippi and was the father of Timothy Dwight, the future President of the College. Two more were the eminent lawyers, Samuel Fitch and David Ingersoll.

Many of the more prosperous merchants, traders and owners of vessels may be found recorded here. One was Jolly Allen, "a shrewd, dashing, thriving man, and a loyalist, body and soul," who died a refugee in 1782 at Wapping, once a busy port on the Thames, and was buried among his forbears. In his will he bequeathed cauls (charms against death by drowning at sea) to his three children, and expressly desired that his body might be disinterred after the war and taken to Boston to be buried in King's Chapel. Prominent figures in the commercial history of Boston are John Borland, Richard Clarke, and members of the Deblois family. John Bryant died at Morden College, Blackheath, on the outskirts of London, justly famous for the beauty of Sir Christopher Wren's building and for its situation. Here, too, William Randall ended his days in peaceful security, spared from the menace of want. One more conspicuous man was Francis Rotch, an influential and enterprising owner of vessels.

Printers, bookbinders and stationers are numbered among the Boston loyalists, in William Cross and in the Scotsman, William McAlpine. An interesting product of the Revolution was Isaac Clemens, engraver, silversmith and watchmaker, of Boston, whose claim to be a loyalist is founded on his declaration that his efforts " to quell the unnatural rebellion " consisted of " harassing and perplexing the rebels " by counterfeiting their paper currency.

Art is represented by Henry Pelham, a pupil of John Singleton Copley, himself a loyalist, and in his own words, " Copley's successor in all the business of a painter without a rival." Pelham engraved a plate of the " Boston Massacre " in 1770, and allowed the famous Paul Revere, silversmith and engraver, to have the loan of it, with the result that Revere made a copy of it and brought upon himself from Pelham a bitter reproach as a man without honour for having deprived the real author of the expected advantages from the sale of engravings as truly as if he had been plundered on the highway.

Music has its representative in David Propert, the Welsh organist of Trinity Church, Boston, and a pioneer in the art in Massachusetts.

Many deserve an honoured place in the military annals of Massachusetts. One such was Phineas Atherton, who with Isaac da Costa and Major Robert Rogers, the celebrated New Hampshire ranger, was concerned in a project for the discovery of a north-west passage. Isaac da Costa had served as a volunteer at the siege of Louisburg in 1745 and afterwards in Colonial regiments. Colonel Thomas Gilbert—afterwards a member of the General Assembly—was in command of a company of Massachusetts forces in the same celebrated siege, where also served his brother Samuel. Ten years later he was Lieutenant Colonel of provincial forces under that gallant soldier Timothy Ruggles, mentioned on an earlier page, in the expedition against Crown Point, and succeeded Colonel Williams, who was killed on that day. Then there are the members of the Goldthwait family, and Francis Green, whose services are chronicled under their names.

Colonel Joseph Goreham was also present at the sieges of Louisburg, Quebec and Havana, and during the American War of Independence was Lieut.-Colonel Commandant of the Royal Fencible Americans. Two other participants in the siege of Louisburg were Captain David Phipps and Colonel Richard Saltonstall, the last of whom served throughout the long and arduous campaigns against the French, which ended in their loss of Canada and of their power on the North American continent.

John Malcolm, who had seen long service in the same war, claims to have been the first victim of the barbaric tarring and feathering in the American Revolution, suffering indescribable tortures for his fidelity to the Crown and behaving with great intrepidity through all.

The last name is that of Samuel Mather, guilty of disobliging the best of fathers (the Rev. Samuel Mather, the eminent Congregational minister, of Boston) by refusing his advice and commands to quit the service of the King and join the Americans.

In Massachusetts, as in other colonies, many loyalists of military
experience and social rank were offered commands in the American forces.
Joseph Adams could have had the command of several vessels, but holding
as he did rebellion in the greatest abhorrence, he definitely refused the
offers. Captain John Bowen, a retired officer in the regular British army,
received and rejected flattering offers of high rank. George Ellison was
offered a captain's commission, and having refused, he was threatened
with violence. Benjamin Pollard declined important appointments in
the American forces, in which his brother, Jonathan, was Quartermaster
General at Boston, but he would rather have a commission in the army of
the King " to the first place in the gift of the rebels " ; he was killed in
the defence of Savannah in 1779, while his younger brother was serving as
Lieutenant in the Royal Navy.

Offers were also made to John Walker, gentleman, of Shrewsbury,
who had seen active service since 1744 and was present at the sieges of
Louisburg, Quebec and Havana.

Governor Hutchinson said of William McAlpine, the Scottish printer,
bookbinder and stationer, at Boston, that if he had not been well affected
to the British cause he would have been singular in differing from the other
Scotsmen in the town, who were almost without exception good subjects
—*i.e.*, loyalists.

The Loyal North British Volunteers—said to have been the first
volunteer company raised in America " in defence of the constitution "—
to the number of about seventy, were formed for the most part from
Scottish settlers in Boston, commanded by James Anderson. Thomas
Alexander and David Black were Lieutenants, while two of the most active
and prominent were the above-mentioned William McAlpine and Archibald Cunningham, a prosperous merchant and treasurer of the Scots
Charitable Society, established in Boston as early as 1657, the books of
which he took away. Of the twenty-seven members of this old charitable
institution in 1775 no fewer than twenty were banished for loyalty.
Governor John Hancock would seem to have had an eye on the considerable
funds of the Society.

An ardent Scottish loyalist was Major Alexander Campbell, an
officer residing on half-pay in Boston, who after serving at Bunker Hill
volunteered for the hazardous voyage to North Carolina with a company
of ninety men, with the object of enlisting the Highland emigrants in
support of the Crown. Walter Logan, confidential friend of Governor
Sir Francis Bernard, is stated to have been the possessor of the most
practical knowledge of farming in or near Boston. One other staunch
Scottish loyalist must be mentioned, though he had fled before the actual
outbreak of war—namely, John Mein, who had started the *Boston Chronicle*
in 1767.

Among other Scotsmen was James Murray, a conspicuous figure in
the Colonial history of North Carolina as President of the Council, afterwards a settler in Boston and exceedingly active as a magistrate during
the revolutionary disturbances.

Irish settlers in the province were no less loyal. Chief among them was John Murray, of Rutland, representative in the General Assembly, Colonel of militia, and a "Mandamus Councillor," whose four sons evinced their practical loyalty by joining Wentworth's Volunteers.

The Loyal Irish Volunteers were formed on December 7, 1775, from Irish merchants in Boston and their adherents, and were distinguished by a white cockade. Their Captain was James Forrest, a prosperous merchant, who gave two sons to the British forces.

Strong in opposition to the well-known Non-Importation agreement of 1770 were the following great merchants : Henry Barnes, of Marlborough ; Ebenezer Bridgham, who claimed to be the first to break the combination in New England ; Ebenezer Cutler ; and William Jackson, who openly defied it and was consequently boycotted by the "Sons and Daughters of Liberty." To James and Patrick McMaster the credit is given for their opposition to the above agreement, and in October, 1770, they were joyfully received by the inhabitants of Boston, the whole town attributing the abandonment of the scheme to the steady opposition of these two Scotsmen.

Ann Hulton, mentioned earlier, maintained that 90 out of every 100 Boston merchants wished to follow the example of the New York merchants and break through the agreement, but were terrified by the tyranny of the inhabitants.

The settlement of Penobscot is frequently mentioned. General Sir Henry Clinton, Commander-in-Chief of the British army in America, was ordered in September, 1778, to take post on the Penobscot River, with a view to establishing a province as an asylum for the loyalists. William Knox, Under-Secretary of State in the American Department, was foremost in the same year in advocating the occupation of the territory for the same beneficent purpose—a scheme which was denounced by Governor Hutchinson as preposterous in a spot described by Admiral Sir George Collier as "infernal." On the other hand, Colonel Thomas Goldthwait expressed favourable views of the scheme, as he could testify to the advantages of the place from many years' personal knowledge. As to the alleged disaffection of the inhabitants, he would pledge himself (as the main cause of their settlement there, to the number of over 2,400 able-bodied men) that he would raise a battalion among them.*

The Rev. Henry Caner was proposed as the first Bishop of the new colony and Chief Justice Peter Oliver as Governor. Dr. John Calef had done much in helping the scheme and was the author of *The Siege of Penobscot by the Rebels in* 1779 (1781).

Many loyalists had fled to Penobscot for safety, in response to invitations from the British Government, and had built houses and huts on their free grants of land. In April, 1783, by the unexpected evacuation of

* *American MSS. in the Royal Inst., op. cit.,* ii, 18-19, 45. The British Museum copy of *The Proceedings of the General Assembly of Massachusetts relating to the Penobscot Expedition,* 1779, is autographed (a) " Samuel Moody's Book a gift of ye Honr. Caleb Cushing Esq.," and (b) " Samuel G. Drake, Boston, 1858."

Penobscot, over 100 families desired to flee to Nova Scotia, there to enjoy, as they had hoped, the blessings of that Government which they still revered and to escape from the resentment and threats of those against whom they had from principle taken up arms in the royal cause. Many of these refugees settled at St. Andrews in New Brunswick.

Two instances at least are here recorded of the dissolution of marriages by the wives of absentee loyalists, with the approval, it is alleged, of Congress, and of their re-marriage.

There were other volunteer corps associated with Massachusetts : the Loyal New Englanders, under the command of Lieutenant-Colonel George Wightman, with Richard Holland (Luther Hatheway's successor) as Lieutenant, and Shadrach Chace as Ensign ; and the Volunteers of New England, commanded by Lieutenant-Colonel Joshua Upham, with Thomas Cutler as Captain, Oliver Arnold as Lieutenant, and John Murray Upham as Ensign. The Royal Fencible Americans, drawn from other colonies, were commanded by Colonel Joseph Goreham, previously mentioned. The Massachusetts Volunteers formed at New York under Colonel Abijah Willard after the evacuation of Boston by the British, are frequently mentioned.

The loss of objects of art, precious old silver and furniture, is beyond description. Moreover, several important personal libraries were destroyed. Chief among them was that of Governor Hutchinson, whose documents relating to the history of his native province were of incredible value. Next in importance was the library of the Rev. Henry Caner. Richard Acklom Harrison, Collector of Customs at Boston, was the owner of 700 volumes, while Joseph Hooper, a spirited loyalist of Marblehead (where five members of this prominent family are claimed as loyalists), deplored the loss of 500 volumes from his elegant mansion, built only 18 months before his flight.

Charles Paxton, Commissioner of Customs, left a large library, neatly bound and gilt, as well as valuable Italian pictures and old furniture ; he had displayed much concern in 1779 at the prospect of being buried in London, where he feared that his bones might be dug up after a few years and be cast into a common heap, in accordance with a general custom, as he had supposed. Paxton told Governor Hutchinson that he would give 100 guineas to be buried by his parents under King's Chapel, Boston. There were also the libraries of James Putnam and William Latta.

Several loyalists from those parts of Massachusetts now comprised in the State of Maine are also included.

Bitter was the disappointment of the loyalists at the violations of the Treaty of Peace and their failure to recover their just debts. Some, in endeavouring to return to their homes in Massachusetts, were not only denied redress but were brutally ill-treated.

" The inability of Congress to enforce its ordinances and the stipulation of its treaties brought the country at once into conflict with Great Britain. By the fourth, fifth and sixth articles of the treaty no impediments were to be put in the way of the recovery of debts ; the States were to be recommended to repeal their Confiscation Acts; and there were to be no further confiscations nor prosecutions of any sort against any person because of the part taken in the late war. But the States gave no heed whatever to these articles. The Confiscation Acts were not repealed; impediments were placed in the way of recovery of debts; and thousands of loyalists were driven from the country. Indeed, the ink was scarcely dry on the treaty when the loyalists, well knowing that its provisions would be set at naught by a people embittered by a desperate struggle, began to flee the country by thousands." (Professor J. B. McMaster in *The United States*, vol. vii. of the *Cambridge Modern Hist.*, 1903, p. 307.)

Of the 501 loyalists whose petitions, memorials and claims are included in the text, no fewer than 282 were of American birth, 50 more were probably born in America, 55 were English, 25 Scottish, 10 Irish, and 8 of other nationalities. These figures are exclusive of the large number in the Appendixes.

In round figures the total amount of the claims for compensation was £731,000 sterling, which were met by the British Government by the payment of £219,000. In addition considerable sums were paid for losses of official incomes and for pensions and temporary allowances to the distressed loyalists.

Included in the claims were large sums for debts due to the loyalists, but as these were supposed to be recoverable under the Treaty of Peace, no compensation was allowed by the Government.

Like the Huguenots of 1685, the exiled American loyalists enriched many lands by their industry and talents; they were the founders of the Canadian province of New Brunswick; they fled in great numbers, not only to the British Isles, but also to other parts of Canada, Nova Scotia, Prince Edward Island and the West Indies, to seek new homes in strange surroundings, friendless, but yet resolved to start new lives "with true loyalty, invincible courage, and unshaken constancy," and, in the words of the motto of Arthur Savage, a loyalist of Massachusetts,

MALO MORI QUAM FŒDARI,

preferred death to dishonour.

ADDENDA ET CORRIGENDA

PLATE IX.   This portrait is from Peter Pelham's engraving mentioned on page 78.

PLATE XXIII.   The portrait of Dr. Stearns is from his book (page 267, footnote).

PLATE XXXIII.   This portrait, by Smibert, is that of John Lovell, the elder, at Harvard (page 201, footnote).

PLATE XXXIX.   Charles Paxton's portrait is by Cornish, 1751, as mentioned on page 230.

PLATE XLVII.   The portrait is by Copley and is in the possession of Miss Grace W. Treadwell.

PAGE 197.   A portrait of Dr. James Lloyd, by Gilbert Stuart, c. 1808, is in the collection of T. B. Clarke, Esq., New York.

All the portraits illustrated are those mentioned in the text.

LIST OF PLATES

BIBLIOGRAPHY

The references to original sources, where not otherwise mentioned, are to documents in the Public Record Office, London.

APPLETON, *Cyclopedia of American Biography.*

FOOTE, *Annals of King's Chapel, Boston.*

FORCE, *American Archives.*

Hist. MSS. Comm. Report on the American MSS. in the Royal Institution.

Hist. MSS. Comm. Report on the MSS. of the Earl of Dartmouth.

Hist. MSS. Comm. Report on the Stopford-Sackville MSS.

Journal and Letters of Samuel Curwen, ed. by G. A. Ward, 1864.

SABINE, *Biographies of American Loyalists.*

Second Report of the Bureau of Archives of the Province of Ontario, 1904.

J. H. STARK, *The Loyalists of Massachusetts.*

STOCKTON and LAWRENCE, *The Judges of New Brunswick and their Times.*

The Frontier Missionary: A Memoir of the Life of the Rev. Jacob Bailey, ed. by W. S. Bartlet, 1853.

The Royal Commission on American Loyalists' Claims, 1783–1785, ed. by H. E. Egerton for the Roxburghe Club, 1915.

The Loyalists of Massachusetts

DR. JOSEPH ADAMS

of Townshend, surgeon and apothecary, whose duty to his Sovereign and attachment to his country led him early in the disputes to take every method in his power to promote the cause of Great Britain and to take care of the sick and wounded British prisoners of war in Massachusetts. For this charitable office he became so obnoxious to the revolutionary party as to be compelled to flee for protection to the British army in New York in September 1777. (A.O. 13/43.)

As early as 1774 he had communicated to Jonathan Sewall (*q.v.*) the private resolves of Committees of Correspondence and their method of secreting magazines of gunpowder and other warlike stores for rebellious purposes. He had also made known the proceedings of town meetings, which had for their object the subversion of the British Government, to Sewall, Colonel Brattle, of Cambridge, and Colonel Jones, of Weston (*q.v.*), and to Daniel Bliss, Esq., of Charlestown, and Abijah Willard, (*q.v.*). At the risk of his life he refused to sign the solemn league and covenant of the people, and thereby lost the esteem of the inhabitants, suffered imprisonment, was unable to recover his just debts, and was confined to his own town for six months, from April 26, 1775, upon the pain of death. Dr. Adams paid several sums of money as fines for refusing to take up arms against Great Britain, and in particular he paid £14 to one James Parks, a rebel lieutenant, of Lincoln, Massachusetts, in March, 1777. At length he was obliged to flee by night, leaving his wife and property to the mercy of the rebels, and was for thirty days on the journey to New York, at the hazard of his life. Here he joined the Massachusetts Company of Volunteers of Colonel Abijah Willard (*q.v.*). (*Ib.*)

With his memorials are his appointment by Commodore William Hotham, of H.M.S. *Preston*, dated May 18, 1778, as surgeon to the store-ship *Greenwich*, in which he served for eleven months ; a recommendation from Christopher Rigby, commander of the *Greenwich*, dated February 29, 1779, to the Commissioners of the Royal Navy, testifying to the good qualities of Joseph Adams as a loyalist and surgeon, and recommending him for promotion ; copies of a letter and certificate, dated May 1, 1779, and an original certificate, dated September 8, 1784, from Major-General Sir Archibald Campbell, M.P., testifying to his loyalty and to his unremitting attention to the relief and comfort of the British prisoners of war in Massachusetts ; a schedule of his real and personal property ; a certificate and letter from Sir William Pepperell (*q.v.*), dated January 3, 1783, and February 5, 1783, stating that Dr. Joseph Adams's wife in America was destitute of the necessaries of life, and appealing for his promotion to naval surgeon from surgeon's mate to the *Tyger* hospital ship at Plymouth ; a letter from Dr. Adams, dated November

A

23, 1786, from Liskeard in Cornwall (whither he had retired from service on April 12, 1783), to John Forster, of the office of the Commissioners of Loyalists' Claims, mentioning several men of Massachusetts who could testify to his loyalty and sufferings, including Daniel Bliss, his attorney, John Semple, mercer, formerly of Boston and now of Glasgow, and particularly Mr. Farnsworth, an attorney who had transacted considerable business for him in New England before the Revolution; and a certificate of Thomas Mein,* surgeon, Royal Navy, February 20, 1787, that he had known Adams for eight years as a man of whom officers in the British Navy and Army had spoken as the victim of most rigid and cruel persecutions for his loyalty. (*Ib.*)

Joseph Adams had buried in the earth all his manuscripts and account books before leaving home, and as they had been much damaged thereby, he was unable to give a detailed account of his losses and debts. (*Ib.*)

The Commissioners in their report state that he was a very meritorious man, very deserving of support, and allowed him £30 per annum. (A.O. 12/99, f. 316; A.O. 12/102, f. 62.)

His estate was forfeited, November 28, 1780. (A.O. 12/82.). He was granted £450 for the loss of his real estate from his claim of £1,127. His claim of £1,871 was disallowed. (A.O. 12/109.)

Dr. Joseph Adams received a pension of £70 per annum until 1804. His wife, Love Adams, received a pension from June 1, 1803, until October 10, 1831. (A.O. 13/83; A.O. 459/7; A.O. 426/20; A.O. 462/191; T. 50/28.)

This loyalist was the son of Captain Joseph Adams (who died at Lincoln, Massachusetts, March 28, 1807), and was born January 4, 1749; he married, September 4, 1770, Love, daughter of the Rev. William Lawrence, of Lincoln, and died in England, February 2, 1807. (*New Eng. Hist. and Gen. Reg.*, i, 260–1.) The town of Townshend contained a large number of Tories, and Dr. Joseph Adams was the most prominent of them. (Drake, *Hist. of Middlesex County*, vol. ii; Sawtell, *Hist. of Townshend*.)

His property at Townshend was advertised to be let, in the *Boston Gazette*, February 14, 1780.

References: Resolves of the General Court, 1783, chap. 106; *ib.*, 1787, chap. 75; Mass. Archives, vol. 154, p. 332; Middlesex Probate Recs., vol. 59, pp. 295, 484; *ib.*, vol. 60, p. 10; *ib.*, vol. 61, p. 269; Middlesex Registry of Deeds, vol. 76, pp. 199–201; Ex inform. Mrs. Evelyn L. Warren, of Townshend.

JOSEPH ADAMS

a mariner, born in Cornwall, England, settled and married in 1757 at Boston. He had served for many years in the Royal Navy, in H.M.S. *Dover*, commanded by Captain Washington Shirley (afterwards Earl Ferrers) in 1747. In 1769 he was employed by the Commissioners of

* Dr. Mein was highly esteemed in his profession. The interesting memoirs of his daughter, Susan Sibbald, ed. by Francis P. Hett, have been published.

Customs at Boston as an assistant tide-surveyor and first mate of the sloop *Liberty*, which was destroyed by an enraged mob at Newport, Rhode Island, on July 19, 1769. Having returned to Boston he was cast into prison for his part in this affair, and was kept there for more than ten weeks. Adams went afterwards to Branford, Connecticut, where he got employment as master of a vessel, but was driven from thence by one Caleb Trowbridge, who, with a number of men, went in pursuit of him, but by the guidance of Providence he escaped capture by hiding himself. He proceeded to New Haven and there took a boat for New York. Here he suffered great distress until his engagement as chief mate in the London ship, *Generous Friends* (George Ross, master), by which he sailed for England. He was now taken into the Royal Navy as master's mate in H.M.S. *Egmont*, from which he was transferred to the *Swan*, in which he sailed to Boston and there obtained the necessary voucher regarding his property. Joseph Adams appears to have been paid off at Portsmouth, England, from the sloop *Viper*, and to have been appointed next to the command of the armed cutter *George*, which was found on arrival at Cork to be unfit for the voyage to Quebec. The next stage in his career was in charge of a Dutch ship, just taken into the Navy, which he was the means of saving at great personal risk and which he conveyed safely to New York. He seems to have left the naval service here, and to have been engaged in supplying the British military forces with provisions. With the proceeds of the sale of an old vessel he bought two prizes, which he fitted out and, after taking on board a cargo, sailed under convoy of H.M.S. *Seaford*, *Renown*, *Grasshopper*, *Signet* and others. On reaching the American coast, Adams sent one of his vessels to New York, and took the other himself to Philadelphia. After an adventure with an American privateer, he had the misfortune to be captured by the *St. John* privateer on July 13, 1778, and was taken to Philadelphia, where he was kept a prisoner until October 4, following. Meanwhile, his other vessel was taken by the French Fleet off Sandy Hook. By the capture of these two vessels he lost over £3,000 currency. Joseph Adams was now offered by the Americans the command of several war vessels, but having always held rebellion in the greatest abhorrence, he utterly refused these offers. On October 4, he went from Elizabethtown, New Jersey, to Staten Island and New York on parole, and sailed for Europe on 20th of the same month. He appealed for assistance to Lord North, who gave him a recommendation to Admiral Rodney, and was given the command of an armed schooner for carrying despatches. On March 30, 1781, he was appointed Lieutenant of H.M.S. *Alcide*, and afterwards of H.M.S. *Hussar*. (A.O. 13/43.) In the schedule of his losses, the names of the two vessels purchased in Antigua are mentioned as the *Lord Drummond* and the *Rosamond*. (*Ib.*)

In his original petition he recounts his experiences and distress since the destruction of the *Liberty* in July, 1769. (Earl of Dartmouth MSS., *op. cit.*, ii, 119.)

Joseph Adams was married, August 25, 1757, to Mary Jeory. (Boston Records, vol. 28.)

His claim for compensation from the British Government was dismissed. (*Loyalists' Claims, op. cit.*, p. 353.)

NATHAN ALDIS

of Franklin, is mentioned in A.O. 12/83, f. 1.

MARTHA ALDRIDGE

describes herself as having been born at Marblehead, Massachusetts, where she had property which would have supported her through life comfortably, but which she lost by the Revolution. She was the widow of Major Christopher Aldridge, of the 40th Regiment of Foot, who had served for nearly thirty-three years in the British army in North America, the last twelve of which as commander of the troops at St. John's, Newfoundland. (A.O. 13/43.) Here he appears to have died. (C.O. 5/116, f. 267.). Accompanying her memorial is a letter from Lieut.-Colonel Adam Williamson, late Captain in the 40th Foot, to Lord Beauchamp, February 16, 1779, relating to her distresses.

She received a pension from the Concordatum of Ireland.

THOMAS ALEXANDER

was for sixteen years a trader in Boston. Early in the Revolution he was one of the Associators under General Gage at Boston. When General Howe succeeded Gage in command of the British troops he joined Howe with a company of merchants and others, entitled the Loyal North British Volunteers, to the number of about seventy, and he was appointed a Lieutenant in this company. The duty was fatiguing, though of considerable utility. At the evacuation of Boston he followed the British Army to Nova Scotia, New York and Philadelphia, and was present at several engagements. In 1778 he accompanied General James Grant's expedition to St. Lucia, and obtained permission to proceed from St. Lucia to Grenada to procure supplies for the military forces. On the return passage he was captured by an American privateer and carried to Martinique, where he was detained until exchanged. He then sailed for England and arrived in June, 1779. Having returned again to America in February, 1781, he was appointed Port and Harbour Master of the ports of Portsmouth and Norfolk in Virginia. At the evacuation of those ports he went to Yorktown, and was appointed by Lord Cornwallis to a similar office for the ports of Yorktown and Gloucester. He was taken prisoner at the surrender of Yorktown by Cornwallis. (A.O. 13/43.)

In evidence he states that he had a distillery and two warehouses on the Long Wharf at Boston, and that he was wounded at the battle of Brandywine. (A.O. 12/99, f. 156.) He was granted a pension of £50 a year, and appears to have settled at Shelburne,* Nova Scotia, in 1784. He claimed compensation to the amount of £419 for the loss of his property and received £220. (A.O. 12/109.)

Thomas Alexander was a Scotsman who emigrated to Boston in 1761. (*Ontario Archives, op. cit.*, pp. 1225–6; *Loyalists' Claims, op cit.*, pp. 110–1.)

JOLLEY ALLEN

was for many years a shopkeeper at Boston for the sale of English goods, and comfortably maintained a large family. As a staunch loyalist he lodged in his house several British army officers during the blockade of Boston. At the evacuation of Boston by the British troops, March 27, 1776, he engaged a small vessel [*Sally*] to transport him and his wife and family of seven children, together with his furniture and personal property to the value of nearly £3,000 sterling. During the night this small vessel parted company with the main fleet, and was driven by a strong wind ashore on Cape Cod, near Provincetown, where the vessel and cargo were immediately seized by the inhabitants, while Jolley Allen and his family were lodged in a miserable and unfurnished room and denied almost every necessary of life until April 19, when his wife, dispirited and broken-hearted by accumulated distresses, died. Allen himself now succeeded in obtaining permission from the Committee of Provincetown to visit Boston for the purpose of soliciting from the General Court the restitution of such personal articles as might be necessary for his family. After much solicitation he procured an order allowing him and his children to reside with his brother at Shrewsbury, Massachusetts, and directing his effects and the vessel to be sold at auction, and £35 of the proceeds to be paid to his brother for the family support. But his effects had been partly plundered and the vessel stripped and burnt by the people of Provincetown. At his brother's house the unhappy loyalist was threatened with assault and was in danger of being murdered in the street, and consequently he deemed it prudent to make his escape to New London, Connecticut, where he was taken on board a British frigate, commanded by Captain Jacobson, who took him to New York, and thence sailed for England. (A.O. 13/43.)

Sabine describes him as " a shrewd, dashing, thriving man . . . a loyalist, body and soul."

He was born in London, and emigrated in 1755 with his father, Nathaniel, a mariner, and his brother, Lewis, both of whom settled in Shrewsbury, Massachusetts, and were staunch loyalists. Jolley Allen was a principal and prosperous shopkeeper in Marlborough Street, Boston, and kept a boarding-house and a stable for horses. (*Annals of King's Chapel, op. cit.*, ii, 314; Ward, *Hist. of Shrewsbury, Mass.*, p. 216.) An " autobiographical fragment " passed into the hands of his executors and is still preserved. (*Mass. Hist. Soc. Proc.*, 1878, p. 67.)

* An article on the settlement of Shelburne is in *Acadiensis*, viii, 35–52.

Jolley Allen was buried, June 7, 1782, at St. John's, Wapping, London, where several relations had been buried. In his will (Gostling, 332), dated November 17, 1779, and proved July 12, 1782, he says, " Being now stripped of all my large property in America at the age of 64 years, which I had accumilated largely through great success in trade I give thanks for a good King & kind government which now supports me or else I must have starved & I trust the said Government will see me & my six poor children redressed when this unhappy trouble shall subside." To his eldest son, Jolley [born December 22, 1766], he writes in this will : " Pray dear child mind your learning fear God and love your Church and do all you can for your Brothers and Sisters and Relations and God will bless you . . ." To his daughter Eleanor [born December 1, 1758] he left her own caul. To his daughter Johanna [born in August, 1762] he also left a caul. To his son Jolley he bequeathed a caul,* which was never to be parted with except to a brother or sister at the hour of death, and portraits of himself and his wife. He expressed a desire that his body may be disinterred and taken to Boston and there buried in vault No. 17 in King's Chapel at the termination of the war.

ALEXANDER ANDERSON

describes himself as a mariner of " the parish of Dartmouth, on Cushant River," where he was the owner of a sloop and boat as well as some inherited land. He was also the owner of a house and garden at Plymouth. He joined the Royal forces at New York in August, 1776, and acted as a pilot until the peace. He says that such was his activity in favour of the British that General George Washington offered a great reward to any party or persons who would bring him or his head to American headquarters. Having sailed for England he joined the Royal Navy and served on merchant ships until incapacitated for further active duty, when he went to relations and friends in Scotland. In consequence of the " cursed and woefull rebellion " he was now reduced to poverty. With this memorial is a schedule of his losses. (A.O. 13/96.)

Alexander Anderson became chief clerk in the Naval Storekeeper's office in Halifax Dockyard, Nova Scotia.

CHARLES WARD APTHORP

A list of debts due by him in Massachusetts and two references to his property in Boston are in A.O. 12/81, ff. 36, 63-4, and A.O. 12/82, f. 15, and about thirty papers regarding his property in Massachusetts, New York and Vermont are in A.O. 13/11. His estate

---

* Early in the nineteenth century cauls were believed to be sure charms against death by drowning at sea, a single specimen selling for £20. In 1917 they were sold at London docks for 50s. as charms against death from German submarines. (London *Times*, March 5, 1917.). For an account of cauls see Brand's *Popular Antiquities*.

in Connecticut was restored to him by the Assembly in 1785. (*Ib.*). In his letter to Sir Brook Watson, dated February 21, 1789, he says he is almost in want, and that his son [Charles*], a Captain in the 23rd Regiment [Royal Welch Fusiliers], was sick and in debt. (*Ib.*). Before the Revolution he was a member of the Council of the Province of New York, and lost considerably in his property by the war. (A.O. 12/75, ff. 163–183 ; A.O. 12/90, ff. 3/7–8 ; *Ontario Archives, op. cit.,* pp. 622-3.)

He was the eldest son of Charles and Grizzel Apthorp and brother of Thomas Apthorp. He settled in New York, and there married Mary, daughter of John McEvers, a conspicuous loyalist. (Stark, *op. cit.,* p. 352.)

THOMAS APTHORP

had been a distiller in partnership with John Scollay at Boston. In 1769 he was appointed Paymaster of the British military forces in America, an appointment which rendered him obnoxious to the prevailing political party. He attended the British army in its movements in America in 1776, when Daniel Chamier (*q.v.*) was joined as his colleague in the American agency of the army contractors, Harley and Drummond. In this same year he resigned his office of Paymaster and in March 1777 he was superseded in the agency without notice. Under the delusion that the rebellion would be speedily repressed he declined further appointments and awaited the time when he could resume his private business, taking up his residence on Long Island, New York. (A.O. 13/43.)

With his memorial are certificates from Generals Gage and Howe to his loyalty and good conduct and to the accuracy of his accounts as Paymaster ; a schedule of his losses ; his letter to the Commissioners, February 4, 1785, relating to his property in America ; his letter, January 30, 1788, that his lands at Thomlinson, Vermont, had been confiscated by the state ; a letter from his brother, Edward Apthorp, dated January 1, 1788, apparently from America, regarding his lands and saying that he (Thomas) was much happier in England than he would be in America, where few or none of his old acquaintances remain. In Massachusetts he imagines Thomas would not be safe. He would be glad to receive a third of £20,000 for his share with Thomas in the lottery (not named) ; a copy of a report on the sale of about 9,000 acres of land acquired by him at Thomlinson, Vermont, in discharge of a debt due to him by Oliver Corey. The sale of this property was held to be illegal, on the ground that Thomas Apthorp had " joined the common enemy," and was consequently vested in the state of Vermont ; and a letter, September 18, 1788, relating to his affairs and mentioning Mary Apthorp, widow of his brother William, and his nephew, John Trecothick Apthorp.

In a copy of his letter of May 16, 1775, he estimated the number of

* His commissions in this regiment were : 2nd Lieutenant, April 19, 1774 ; 1st Lieutenant, March 2, 1776 ; Captain-Lieutenant, November 8, 1778 (the regiment in America) ; and Captain, August 8, 1780. He was Lieut.-Colonel of the 38th Foot from 1795 until his retirement in 1800.

armed men as shortly to be collected round Boston in the American
service at about 30,000. (T.I.515.)

From his claim of £977 he was allowed £400. (A.O. 12/109.)

In reporting on his appeal for bounty, November 25, 1784, the Commissioners state as follows : " This is a very extraordinary Application
from a Servant of the Crown in whose Loyalty there is no Merit and who
confesses that he has made as much by the War as he has lost by it even
supposing that he never recovers a Shilling of his Debts for besides supporting himself during the War he has transmitted into the Funds of this
Country as much Money as gives him a Capital in the 3 p Cents of between
£5,000 and £6,000." Even if he had lost £20,000 he would not be an
object of bounty because he has an income sufficient to support himself
as a single man with great comfort. Moreover, it was presumed that he
had been guilty of bad conduct in his office, having been turned out of it
in 1777.* (A.O. 12/101, f. 150.)

* Correspondence regarding his careless method of keeping his accounts as Deputy
Paymaster is preserved in the Royal Institution. (*Am. MSS. in Royal Inst., op. cit.,*
i, 14–15, 37, 46–7, 64–5, 70, 71, 74, 83.)

Thomas Apthorp died at Bath, England, April 31, 1819, aged 78. (*Gent. Mag.,*
1819, p. 284.)

Reference : Stark, *op. cit.,* p. 353.

WILLIAM APTHORP

merchant, Boston, finding all business suspended, sailed on December 26,
1775, for England with his wife, leaving four young children behind.
With this memorial are certificates to his loyalty from General Gage,
Governor Hutchinson and Lieutenant-Governor Thomas Oliver, dated
1778. (A.O. 13/43.)

His estate was not confiscated and was restored to his wife [Mary
Thompson]. (A.O. 12/81, f. 35 ; A.O. 12/82, f.9.)

Reference : Stark, *op. cit.,* p. 354.

Mr. William C. Bond, of Boston, is the owner of portraits of the Apthorp family.

FRANCIS ARCHBALD

is described as of Fort George, Penobscot. In May, 1779, General
Francis Maclean and his British troops arrived there and issued a proclamation requiring all loyal inhabitants to join him. Archbald joined
immediately and took the oath of allegiance. He was soon afterwards
appointed to assist Captain Thomas Hartcup, the Engineer, and served
until the evacuation of Fort George. Having been assured of the intention
of the Crown to hold Penobscot at the conclusion of the war, Archbald
and many other loyalists built houses upon the lots of land assigned to
them, all of which they lost at the evacuation. He was at Fort George
in January, 1784, and appears to have died there on October 8, 1785. He
had 100 acres of land on Orphan Island, Penobscot River. With his
memorial is an inventory of his losses. (A.O. 13/43.)

His widow, Mary, claimed £424 for the loss of his property at Penobscot and was awarded £100. (A.O. 12/109.)

Brigadier General Francis Maclean and his detachment arrived at Penobscot on June 12, 1779, and "finding that the people had been artfully led to believe that his Majesty's troops were accustomed to plunder and treat the country where their operations led them with the greatest inhumanity," a proclamation was issued, with the result that about 500 inhabitants took the oath of allegiance. (*Am. MSS. in R. Inst.*, *op. cit.*, i, 458–463.). For the Penobscot Loyalists, see *Acadiensis*, iii, 172–182 ; and Professor W. H. Siebert, *The Exodus of the Loyalists from Penobscot to Passamaquoddy*, in *Ohio State Univ. Bulletin*, Apr., 1914.

Francis Archbald, the son of Francis and Anna (Gale) Archbald, was born October 19, 1750, and died October 8, 1785, and was buried in the family vault, Tomb No. 2, in the Granary burial ground in Boston. His death is announced in a letter dated December 29, 1785, from Jonathan Lowder to Archbald's father-in-law, Thomas Goldthwait (*q.v.*). His wife's name was Mary. (With the Goldthwait papers in A.O. 13/84.)

JOHN ARNOLD

states in his memorial, dated Boston, April 3, 1786, that his losses by the Revolution included an entirely new brigantine of 175 tons burden and a library of 183 volumes. (A.O. 13/24.). In a letter, dated Onslow, Nova Scotia, April 8, 1786, he says that at the commencement of the war he entered the American service as Adjutant and Lieutenant and was soon promoted Captain and finally Major. Upon the arrival of the British Peace Commissioners in 1778, he deserted from the American army, but succeeded in evading arrest as a deserter until June 7, 1779, when he was apprehended on a charge of high treason. He remained in prison without trial until June 27, 1780, when he escaped to New York. Meanwhile, all his property was confiscated and sold. At New York he took the oath of allegiance to the King and there remained until he went to Nova Scotia, where he was granted 1,000 acres of land at Onslow. (A.O. 13/24.). His petition for bounty and his claim are endorsed " Rejected, December 13, 1786." (*Ib.*)

One John Arnold married Abigail Foster, March 10, 1763. (Boston Records, vol. 28.)

The only Massachusetts man of this name recorded in Heitman's *Continental Officers* was an Ensign in the 15th Continental Infantry, January 1, 1776, who deserted in August 1776.

JAMES ASBY

was born at Penrith in Cumberland and served during the previous war (presumably in America) under Captain Deane and others. At the peace he was settled at Boston as a watchmaker and was in comfortable circumstances until the outbreak of the Revolutionary war. His natural love of his country and his duty to his King induced him to risk everything in favour of Government, and to join the Loyal North British Volunteers. at Boston, in which he served as Lieutenant from June, 1775, to March, 1776, at his own expense. At the evacuation of Boston by the British troops he sailed for Halifax, Nova Scotia, where he was employed in a marine department. From Halifax he went to New York and there served in the army until January, 1777, when he was granted leave to return to England. (A.O. 13/43.)

With his memorial is a schedule of his property, and a pathetic letter from his eldest daughter, Ann, dated London, April 14, 1788, stating that while her father was in the West Indies, master of the ship *Alexander*, she and her sisters and infant brother were in great distress, motherless and virtually fatherless. Ann Asby became Ann Bond. (T. 50/6; A.O. 460/15; A.O. 462/3.)

James Asby gave evidence in London on August 19, 1788, in support of his claim for compensation. His witnesses were Frederick Roberts, formerly of Boston, and William Bowes (*q.v.*). He was granted a pension of £20 per annum (A.O. 12/102, f. 133) and was allowed £200 from his claim of £280. (A.O. 12/109.)

His wife, Mary, died in London in 1787. (A.O. 13/137.)

James Asby was the son of John Asby, parish clerk, of Penrith, Cumberland, and was baptized in the parish church there, May 12, 1739.

PHINEAS ATHERTON

was born in Lancaster, Massachusetts, where he was the owner of a house and 100 acres of cultivated land. In 1755 he was a volunteer in the expedition against the Acadians in Nova Scotia and in 1757 he was present at the capture of Fort Cataraqui [in Captain Thomas Hartwell's company in Colonel Joseph Frye's force]. In 1760 he participated in the campaign against Swagalia, Montreal, Niagara and Detroit. For his exemplary conduct he was appointed by General Amherst an ensign in Wendell's Corps of Rangers and in the same year he was promoted Lieutenant in Waite's Corps of Rangers. Atherton was appointed in January, 1777, Lieutenant in the King's Royal Regiment of New York and in July following Provost Marshal to Burgoyne's army. With this army he was taken prisoner in October, 1777, and was detained until November, 1782, " labouring under every inconvenience that his incensed neighbours could devise." (A.O. 13/43.)

A letter from Colonel Abijah Willard, January 26, 1784, states that he had known him for many years and that he was a firm loyalist. (*Ib.*)

In 1788 Phineas Atherton was in prison for debt in the Marshalsea Prison in London, where, according to his petition, he had lain for over two months in great distress and destitute even of the common necessaries of life. On November 14 of the same year he wrote a letter regarding his property. (*Ib.*)

On July 26, 1784, he gave evidence in support of his claim and of his application for a pension. It would seem that he was in England at the outbreak of the American War of Independence and returned home immediately. (A.O. 12/101, f.11.). His claim of £140 for the loss of his property was met with a reward of £110. (A.O. 12/109.)

Phineas Atherton was a signatory to the memorial of Jonathan Carver, Moses Park and Isaac Da Costa (q.v.), dated May 18, 1772, praying to be appointed members of a proposed expedition under Major Robert Rogers, the celebrated Ranger of New Hampshire, to attempt to discover a northwest passage. (T.I. 484 (409).)

He was born February 17, 1740, the son of Amos Atherton and his wife, Elizabeth Harris. (Ex inform. Mr. J. C. L. Clark, of Lancaster.)

References : Nourse,. *Military Annals of Lancaster*, p. 42 ; *Massachusetts Archives*, vol. 78, p. 81 ; *Ontario Archives, op. cit.*, pp. 1181–2 ; *Loyalists' Claims, op. cit.*, p. 90.

GIBBS ATKINS

Thomas Atkins had a claim of £571 12s. 5d. against his estate. The total proceeds of the sale were £712 19s. 6d. and the claims, £946 19s. 5d. (A.O. 12/82, f.4). Judgment was rendered against his estate in the Court of Common Pleas of Suffolk County. (A.O. 12/83, f.1.)

Gibbs Atkins died in 1806, aged 66.

HENRY ATKINS

was born in Boston and from 1771 he was clerk to Richard Reeve, Secretary to the Commissioners of American Customs, and from May 1, 1772, weigher and gauger of Customs at Newburyport. On July 27, 1775, he was prevented by the revolutionary party from performing the functions of his office. In May, 1777, he was apprehended for refusing to bear arms against Great Britain and in April, 1778, he escaped from prison with his son, Henry, and reached Halifax, Nova Scotia. (A.O. 12/10, ff. 316–320 ; A.O. 12/61, f. 97 ; A.O. 12/99, f. 26 ; A.O. 13/43 ; A.O. 13/59 ; A.O. 13/96.)

A certificate from Captain Edward Barron, late of the 4th Regiment, November 3, 1783, states that Atkins was a prisoner of war with him in the same cell and that he (Atkins) was denied all communication with friends by letter or otherwise and not suffered even to receive visits from his own children.

Henry Atkins died at Walthamstow, Essex, England, on May 24, 1786, and was buried in the parish of St. Mary's. His neighbour at Walthamstow was Henry Goldthwait (q.v.), who with other friends comforted him with necessaries during his last illness. His eldest son, Henry, was in the Paymaster General's office at Halifax, Nova Scotia, where he died, February 13, 1823, aged 70, and was buried in old St. Paul's cemetery.

Reference : *Ontario Archives, op. cit.*, p. 190.

JOHN ATKINSON

settled at Boston in 1767 as a merchant in partnership with one Smith. In 1775 he joined the company of Associated Volunteers at Boston commanded by Francis Green (*q.v.*). From 1778 to 1780 he bore arms in New York, in Colonel Abijah Willard's company of Massachusetts Volunteers. Here he fitted out armed vessels to distress the Americans. With his memorial is a long list of the debtors of Smith and Atkinson, and a certificate of Francis Green (*q.v.*), March 4, 1784. (A.O. 13/43.)

Reference : *Loyalists' Claims, op. cit.*, p. 186.

ROBERT AUCHMUTY

From his memorial (c. 1786) :

"That about twenty years ago, your Memorialist then being a Counsellor at Law, and at the barr, was selected by the Governor of the Massachusetts Bay, the late Sir Francis Bernard, to whom your Memst then was an entire stranger, to fill the place of Advocate General in that province. That said office was extremely obnoxious to the people, from the nature of it, and hazardous from the furious spirit of the times. That prior to the offer of it to him, he was earnestly sollicited to reject it, when offered. That soon after your Memst was urged by the said Governor to undertake that trust. The arguments used for that purpose were various. Some of which relate so intimately to the professional character of your Memst as to enjoin silence on him as to such. The others were founded on the urgent necessity, occasioned by the licentiousness of the times, of a confidential servant of the Crown in that department, and the peculiar merit such a character would acquire in voluntarily, and without any salary, engaging to support the interest of his Majesty and government, by maintaining and defending their laws and Officers, in times seriously perplexing, and rapidly approaching to real danger. The task your Memst well knew would be extremely unpleasing and arduous. And would also necessarily engross too much of his time, of which, both his health and interest compelled him to be very frugal, his common law practice, on which his bread depended, demanding by far the greatest part of it. To his loss of time, he knew a pecuniary one necessarily succeeded. And that on his acceptance of an office, so peculiarly obnoxious to all orders of the people, followed a very interesting risk ; especially as he was informed, which he then and now believes, that some persons of weight and consequence were determined, if in their power, to ruin the practice of any gentleman who should accept the office of Advocate General. These difficulties your Memst seriously weighed in his mind. And opposed to them the consciousness of the duty which he justly owed his Sovereign, and that government to whom he, his Ancestors, Connections and fellow-subjects were indebted for the parental care of a mother country, and the blessings of ease and plenty. He also considered that some body must encounter the danger, and that, as he had the honor of being pitched on by his Majesty's Representative for that purpose, a denial, under such peculiar circumstances, would greatly aggravate his criminality, in withholding his slender abilities, when demanded, from those, to whom in honor, in duty, and gratitude, such were due. These considerations immediately determined your Memst, at all hazards, to engage in the service of the Crown. And in consequence thereof he was appointed Advocate. That he continued such about five years : during which time he had neither salary, or an allowance of five or any Per Cent on condemnations. That the emoluments of said office being small, and he always held on the Crown's side, he was annually a sufferer in point of profit ; besides his great loss of time, then very essential to him in his extensive practice at the barr. That he ever discharged his official duty with fidelity. And as the best proof of it, he begs leave to assure you Gentlemen Commissioners, that he does not recollect a single instance of a libel exhibited by him, which failed. And that there were more for breaches of the laws of trade, and those for the preservation of the King's Masts, all of which were instituted, conducted, and argued by him *alone*, in his department than in any two or three others on the Continent of America. That while he remained the King's Advocate, he never received any assistance, as such, from any Gentleman of the profession, either in forming a libel, arranging the evidence, or arguing a cause ; but was always, in disputed cases of which there were many, opposed by two, and sometimes three of the principal characters at that barr. That in that time an attempt was made in the common law Courts to annihilate in part the legal powers of the Court of Vice Admiralty, and of the Officers of the customs. For the first of which purposes a suit was commenced against the Marshall of said Court. And for the second, an objection was taken and argued before the Judges, to their granting writs of Assiastance to such officers. The first cause your Mem^{st.} defended without the assistance of any one. In the last, he had a Gentleman of learning with him, and succeeded in both.

"That on the death of Judge Russel* your Memorialist was appointed by the late Sr Francis Bernard Judge of the Court of Vice Admiralty in the Massachusetts Bay. And in about fifteen months after, he received a patent from the Lords of the Admiralty constituting him not only Judge of that Court ; but also in the province of New Hampshire. That he continued under those appointments to act about three years, during which time, he had not any salary. And though there was more than a common share of business, yet the fees of office never amounted annually to thirty pounds.

"That after serving as Advocate and Judge for near eight years, not only without salary, but at an annual loss, and in very troublesome times ; insomuch that while he was Advocate, and merely for his being so, he was once obliged to remove his books and furniture to prevent the danger of their being destroyed by the Mob, his Majesty was graciously pleased to honor your Mem^{st.} with his last patent. And which he confesses was

---

* Judge Chambers Russell died in 1767.

extremely agreeable to him. As he from thence concluded, being unknown in person, and without any connections here, his Royal Master's
approbation of his past conduct. The honorary notice and attention
thereby paid him he flattered himself proceeded immediately from some
degree of merit in him, as it certainly could not flow from any private
interest. That on the receipt of the same, he, and his Majesty's principal
servants, then in Boston, were clear in opinion that your Mem^{st's.} continuing as a practicer at the barr would be incompatible with, and derogatory to the rank his Majesty had been pleased to advance him to. In consequence of which he quitted it ; though certainly the emoluments thereof
were materially more than those of his patent. And never again reas-
sumed it, except occasionally, in defence of his Majesty's civil and military
Officers, which, in effect, was in support of his authority and dignity.

"That as the said patent contained an *express Grant* from his Majesty
of an annual salary of six hundred pounds, which was all your Mem^{st.} could
reap by the appointment. Because he was commanded by the patent not
to take any fee or reward for any business to be done by him in said office,
which injunction he sacredly obeyed, and for the payment of which an
existing fund was appropriated, That your Mem^{st.} neither did or could
possess an idea of loosing that support, unless by his neglect of duty, or
mal-feazance in office. In fact he was convinced it was for life ; unless
forfeited by misconduct, both by the rules of justice, and the constant
practice relative to Gentlemen in the law line here, in similar cases. His
professional business he knew to be certain, on which he had founded his
hopes not only of present support, but of making up a competency to have
retired on in easy circumstances, when his age or inclination might have
required it. Had he in the least mistrusted that he was about to quit a cer-
tainty and thereby relinquish the above grand object of life, and rest his
hopes on any fortuitous event, in which he had no concern, he humbly
submits to you Gentlemen whether he would have acted prudently. This
being your Memorialist's idea, which was confirmed by every other
gentleman whom he consulted on the subject, he preferred obeying his
Sovereign's commands, though attended with less profit, to the pursuit of
his profession And these circumstances, he humbly conceives, materially
differ his case from most, if not all others. That though several appeals
from his decrees, on clauses of intricacy, were claimed, and the proper
stipulations entered into to prosecute the same, he ventures, on his honor,
to assure you Gentlemen, not one was reversed. And that he never was
served with a monition for that purpose. These facts he mentions as the
most conclusive evidence, in his humble opinion, of his faithfull and legal
discharge of duty.

"That after he had given up his practice he was too frequently, for
his own interest and safety, obliged to appear as Council in the defence
of the Servants of the Crown, particularly in the dangerous trial of Capt.
Preston, and two under Officers of the customs, all charged with murder.
Also in civil suits brought against others. And was happy in having his
endeavours crowned with success : though such conduct rendered him,

having in general left the barr, particularly obnoxious to the populace. A most disagreeable situation in the riotous times at Boston. In fact, that he, on all occasions was ready by Council or speaking to assist, as far as his abilities would admit, all servants of the Crown, who did not exceed their duty. And for which purposes he was too often applied to and employed particularly to mention.

" That as the first seven or eight years of his services were impossible to be bottomed in, or influenced by any sinister or lucretive motives. And as from the time of his last patent, he was no gainer in point of profit, he humbly trusts, he may assume to himself, the honor of having acted on unsullied principles. And therefore he cannot entertain a doubt either of the justice or humanity of Goverment ; especially as his fate principally depends on the enquiry and report of Gentlemen of abilities and character. Nor has he any idea that an old faithfull officer of the Crown can be abandoned to misery ; especially as his sufferings flow immediately from his loyalty to a most gracious Sovereign, his due discharge of duty, and his disinterested attachment to Goverment.

" That the feelings of a gentleman in the sixtieth year of his age. And who was long acquainted with ease, affluence, and a style of life which mett his wishes ; but now almost spiritless by the pressure of many and various misfortunes, are more easily conceived by the virtuous, than expressed by the unhappy object.

" To you Gentlemen therefore your Memorialist most chearfully submits himself and his fortunes ; being confident that your report to the Right Honble the Lords Commissioners of his Majesty's Treasury, and to his Majesty's principal Secretaries of State, on his case, will be in conformity to his situation, his past services, rank in life, loss of profession or Office, and in every respect founded in equity. . ." (A.O. 13/43.)

Another memorial, dated March 9, 1783, incorporating some of the above facts, concludes with these words : " That the feelings of a gentleman advanced to near fifty nine years of age, formerly used to ease and affluence, to a stile of life which mett his wishes, but now bending under the pressure of misfortunes, exposed to poverty, and in apprehension of beggary, are wretched beyond description." (Ib.)

With his memorials are the following :

A copy of an extract from a letter of Governor Bernard to the Earl of Halifax, dated May 17, 1766, in which it is stated that William Bollan, the Advocate General, was an absentee in England and had appointed a deputy who deserted his post and put himself at the head of the attack on the King's officers. At this disturbed time it was difficult to procure a proper person for this very discouraging office, which required a man of great resolution as well as learned in the law. Not only was a popular torrent to be stemmed, but all the best lawyers of the province to be combated. In this anxious time the Governor appointed Robert Auchmuty to this office, a lawyer who not only fully came up to but much exceeds his expectation and who was firm in engagements, learned and eloquent in his arguments, and, more extraordinary, has never failed in one prosecution he has undertaken.   Governor Bernard hopes that there is no truth in the report that another gentleman is to be appointed over the head of this zealous man and master of the business.   Only one other gentleman in Massachusetts is equal to the office and he does not desire it.

Copies of extracts from two letters to the Earl of Shelburne from Governor Bernard, one dated October 12, 1766, and the other October 15. In the former he says that "The Court of Admiralty is the Palladium of the American Laws of Trade" and recommends adequate payment of its officers ; and in the second he recommends making the office of Advocate General desirable by the grant of an adequate salary and occasional fees, in order to tempt a first rate lawyer.   Robert Auchmuty had been offered fees ten times larger than those received from the Crown, had accepted office at a dangerous and difficult time, exerted himself with resolution and steadiness, and had shown himself superior to the threats of the people in times of danger and to their attempts to seduce him in times of quiet.   In the duties of his office he had been generally opposed by the first lawyers of the country and had manifested such distinguished skill and abilities that if he should resign he knows not where to replace him to any degree of public utility.

A schedule of mortgages and bonds, real and personal estate, and a schedule of his notes of hand, with the interest due.

A list of claims against his estate, some of which he does not acknowledge as due. Auchmuty gives reasons for the claimants taking advantage of his absence from America, namely, that the law under which some of these claims was made was founded in cruelty and injustice and deprives the loyalist absentees of any chance of being heard and consequently left them at the mercy of people who think there is no crime in plundering loyalists in general, and especially those declared as "notorious conspirators."

A number of certificates from Registers of Deeds of Suffolk County relating to conveyances of property to Robert Auchmuty at various dates before 1775 and other documents relating to his personal affairs.

A certificate from Robert Hallowell to his fidelity in his office in face of difficulties and to his eminence at the Bar of Massachusetts. Auchmuty had altered his house at Roxbury at considerable cost, until it became more complete than any other seat in the neighbourhood.

Certificates from several British military officers, to the effect that he was at the head of his profession and that officers of the Crown and others reposed great confidence in him.

Robert Auchmuty was one of the Commissioners appointed to enquire into the destruction of the schooner *Gaspée* by the mob in 1772.

He appealed for an office in any new settlement in North America. (H.O.Dom. 42/1.)

He was granted £300 per annum from May 13, 1783 (A.O. 12/99, f. 23.), and was granted £1,775 compensation from his claim of £3,075, as well as £600 for the loss per annum of his professional income during the war. (A.O. 12/109.)

In a letter from Auchmuty to Governor Hutchinson, dated Boston, March 3, 1775, he expresses the view that he has no reason to expect restoration of peace in this miserable province until the fatal experiment of arms is tried. Such a strange infatuation prevails as scarcely can be credited and never yet to be paralleled. No absurdity in politics, however gross or impossible, but meets with entire assent, as soon as it is propagated by the flagitious disturbers of American liberty and loyalty. No treatment is too bad for the friends of Government, except taking away their lives. He very much suspects that even the horrid crime of murder will soon be deemed and openly published as a meritorious act. Appearances indicate a spirited and obstinate resistance in the people to the measures of the Crown, but if a proper military force be marched against them with vigour, their courage would soon abate and in time be totally extinguished. But on a supposition of the contrary, they cannot long maintain a war for which they are **too** ignorant and destitute of the means. On the whole, bloodshed and desolation seem inevitable, though on cool reflection he is astonished how the monster of rebellion hath reared its head so high against the dictates of reason, gratitude and interest. Surely, Heaven hath been pleased to interfere. All that can be said is : *Quos Deus vult perdere, prius dementat.* The letter concludes with advice to Governor Hutchinson to remain in England, despite his inclination to return to his native country. (British Museum : Egerton MSS. 2559, f. 141.)

Robert Auchmuty was the son of Robert Auchmuty, the distinguished lawyer, of Boston, and member of the Middle Temple, who died in 1750.

In a letter to the Commissioners from his widow, Deborah Auchmuty, dated January 14, 1788, she announces his death on December 11, 1788 [in London], and appeals, at the age of 65, for a loyalist's pension. (A.O. 13/97.)

Robert Auchmuty's will (Calvert, 573) is dated February 9, 1785, and was proved December 29, 1788. In it he mentions his wife's sisters, Catherine Brinley and Sarah Cradock ; his nephew, Samuel Auchmuty (afterwards General Sir Samuel) ; his brother, James Smith Auchmuty, and the latter's son, Robert. To his nephew, Robert Nicholls Auchmuty, he left one shilling.

The above Mary Cradock was granted an allowance for her support from the estates of her two sons-in-law, Robert Auchmuty and Thomas Brinley (*q.v.*), by order of the General Court of Massachusetts, March 25, 1780. (A.O. 12/82, f. 10.)

Auchmuty made in defence of Captain Preston, of " Boston Massacre " fame, a plea so memorable and persuasive as " almost to bear down the tide of prejudice against him, though it never swelled to a higher flood." (*Journal of Samuel Curwen,* op. cit., Appendix.)

References : A.O. 12/81, ff. 61–2 ; A.O. 13/83 ; Stark, *op. cit.,* pp. 301–5.

B

THOMAS AYLWIN

left England in 1763 with merchandise for Quebec and there settled as a merchant. In 1770 he removed to Boston, and on the day of the skirmish at Lexington General Gage asked him to enrol himself as a volunteer for the defence of Boston ; he was discharged from this duty later in the day. A few days later he sailed for Quebec, accompanied by his wife and family, and settled there. He was appointed a magistrate, and when the province and city of Quebec were threatened with invasion by the Americans he was appointed a Lieutenant in the militia and did duty until disabled by ill-health. His brigantine, *Little Lucy* [named after his wife], with a cargo was despatched from Quebec bound for Antigua in 1776, in charge of one Edmund Dwyer, who treacherously disposed of part of the cargo in Antigua and agreed with Americans at St. Lucia to take possession of the vessel. His claim, £3,173 2s. 10d., for this vessel and cargo was rejected. (A.O. 13/81.)

Thomas Aylwin married in 1771 Lucy, daughter of Hon. John Cushing.

According to the records of the Goldsmiths Company of London, Thomas Aylwin was the son of Thomas Aylwin, of Romsey, Hampshire, and was apprenticed to Richard Sharp, goldsmith, of London, for seven years from June 4, 1752. He received the honour of the freedom of the Goldsmiths Company, March 6, 1782.

Thomas Aylwin died in Quebec, April 14, 1791.

EBENEZER AYRES

of Worcester County, farmer, served as a soldier in the Prince of Wales's Volunteers in 1777–8 in America and acted as a scout. His claim for compensation was rejected. He was at Montreal in 1783–4. (A.O. 13/81.)

A man of this name was one of Captain John Lovewell's brave company in the " Great Fight." (Sylvester, *Indian Wars of New England*.)

CAPTAIN JOHN BAKER

of Northampton, suffered greatly for his loyalty and for refusing to resign his military commission held under the Crown at the commencement of the rebellion. He was fined several times and suffered persecution in other ways. Witnesses to his loyalty were Aaron Wright and Hains Kingsley, loyalists, of Northampton. (A.O. 13/80.)

A man of this name was sergeant at Northampton in 1720 and Ensign, 1722–34; Lieutenant, 1736–8 ; and Captain, 1739–52. (Ex inform. Mr. Clarence D. Chase.) One Captain John Baker died February 3, 1802, aged 87.

Henry Barnes

PLATE I

PLATE II   Mrs. Henry Barnes

SARAH BAKER

was a daughter of Andrew Hawkins, butcher, of Boston, who suffered imprisonment for his loyalty and for serving as a volunteer under Gage during the blockade of Boston. At the evacuation of Boston by the British troops she accompanied her husband, Benjamin Baker, to Nova Scotia, and thence to New York, where they remained until 1783. In this year he left New York on a privateering expedition and is believed to have been lost at sea. Sarah Baker was sent in 1784 by her landlady in London into a sponging house* and finally to Newgate gaol for debt. During her imprisonment her benefactors included the Rev. Samuel Peters, the well-known Connecticut clergyman, and Thomas Coffin. In a long letter from this clergyman, dated November 20, 1784, he says that he had approached John Young, master of the ship *Hero*, of Boston, about taking back Mrs. Baker to her father at Boston. Young, upon hearing that she and her father were loyalists, he as a " violent rebel " refused to accept her and her children, because " such lumber ought to remain under that Government to which they had fled for protection." The proverb of Solomon, " the poor man's curse is his poverty," applies to this unhappy family, says the Rev. Samuel Peters, who exerted himself in divers ways to relieve their distress. (A.O. 13/43.)

Benjamin Baker was a native of America, and served on board a privateer for the greatest part of the war. (A.O. 12/101, f.135.)

AARON BANKS

was from 1779 to January, 1784, a yeoman at Penobscot, where his losses included six head of black cattle. At the latter date he was at Fort George, Penobscot. (A.O. 13/90.)

ANDREW BARCLAY

took an early and active part against the rebels at Boston, by taking up arms in the Loyal North British Volunteers. At the evacuation of Boston by the British troops in March, 1776, he sailed for Nova Scotia and thence to New York, where he remained until the evacuation, when he was honoured by Sir Guy Carleton, commander-in-chief, with the charge of a company of loyalist refugees bound for Shelburne, Nova Scotia, and settled there. (A.O. 13/24.)

One Andrew Barclay and Mary Bleigh were married, October 15, 1761, at Boston. (Boston Records, Vol. 28.)

HENRY BARNES (Plate 1)

His loyalty to Great Britain and his opposition to the Non-Importation agreement† in 1770 " drew upon him the resentment of his countrymen,

* A sponging house was a place of preliminary confinement for debt.

† See Professor Charles M. Andrews's article in *Publications of Colonial Soc. of Mass.*, xxiv, 159–259.

and occasioned his business to be obstructed, his merchandise seized and his life threatened," insomuch that he judged it necessary to absent himself for some time.* In the winter of 1775 he became still more obnoxious by his protection of Captain Brown and Ensign D'Bernicre, the two British officers who were sent to survey the country around Marlborough. Soon after this event it was necessary for his own safety to seek the protection of the British troops in Boston [on April 17, 1775]. (A.O. 13/43.)

He was a justice of the peace for the town of Marlborough. For his support of the British cause he was advertised in the Boston newspapers as an infamous importer of British goods and an enemy of his country. His house at Marlborough was beset every night and the lives of himself and his family were threatened in the following " incendiary letter." Henry Barnes fled to England in November, 1770, for protection, returned in 1771, and lived in tolerable quietness until [February] 1775, when he was called upon as a magistrate to issue orders for billeting the King's troops [a sergeant and a party who had gone in search of deserters], a duty which he carried out at the risk of his life. The event which finally enraged his persecutors was his help in effecting the escape of the two officers mentioned above. Having received news of the death of his uncle, Jonathan Perrie, at Hampstead in London, and of his legacy to him of £1,925, he sailed with his family to England in February, 1776. His wife and niece had previously sought refuge in Rhode Island. He applied to Government for relief, and to his mortification was granted £50, which was afterwards increased to £100. (Ib.)

He was an importer of British goods at Boston, and shipped to London large quantities of pearl ash of his own manufacture and of which he was the sole inventor. For his loyalty he was obstructed in his business, his workmen inveigled from him, and the inhabitants refused to supply his works with necessary fuel. His inventory of his real and personal property includes his pearl ash works and distillery ; 5,000 acres of land bought of General Winslow for £250 ; 3,000 acres of land bought of Captain Joshua Barker ; six valuable family portraits ; a library ; a quantity of silver plate ; a coach and chaises. (Ib.)

With his memorials is a copy of his petition to Governor Hutchinson, June 9, 1770, regarding his persecution and losses as an opponent of the Non-Importation agreement, and pleading for protection ; and a copy of the " incendiary letter " mentioned above : " Henry Barnes I understand you are about carrying your Old dam'd Booby Hutt† to the General

* A letter from Mrs. Barnes, dated March 13, 1770, says that the vile town of Marlborough had put up a notification, warning the inhabitants against importing British goods. " It does not give us much uneasiness, for as a guilty conscience needs no accuser so conscious innocence fears none." (Letters of James Murray, Loyalist, 1901, p. 174.)

† A body of a coach upon runners, which the revolutionists cut to pieces. References to this coach and to the burning of Henry Barnes's effigy as an infamous importer are in Letters of James Murray, Loyalist, 1901.

Court and from thence Home to England to get recompence for all the damage you have sustained since you have been an infamous Importer or a common Enemy to the Country—Therefore if you only want recompence for the damage you have done the Country in Importing goods contrary to the Agreement of Body of Merchants on this Continent I will recompence you without going there or any where else for I am determined to fetch you to terms even if I do it at the expence of my own Soul, or the Cost of a Sore Back or any other punishment in this World only for the good of my Country, for I stile myself a Son of LIBERTY, therefore if you will Shut up your Store and Sell nothing out, nor Import any goods till the Importation takes place you shall sustain no more damage But if not I will Fire your House and Store and destroy all your substance you have on the earth, And I will take your Body and I will Tar it, and if nothing else will do but Death you shall have it certainly, and so you will have no more Notice and if you do it by the 20th June 1770 Good and well, and if not you may depend upon my being as good as my word and so I will never write no more and so I stile myself Inspector General." (*Ib.*)

Two letters from Samuel Blackden to Henry Barnes, dated London, January 25, and February 4, 1784, state that while passing through Marlborough about three years previously he found Barnes's property put up for sale by public auction by authority of the state, and he bought it. He now offered it to Barnes with the assurance that if he should return to his old home he would be cordially received, as no person ever left a better character behind him than Barnes for integrity, benevolence and public usefulness, politics having now happily subsided. He refers to the sale of other portions of the Barnes property and to his conversations with inhabitants of Marlborough between March, 1781, and November, 1783, all of whom declared that Henry Barnes by his attention to business and the improvements effected by him had been of great benefit to the town, and that they had not appreciated his worth until after his enforced flight. Blackden offered him his property for £1,000, the amount which he had paid for it. (*Ib.*)

The estate of Henry Barnes was forfeited, November 28, 1780. (A.O. 12/82.). His claim amounted to £1,700 and the award to £730. (A.O. 12/109.). He received a loyalist pension of £60 until his death, and his widow one of £40 until April 5, 1808. (T. 50/6; T. 50/10; A.O. 462/21.)

This loyalist was the son of John Barnes, a prosperous Boston merchant, and his wife, Elizabeth Perrie, and was born in Boston, November 20, 1723. He married in 1740 Christian, daughter of John and Abigail Arbuthnot. His portrait and that of his wife, by Copley, as well as some family silhouettes, have descended to Miss Susan B. Willard, of Hingham, Massachusetts, who is also the owner of the diary and correspondence of Mrs. Barnes. (Plate 11.)

Catherine Goldthwait, daughter of Colonel Thomas Goldthwait (*q.v.*) and niece and adopted daughter of Henry Barnes, whom she accompanied into exile in England, petitioned on December 13, 1775, the House of Representatives of Massachusetts for their interposition to prevent the sale of the remaining contents of the home at Marlborough for her use, but her petition was dismissed. (Force, *American Archives*, Series IV, vol. iv, pp. 1335, 1343.) This lady became the third wife of Dr. Sylvester Gardiner (*q.v.*).

References : A.O. 12/105, f. 53 ; C.O. 5/246, f. 31 ; Suffolk Deeds, vol. 85, p. 513, vol. 90, p. 293 (for his property) ; Stark, *op. cit.*, pp. 399–402.

COLBORN BARRELL

was for several years a merchant at Boston, " where his business afforded him a competent and genteel support for his family, but from his uniform and openly avowed utter abhorrence of the licentious principles and seditious practices of his ungrateful Countrymen, he rendered himself so exceedingly obnoxious to them, that he found it necessary for the quiet in which he would always wish to live, more than two years since, to leave his native Country, and retire to this. And to avoid the fury of the Sons of violence, he was constrained to send his wife, tho' in an ill state of health, from Boston to Philadelphia with a Servant, not daring himself to travel openly, and when he did leave Boston it was at Midnight, and he went thro' the Country in the most private manner, in constant terror lest he should be discovered and insulted. That when he got to Philadelphia the sons of violence had found means to stir up the Populace against him, and to defeat him of a Cargo he had engaged for a Ship he then had waiting at Perth Amboy. That he was glad to leave the place undiscovered, when he escaped to his Ship with his Family and went to South Carolina, where thro' the industry of the same Sons of violence, pointing him out as an addressor of Gov : Hutchinson and Gov : Gage, he was repeatedly on the point of being publickly insulted, and again, frustrated in his voyage." The memorial goes on to say that after these and many more dangers and difficulties he arrived in England in 1775 and there, in a destitute condition, awaited the return of happier times, when he might embark for his native country. (A.O. 13/43.)

At the peace he was a prisoner of war at Philadelphia, and upon his release he repaired to New England, there to find that all his real estate had been confiscated and sold. By taking legal proceedings he obtained recovery of his property in Connecticut, though with considerable loss. With this memorial is an inventory of his losses. (A.O. 13/68.)

Colborn Barrell in evidence on August 15, 1788, stated that he left Boston in September, 1774, and arrived in England in February or March, 1775. He returned to New York in 1777 and came to England from Boston in January, 1787. In March following he was a bankrupt, though he could have discharged all his debts but for his losses arising from the war. The Commissioners in their decision state that they were not justified in recommending him for temporary support. On the score of loyalty he appeared to have no particular merit, and with respect to his property, his estate had been restored to him. (A.O. 12/102, f.146.)

In a letter of August 16, 1788, to the Commissioners he says that after the capitulation at Yorktown he.went thither from New York in his own vessel under a flag of truce from Admiral Digby for some tobacco to which he was entitled by the terms of the capitulation, but he was met at sea by American armed boats and was plundered. His vessel was afterwards seized at Alexandria in Virginia for having on board some goods sent by Virginia loyalists to relatives and friends there. With the memorial is a list of his notes of hand and a paper relating to his Connecticut property. (A.O. 13/41.)

Colborn Barrell was the son of John Barrell, of Boston, and his wife, Ruth Green, and was born, November 6, 1735. He was a frequent correspondent of Robert Sandeman. (*Letters . . . by Robert Sandeman, John Glas, etc.*, 1851.) In a list of members of the First Church of Christ, constituted at Portsmouth, New Hampshire, in 1765, are the names of Robert Sandeman himself and James Cargill, both elders from Scotland, Nathaniel and Colborn Barrell, merchants, and William Barrell, clerk. (*Ib.*, p. 99.) He was educated at the Boston Latin School, and was a member of the Sandemanian Church in Boston, with Benjamin Davis (*q.v.*), Edward Foster (*q.v.*), and Isaac Winslow (*q.v.*). (H. H. Edes's account of this Church in *Publications of Colonial Soc. of Mass.*, vi, 109–130.) John Andrews was his brother-in-law. (*Letters of John Andrews*, 1772–6, ed. by Winthrop Sargent, 1866.)

Hamilton Usher St. George, a Virginia loyalist, says that Lord Cornwallis in 1782 gave him £460 for the support of his wife and family, which sum he entrusted to Colborn Barrell, who kept the money and gave only sixty dollars to Mrs. St. George. (*Loyalists' Claims, op. cit.*, p. 344.) His brothers were Theodore, Joseph and Walter Barrell.

MARY BARRELL

was an Englishwoman who settled in the Island of Grenada about 1763, and sustained heavy losses there by fire in 1770 and again in 1775. She removed to St. Eustatia in 1776. In 1777, in attempting to go to Philadelphia, then in possession of British troops, the vessel was badly damaged in three different actions with American ships, and being unable to weather a storm, went to pieces off Egg Harbour, when she and her children were saved by boatmen. Upon reaching Philadelphia she was not permitted to reside there, and left forthwith. On the journey, she was captured by a party of rebels, who made a prize of everything, even to her horses and carriage, and in depriving her of her possessions observed that she was fortunate in not being cast into gaol, agreeable to General Washington's proclamation. During her detention of 34 months, Admiral Rodney took St. Eustatia, whereby she lost furniture, a library, horses, etc., to the value of £4,000, besides several vessels captured in the course of the war. In 1780, after repeated applications, she was per-

mitted to leave Boston in a cartel, " under an absolute prohibition " of
returning. She sailed to England and started business, which was unsuccessful. She prays for a grant of land in New Brunswick. (A.O. 13/79.)

Mary Barrell gave evidence in London on September 23, 1784, in
support of her claim for compensation. She stated that she had married
Theodore Barrell of Boston in Grenada. She left him in Boston in 1780,
the Congress having refused him permission to accompany her to England,
and she had not heard from him for three years. The Commissioners,
in announcing their decision, stated that she was not an American sufferer
by the rebellion. Although she declared the loyalty of her husband, they
conjectured he was a rebel as he was in Boston in 1780, and all those who
lived there since the evacuation of that town by the British troops in
1776, whatever their former sentiments may have been, must have become
advocates of rebellion. (A.O. 12/101, f.91.)

She was arrested for a debt of her brother, to whom she had lent her
name as security, and was in the King's Bench Prison from July 22, 1786,
and was still there in 1790 with her two fatherless children, one a boy of
14, who writes a fair hand and for whom she is anxious to find a situation
suitable to his tender age. (A.O. 13/137.)

Theodore Barrell was a brother of Colborn and Walter Barrell (q.v.)

WALTER BARRELL

had been employed in the office of the Inspector of Imports and Exports
and Registrar of Shipping for New England since 1769, and from November 1771 until October 1774 he conducted the duties of this office in the
absence of the Inspector himself. When the " Lexington affair of the
Rebells firing on His Majesty's Troops " occurred, he voluntarily associated
with a number of friends to Government who offered their services to
General Gage in any capacity to oppose the rebels. Walter Barrell himself did duty every fifth night throughout the winter, to prevent disorder
and other evils threatened by the rebel party. During the blockade of
Boston, the cost of necessaries of life became " so enormous " that his
income was insufficient for the bare support of his family, and he was
obliged to run into debt. At the evacuation of Boston he accompanied
the British army to Halifax, Nova Scotia, together with his family of
seven. (A.O. 13/43.)

After the Lexington affair the inhabitants of Boston were thrown
into a great state of confusion, and even the troops were much alarmed.
The enemies of the British Government he estimated as not short of four
to one and growing more and more furious, threatening destruction to
the troops and the loyalists. At this critical juncture, all the loyalists
who dared to show their faces assembled and entered into an association
to support the troops by relieving them of night duty. (A.O. 13/74.)

He was appointed on April 5, 1781, clerk in the office of the Secretary
of State for the American Department, where he had been employed as
an extra clerk for some time previously, and remained there until that

office was abolished. (A.O. 12/105, f. 31 ; A.O. 13/85 ; H.O. Dom. 42/1.) In 1788 he was a temporary clerk in the East India Board of Control. (A.O. 13/83.)

In a letter dated Boston, August 14, 1775, to Joseph Green in London, Walter Barrell relates some of the " foolish proceedings " of the rebels, especially in setting fire to the lighthouse, and promises to take measures to preserve Green's house from destruction. Considering the enthusiasm of the rebels, he questions whether Great Britain will overcome them now or at all. (*Earl of Dartmouth MSS., op. cit.*, ii, 352.)

Walter Barrell was born in Boston, August 25, 1737. His brothers were Colborn, Joseph and Theodore Barrell. His name is recorded as a member of the Sandemanian Church in London from about 1783 to July 26, 1805, when he died at the age of 68. The Meeting House of this body was removed about 1783 from Glovers Hall in Beech Lane, Barbican, and the congregation met in what was formerly the Quakers' Meeting House, St. Martin's-le-Grand, subsequently part of the Bull and Mouth Tavern. He was buried in the famous Bunhill Fields Burial Ground, as was his wife, Euphan, who died September 12, 1794, aged 53. (Guildhall MS., 897/6 ; Ex inform. Mr. D. J. Blaikley.)

References : C.O. 5/116, f. 141 ; *Loyalists' Claims, op. cit.*, p. 20.

JAMES BARRICK

For openly avowing his principles in support of Government, especially as a juror in the trial of Captain Preston in 1770, when he had the grati-fication of faithfully discharging his conscience in clearing an innocent officer, he suffered in his interests and was rendered obnoxious to all his business supporters, who associated to withdraw their business from him, particularly John Hancock, with whom he was largely connected. But he has the pleasing reflection in his breast that he had discharged his conscience to God and to his King. In the recital of these incidents in his career he claims no merit, being sensible that he had done no more than his duty. (A.O. 13/43 ; A.O. 13/102.)

He was born in Boston and served his apprenticeship there with a merchant. For twenty years from the age of 24 he was in business as a ropemaker. For many years he was a member of the Governor's Company of Cadets and as such did duty in patrolling the streets during the Stamp Act riots and for a month in protecting the Custom House. As the political troubles increased, jealousies and divisions arose in the company, and by his steady support of Government he became obnoxious to many members, particularly John Hancock, his clients in business, which he was in consequence obliged to relinquish. Being desitute of the means of support he was given appointments in the office of the Inspector of Imports and Exports at Boston and in the Custom House. He also assisted Richard Lechmere (*q.v.*) as accountant. (*Ib.*)

Two of his sons were in His Majesty's service. (A.O. 12/105, f. 32.)

He was granted compensation, £56, from his claim of £100 and received £100 per annum for the loss of his offices mentioned above. (A.O. 12/109.) A pension of £50 was granted to him from 1788 to 1808. His widow, Susannah, received a pension of £29 from November, 1807, to about 1811. (T. 50/22; A.O. 463/23.)

James Barrick was born April 9, 1731, the son of Thomas and Elizabeth Barrick, and was married, November 24, 1757, to Susannah Winkley in Boston. Henry Leddel (*q.v.*) married Elizabeth Barrick (probably his sister) at Boston in 1745–6.

His son, James, is believed to have been appointed Lieutenant in the 60th Regiment of Foot, September 24, 1787.

THOMAS BEAMAN

lived at Petersham, and during the winter before the blockade of Boston, he, at the request of General Gage, frequently travelled through the country to discover the real designs of the leaders of the rebellion, and on April 19, 1775, he was a volunteer [as a guide to Lord Percy] with the military detachment to Concord. In May, 1775, he was appointed waggon master to the army and faithfully discharged his duties until his death in November, 1780, at Bedford, New York. His estate was confiscated and sold. His widow, Elizabeth, and children settled at Digby, Nova Scotia. (A.O. 13/51; A.O. 12/11, ff. 49–50.)

A schedule of his real property, including a farm and mansion at Petersham, and land in Murrayfield and Lancaster, Massachusetts, is in A.O. 12/11, ff. 51–6. His eldest son, Thomas, was a mate on board a sloop belonging to St. John, New Brunswick, after the Revolution and was the owner of a farm. (*Ib.*)

His widow was granted compensation, £600, from her claim of £805 17s. 6d. (A.O. 12/61, f. 63; A.O. 12/109.)

Thomas Beaman, who is described in the Banishment Act of Massachusetts as a gentleman, was a Lieutenant in the First Company of Loyal American Associators raised in Boston, November 17, 1775. (*Ontario Archives, op. cit.*, pp. 878–80.)

His name appears in a list of associates of Jacomiah Allen in a petition to Governor Tryon, of New York, September 29, 1772, for the grant of a tract of 80,000 acres in the north of that province, beginning at Bessborough. (A.O. 13/100.)

Thomas Beaman was present at a meeting on January 2, 1775, at Petersham, when Joshua Willard, Esq., William Barron, Esq., Joseph Stevens, Moses McClallan, Luke Lincoln, Joseph Smith, James Jackson, Samuel Frizzell, David Stone, Robert Goddard, Ebenezer Bragg, Seth Hapgood and Dr. Ephraim Whiting entered into a combination that they would " not acknowledge or submit to the pretended authority of any Congress, Committees of Correspondence, or other unConstitutional Assemblies of men but at the risk of our lives if need be oppose the forcible exercise of all such authority "; and that they would stand by each other and repel force with force, in the event of any of their persons or property being invaded or threatened by any committees, mobs or unlawful assemblies. (Town Records of Petersham.)

GEORGE BEATTIE

took up arms at Boston in 1775 in the Loyal North British Volunteers. At the evacuation of Boston by the British in March, 1776, he went to Halifax, Nova Scotia, thence to New York, where he remained until May, 1783, when he accompanied the loyalist refugees to Shelburne, Nova Scotia. (A.O. 13/24.)

ELIZABETH BELCHER

" That your Memorialist Exclusive of the Abovementioned property was also in her own Right Possest of a very Considerable Farm, situate at Milton Near Boston, where she Resided the Value of Which upon a Moderate Computation amounted to £5000.

" That on the day after the Battle of Lexington Your Memorialist's House was by a party of American Soldiers, plundered of plate, Linnen, Furniture, & Horses, to the Value of £1000, & that at the time of the Blockade of Boston, her said house having by Accident Caught Fire, her Goods & Effects were Carried away by the Americans, who in Consequence of her Attachment to His Majesty's Government refused to Use any Endeavours Whatever to Extinguish the Flames, which might have been with great Ease effected ; the House being situated Close to two Springs & a Large Pond of Water.

" That Your Lordship's Memorialist Notwithstanding these Losses (being desirous to Avoid making any Application to Government) Still Continued to Reside On the Small Remains of her property, for which Indulgence she was repeatedly obliged to pay very Considerable Sums, & at length being totaly Unable to discharge the Tax of £1500, Sterling Imposed on her Estate in the year 1781 she was reduced to the Necessity of disposing of her Lands for that Purpose & also in the year 1782 to Solicit for Leave to Come to England, which with difficulty she Obtained upon the Express Condition, (as appears by the Inclosed paper) of taking with her such Effects only as were Absolutely necessary for the Voyage.

" That your Memorialist arrived in England in November last & at the advanced age of Sixty three Years, finds that she is entirely deprived of that Ample Competency, which her Family & herself had very long Enjoyed, & after having suffered much hardship and Oppression, on Account of her Loyalty to her Sovereign & her Attachment to this Country, is reduced to the Necessity of Imploring your Lordships to grant her such Releif & Support as she may appear Intitled too, in Consideration of her great Losses & present distrest Situation." (A.O. 13/43.)

With her above memorial is a copy of a resolution of the House of

Representatives, September 26, 1782, granting her leave to depart the State, not to return again without leave of the legislature, and to take a servant and such appendages only as may be necessary on their passage. She was ordered to be carefully searched and especial care taken that no letters of intelligence be conveyed by her to the enemies of the United States. There is also a letter from Peter Oliver, Chief Justice of Massachusetts, dated Birmingham, May 15, 1783, estimating the value of her land at Milton at about £10 Sterling an acre [336 acres]; and a copy of a certificate, dated August 19, 1747, and signed by Matthew Livermore, Clerk to the Proprietors of the town of Kingswood, New Hampshire, that Andrew Belcher [husband of Elizabeth Belcher] was admitted an associate in the said town on October 31, 1737. (A.O. 13/43.) Kingswood was chartered by the Province of New Hampshire in 1737, but the township was not settled or incorporated. The names of the grantees are in the New Hampshire State Papers, XXV, 186.

Further, there is a copy of Andrew Belcher's memorial to the House of Representatives of Massachusetts, April 14, 1762, regarding the grant of land made to his father, Governor Jonathan Belcher; a copy of a resolution of that House relating to this grant; and a copy of a grant by George II. of 23,000 acres of land in New Hampshire, with conditions, February 13, 1752. The names of the grantees are not given. (A.O. 13/43.)

She was granted in 1783 the sum of £60 for her support (A.O. 12/99, f. 229); and later received compensation, £910, from her claim of £4,860. (A.O. 12/109.) Her loyalist pension was paid until 1787. (T. 50/8; T. 50/9; T. 50/10.)

Andrew Belcher, husband of this loyalist, was Registrar of the Admiralty in New England and died January 24, 1771.

WILLIAM BELLINGER

was " born in the Army " and served many years as sergeant. During the American Revolution he was drafted from the 70th Foot into the 74th Foot and served as sergeant-major until the peace. He was expecting a commission in the 74th Regiment, on duty at Penobscot, and was ready with the necessary amount of money to purchase it. Encouragement having been given by the commanding officer of that post to make settlements there by granting lots of land, he bought a lot for £15 and built three houses at a cost to him of £300. By the evacuation of this settlement he lost all his property and received no compensation. He was an out pensioner of Chelsea Hospital after the war. (A.O. 13/99, and A.O. 13/96.)

GOVERNOR SIR FRANCIS BERNARD, BARONET (Plate III)

In A.O. 13/74 are the following four letters :—

(a) In his letter of November 25, 1765, he says that in the performance of his public duty he had lost the good will and good opinion of the people, not by his own acts but by the unavoidable obligations of his office. He earnestly wishes that, if it can be done consistent with the dignity of Parliament, the Stamp Act may be abandoned. In another letter, dated January 25, 1766, he expresses similar wishes regarding the Stamp Act. (British Museum, Addl. MSS., 15488, f. 164.)

(*b*) From Walter Logan (his agent), dated Boston, November 5, 1770, relating to the fatal illness of his son [Francis] Bernard. Another letter, dated 18th, states that this son was buried in a brick grave adjoining that of his brother, Shute.

(*c*) From his son, John, dated Boston, November 5, 1770, referring to the death of the above [Francis] Bernard on that day.

(*d*) From Walter Logan, November 18, 1770, mentioning the " affair of the plate," which some gentlemen wished to have ended. Logan was desirous to save former friends from reflection and to impute what they have done to indiscretion. He also mentions a dispute which had occurred between Logan and Mr. Loring, and that the disorders in Boston had ended sooner than could have been expected. (A.O. 13/74.)

Sir Francis Bernard was appointed Governor of New Jersey in 1758, and in 1760 was transferred to Massachusetts. In 1768 he returned to England to report on the condition of the province and did not resume his office. He was succeeded by Thomas Hutchinson (*q.v.*), who declared that he would have been spoken of as one of the best of New England Governors if he had left America just after the gift of Mount Desert to him.

He died, June 16, 1779. In his long will (dated September 23, 1778, and proved July 10, 1779), oblivious of the pending confiscation of Mount Desert by the State which had given it to him, he bequeathed the Island in trust for his eldest son, John, and afterwards, in default of male issue, to his second and third sons, Thomas and Scrope. Provision is made for the letting of the lands to settlers on the Island. (Warburton 287.)

SIR JOHN BERNARD, BARONET.

From the case of Sir John Bernard,* sent in and signed by his younger brother, Thomas Bernard, January 28, 1781 : —

In the beginning of 1774 he (John) held the lucrative appointment of Naval Officer of Massachusetts [to which he had been appointed, September 19, 1770]. In consequence of his engagements in trade at Boston during his elder brother's life, and before receiving this appointment, he was indebted (and still is) to his correspondents in England for £3,000. As security he held real and personal estate, as well as debts due to him in America, to the amount of nearly £6,000. The Boston Port Bill, and the events following it, having put an end to his office, he retired in the spring of 1775 to his little estate at Kennebec, where he was seized by the rebels

* Sir John Bernard succeeded to the baronetcy on the death of his father, June 16, 1779. He died in the West Indies in 1809, and was succeeded, as third baronet, by his brother, Thomas, a graduate of Harvard College.

and confined as a prisoner until he found security for £4,000.   From that time he has continued on parole and with difficulty subsisted.   Governor Sir Francis Bernard, in his partiality for New England, had laid out over £5,000 in the purchase of lands there, which, together with the Island of Mount Desert* (granted to him for his services), were valued at £10,000 at the Governor's departure from the province in August, 1769.   All this property was in the hands of the rebels or of the purchasers at auction. Sir John Bernard inherited a barren title without any income whatsoever to support an honour granted to his father for his public services.   (A.O. 13/43.)

In a letter to the Commissioners, dated November 4, 1782, regarding the above claim, Thomas Bernard speaks in strong terms of the cruel and unjustifiable reflection on the memory of his father by the neglect in not granting compensation to Sir John Bernard, especially as some persons (whom he had remembered in Massachusetts, in inferior situations and of doubtful characters if not inimical to government) had been granted pensions or compensation.   (*Ib.*)

Certificates from Colonel Thomas Goldthwait (*q.v.*) and Sir William Pepperell, testify to the truth of the above memorial.   (*Ib.*)

Thomas Bernard on June 11 and 13, 1783, gave evidence before the Commissioners in London, in support of the claim of his brother, Sir John Bernard (then living on a small farm at Kennebec) and valued the whole of the late Governor Sir Francis Bernard's property in America at £12,000 sterling.   The Commissioners in their report state that the losses of Sir John were undoubtedly great, but as he was resident in America, with sufficient for his support, they could not recommend him any allowance. (A.O. 12/99, f. 319.)

From a petition of [Sir] John Bernard, then of Bath,† Lincoln County, Massachusetts, dated January, 1785, to the Senate and House of Representatives :

He has resided in the State of Massachusetts before, during and since the war.   During the war he " invariably demeaned himself as became a Citizen of this State, in proof of which, he most humbly begs leave to refer your Honors to a Testimony of many of the inhabitants in the neighbourhood of his place of residence, and also to his well-known and general Character."   By the war and the confiscation of his father's estate he has suffered a serious diminution of his property and in consequence has been reduced to real indigence.   As his father had left Massachusetts in August, 1769, and had retired from public life for several years before the Revolution and had never taken an active part in politics in England relating to American affairs, he ventures to submit to the consideration of

* This Island was granted by the Province of Massachusetts to Governor Bernard in 1762, for his services to the province in the war with the French in North America. The grant was confirmed by the King in Council, March 28, 1771.   Mount Desert was included in the Massachusetts Confiscation Act for the confiscation of the property of loyalists in 1779.

† Now in Sagadahoc County, Maine.

Governor Sir Francis Bernard, Bart.   PLATE III

PLATE IV

Sampson Salter Blowers

the legislature whether it is needful to involve his ruin and destruction in "the system of exemplary Justice, necessarily and wisely adopted by this Country." He hopes, therefore, that he may be permitted to take possession of the property devised to him in the last will and testament of his deceased father and thereby be released from the gloomy condition of penury and want into which he has been thrown by a long succession of misfortunes. (A.O. 13/74.)

Sir John Bernard's above petition to the General Court in January, 1785, was unfavourably received and he was obliged to withdraw it. A new election having been held in May, 1785, he again presented it and in June he obtained a grant of a moiety of Mount Desert, with a proviso that he should convey unto each and every person then in possession such quantity thereof and upon such terms as the Committee named should direct. This committee directed that to every person in possession of land before January 1, 1784, 100 acres shall be conveyed and as about eighty was the number, they got about 8,000 acres, and not unnaturally selected the best and most valuable land. (*Ib.*)

Sir John Bernard was in England in 1787. Whether he returned to America or not depended upon the decision of the Commissioners on his claim for compensation. He had mortgaged a moiety of Mount Desert for about half its value. (Letter from Thomas Bernard to the Commissioners, dated June 21, 1787.) (*Ib.*)

From an affidavit of Sir John Bernard, sworn in London, July 6, 1787 :

At the end of 1783 and early in 1784 he consulted John Lowell, lawyer and senator, respecting his proposed petition to the General Court for the restitution of Mount Desert.* By Lowell's advice he prepared a draft of this petition, but Lowell advised postponement until a more favourable time, when the ferment and animosity arising from the war should abate. Shortly afterwards he consulted William Lithgow, junior, lawyer and senator, of Georgetown in Lincoln County, who advised him to procure from the inhabitants of Kennebec River and the neighbourhood a written testimonial to his character, for presentation with his petition. Lithgow prepared a draft of the testimonial [of which there is a copy in this affidavit] certifying that he is an honest and upright man, and that his moral and political conduct has been uniformly unexceptionable. Lithgow not only signed it himself but also procured the signatures of the justices and civil officers assembled at the General Sessions for Lincoln County in or about June, 1784. Having obtained this testimonial he was advised by John Lowell to consult James Sullivan [the distinguished Massachusetts lawyer], who added to the ninth paragraph of the draft, " And having never since he left this State taken any Part in the politicks of his Country respecting America, your petitioner would humbly submit . . . whether it is needful to involve his ruin and destruction in the system of exemplary Justice necessarily and wisely adopted by this

---

* For Sir Francis Bernard and Mount Desert, see *Publications of Colonial Soc. of Mass.*, xxiv, 197–254.

Country." Sullivan said that this clause was necessary and would have a good effect in pointing out the injustice of the confiscation of the late Sir Francis Bernard's estates. The petition and testimonial were presented in January, 1785, but, the temper and disposition of the majority appearing to be unfavourable, he was advised by several of those members who were favourable, not to hazard it that session. Upon a new election in May, Edward Hutchinson Robbins, a lawyer and member of the General Court, offered his assistance to Sir John Bernard in carrying the petition through the House and it was referred to a committee, which included Robbins. This committee reported in favour of a grant of a moiety of Mount Desert with certain restrictions, and consequently the resolve, previously prepared by Robbins, passed the General Court in June, 1785. Sir John Bernard now goes on to swear in his affidavit that during the war he had not taken any part with the Americans, or aided or abetted or assisted them in any respect whatsoever, but on the contrary did give such information and assistance, so far as his situation at Kennebec permitted, to Edward Parry (agent for procuring masts for the Royal Navy) who was the only British subject in or about Kennebec to whom he could be of any service. He verily believes, from information received from several members of the General Court, that what induced that Court to grant him part of Mount Desert was the prevailing opinion in Massachusetts that in view of Sir Francis Bernard's departure from the province in 1769 and his retirement from public life, the confiscation of the Bernard estates was illegal and unconstitutional. (A.O. 13/74.)

The following extracts from a Journal of Edward Parry, just mentioned, were submitted by Sir John Bernard in proof of this loyalty. (A.O. 13/74):

21 April, 1775. Information was given to him by John Bernard, Esq., warning him to be on his guard against his landlord (Luke Lambert), who was " leagued " against him and had sworn to Captain Hubbs, Hobby and others that he wished the Committee would carry Parry off, and was ready with his gun. This perfidious rascal, only a day or two previously, had been endeavouring to ingratiate himself with Parry by declaring his abhorrence of, and his refusal to sign, the solemn league and covenant, although incurring thereby the displeasure of his brother, Joseph Lambert. This declaration of Luke Lambert was confirmed by Captain Hubbs in the presence of Parry.

29 April, 1775. Mentions various schemes to destroy the masts and trees at Georgetown, ready to be shipped.

3 May, 1775. Edward Parry was sent for to the tavern of Joseph Lambert, where Colonel Samuel Thompson and fifty armed men were gathered, one playing " miserable music of a miserable hautboy," and a lad thumping a drum. Parry soon perceived Thompson's irritation against him, for his alleged unbecoming treatment of a person (Thompson) of his imaginary consequence. Thompson was very clamorous and violent and said that Parry was no more worthy to be treated like a gentleman. A committee was formed, with Timothy Langdon, attorney, of Wichcasset (afterwards a Judge of the American Admiralty) as their clerk.

4 May, 1775. Parry was taken into the custody of Thompson as a suspected enemy of the rights of America. Mentions the arrest of John Bernard, who was searched on suspicion of conveying letters from Parry to Captain Mowat (*q.v.*) and other British officers, and was ordered to find a bond for £2,000, Thompson tauntingly adding that he (Bernard) should plant potatoes for him at Topsham.

12 May, 1777. John Bernard informed Parry that 31 masts had been removed by order of the Boston Board of War.

The following affidavits are in A.O. 13/74 :

(*a*) Affidavit of James Sullivan, lawyer and member of the House of Representatives, that John Bernard had applied to him for advice respecting his petition to the General Court and his opinion thereon. This opinion is not, however, here.

(*b*) Affidavit of William Lithgow, lawyer and senator, that John Bernard and his property were seized in 1775, in consequence of his attachment to British Government ; and that the said testimonial was prepared and procured for Bernard by Lithgow.

(*c*) Affidavit of John Lowell, lawyer and senator, who advised John Bernard that his claim would not be injured in England by the presentation of his petition to the General Court, but was a previous step to establishing it.

According to a long statement, Sir John Bernard's loyalty and attachment to the Crown had been proved to the satisfaction of the Commissioners, but that a question had arisen as to whether he had ceased to be a British subject by reason of his petition to the State of Massachusetts, or by his residence in America from July, 1785, to January, 1787, and thereby forfeited his right to compensation from the British Government. Sir John Bernard's explanation was that he had spent that time mostly in obtaining vouchers and certificates of his father's vast estates—which was a long and tedious business, involving much travelling—in response to requests from his father's executors. (A.O. 13/74.)

With the Bernard papers in A.O. 13/43 are many certificates, affidavits and schedules relating to Governor Sir Francis Bernard's vast landed property in New England, which was confiscated and sold. There are other references to the Bernard affairs in A.O. 12/81, ff. 67-8 and A.O. 13/137.

The executors of Governor Bernard claimed £5,800 compensation from the British Government and were awarded £2,500 for the loss of the real property. (A.O. 12/109.)

A portrait of Governor Bernard is at Christ Church, Oxford, where he was educated.

References : *Life of Sir Francis Bernard* . . . . [by his son, Thomas] 1790 ; *Barrington-Bernard Correspondence*, 1760-1770, ed. by E. Channing and A. C. Coolidge, 1912 ; Stark, *op. cit.* 191-204; Mr. W. Otis Sawtelle in *Trans. of Colonial Soc. of Mass.* xxiv, 197-254; *American Members of the Inns of Court*, by E. Alfred Jones, 1924.

JOHN BERNARD

was a German who settled in Boston in 1770 as a furrier. Early in the war he was invited by the rebels to join them, but he refused and joined the Associated Loyalists in Boston in 1775. (A.O. 13/43; A.O. 13/74; A.O. 12/99, f. 291.) His claim of £63 10s. was met by a grant of £10. (A.O. 12/109.)

Reference: *Loyalists' Claims, op. cit.*, pp. 231-2.

ROBERT BETHELL

was for many years an officer in the Customs at Boston. As a strong, active and spirited loyalist, he joined the King's Orange Rangers* at Paulus Hook in 1777 and received a commission as lieutenant and quartermaster. In October, 1777, this regiment was attached to General Sir Henry Clinton's abortive expedition up the North River, New York, intended to effect a junction with Burgoyne's army, and was present at the reduction of Forts Montgomery and Clinton. In October, 1778, the regiment was ordered to Nova Scotia, and in 1782 Bethell was promoted Captain. At the reduction of the regiment he was placed on half pay and settled first at Chester, Nova Scotia, from predilection, as being the name of his birthplace in England, the historic city of Chester. From this place he removed to Halifax and finally to Lunenburg, Nova Scotia, where he died, February 11, 1816, at the age of 63, leaving his widow, Margaret Honey (whom he had married at Lunenburg, October 12, 1792) in great distress. (W.O. 42/B12.)

DAVID BLACK

was of Scottish birth and settled in 1770 in Boston as a merchant. He utterly abhorred and detested the principles and conduct of the rebels and exerted himself by every possible means to suppress the rebellion. He was granted a commission as Lieutenant in the Loyal North British Volunteers, " which was the first Company raised in American in defence of the constitution." The conduct and bravery of this corps drew from his Excellency the General repeated thanks both publicly and privately, during the blockade of Boston. In 1775 he contracted for two different brigantines at that time being built, one in Kennebec River, bought from Alexander Inglish, of Boston, and the other at Liscomtown, Taunton, from Nehemiah Liscom. The revolutionary troubles prevented the fulfilment of the contract for delivery. Liscom, a zealous loyalist, was imprisoned, cruelly treated and banished, and fled to New York, where he

* John Coffin, of Boston, raised and commanded the King's Orange Rangers, and distinguished himself throughout the American War of Revolution in this and other Loyalist regiments as an intrepid and gallant officer. After the war he settled in New Brunswick, where he reached the rank of General in the British army. (Stark, *op. cit.*, 235-9.)

suffered much and was murdered at Kingsbridge by two ruffians, who were captured and executed. David Black engaged one Captain James McEwen (afterwards a justice of the peace at Shelburne, Nova Scotia) to endeavour to get the Taunton brigantine finished, butMcEwen himself (the intended commander of this vessel) was obliged to flee in June, 1775. Sinking under the weight of his accumulated losses and misfortunes, this Scotsman was forced to call together such of his creditors as were available in New York in December, 1779, and compound with them for 4s. in the pound. He remained in that city and did duty in defence of the garrison whenever required. In May, 1783, he returned to Boston in the hope of recovering a share of his debts, but soon after landing he was arrested and taken before the Committee of Safety, who treated him very roughly and threatened him with the rigour of their laws as a proscribed traitor and finally committed him to gaol, where he was kept for eleven months. He would have been liberated but for fresh prosecutions arising from the alleged plundering by the Loyal North British Volunteers during the blockade of Boston. He offered to give security for the payment of all damage alleged to have been done, upon a fair trial. With this memorial is a schedule of his losses. (A.O. 13/50 ; A.O. 12/10, f. 262–270.)

His witnesses in support of his claim were George Graice (or Gracie), who called upon him in Boston gaol ; Alexander Selkrig ; and three Loyal North British Volunteers : Andrew Barclay, George Beattie and William Black. He settled at Shelburne, Nova Scotia.

David Black was granted £480 as compensation from his claim of £1,935. (A.O. 12/61, f. 36 ; A.O. 12/109.)

He sent a deposition to the Privy Council regarding the " tea riots " at Boston. (*Acts of the Privy Council, Colonial* (printed) vi., 550–5.) In 1776 he was captured by Manly with a vessel load of Tories, including " brazen-head " Jackson and Hill, the baker. (Abigail Adams to John Adams, April 14, 1776.)

Reference : *Ontario Archives, op. cit.*, pp. 569–61, 664.

LANDON BLACK

was born in Boston. In the Revolutionary War he was forced to carry arms in the American militia. He afterwards joined the Royal Navy. (A.O. 13/43 ; A.O. 12/99, f. 86.)

JOHN BLAIR

of Boston, baker. In April, 1786, he was at Shelburne, Nova Scotia. His claim is endorsed : Rejected 18 April, 1786. (A.O. 13/25.) His estate in Boston was bought, September 29, 1787, by Victor Blair. (Suffolk County Recs., Lib. 161, p. 79.)

DANIEL BLISS

In A.O. 12/82 is a copy of the libel against his estate in the Inferior Court of Common Pleas held at Cambridge, November 28, 1780, signed by

John Hancock and John Avery, junior, showing that his estate was forfeited.

He was a signatory to the address from the barristers and attorneys
of Massachusetts to Governor Hutchinson in 1774 and is named in the
Banishment Act.

Governor Hutchinson, in a letter to Lord North, September 25, 1776,
recommending Daniel Bliss, said that he made him a Justice of the Peace
and that he was a very active loyalist. (A.O. 13/46.)

Daniel Bliss was born in 1742 at Concord and graduated at Harvard
College in 1760, in the same year as Daniel Leonard (*q.v.*). He married
Isabella, daugher of Colonel John Murray (*q.v.*). As an active loyalist he
served as Assistant Commissary-General with General Burgoyne's army
and afterwards was in charge of the whole commissariat from Niagara to
the most westerly British post. At the end of the war he was appointed
a member of the Council and a Judge of the Court of Common Pleas
in New Brunswick, where he died in 1806. His brother, Jonathan,
graduated at Harvard in 1763 in the same class as four loyalist lawyers, Sampson Salter Blowers, William Parker, Samuel Porter and Joshua
Upham, and died as Chief Justice of New Brunswick in 1822. (Sabine,
op. cit. ; Judges of New Brunswick, op, cit., pp. 231–2, 239–41, 253–6,
267.)

SAMUEL BLISS

of Greenfield. Before the skirmish at Lexington he was obliged to take
shelter in Boston, on account of his exertions in opposition to the measures
of the revolutionary party. He accepted a commission as lieutenant in,
and recruited several hundred men for, the Royal Highland Emigrants,
and served in the corps until it was disbanded. Under the provisions of
the Treaty of Peace he sailed for New York, to endeavour to recover his
property, and in 1786 he was about to embark a second time for America,
to close his affairs in Massachusetts. This memorial is endorsed " Rejected 29 November, 1786." (A.O. 13/32.)

His commission as lieutenant in the Royal Highland Emigrants is
dated June 14, 1775. This regiment was raised in June, 1775, and was
formed for the most part of emigrants to America from the Highlands of
Scotland. In 1779 it was placed on the British establishment as the 84th
Regiment of Foot. (C.O. 42/39, f. 65 ; Force, *American Archives*,
Series IV, vol. iii, pp. 4–5.) According to the index of Charlotte County,
New Brunswick, Samuel Bliss was the owner of property at St. Andrews
in that county.

SAMPSON SALTER BLOWERS (Plate iv)

was born at Boston. In 1769 he was admitted a barrister and continued in
his profession until the autumn of 1774, when he left Boston. Having
been frequently engaged on the side of the Crown in unpopular contro-
versies previous to the Revolutionary war, especially as attorney for
Captain Preston and the soldiers of the 29th Regiment in their second trial,

he, soon after the commencement of hostilities, was proscribed, though absent in England, and such of his estates and effects as could be discovered were seized by the committee of sequestration. Towards the end of 1776, being unable to support himself and his family in England, he applied to the Treasury for relief and was granted £100 per annum. On the reduction of New York and Rhode Island by the British army, imagining he could be useful to Government as well as to himself by residing in America, he left England in August, 1777, for New York. On his visit to Boston in 1778 he was thrown into gaol with four or five common felons, and was detained for eight days. It was judged expedient to establish in 1779 a Court of Admiralty in Rhode Island, and he was honoured with a commission of appointment as Judge of that Court, and repaired thither, but within a few days of landing orders were received for the evacuation of the garrison, and he was obliged to return to New York. In the spring of 1780 he sailed again for England, with a view to solicit compensation for the loss sustained by him in the evacuation of Rhode Island, but he failed to obtain pecuniary satisfaction. He was, however, honoured, through the influence of Lord Sackville, with the appointment of Solicitor General at New York, and immediately returned. By this appointment and his own profession he was enabled to procure a decent support for his family. At the evacuation of New York he moved to Halifax in Nova Scotia. His profession for seven years before the Revolution produced him £500 lawful money per annum. By his marriage [in 1774 to Sarah, daughter of Benjamin Kent] he got £5,000 sterling and £1,000 more in slaves, household effects, etc. The estate of Mrs. Blowers consisted of houses, but chiefly of money lent on personal and real securities. In consequence of his proscription and the risk of any legacy being confiscated by the United States, his grandfather altered his will and left property worth £1,500 to his sisters. (A.O. 13/50; A.O. 12/10, ff. 1, et seq.). There is a schedule of the bonds and securities, just mentioned, with the names of the debtors and the amounts. (Ib.)

His claim of £1,200 for real estate and of £3,591 16s. 3d. for personal property was disallowed. A pension of £100 was granted. (A.O. 12/61, ff. 1-2; A.O. 12/105, f. 54; A.O. 12/109.)

His Boston estate was bought in 1784 by Elisha Sigourney (*Suffolk County Recs.*, Lib. 145, p. 124).

Sampson Salter Blowers was born March 10, 1741, the son of John Blowers, silversmith, and his wife, Sarah, daughter of Sampson Salter, and graduated at Harvard College in 1763. He studied law in the office of Governor Hutchinson, in whose diary he is frequently mentioned. His high sense of honour, sound judgment and zealous loyalist principles, as well as his ability as a lawyer, were such as to induce the British Government to appoint him as Attorney General, Judge and Chief Justice (from 1797) successively, in Nova Scotia. In his letter to the Treasury, dated London, May 2, 1777, he expresses his desire to reside in Rhode Island, provided he could have a passage out and his loyalist allowance continued until he could return in peace and safety to his estate at Boston. He is inclined to make this application as there would seem to be a very great probability of an early conclusion of the rebellion. (A.O. 13/43.) In his letter to the same, dated June 5, 1777, he prays for a sum of money for the passage of himself and family to New York, as the interest of many clients, loyal subjects, and his own private affairs, render it necessary for him to embrace the earliest opportunity of getting to Boston after the peace and the restoration of the King's government. Furthermore, he flatters himself that by the influence which his profession has given him in Massachusetts, and his former connections there, it may be in his power to render service to Government by residing near Boston, whereas in London he can only drag on a useless life of indolence and inactivity. (*Ib.*)

DEAR BLISS,   New York Novem^r. 24th 1778.

A few days after the date of my last from R^d. I^d. in which I enclosed Judge Sewalls Note for £8 Ster^g. I left the Island with design to pay a visit to M^{rs}. B. who had been for some time past and then remained extremely ill, intending also if I found the passions of the people moderated and a prospect of living quietly there, to continue amongst them, with a view of preserving my estate, serving my friends and contributing by my vote and influence to the restoration of peace and good government.

On my arrival at Providence I waited on Genl. Sulivan who has the command there and ask'd his permission to go forward to Boston. He told me he was surprised I should think of appearing there after the part I had taken in the present contest—That from the information he had received respecting me, he had reason to think I had taken a very decided part agst. them, and that I should find the people of Boston generally of that sentiment—I desired him to tell me what particular charges had been alledged agst. me, to which he answer'd that I had wrote several letters wherein I had express'd myself explicitly in favor of the enemy and agst. the country, & that he had heard I had been a writer in the publick papers in vindication of the measures of the Par^{lt}. of G. B. The charge of writing in the papers I denied and as to private letters I told him I could say nothing unless I saw them or was acquainted with their contents ; that I was however ready to acknowledge that my sentiments respecting the present dispute had not comported with those of my countrymen in general, though I took upon to affirm, that nothing which I had wrote or said could be fairly construed into a proof of inimicality to my country for which I had ever felt a most cordial attachment—that at any rate I had taken no active part whatever in the war & that I hoped in a land of liberty I should not be condemn'd for opinions only—Several other things were said in the course of which he was pleased to say, that as an individual he esteem'd me & should be glad to hear I had made peace with my townsmen, though he believed I should not meet with a favorable reception —That I should have a pass and that when I got to Boston he expected I would make my arrival known to the council at Boston—I took his pass— thank'd him for his politeness & parted with telling, that the situation of my wife and her great desire to see me were sufficient to carry me to Boston at any risk—I set off that day on horse back and arrived the next day, having spent nearly two days on the journey and stop'd at almost every farm house and tavern on the road I found the farmers full of complaints against the scarcity of cloathing & the enormity of the taxes which they said must very soon ruin them. There was few who did not throw out some bitter expression against the french or who omitted to express his wishes for peace and for a treaty of commerce with G^t. B^n. The morning after my arrival at Boston I sent the council notice of my being there and by their direction Justice Pemberton was made acquainted with it. About 12 o'Clock I went to his house where I found Justice Gardiner. These Gentlemen treated me civilly and discovered a disposition to serve me as far as they dared. They allowed me to return to my own house and took my word for my appearance again before them at 6 o'Clock—I had been at home but a very short time when the Com^e. of Correspondence he having obtain'd notice of my being in town sent an officer to summon me before them at Farnwell hall* at 3 o'Clock. I wrote them a short note in which I told them I was already in the hands of justice and could not attend them, soon after which word was brought me that the Com^{ee}. was mustering their forces and were determined to send 500 Men to bring me before them unless I prevented it by $appear^s$. at the hall at the time fixed—As I dreaded above all things the consequences to M^{rs}. B of such an alarm, at 3 o'Clock I walk'd down to the *Gentl*". Nat Barber was their president and I soon found that all they wanted was to raise a mob about me & to make my commitment as publick and ignominious as they could. While I was before them Bill Cooper† & Edes‡ the printer were collecting a sufficient number of choice spirits to huzza me through the streets—to insult & perhaps to murder me which was frequently threaten'd. With these people at my heels and Cudworth at my elbows I went from the Hall to the Jail and was put into a dismal stinking lower room, with grated windows & without a chimney or any place for fire except a wooden tub lined with brick & here kept 7 days § & then sent on board a cartel ship bound to Halifax but brought by the prisoners on board to this place.

During my confinement I was visited by many of the Merchants & gentry of the town who all expressed a disapprobation of the late law and the barbarous manner in which it was executed ag^{st}. me. They were very sure that the Genl. Court would very soon repeal it & that permission would be granted for the greater part of those proscribed in that act, to return—Several of them urged me to petition the council & board of war for permission to remain there untill the Genl. Court met when they were confident I should get released from confinement & liberty to continue in the country but I absolutely refused & told them that after the treatment which I had received I could have but one wish, which was to get out of

---

* Faneuil Hall.

† William Cooper, Town Clerk of Boston.

‡ Benjamin Edes, of *The Boston Gazette and Country Journal*.

§ Eight days is stated in another document.

the country as soon as possible—Mr Nichborn and Mr M. Brimmer *
interested themselves very warmly in my favor and took great pains to
procure me a more comfortable appartment and liberty to return by
land to New Port or New York, but all to no purpose.

I suffer'd exceedingly on board the cartel which was crouded chock
full as the sailors say. I have however escaped with the loss of a few
pounds of flesh. Notwithstanding all I have suffer'd I am now glad I
have made the experiment, because it has convinced me that very material
changes must take place in that country before long. Divisions and
animosities abound more than ever and the mischiefs produced by the
war become every day more apparent. The french alliance is extremely
disagreable to the common people who have the same antipathy for the
french they ever had. The country is thin'd of its inhabitants & much
wasted by the war and the paper money is every day grow^{r}. worse. 25
Dollars is the current price for a Guinea & if pains is taken 30 can be got—
The principal shops & stores are kept by french men who exchange the
paper they receive at any discounts—

I ought to have mentioned that projett of going to Boston was approved
by Sir Robt. Pigot to whom I stated my reasons at large. I had also
Genl. Prescotts permission to leave Rh^{d}. Island for Boston—I am fully
satisfied that if I had been permitted to remain at Boston I could very
soon have made myself usefull & have been inabled to render essential
services to my friends &c—I shall not have time to forward a certificate
for Mr. Rowe† but will do it after the first of Janry.

I expect M^{rs}. Blowers will be here as soon as she is able to travel and
heaven only knows how I shall procure the means of living—Should a civil
government be established for this place I shall try to live by the law—

Adieu Beleive me always   Your affectionate friend
(A.O. 13/43.)   S. S. BLOWERS.

The story of his challenge to a duel to Richard John Uniacke, Attorney
General of Nova Scotia, arose from a fight in the streets of Halifax
between Uniacke and Jonathan Stearns, a Boston loyalist and friend of
Blowers. Uniacke, a strong man, beat Stearns, a weak and sickly man, to
death. Stirred to anger, Blowers challenged Uniacke to a duel and the
challenge was accepted. But Uniacke secretly sent his wife to inform the
magistrates, and both these Law Officers of the Crown were bound over
to keep the peace. (W. J. Stirling, in *Diary and Letters of Governor
Hutchinson*, i., 341–2.)

He died in 1842, aged 100, and was buried in the historic church of
St. Paul at Halifax, where there is a monument to his memory. His
portrait by J. P. Drake, 1820, in his scarlet robes as Chief Justice, hangs
in the County Court House, Halifax.

References: A.O. 13/83; Sabine, *op. cit.*; *Journal of Samuel Curwen, op. cit.*,
pp. 501–3; *Ontario Archives, op. cit.*, pp. 490–1.

* Martin Brimmer, merchant of Boston.

† Probably John Rowe, Boston merchant, whose Diary was edited by E. L.
Pierce in 1895.

ANNA BORLAND

was the widow of John Borland, Esq., a gentleman possessed of an estate of £2,000 sterling per annum, who for his well-known loyalty was obliged in September, 1774, to quit his house and property in the country and with a numerous family remove for protection to Boston. He died during the blockade of that place, leaving nine children. To avoid other distresses and to prevent her children from being forced into the rebel army, Anna Borland sailed for England. Two sons entered H.M. service, one [John Lindall] as an Ensign in the 22nd Regiment, and the other [Francis*] as a surgeon's mate in the Military Hospital at New York. Her husband's American estate having been confiscated, she was obliged in her poverty to appeal to Government for relief. (A.O. 13/43.)

Having received several encouraging accounts of a favourable disposition in some of the people of Massachusetts towards her, and wishing no longer to be a burden to Government, she applied for leave to sail to New York, where she would have a more speedy communication with those who may be disposed to relieve her, and be better able to take advantage of such disposition to recover part of her husband's estate. (Ib.)

Her son, John Lindall Borland, stated in evidence that his mother had sailed for America with one son, Leonard, and had gone to her two married daughters at Charlestown in Massachusetts. She inherited £20,000 after his father's death. Sir William Pepperell stated that John Borland was a retired merchant and died in 1775† from the effects of a fall from a ladder. (A.O. 12/105, f. 99.)

John Borland was the son of Francis and Jane Borland and was born in Boston, September 5, 1728. He married, February 20, 1749, Anna Vassall, of Charlestown, Massachusetts. A copy of his will is in A.O. 13/74.

His estate having been restored to Mrs. Borland, her bounty of £200 per annum from the British Government was consequently stopped about the end of 1783. (A.O. 12/81, f. 37 ; T. 50/6 ; T. 50/7.)

According to Peter Oliver's letter of March 5, 1784, Anna Borland married a Mr. Knight, of Rhode Island, who first courted her. (Gov. Hutchinson's *Diary*, ii, 403–5.)

John Borland's Boston estate was bought by his son Leonard Vassall Borland (1759–1801) (*Suffolk Recs.*, Lib. 172, p. 55), who married in 1785, Sarah, daughter of Dr. James Lloyd (*q.v.*). Her portrait, painted by Gilbert Stuart, is in the possession of Mr. William Augustus Jeffries, of Boston. (Lawrence Park's *Gilbert Stuart*, 1926.)

Her daughter, Phœbe, was the wife of George Spooner (*q.v.*), and another daughter married Jonathan Simpson the younger (*q.v.*), who lived in John Borland's house, originally Apthorp House, which is illustrated in Drake's *Hist. Mansions and Highways around Boston*, 1899.

---

* Francis Borland was appointed surgeon's mate to this hospital, July 11, 1777. (Kemble Papers, in *New York Hist. Soc. Colls.*, 1883, p. 469.)

† June 5, aged 47. (*Proc. of Mass. Hist. Soc.*, 2nd Ser., x, 412.)

JOHN LINDALL BORLAND

joined the Associated Loyalists in Boston in 1775, though under age, and was possessed of a fortune of £600 per annum. He accompanied his mother, Anna Borland (*q.v.*) to England. General Gage gave him a commission as Ensign in the 22nd Regiment and afterwards borrowed money to buy a commission in that regiment. He was present in the action of August 27, 1776, on Long Island, New York, and served with his regiment until August 29, 1778, when he was wounded by a musket ball, which lodged in his right shoulder and incapacitated him from further active service, except recruiting. He is now obliged to make an application for relief, being unable to subsist any longer. With this petition are certificates to his loyalty from General Gage and Governor Hutchinson. (A.O. 13/43 ; A.O. 13/74.)

The Commissioners reported on his case that he had been very active in the cause of Government and recommended the continuance of his allowance of £100. (A.O. 12/105, f. 5.)

Under the will of his great-grandfather, Timothy Lindall,* of Salem, Massachusetts, he was entitled to considerable real property, including a farm at Freetown (a plan of which is here and is called " alias Damon's farm ") ; farms at Danvers and Middleborough, and land at Raynham and Lunenburg, valued at between £6,000 and £7,000, some of which was confiscated and sold by the State. He was entitled to about £5,000 under the will of his father, who was the owner of valuable estates in Massachusetts and Rhode Island. (A.O. 13/74.)

John Lindall Borland claimed £6,129 for the loss of his property and was awarded £3,887. (A.O. 12/109.) He is described as a gentleman of fortune from Boston, and was granted a benevolent allowance of £100 from 1782 to about 1785. (T. 50/6 ; T. 50/8.)

With the Borland documents are copies of the wills of his great-grandfather, Timothy Lindall, and of his father, John Borland ; several copies of conveyances of land to Timothy Lindall between 1712 and 1715 ; certificates of the sale of the confiscated property ; a copy of a certificate that part of the Rhode Island property was assigned to Colonel William Barton with other estate for the payment of wages due to him ; and many other certificates and copies of conveyances relating to the Borland estates. (A.O. 13/74.) For the Rhode Island property, see *Rhode Island Col. Recs.*, vii, 377–8, 394, 556 ; viii, 66, 204, 626–7 ; ix, 420.

The commissions of John Lindall Borland in the British army are as follows : Ensign in the 22nd Foot, September 24, 1775 ; Lieutenant, August 14, 1778 ; Captain in the 38th Foot, February 28, 1792 ; Brevet Major in same, October 18, 1797. He sold out April 9, 1807. (Ind : 5440.)

* Timothy Lindall (1677–1760) was a prominent merchant and a conspicuous figure in the public life of Salem. A silver beaker, his gift to the Second or East Church, Salem, is still preserved. (E. Alfred Jones, *The Old Silver Vessels of the American Churches*, 1913, p. 425.)

He married a lady of Bristol, worth £1,500. (Letter of Peter Oliver, of March 5, 1784, in Gov. Hutchinson's *Diary*, ii, 405–6.) He was married in December, 1783. (Journal of Lieut. George Inman.) John Lindall Borland died in London. In his will, dated November 21, 1814, and proved March 21, 1826, he bequeaths all his property to his wife, Elizabeth. (Swabey, 139.)

DR. THOMAS BOULTON

had enjoyed a good practice as a surgeon at Salem for several years before the Revolution. His active and unwearied endeavours in favour of his Majesty and his many writings in support of Government, made him particularly obnoxious to the rebels, who entirely destroyed his house and furniture and robbed him of everything in his possession. He joined the royal forces as a volunteer and was present and particularly active at Lexington and Bunker Hill, where he was dangerously wounded. Such was his zeal that Lord Percy (to whom he had greatly recommended himself) sent him from Halifax to Quebec, where he was present in almost every skirmish in and about that city, as well as serving during the whole siege. The recovery of Canada having been accomplished, and finding his life in danger from his many wounds, he returned to England and was granted his Majesty's bounty of £50 per annum. He died in great misery, July 27, 1777. (A.O. 13/43 ; A.O. 13/74.)

A certificate, dated Quebec, May 25, 1776, from Captain Robert Lester, R.N., testifies that Boulton joined his company in the British militia in Quebec and stood the fatigues of the whole winter's siege with exemplary zeal and patriotism* ; and another certificate, July 7, 1776, of Lieut.-Colonel Henry Caldwell, in command of the British militia in Quebec, testifies to his good service there. (A.O. 13/43.)

James Rivington, the well-known printer and publisher of New York, in his certificate of July 13, 1776, states that Dr. Boulton exhibited after Dr. Warren's treasonable oration at the Brick Meeting House at Boston on March 5, 1775, a humorous and satirical parody on this oration at the British Coffee House,† in Boston, which was afterwards printed and published at the request of many principal officers of the army and by them sent to New York, where it was reprinted and became serviceable to the cause of Government.‡ (*Ib.*)

Rivington in a letter to William Knox, dated July 15, 1776, says that Dr. Boulton was advertised in the *London Gazette* for a second time as a fugitive returned from Quebec to secure the benefit of the late Insolvent Act.§ He advised Dr. Boulton to surrender himself to the Secondary of

* John Coffin (*q.v.*) was present during this siege.

† The British Coffee House was kept by Hannah Cordis (*q.v.*). See *Letters of John Andrews*, 1772–6, ed. by Winthrop Sargent, 1866, p. 87.

‡ Entitled *An Oration delivered March Fifteenth*, 1775, *at the Request of a Number of the Inhabitants of the Town of Boston. By Dr. Thomas Bolton.*

§ An Act for the relief of Insolvent Debtors ; and for the relief of Bankrupts in certain cases (G. III., 16.). See *London Gazette*, 6–9 July, 1776.

Wood Street Compter* and thereby secure his discharge from many embarrassments. (*Ib.*)

From two letters from Dr. Boulton to Rivington:

(*a*) Solicits him to plead his cause in his distress. The American rebels had destroyed his all, tarred and feathered him and cast him into prison, but these outrages are not comparable to the inward anxiety of being separated from his wife and family. Would to God that every person under his Majesty the King had as just a title to his bounty and protection as he had. His debt in Liverpool amounts only to £138, whereas his losses in America are more than double that sum. (*b*) Dated July 27, 1776. His most pressing creditor is one Yates for £52. He asks Rivington to speak a word in his favour, as one who in the defence of his Sovereign had lost his all. (*Ib.*).

William Knox in a letter to the Treasury, dated July 31, 1776, says that he had advanced the sum of 7½ guineas to Boulton, by direction of Lord George Germain for his immediate subsistence, until he should be discharged from his creditors in consequence of the Insolvent Act. Having failed to obtain the benefit of that Act, Lord G. Germain recommends his petition to the Treasury as a loyalist deserving of the support and protection of Government. (*Ib.*)

His wife, Ellen Boulton, who appears never to have been to America, was granted a loyalist pension of £40. (A.O. 12/105, f. 100.) She was afterwards Mrs. Ellen Edgar. (T. 50/6; T. 50/9; T. 50/11; T. 50/28.)

JAMES BOUTINEAU

At the alteration made in the charter of Massachusetts Bay in 1773, he was appointed [in 1774] one of the new Council. Although many gentlemen who were appointed at the same time declined to act, and others, after accepting, resigned from the Council, he thought himself bound to support Government, as he had always done so far as lay in his power, and notwithstanding his advanced age and the threatening aspect of the times, continued to discharge his duties until August, 1775. Finding that there was no probability of the early restoration of peace and order and that his presence would be of no avail, he intimated to General Gage his desire to embark for England, where he arrived at Bristol on September 22. Here he was reduced from a state of ease and affluence to the necessity of soliciting assistance from Government. (A.O. 13/43.)

From a memorial of Susannah Boutineau, dated Bristol, May 23, 1778:

She is the widow of the above James Boutineau, who had died May 9, 1778. After reiterating most of the above memorial, she sends a schedule of her husband's property in Boston, with mortgages, bonds and other securities, to the estimated value of £7,801. (*Ib.*)

In a letter from her son-in-law, John Robinson, dated May 29, 1778, to the Treasury, regarding her deplorable state, he states that she lost

* A preliminary place of detention for debtors before removal to prison.

the £14,000 sterling which she had brought to her husband at her marriage. (*Ib.*)

Harrison Gray, junior, in a letter of March 27, 1787, says that he resided for over three years in the same house with Mrs. Boutineau at Bristol. He knew James Boutineau as a gentleman of independent fortune, unconnected with business. (*Ib.*)

With another memorial is a long list of deeds of property and a letter of no interest from her granddaughter, Ann Piercy, wife of Lieut. Richard Piercy, R.N., dated January 30, 1788. (A.O. 13/74.)

Her claim of £1,824 was met by a grant of £1,500. (A.O. 12/109.) She received a loyalist pension until 1788. (A.O. 12/105, f. 101 ; T. 50/6 ; T. 50/9 ; T. 50/10.)

A memorial was presented in 1799 on behalf of Susanna Boutineau by Harrison Gray Otis, for a promissory note, dated 1774, for £1,120 and interest due to her late husband from the Province of Massachusetts. (T. 79/21.)

James Boutineau (born January 27, 1710) was the son of Stephen Boutineau, an elder of the French Protestant Church in Boston, and married his wife, Susannah, a sister of Peter Faneuil (*q.v.*), July 26, 1738. He was an attorney at law and acted as counsel for his son-in-law, John Robinson (who married his daughter, Anne, October 5, 1769) in the celebrated action brought against him for his assault on James Otis at the British Coffee House in 1772.

Reference : Sabine, *op. cit.*

CAPTAIN JOHN BOWEN

served throughout the war with the French in North America and having been placed on half-pay after the peace he purchased [in 1767] an estate at Princeton in Massachusetts for £250, and laid out £1,000 upon it. Upon the arrival of General Gage as Governor, the concerted plan of the people at large was to compel every person whose sentiments were in favour of Great Britain to change them, otherwise they were treated in such a manner as obliged them to quit their property. In August, 1774, he was detained as a prisoner in his own house by a numerous armed mob, who accused him of being an enemy to America and a dangerous man, and threatened to cast him into gaol, in irons, if he persisted in joining General Gage at Boston. In consequence of this treatment he was obliged to leave his estate and seek the protection of Gage, who from that time employed him to go into the country for intelligence—a dangerous service, which only his zeal for the King caused him to undertake. (A.O. 13/43.)

Gage having failed to procure a guide for Lord Percy's brigade, he (Bowen) volunteered for the duty and conducted the force to Lexington and he was taken prisoner in returning from that skirmish. He was the first person in Massachusetts to take an active part in favour of the Crown, and during the blockade of Boston he was employed in a confidential capacity by the British force. His land (205 acres) was wild when he bought it and did not produce more than one load of hay, but after eight years' labour in clearing, fencing and improving it, twenty-five loads were harvested. He built a house and repaired another. Later in the war he was given a Captain's commission in the Prince of Wales's Volunteers.* With his memorial is a schedule of his losses.

In October, 1774, proposals were made to him in Boston by a member of Congress [Moses Gill]† in the presence of John Hancock, to serve in the American Army under General [Charles] Lee and to have the nomination of his rank and appointments. The ideas of high rank and the possession of his estate were very flattering and the temptation great, but his duty to his King and country forbid him to serve any power opposed to them. In consequence of his loyalty he lost his estate, which was the sole support of his family. (A.O. 13/43 ; A.O. 13/74 ; A.O. 12/99, f. 230.)

There are several letters of no consequence from him, the last being dated July 2, 1787, and is sealed with arms (A.O. 13/74 ; A.O. 13/137) ; and a certificate from Captain R. Donkin that he was active in procuring intelligence in 1774-5. (A.O. 13/100.)

He was put on half-pay as Captain and was granted a pension. (A.O. 12/100, f. 331 ; A.O. 12/101, f. 278.)

John Bowen was born in England about 1733. (Ind.: 5605-6.) He was gazetted Ensign in 45th Foot, October 15, 1754, and was promoted Lieutenant in the same regiment, in America, June 30, 1755. (Army Lists.)

HENRY BOWERS

of Swansea, was by religious profession a Quaker and as such had " ever uniformly comported himself obedient to the Laws and Government under which he was born and educated, having never swerved by Act or Deed therefrom." With this memorial is a long list of vessels, with their names, which were taken at sea by the Royal Navy and condemned under the Prohibitory Act, and for which he claimed compensation. His claim was, however, rejected, May 29, 1786. (A.O. 13/24.)

An anonymous letter (mutilated and altered) says that Colonel Bowers (presumably Henry Bowers or a family connection) built the first two privateers which sailed from Swansea. (Ib.)

JERATHMEL BOWERS

of Swansea, suffered in his rights, properties and possessions during the rebellion in consequence of his loyalty, and from 1776 to 1779 was the perpetual subject of insult and oppression from minute men and committees of correspondence. Early in the political dissensions he was removed by armed men from his wife and children to a prison and closely confined within its walls and was denied intercourse with his family and friends for many months. To the losses from the rebels must be added

* A loyalist regiment raised in America in October, 1776.
† Loyalists' Claims, op. cit., p. 169.

his losses from the Royal Navy and army of a ship and cargo, and in 1777–1779 from the encampment of British soldiers on his property on the Island of Conanicut, Rhode Island. This memorial is endorsed : Rejected May 29, 1786. (A.O. 13/24.)

A copy of a resolve, dated April 4 and 7, 1777, of a committee of both Houses of the State of Massachusetts that he at divers times had artfully evaded the acceptance of American currency in payment for his securities against individuals ; that he had positively refused to take it and had spoken of it in a very contemptuous manner, declaring that he esteemed it of no more value than chips ; that he had publicly affirmed in December, 1776, his opposition to the Independence of America ; and that he was determined to resign his offices under the Government of Massachusetts. (*Ib.*)

A copy of a petition to the House of Representatives, June 10, 1778, from General Sullivan that Jerathmel Bowers, Esquire, is too great an enemy of the American cause and too dangerous a person to remain near the army in Rhode Island and desiring his removal from the seat of war. Resolved that the sheriff of the county of Bristol be directed forthwith to apprehend Bowers and bring him before the Council of State. (*Ib.*). In an affidavit of Benjamin Tale, Bowers is called " Honorable " and as the owner of a farm called Beaver Tale on Conanicut Island, occupied by the British army. (*Ib.*)

According to an affidavit of David Huntington, the brigantine *St. James*, owned by Bowers and commanded by Huntington, was taken by H.M.S. *Rose* in Newport Harbour, Rhode Island, September 23, 1775. (*Ib.*)

Jerathmel Bowers was accused in 1775 of acting a part inimical to the rights and liberties of America, but was acquitted of these charges by a committee. (Force, *American Archives*, Series IV, vol. iii, pp. 160–1, 1436.) He was a member of the Committee of Correspondence in 1773 and of the House of Representatives of Massachusetts in 1775.

According to Sabine (*op. cit.*) he was elected in 1783 a member of the General Court, but was disqualified on a petition from Rehoboth that he had not shown himself friendly in the late struggle [for independence].

He was a boon companion of Daniel Leonard (*q.v.*).

A charming portrait of his wife, Mary Bowers, by Copley, is in the Metropolitan Museum, New York.

LLOYD BOWERS

was of Swansea and a Quaker. His memorial begins like that of Henry Bowers (*q.v.*). He was part owner of certain vessels captured by the Royal Navy in 1778 and 1779 and condemned under the Prohibitory Act. His claim was rejected, May 29, 1786. (A.O. 13/24.)

WILLIAM BOWES

from about 1750 was a merchant and underwriter in Boston, and from the earliest period of the political dissensions he was a loyalist and during the siege of Boston he did military duty. He left Boston at the evacuation by the British troops, abandoning a large property. With his memorial is a schedule of his real estate, which included 100 acres in Pomfret, Connecticut, derived from William Stoddard, father of his [second] wife [Mary Stoddard, who died, May 9, 1774]; and pew No. 53 in the New Church, Brattle Street. There are also letters to him from Thomas Parker, dated Boston, July 4, 1783, and from Benjamin Clarke, of Boston, August 20 and September 18, 1784, as well as several papers regarding his property. A letter from Clarke, dated October 9, 1788, states, *inter alia*, that the demand of Governor John Hancock upon the estate of Bowes would swallow it all up. (A.O. 13/74.)

He was allowed £1,800 from his claim of £2,075. (A.O. 12/109.) Debts due by him amounted to £995 11s. (A.O. 12/81, f. 66.)

William Bowes was the son of the Rev. Nicholas Bowes, minister at Bedford, Massachusetts, and his wife, Lucy Hancock, aunt of Governor John Hancock. He inherited considerable property in 1764 from his uncle, Thomas Hancock. He died in 1805, aged 71.

References: Sabine, *op. cit.* ; Stark, *op. cit.*, p. 225.

NICHOLAS WARD BOYLSTON (Plate v)

In October, 1773, he was obliged by ill-health to leave Boston, where he left considerable property in bonds and personal securities. By the persuasions of American friends he was prevailed upon, in view of the political disturbances, to remain in Europe. The Courts of Justice having been closed soon afterwards, his attorney was prevented from recovering more than a small part of his property, and since March, 1775, he has not received a shilling therefrom or from any part of America. He had depended for his support on monies deposited with a merchant in London, by whose recent failure he is now without a farthing. (A.O. 13/43.)

A certificate from Benjamin Hallowell (*q.v.*), dated April 6, 1778, states that Nicholas Ward Boylston was his eldest son, and had assumed by royal licence the name of a deceased uncle, Nicholas Boylston, who was well known to have been a firm adherent of the British cause, both in opinion and practice, and from whom he had formed considerable expectations. (*Ib.*) A certificate from Governor Hutchinson, April 27, 1778, states that Boylston was known personally to him as well affected to Government, and as generally understood to have been a man of property who was reported to have had a legacy of several thousand pounds from his uncle. (*Ib.*)

In his letter to the Treasury, September 3, 1778, he repeats the

Nicholas Ward Boylston   PLATE V

PLATE VI   Ann Browne

above memorial, with the addition that the vessel bringing some of his effects from Nova Scotia had been captured by an American privateer. (*Ib.*)

According to his letter to the Commissioners, dated Yarmouth, England, October 26, 1782, he was prevented by his military duty from answering their summons to attend, having procured a commission in the [East Norfolk] militia, and though obliged at considerable and unavoidable expense to take the field, and though he had served in four campaigns as a subaltern, he has had the mortification of seeing the promotion of his juniors over him, owing to his inability to rise higher by lack of money. For ten months past he had been detached upon a very severe duty, exposed to all weathers and injurious to his health. (*Ib.*)

A certificate from Major-General William Tryon, formerly Governor of New York, dated October 25, 1782, states that Boylston, as a Lieutenant in the East Norfolk militia in the Engineer's department, could not be spared from his duties without inconvenience to the service. His ability, attention and diligence were much approved. (*Ib.*)

A certificate from Colonel Sir John Wodehouse, baronet, October 30, 1782, declares that Boylston had served as Lieutenant since June, 1779, and by his diligence and activity had proved himself a good and useful officer. (*Ib.*)

On the outbreak of war between England and France he got a commission in the East Norfolk militia, and was engaged, except during the last year of the war, in erecting defensive works at Yarmouth. He served until the disbandment of that regiment. With his memorial is a schedule of notes of hand and book debts due to him in Boston, as well as details of the cost of the brig *Nancy*, in 1773, with the names of men who supplied or made certain parts, *e.g.*, James Barrick (*q.v.*) for rigging, and Edward Burbeck for carving the head, £5 1s. 10d. (*Ib.*)

The notes of the Commissioners on the evidence of his father, Benjamin Hallowell, are as follows : His uncle, Nicholas Boylston, left him £3,000 worth of property,* and Nicholas Ward Boylston himself was worth £3,000 to £4,000 more. Thomas Flucker (*q.v.*), who knew him very well, says that he had nothing of his own in America ; he took the name of Boylston to recommend himself to his uncle [Nicholas], who was much offended thereby and left him only £3,000, which he believes he spent in travelling to Egypt and elsewhere. Boylston himself says that he has an uncle in London, a bachelor, named [Thomas] Boylston, reputed to be worth £100,000, who has come on leave from Congress, to whom he is "rather inclined." (A.O. 12/105, f. 6.) His claim of £333 was disallowed. (A.O. 12/109.) He received a loyalist pension until his death, January 7, 1828 [at Roxbury, Massachusetts]. (T. 50/6; T. 50/9 ; T. 50/10.)

Nicholas Ward Boylston was the eldest son of Benjamin Hallowell

* Nicholas Boylston bequeathed him £4,000 in his will, proved August 30, 1771.

D

(*q.v.*), and his wife, Mary, daughter of Thomas Boylston, and was born in Boston in 1749. He changed his name by royal licence, March 21, 1770.

His portrait, painted by Gilbert Stuart in 1825, hangs in the Harvard Medical School.   Another portrait by the same artist, in 1825, belongs to Mr. Ward Nicholas Boylston, junior, and his sister, Miss Barbara H. Boylston.   (Lawrence Park's *Gilbert Stuart*, 1926.)

References : Curwen's Journal, *op. cit.*, pp. 35, 36, 56 ; *New England Hist. and Gen. Reg.*, April, 1853, pp. 145–150 ; Stark, *op. cit.*, pp. 282–3.

BENJAMIN BRADFORD

From an affidavit made February 28, 1786, by him and John Dowling, gentleman, and Waldo Dickey (or Dickie), mariner, at St. Andrews, New Brunswick :—

On or about April 1, 1782, Captain Henry Mowat (*q.v.*), in command of H.M. sloop *Albany*, at Penobscot, having received intelligence that the sloop *The Thorn* (captured from the British by the Americans), was fitting out at Marblehead or Salem, and having reason to think that an attempt to seize her might succeed, he ordered Robert Piercey, then master's mate of the *Albany*, John Dowling, as a midshipman, and Waldo Dickey, with thirty sailors of the *Albany* to hold themselves ready for this duty. Delay occurred for want of a pilot.   Bradford, a mariner and loyalist, of the vicinity of Penobscot, and master and owner of the schooner *Three Friends*, of seventy tons burden, volunteered for the duty of pilot, and offered his vessel to promote the King's service and to distress the enemy. On April 15, these officers and men embarked with Bradford on his schooner and set sail for Marblehead, where he landed them under the cover of night.   The party were discovered by a straggler, who alarmed the town and the scheme was frustrated.   Bradford had put to sea, leaving the party on land, it being no part of his engagement to await their return.   He himself was taken by Captain Thornborough, of H.M.S. *Blond*, and in his sudden flight from Marblehead he was prevented from procuring the necessary papers [he says in his petition that he destroyed all his papers to avoid identification] to prove his loyalty and duty.   This officer ordered his schooner to be burnt, and said that on proof of the service of Bradford on the expedition to Marblehead, he would be compensated with a better vessel.   But the *Blond* having been cast away and the Captain called home, he had never been compensated for the loss of his vessel.   With this affidavit is a certificate of Robert Pagan (*q.v.*) that Bradford had been employed during the war as a pilot in the Royal Navy, and served on many occasions in privateers and armed ships. (A.O. 13/50.)

According to his petition he had 300 acres of land on Long Island in Penobscot Bay.   (*Ib.* ; A.O. 12/11, ff. 163–8.)

His claim of £355 5s. 6d. was disallowed, as most of it was for his schooner *Three Friends*, which was condemned under the Prohibitory Act.   (A.O. 12/61, f. 91.)

According to the Index of Charlotte County, New Brunswick, this loyalist owned property at St. Andrews, as did John Dowling and Waldo Dickey. A list of the 430 grantees of land at St. Andrews, dated August 12, 1784, is printed in *Acadiensis*, vii, 216–9. Dowling had served in the Nova Scotia Volunteers and in the King's Rangers before joining H.M.S. *Albany*. (*American MSS. in Royal Inst., op. cit.*, iv, 40.)

MARY BRADSTREET

Her husband, Major-General John Bradstreet, at his death in 1774, was possessed of very considerable real and personal estate in America, which he bequeathed for her benefit and that of his daughters, Philip Schuyler being appointed executor and trustee. Schuyler immediately took possession of all this estate and the effects and never accounted for or remitted one single farthing to her or her children. The rebellion having broken out, and Schuyler having been appointed an officer in the American army, she and her daughters were deprived of the support from General Bradstreet's estate and of the means of recovering it, to their great distress. Mary Bradstreet presented a petition to the King, who was graciously pleased to put her name on the pension list of a colonel's widow. She petitions that she and her family, having been deprived of their property in their native country of America, may be granted the Parliamentary bounty to loyalists. (A.O. 13/43.)

Her daughter, Elizabeth, married [in 1780] Peter Livius, Chief Justice of Quebec [formerly of New Hampshire], and therefore relinquished her loyalist pension. Elizabeth Livius's brother, Major Samuel Bradstreet, of the 40th Regiment of Foot, lost his life in the service of his King, in Antigua, December 18, 1779, leaving two young children unprovided for. She prays that her pension may be transferred to them. In consequence of the recent deaths of her mother* and sister, Martha Bradstreet, two loyalist pensions were extinguished. She mentions the long services in the British army of her brother, her uncle and grandfather, all of whom died in the rank of Major in the 40th Regiment, as well as the distinguished services in America of her father, an officer in this regiment. (*Ib.*)

Agatha Du Bellamy, eldest daughter of General John and Mary Bradstreet, in a letter dated Bury St. Edmunds, October 26, 1782, refers to Sir Charles Gould, Judge Advocate, her father's intimate friend and correspondent, who would testify to his property as being in the possession of General Philip Schuyler, and hopes the bounty would not be withdrawn from her, inadequate as it is to the style in which she was brought up ; this bounty would be preferable to returning to her native country in the present unhappy conditions. (*Ib.*)

Elizabeth Livius, in a letter to the Commissioners, dated Bath, November 4, 1782, mentions her father's services in America and to the retention of his property by Schuyler. (*Ib.*) In her evidence she stated

* Mary Bradstreet died in March, 1779.

that her father, General John Bradstreet, was reported to have died worth £100,000, but she estimates the value of his estate at about £50,000. From the evidence of Chief Justice Livius it appears that the two children, Samuel and Martha Bradstreet, mentioned earlier, were the natural children of Major Samuel Bradstreet and were entitled to a legacy under the will of their aunt, Miss [Martha] Bradstreet [who died, March 25, 1782] in America, but this is lost. (A.O. 12/105, f. 7.) These two children were born in 1775 and 1780 respectively, and in 1783 £30 per annum was granted for their education, and was continued until 1801. (A.O. 12/99, f. 232 ; T. 50/8 ; T. 50/17.)

On March 24, 1783, Charles Du Bellamy* in evidence stated that his wife, Agatha, may receive her estate by returning to America, as she had not taken any active part in the rebellion on the loyalist side. He therefore applied for £200 to enable her to return. On April 8 he stated that his wife would be satisfied with £50 for the voyage, and this sum was granted. (A.O. 12/99.)

There are letters from Charles and Agatha Du Bellamy of no interest in A.O. 13/44.

The first commission of Major-General John Bradstreet in the British army appears to have been that of Ensign in Phillips's Regiment of Foot (afterwards the 40th) on August 23, 1735, at the age of 24. He served in this regiment until September 4, 1745, when he was transferred as Captain to Sir William Pepperell's Regiment of Foot. In 1746 he was appointed Governor of St. John's, Newfoundland. Bradstreet served on Braddock's staff and was Adjutant-General to Governor Shirley of Massachusetts. He served with distinction in several actions in America and became Colonel of the Royal American Regiment (now known as the 60th, or King's Royal Rifles). He was promoted Major-General, May 25, 1772. (Army Lists). Bradstreet was the owner of a large tract of land in Albany County, New York, on which he had expended £7,000 before 1772. (*Earl of Dartmouth MSS.*, *op. cit.*, ii, 120, 153.). After a life-long service in the British army in America, General John Bradstreet died

* Du Bellamy (stage name in America, Charles John Evans) made his first appearance at Covent Garden Theatre on November 12, 1776, as Young Meadows in Bickerstaffe's opera, *Love in a Village*. His first wife appeared in the same theatre a week earlier in the character of Lavinia in *The Fair Penitent*. He married, May 11, 1777, Agatha, daughter of Major-General John Bradstreet, and widow of one Button, a merchant. Early in 1777 he quitted Covent Garden and was giving concerts at Bath in April. An engraved portrait of Du Bellamy as Young Meadows, with Mrs. Cargill as Rosetta, appears as a frontispiece to the opera, *Love in a Village*. He died in August, 1793, at New York, where he had lived for about nine years, and where his social disposition and reputable character had rendered him popular in a large circle of the politer inhabitants. By his will of April 11, 1793, he left everything to his beloved wife, Agatha. (A.O. 12/105, f. 7 ; *Notes and Queries*, 12 S. II, p. 257 ; *Gent. Mag.*, vol. lxiii, p. 1149 ; *New York Hist. Soc. Colls.*, 1905, pp. 240, 243). He was probably the Brother Du Bellamy who sang an anthem at the dedication of Freemasons' Hall in Great Queen Street, London, on May 23, 1776. (*Gent. Mag.*, 1776, p. 219.)

at New York, September 25, 1774. (W.O. 25/3091.) According to his will, dated September 23, 1774, General Bradstreet left £1,000 to Elizabeth Bradstreet (his wife's daughter) ; a farm, his arms, books and apparel to John Bradstreet Schuyler, son of Colonel Philip Schuyler (one of his executors) ; his horses and carriages to Mrs. Philip Schuyler ; money to Margaret, daughter of the said Colonel Schuyler ; and the remainder of his estate, both real and personal, to his two daughters, his wife to receive an annuity of £100 therefrom. (*New Eng. Hist. & Gen. Reg.*, 1862, p. 315.)

THOMAS BRATTLE

There are no original memorials of this loyalist. He received a licence to reside in Massachusetts (A.O. 12/83, f. 27), having returned from abroad in 1779, and his name removed from the Banishment Act and his estate restored to him. Thomas Brattle was the son of William Brattle (*q.v.*), and graduated at Harvard College in 1760. (Stark, *op. cit.*, pp. 296–7.)

WILLIAM BRATTLE

The only references to this loyalist are copies of a libel against his estate in the Inferior Court of Common Pleas, held at Concord, in March, 1782, showing that his estate was forfeited (A.O. 12/82) ; and of a judgment in the Inferior Court of Common Pleas of Suffolk County against his estate. (A.O. 12/83, f. 1.)

Theologian, physician, soldier and lawyer, this loyalist graduated at Harvard College in 1722. He accompanied the British forces at the evacuation of Boston in March, 1776, and died at Halifax, Nova Scotia, in October of the same year. His estate was confiscated. His son was Thomas Brattle (*q.v.*). (Sabine, *op. cit* ; Stark, *op. cit,*. pp. 294–6.)

EBENEZER BRIDGHAM

was born at Boston about 1745, and had a large and lucrative business there.

From principles of loyalty and attachment to the British Government, inherited from his father (who fell a sacrifice to his allegiance to the Crown), he took an early and active part as a loyalist in the Revolution. Early in 1770, in open defiance of the Non-Importation agreement, he sailed to England with the avowed intention of returning with a cargo of British manufactures and was the first to break the combination in New England. He continued thereafter in a lucrative and increasing branch of commerce, by which he cleared never less than £1,000 a year until the rebellion in 1775. During the siege of Boston he took up arms in support of the British Government and acted as Lieutenant and Adjutant in the loyal militia embodied under Brigadier-General Timothy Ruggles, without pay or rations. Abuses and irregularities having crept into the Provincial forces in Nova Scotia, he was ordered thither and incurred heavy expenses for which he had not been compensated. He is now in great distress, and his family, consisting of his wife, a sister and three children, are compelled to reside in France, on account of the cheapness of living there, while he is in the unhappy position of being unable through his poverty to return to them or fetch them to England. His health, greatly impaired by his hardships in Nova Scotia (having been shipwrecked three times) and the torture of mind under which he has so long laboured between hope and despair, is now rapidly declining, and he has no hope of saving himself and his family from perishing in a prison but in the justice and humanity of the British Government. (A.O. 13/74.)

Disdaining to remain an idle spectator of so important a contest, and unwilling to remain a burden on the bounty of Government, he embarked as a volunteer on General Sir William Howe's expedition to New York in 1776. In November, 1777, he was honoured with the appointment of Deputy Inspector-General of the Provincial forces, with a salary of 10s. a day, which, though inadequate for the support of himself and his family (and in his humble opinion not equal to the importance of the trust), he accepted it, and continued to discharge his duties with a diligence and integrity which secured the approbation of the Generals, until December, 1783, when the provincial corps were disbanded and his salary ceased. He is now under the disagreeable necessity of soliciting the bounty of Government for the immediate subsistence of himself and his family. (A.O. 13/43.)

The following documents are in A.O. 13/74 :—

(a) A contract of John Hobby, undertaking to procure for and deliver to him at the landing place at George Town,* Lincoln County, on or before October 1, 1774, a quantity of oak planks, which are described.

(b) A long letter from Joseph Stokes, dated Liverpool, May 27, 1774, announcing the sailing of a cargo bound for Philadelphia for Bridgham's account, and deploring the shutting up of Boston harbour, as such an act of revenge will avail but little to distress or ruin so capital a place of trade and will fall upon the traders of England.

(c) A letter from Francis Rotch (q.v.) dated September 24, 1774, deploring his failure after repeated attempts to enter upon a cool and dispassionate conference with him (Bridgham) regarding his intention to leave his (Rotch's) store, which is now useless to him in the prevailing disturbed conditions. Rotch announces that he has let the whole building for the use of the British military forces and requests Bridgham to remove his goods within ten days.

(d) An affidavit of Captain John Clarke and Sergeant Richard Knowles, dated Chester, England, June 18, 1787, that a large party of soldiers were engaged for several days in 1774 in removing a quantity of china, glass and Staffordshire ware, the property of Bridgham, from the " Staffordshire Warehouse " in Boston, which was afterwards fitted up as a barracks for the 59th Regiment.

* Now in Sagadahoc County, Maine.

He claimed £14,111 for the loss of his property, and was granted £900. (A.O. 12/109.) He received a loyalist pension. (T. 50/8; A.O. 12/102, f. 8.)

He submitted a plan for forming the Fencible Americans, the King's Orange Rangers, and the King's Rangers into one corps, October 24, 1782. (*American MSS. in Royal Inst., op. cit.*, iii, 183.)

His Boston estate was bought in 1794 by Benjamin Tupper. (*Suffolk County Recs.*, Lib. 178, p. 244.)

Ebenezer Bridgham married Desire Hatch at Boston, February 7, 1768.

References: Ind. 5605-6; A.O. 13/43; A.O. 12/100, f. 253; Chatham Papers, 225; Sabine, *op. cit.*

THOMAS BRINLEY

was born at Boston, and from the earliest days of the Revolution he took a decided part in support of Government, to prevent those evils which have since, unhappily, occurred. He had real estate of the value of £1,800, consisting of a dwelling house and a distillery and a large wharf, besides an interest in lands in Massachusetts and New Hampshire. At the evacuation of Boston by the British troops he sailed for Halifax, Nova Scotia, and thence to England. In October, 1776, he signed the memorial of about thirty Massachusetts loyalists to the Treasury and was granted a bounty of £100, subject to a reduction of 2½ per cent. (A.O. 13/43.) This bounty was continued to him. (A.O. 12/105, f. 121.)

With this memorial are certificates to his loyalty from Sir William Pepperell and Thomas Flucker, and Harrison Gray, junior, who added that Brinley and his wife were descended from the first families in New England. (A.O. 13/43.)

His losses included a quantity of salt, value before the war at 2s. a bushel sterling, but from scarcity rose suddenly to 18s. He was part owner of the sloop *Dolphin*, fitted out in April, 1775, for a whaling voyage, which was seized in an American port. Another part owner was his brother, George Brinley, commissary at Halifax in Nova Scotia. In a schedule of his property is a pew in King's Chapel at Boston. (A.O. 13/74.)

According to a memorial of his widow, Elizabeth, he died October 7, 1784. She prays for the bounty of Government in her distressed condition. (A. O. 13/43.) She claimed the sum of £2,576 2s. for the loss of his property, and was awarded £803. (A.O. 12/109; A.O. 13/87.) A part of the confiscated land was sold by the State to Gustavus Fellows for £1,152 16s. 7d.

This loyalist was the son of Francis Brinley, of Boston, and graduated at Harvard College in 1744. His wife, Elizabeth, was a daughter of Judge Cradock, of Boston. She died in London early in 1793. In her will (Dodwell, 180), dated June 14, 1791, and proved April 4, 1793, she mentions her sister, Deborah, wife of Robert Auchmuty (*q.v.*) ; Mary, wife of the Rev. John Breynton, D.D., Rector of St. Paul's, Halifax, Nova Scotia ; her sister, Sarah Cradock; and Catherine, wife of Nathaniel Brinley. She also mentions her husband's four brothers, Francis, Edward, Nathaniel and George Brinley.

References : Sabine, *op. cit.* ; *Loyalists' Claims, op. cit.*, p. 336 ; An Old Newport Loyalist, by Katharine J. Wharton, in *Bulletin of Newport Hist. Soc.*, April, 1920.

HAYES ROBERT BRISTOW

After nearly four years' service as clerk in the office of the Comptroller-General of Customs in London, he was appointed chief clerk to James Porter, Comptroller-General of Customs in America, and started duty at Boston, July 30, 1773, and continued until August 19, 1775, when he was obliged by illness arising from the fatigue of patrolling the town under arms at night, to return to England. (A.O. 13/73.)

JOHN BRODERICK

was a tailor in Boston, and accompanied the British troops to Halifax and New York, where he served in the loyal militia from 1777 until 1783. On the voyage to England he was captured by an American ship and taken to Boston, where he was kept in prison for three months and lost his eyesight by a violent fever. Having been exchanged, he sailed for England. His wife was Mary Broderick. (A.O. 13/43 ; A.O. 12/101, f. 122 ; T. 50/8.)

DAVID BROWN

was a Scotsman who settled in 1770 at Bridgewater. He was obliged to flee from Boston in 1778 and take refuge in the British lines in Rhode Island. He lost his only son, an apprentice in the Royal Naval Hospital in Rhode Island. At the end of the war he settled at Shelburne, in Nova Scotia. (A.O. 13/50 ; A.O. 12/10, ff. 248-9.)

His claim of £300 was disallowed. (A.O. 12/61, f. 28.)

Reference : *Ontario Archives, op. cit.*, p. 656.

MARGARET BROWN

was of Charlestown, where her husband, John Brown, for more than fifteen years a seaman in the Royal Navy, was settled, and where her house and furniture were burnt at the Battle of Bunker Hill. Having no home, she lived for thirteen months on board Admiral Graves's ship, *Preston*, on which her husband was serving. She eventually went to England, and there entered domestic service rather than be a burden to Government. Governor Hutchinson testified to the truth of her petition, March 26, 1779. (A.O. 13/43.)

Compensation to the amount of £594 was granted to her from her claim of £906 11s. (A.O. 12/109.)

PETER BROWN

of Boston, had for twelve years prosecuted his business there with reputation and fidelity, and saved £400 sterling. His wife, Mary, a fruiterer by trade, made many hundred dozen shirts for the British soldiers, at a time when few persons dared to assist the King's army. Having refused to bear arms against his Sovereign Lord the King, he was obliged to embark with his wife and family for England, leaving his property in the hands of the rebels. Mary Brown became a servant to Walter Barrell (*q.v.*) at Halifax, Nova Scotia. (A.O. 13/43.)

THOMAS BROWN

of Boston, was a merchant and an active loyalist. Not choosing to subject himself to any other government, he left this town at the evacuation by the British troops, accompanied by his wife and two children, his wife's sister, and a man servant. A schedule of his property includes land at Woolwich, in Lincoln County [Maine]; and property in Lynn, as heir of his grandfather, Thomas Brown, of Lynn. From May, 1775, to March, 1776, he was Coroner under the Crown, Lieutenant of the North Battery at Boston, and Master of the fire engine. (A.O. 13/90; A.O. 12/10. ff. 47–55.)

In his letter, dated Halifax, Nova Scotia, December, 1783, to the Rev. Samuel Peters in London, he says that from the memorable April 19, 1775 [the skirmish at Lexington], to March 10, 1776, he was not a single week free from public calls to act in a civil or military capacity, and never failed to respond, to the detriment of his own private concerns. Upon application to General Gage for repayment of money expended in paying jurors at inquests, coffin makers and grave diggers, the General begged to be excused from doing so out of his own pocket, and told him (Brown), in the presence of General Burgoyne, that he would be rewarded in Heaven. All his effects in Boston were confiscated. He had barely got settled at Halifax when he was called upon by General Massey, Commander-in-Chief in Nova Scotia, to act as superintendent of all the loyalist refugees, for which arduous duty he received only thanks. (A.O. 13/90.)

In giving evidence before the Commissioners at Halifax on December 10, 1785, he stated that he was born in Boston. He produced a commission from General Gage, dated June 5, 1775, appointing him first Lieutenant in a company of loyal militia under John Erving (*q.v.*); and a letter from General Massey, stating that he had consulted Brown on the defence of Halifax in a confidential manner, and speaking in high terms of his loyalty. His sister, Rachel Bernard, is mentioned. (A.O. 12/10, ff. 47–55.)

Thomas Brown claimed £915 for the loss of his property and £445 for debts, and was allowed £50. (A.O. 12/61, f. 9; A.O. 12/109.)

Two letters of no interest are in A.O. 13/50.

He was doubtless the man of this name who started business in Halifax, but soon failed, and established a school there. The Rev. Jacob Bailey wrote in 1781 : " This poor gentleman is still detained under complaint of his unmerciful creditors." (*The Frontier Missionary, op. cit.*)

Reference : *Ontario Archives, op. cit.*, pp. 39–41 ; *Colls. of N. Scotia Hist. Soc.*, xiii, 25, 34.

ANN BROWNE (Plate vi)

was the widow of Colonel Arthur Browne, and daughter and devisee of Dr. Sylvester Gardiner (*q.v.*). She was allowed compensation, £470, from her claim. (A.O. 12/109.)

She married this officer, Colonel of the 28th Foot, and son of the first Earl of Altamont, in 1766 ; he died in 1779, and she died in July, 1807.

Her portrait, by Copley, is in the possession of Robert H. Gardiner, Esq., of Gardiner, Maine.

WILLIAM BROWNE

The following extracts have been made from the large number of documents of this distinguished loyalist.

In 1762 he was elected to represent his native town of Salem in the General Assembly, of Massachusetts, and was annually elected until 1768. Upon the King's request to rescind an obnoxious vote of the Assembly, he was among the virtuous few who thought this vote calculated to promote the disorders which have since overwhelmed the unhappy people of Massachusetts.* By this action he instantly lost the confidence of his constituents, was persecuted with every calumny that malice could suggest, and was exposed in every public paper on the Continent of America as an object of universal detestation, and treated accordingly. He was afterwards persuaded to take the command of a regiment of militia, but he could safely say that he did not thereby defeat the designs of the

* On February 13, 1768, an Act of Parliament was passed, imposing duties on certain articles imported into the Colonies. The House of Representatives in Massachusetts protested, and addressed a circular letter to the other provincial Assemblies. On June 21, Governor Bernard informed the House that he was instructed to require them to rescind the resolution which gave birth to their circular letter. On the 30th the House informed him that they had voted not to rescind by a vote of 92 nays and 17 yeas. The following were the sixteen other members of the House of Representatives who voted in favour of " Rescinding," agreeable to his Majesty's requisition :—Peter Frye, for Salem ; Dr. John Calef (*q.v.*), for Ipswich ; Jacob Fowle, for Marblehead ; Richard Saltonstall (*q.v.*), for Haverhill ; Jonathan Bliss, for Springfield and Willbraham ; Hon. Israel Williams, for Hatfield ; Jonathan Ashley, Jr., for Deerfield ; Captain Joseph Root, for Sunderland ; John Ashley, for Sheffield and Great Barrington ; John Chadwick, for Tyringham ; Hon. Timothy Ruggles (*q.v.*), for Hardwick ; Chillingsworth Foster, for Harwich ; Jonathan Sayward, for York ; William Jennigan, for Edgartown ; Matthew Mayhew, for Chilmark ; and Josiah Edson (*q.v.*), for Bridgwater.

British Government, for having none of the talents of a soldier himself, he never encouraged a military spirit in those who had a little of that spirit. A short time before the violences of 1774 he had the honour to be appointed a Judge of the Superior Court of Massachusetts and a member of the Provincial Council. When it was no longer safe for an officer of the Crown to live without military protection, he resorted with his family to Boston, where he lived, or rather existed, for eighteen months. He refrains from repeating the sufferings of the loyalists during that time. He sailed for England in the *Lord Hyde* packet, taking with him the despatches of General Sir William Howe. His wife went to Rhode Island, and was daily persecuted for payment of a bill of £100, which she was obliged by her necessities to draw in his name. (A.O. 13/43.)

In another memorial he mentions the large property lost to him in consequence of his loyalty, namely, a mansion house, gardens, wharfs and stores in Salem; another house and land in Salem, at a place called Stage Point, improved for curing fish; a farm of about 170 acres four miles from Salem; a large tract of land in Hartford, Connecticut; a township called New Salem, about twelve miles from New London, Connecticut; and other property. (A.O. 13/90.)

In A.O. 13/50 are letters from Samuel and Benjamin Huntington, dated 1784 and 1785, regarding his property in Connecticut; a letter from Joseph Blaney, dated Boston, June 10, 1786, concerning his estate; and an inventory of his estate, including 9,663 acres in Lyme, Colchester and New London, Connecticut. A copy of the latter inventory is in A.O. 12/10, f. 220.

From his memorial, dated Bermuda, March 1, 1786:

After repeating a part of his previous memorial, he adds that when the tumults happened at Cambridge, Massachusetts, in August, 1774, he was attending his duty as Judge at the Superior Court at Boston, where he was from that time obliged to reside until the evacuation of the town by the British troops. Since he left his home at Salem in August, 1774, he has been entirely without assistance from his private fortune, and has depended for support solely upon the bounty of the British Government, whose care and tenderness towards him he thankfully acknowledges. By his proscription and the confiscation of his estates he has lost a fortune, estimated at a moderate computation to have been worth over £33,000 in 1774. (A.O. 13/50, with a copy in A.O. 12/10, ff. 217-9.).

In evidence on June 8, 1786, he stated that he was the representative of two respectable families in Massachusetts on his father and mother's sides, one Browne, the other Dudley, both remarkable for their attachment to the British Government. He was bred to the law, but turned his attention to the improvement of his estate. He lost his seat at the next election after 1768 for voting for rescinding the resolution. His appointment as Colonel of militia was made by Governor Hutchinson in 1771, and that of Judge of the Superior Court by General Gage in June, 1774. He produced *The Massachusetts Gazette* for June 15, 1774,

containing a resolve of the Committee that he should be requested to
resign his office as Mandamus Councillor, with his answer to this resolve
that he would not from persuasion or threat do anything derogatory to
the character of a Councillor of His Majesty's province.   He produced
many deeds and particulars of his great estates in Massachusetts and
Connecticut and a copy of the will of his grandfather, who devised all
his Connecticut lands in Lyme, Colchester, and New London to his
eldest son, Samuel Browne [father of this loyalist] in tail male.   His grandfather was one of the associates in the grant of 600,000 acres of land in
Maine, known as the Muscongus Patent.* A witness at Halifax was
Dr. Jonathan Prince, who declared that he remembered William Browne
living at Salem in the large house built by his grandfather.   It was three
stories high, with seventeen large and handsome rooms and a garden and
stables, and was thought to be the best house, and in the best situation in
the town.   This house was bought since the confiscation by a relation
[Elias Hasket Derby] of Dr. Prince for about £2,250 sterling.   (A.O.
12/10, ff. 221-243.)

According to a deposition, dated June 25, 1786, of Ebenezer Backus,
junior, of Norwich, Connecticut, the Browne estate in Connecticut was
of great extent, and the timber was superior in size and quality to any
other in that part of the state, and for that reason most of the timber used
in building the Continental frigate, *Confederacy*, in 1779, was procured
from this property.   (A.O. 13/50.)   With this deposition is a list of the
tenants on this estate, and their tenure and rentals.   (*Ib.*)   A letter from
Samuel Huntington to Browne himself, dated September 17, 1786,
refers to this same estate.   (A.O. 13/83.)

In A.O. 13/50 is an inventory of furniture, a list of debts due on notes
of hand, many copies of conveyances of property, certificates of the sale
of his confiscated property and other papers relating to the Browne
estates.   The proceeds of the sale of his confiscated property in Massachusetts amounted to £10,025, and the claims against it to £3,843 5s.
The British Government awarded him compensation to the amount of
£7,658 from his claim of £32,256.   (A.O. 12/61, ff. 34-5; A.O. 12/109.)
A description of the great estate of this loyalist has been published in
The Essex Institute Hist. Colls., xliii, 290-302.

A letter from William Hubbard to James Putnam (*q.v.*), dated Boston,
July 1, 1787, states that Judge Sullivan was decidedly of the opinion that
the Act [of 1779 against "certain Notorious Conspirators"] forever
debarred all heirs from any benefit from the Browne estate.   (A.O. 13/11.)

William Browne was born at Salem in 1737 and graduated at Harvard
College in 1755.   (Stark, *op. cit.*, 449-51.)   So great was his popularity
that the dignified office of Governor of Massachusetts was offered to him
by the Committee of Safety as an inducement to forsake his loyalty to
the Crown.   (*Journal of Samuel Curwen, op. cit.*, p. 505.)   On January 19,

* For the names of the associates of the Muscongus Patent, see York Deeds
(printed) x, 245.   Another account is in Burrage's *Beginnings of Colonial Maine*,
p. 204.

1781, he received the appointment of Governor of Bermuda in recognition of his loyalty and in appreciation of his high character and abilities, and held this office until 1788. A silver bowl, made in London in 1782, was presented by him to St. George's Church, Bermuda, and is still preserved there. He died in London in 1802. By his will (Kenyon, 167) he left legacies to his two daughters, Catherine and Mary Browne.

His son was William Browne, junior (*q.v.*)

References : Sabine, *op. cit. ; Ontario Archives, op. cit.*, pp. 638–46, 720–1, 1272.

WILLIAM BROWNE, JUNIOR

He was the only son of William Browne (*q.v.*) and was born at Salem and received part of his education at Winchester College. In his memorial of December 16, 1780, he states that his father (whom he had accompanied through all the scenes of want and distress to which he was exposed) had been obliged for economical reasons to conceal himself among the rugged mountains of Wales. He is now an ensign in the 58th Regiment of Foot, which he is about to join at Gibraltar, and hopes by his education in principles of loyalty to distinguish himself by his good conduct and bravery. (A.O. 13/43.) Governor Hutchinson wrote to the boy's father on April 7, 1779, at Cowbridge in South Wales, asking him to send his son to London to be measured for his military uniform by the Governor's tailor. He was gazetted ensign in this regiment on April 22, 1779, and served in the celebrated siege of Gibraltar, the subject of a well-known picture (in the National Gallery in London) by an artist of American birth, John Singleton Copley. Another American, in the person of Prestly Thornton, of Virginia, served as an ensign and lieutenant in the 12th Foot in the same siege.

William Browne put an end to his life by hanging himself, April 30, 1786. Dr. Peter Oliver describes him in a letter as a most worthless character. (Printed in Governor Hutchinson's *Diary and Letters*, ii, 423.)

JOHN BRYANT

In his young days he fought in defence of his King and country, as the marks which he bears are an ample witness. He resided for thirty years in Boston, as master and owner of vessels, and a dealer in groceries and spirits, and from the fruits of his industry he had acquired a real estate adequate for his family's support. He continued to enjoy the advantages of his prosperity without interruption until April 20, 1775, when communication between Boston and the country was cut off. In the convulsed state of affairs he decided to embark for England on April 24, and remained there in a state of hope and expectation for the restoration of tranquillity in America, but all his hopes were frustrated, and he was reduced to want and a sufferer from blindness. (A.O. 13/43 ; A.O. 13/90.) With the second memorial is a schedule of his property in Boston, including a new brick house of three stories, built in 1770.

Governor Hutchinson certified on August 17, 1778, that John Bryant was known to him as a master of a ship trading between London and Boston and as a man of good character and a loyalist. (A.O. 13/43.)

Bryant in evidence stated that he was an Irishman by birth, that his wife and two daughters were in America, and that he was struck blind by lightning in 1771 in the channel. His pension of £40 was continued. (A.O. 12/105, f. 55.)

John Bryant was elected a member of Morden College at Blackheath, March 20, 1777, and died there, February 27, 1785. The College was founded in 1695 by Sir John Morden, baronet, for the reception of " poor, honest, sober and discreet merchants who shall have lost their estates by accidents, dangers, and perils of the seas, or by any other accidents, ways, or means, in their honest endeavour to get their living by merchandising." This haven of rest, justly famous for the beauty of its building and situation, was designed by Christopher Wren and completed in 1702. (T. F. Green, *Morden College, Blackheath*, 1916.) Two other members were Captain Samuel Ball, for many years in the Carolina trade, who died there in 1782 ; and William Randall (*q.v.*)

THOMAS BUFFTON

was a native of London who lived at Salem for twenty-three years and by industry and economy saved several hundred pounds. When the " rebellious fire " broke out, he was importuned several times by the rebels to take a commission under Congress as a privateersman, to fight against his King and country, but he absolutely refused. On March 16, 1777, four of the leading " Insurrecters ' came to his house and threatened that if he did not within six days join the army or privateers of the American Congress, he must expect such treatment as Tories deserved. Dreading the savage and barbarous treatment which had been inflicted upon many other loyalists, he collected £300 of his money and took the first opportunity to sail for South Carolina and thence for England. On this passage the ship was taken by H.M.S. *Prince George*, and both the ship and cargo were justly condemned under the Prohibitory Act. He left his wife and eight young children at Salem "to the mercy of the Rebels." (A.O. 13/43.)

Thomas Buffton married, August 22, 1758, Mary Coffen (Salem Town Records.) The baptisms of his eight children are recorded in St. Peter's Episcopal Church, Salem.

SOLOMON BUNNELL

of Lanesborough, joined the army of General Burgoyne as a volunteer, and on August 16, 1777, was taken prisoner at the battle of Bennington. For most of the time he was kept a prisoner in irons until December 22, 1780, when he escaped and eventually got to New York. His property was confiscated. (A.O. 13/50 ; A.O. 12/10, ff. 379-381.) His claim for compensation for this property was rejected. (A.O. 12/61, f. 51.) He went to Digby, Nova Scotia, in 1782, and appears to have settled there. (A.O. 13/50.) According to Sabine, he shot two of his neighbours at the battle of Bennington, and was sent to Northampton gaol. This statement is confirmed by the Town Records of Lanesborough, where there are two entries, heavily draped in black, recording the deaths of Lieutenant Abel Prindle, of Lanesborough, by a shot supposed to have been fired by Solomon Bunnell, a Tory and former neighbour, and of Lieutenant Isaac Nash, also shot, supposedly by Bunnell, a Tory, who, like Judas Iscariot, turned to the enemy and betrayed his friend. (Ex inform. the Rev. C. J. Palmer.)

Reference : *Ontario Archives, op. cit.*, p. 755.

WILLIAM BURCH

was one of the five Commissioners of Customs in North America appointed under the Act of Parliament in 1767, and was stationed at Boston. His name is included in the Banishment Act of Massachusetts, 1778. He was granted a pension of £250 from 1785. (T. 50/9.) The name of this official is mentioned several times in the Diary of Governor Hutchinson.

William Burch died at Brandon in Suffolk, and was buried there August 6, 1794. His wife, Ann, was buried there, February 17, 1806. Charles Paxton (*q.v.*), his fellow-Commissioner at Boston, died at the seat of William Burch, and was buried at Brandon, January 25, 1788.

THOMAS BURDEN

was obliged to flee to the British army in Rhode Island in 1776, and was afterwards employed as a guide in the army. For his services he was commissioned Lieutenant in command of a company, and went out of the lines at divers times after the rebels, by directions of the commander-in chief. With this memorial is a schedule of his lost property. He went to live at Burton, Sunbury County, New Brunswick, after the war. (A.O. 13/22.) His grant of land there is dated September 14, 1784, and is re-corded in Book A. (Ex inform. Mr. R. W. L. Tibbits.) His widow was granted £10 as relief in 1846. (Revolutionary War Pensions of New Brunswick ; Journals of the House of Assembly, February 24, 1846.)

SIR CHARLES BURDETT, BARONET

Early in 1775, while holding the appointment of Collector of Customs at St. Augustine, East Florida, he was on a visit to his family at Roxbury, Massachusetts.* On the journey from Boston to Roxbury on April 19 he was taken prisoner by the Americans on suspicion of riding into the

* He was at Roxbury on June 2, 1774, the date of his letter to Lord Dartmouth, praying for a better appointment as collector than that at St. Augustine. (*Earl of Dartmouth MSS., op. cit.*, ii, 212.)

country " to prevent the Americans coming down to fight against the King's troops, by reporting that it was a false alarm that an engagement had begun between the King's forces and the Americans." Having miraculously escaped with his life, he embarked at the earliest opportunity for England, with his wife and family. In right of his wife he was entitled to 3,500 acres of land on the Penobscot River, in the Muscongus Patent,* which he values at 9s. an acre. He was also entitled in right of his wife to a share in the Water Grist Mills at Boston, in which Robert Auchmuty (*q.v.*), or his sister-in-law, Mrs. Cradock, had a like share. From the same source he got a share of two brick houses in School Street, Boston, which had been let on lease in March, 1775, to James Lovell and Samuel Hollbrook, and which were seized by the next heir-at-law. These houses had been inherited by his wife, Lady Burdett, on the death of Mrs. Phillips (aunt of John Erving, junior (*q.v.*)), in March, 1775. Lady Burdett's first husband was Elisha Cooke Phillips, son of the said Mrs. Phillips.

Had not the Revolution broken out, Sir Charles Burdett would have obtained, upon petition to the General Assembly of Massachusetts, a grant of a township of 12,000 acres in right of his wife as granddaughter of Admiral Eldridge,† in conjunction with five other parties, descendants of the Admiral, which grant was voted by the General Assembly for his services in the expedition against Canada with Sir William Phipps. His wife's share would have been 1,500 acres, valued at 9s. an acre. Captain David Phipps (*q.v.*) had inherited a similar grant from his ancestor, Sir William Phipps. Sir Charles Burdett's attorney was John Adams, who could prove to this property at Boston. (A.O. 13/43.) With this memorial is a long schedule of the various properties mentioned.

The Commissioners rejected his claim of £3,612 for the loss of this property, for lack of satisfactory proof of its loss by confiscation or other means. (A.O. 12/109).

Sir Charles Burdett, fourth baronet, was born in 1728, and married, as his second wife, Sarah, daughter of Joseph Halsey, of Boston, whose previous husband, Elisha Cooke Phillips, mariner, of Boston, left her all his property by will, dated September 19, 1763, and proved February 16, 1766. This mariner was apparently the son of John and Margaret Phillips, of Boston. No mention is made of Lady Burdett in Margaret Phillips's will of June 4, 1771 (proved March 31, 1775.) The fifth baronet, Sir Charles Wyndham Burdett, was a son of this American marriage. Sir Charles Burdett died July 19, 1803, and was buried in the Church of St. Mary, Castle Gate, York.

* See p. 60, f.n.

† The only officer of this name in this expedition in 1690 was Captain Joseph Eldridge, commander of the transport *The American Merchant*. He was one of a committee appointed to secure vessels for the expedition. (Year Book of the Mass. Soc. of Colonial Wars, 1898.)

Rev. Mather Byles, Senior

PLATE VII

PLATE VIII

Rev. Mather Byles, Junior

CONRAD BURGHED (or BURGHARDT)

lived in Great Barrington, where he was taken from his family by the revolutionists and confined in Springfield gaol, and afterwards in Great Barrington gaol. According to a certificate of the Committee of Correspondence for 1777, signed by Daniel Nash, John Burgheardt and Benedict Dewey, he was confined in Great Barrington gaol as a person dangerous to the liberties of America. (A.O. 13/80.)

BENJAMIN BURNS

He was a native of America, and took up arms on the British side and was driven from his property. (A.O. 13/79.) In his evidence on September 3, 1783, he says that he was born at Cape Hand [Cape Ann], thirty miles from Boston, and was living there at the outbreak of the rebellion. Having been ordered to take up arms for America, or pay a fine of £50 as a substitute for military service, he as a loyalist fled to the Royal Navy, in which he served until July, 1783. (A.O. 12/99, f.31.)

CAPTAIN GEORGE BURNS

was born in North America, and was all his life a faithful and loyal subject, firmly attached to his Sovereign and to the laws and constitution of Great Britain. He held a commission in His Majesty's service for twenty-nine years.* In 1769, when the world was in a state of profound peace, he retired to America to spend with his family the remainder of his days in tranquillity upon his estates at Salem, Massachusetts, where he was the owner of an excellent house, a coach house, stables, a garden and fields, as well as a grist mill producing great profits. He was likewise the owner of several well cultivated farms at Lyndborough, Souhegan and New Salem, all in New Hampshire, formerly the property of Joshua Hicks, Esquire,† of Salem, which had passed to him (Burns) on his marriage to the granddaughter of Hicks, and all of which he had been deprived because of his loyalty. (A.O. 13/90.)

He joined the army very young, and served from Braddock's first service in America. He sold an estate in England, acquired through his wife, and emigrated to America, where he laid out his all and where he was comfortably settled at the outbreak of the Revolution. His uncle, " whose head had grown grey in the service of his Sovereign," was residing in America on half-pay and for his loyalty suffered such ill-usage as ultimately

* He was commissioned Ensign in Captain Henry Livingston's company of volunteers, raised for an expedition against Canada, July 1, 1747, though only about nine years of age. (*American MSS. in Royal Inst., op. cit.*, i, p. 1.)

† From the records of Essex County in the Probate Court at Salem it would appear that in the division of the estate of Joshua Hicks, the following persons are named : his daughters, Mary Hicks and Elizabeth Mackey (wife of Captain Samuel Mackey) ; and his granddaughter, Martha Hicks, daughter of his deceased eldest son, John. No will of Joshua Hicks is recorded.

cost him his fortune and his life.   He had the command of Fort Cumberland [Nova Scotia] for four years before the Peace of 1783, and was then a Captain in the Royal Fencible American Regiment.   His eldest son, " as fine a young man as most in the line," lost his life on the British side in the American Revolutionary war.   His mother, now aged 81, and a wife and three children are still alive.   (From his printed petition in the Chatham Papers, Bundle 225.)

In a letter of February 25, 1783, he states that inducements were offered to him by the Americans to join them.   (*American MSS. in the Royal Inst., op. cit.*, iii, 373.)   Captain George Burns is described as in the Royal Fencible Americans, as having been born in America in 1738, and as having been in the 60th Foot [the Royal American Regiment] in 1770.   He died August 21, 1801.   (Ind. 5606 ; W.O. 25/3091.)   He was married, May 29, 1766, to Mary Stukeley, lady of a manor in Lincolnshire,* at St. James's Church, Piccadilly, London, and died at Dublin, in Ireland, where he was buried at St. Paul's Church.   (W.O. 25/3091.) George Burns was gazetted Ensign in the 45th Foot in America, July 3, 1755, and Lieutenant August 14, 1759.   He was gazetted Lieutenant in the 60th Foot in America, July 14, 1769.   (Army Lists.)

In his will (at Dublin) he is described as of Montpelier Hill, County Dublin, formerly of Charlotte Town, Prince Edward Island.   He left all his estate in that island to his wife, Mary, with whom he got a considerable fortune on his marriage.

One Captain George Burns was granted Lot 40 in St. John's Island (now Prince Edward Island), July 23, 1767.   (*Acts of the Privy Council, Colonial* (printed 1912), v, 63.)

Captain George Burns settled at Charlottetown in Prince Edward Island after the Peace of 1783 and left there between 1789 and 1792. His name is recorded on about seventy deeds there.   One George Burns, late of Spring Gardens, Westminster, gave a deed in 1771 to George Burns, late of the City of New York, but then of Stukeley Town, of Lot 39—land commonly known as Stukeley Town, but formerly called St. Peter's in King's County, Prince Edward Island.   (Ex. inform. Mr. Æneas A. Macdonald, Judge of Probate in Charlottetown.)   In 1818 administration was granted in Prince Edward Island to the estate of Mrs. Mary Burns, widow.

It would seem that there were two officers of this name.   The Captain Burns who was born in America and married the granddaughter of Joshua Hicks, was perhaps the uncle (" whose head had grown grey in the service of his Sovereign ") of the other, who married the Lincolnshire heiress, Mary Stukeley.

Mary Burns, widow of Captain George Burns, in her memorial of February 27, 1810, states (after mentioning the military services of her husband) that her three sons, William Stukeley Burns, born in 1795, a cornet in the 26th Dragoons, Charles Burns, who served in the 45th Foot,

* This was probably Stukeley House, Holbeach, which had been bought by Squire Stukeley from one Thacher.

and George Burns, in the 54th Foot, lost their lives valiantly in the service of their King and country. Having been thirty-six years with her husband, both in the torrid and frigid zones, suffering various accidents incident to the fate of war, being now sixty-six years of age, very lame, infirm and destitute of life's support and a home, she implored the grant of the usual pension of a Captain's widow. She died in 1818. (W.O. 25/3074; W.O. 25/3091.)

REV. MATHER BYLES, D.D. (Plate vII)

On July 19, 1785, Mr. Temple appeared before the Commissioners to give evidence in support of his claim and stated that this aged loyalist was stricken with the palsy and had been dismissed from his Church in Boston because he was a Tory or friend to Great Britain. He had continued loyal to the Crown to this hour and now subsists on the daily charity of the loyal subjects in Boston, where he is the only clergyman, attached to Great Britain, in that part of America. (A.O. 12/101, f. 232.)

This distinguished divine, one of the few loyalist pastors outside the Episcopal Church, in New England, was deprived in August, 1775, of the pastorate of Hollis Street Church in Boston, where he had laboured from the foundation of that Church in 1732. (Stark, op. cit., 275-9.) Several vessels of silver, presented to this Church and engraved with his name as pastor, have survived to this day. (E. Alfred Jones, The Old Silver of the American Churches, 1913, pp. 80-3.) He died, July 5, 1788, aged 82. His portraits by Copley and Peter Pelham are in the possession of the American Antiquarian Society, Worcester, Massachusetts.

His son was the Rev. Mather Byles (q.v.).

REV. MATHER BYLES, THE YOUNGER (Plate vIII)

His ancestors early in the seventeenth century removed from England to Massachusetts and settled at Boston, to enjoy what they deemed liberty of conscience and the rights of Protestant Dissenters, but not to become aliens to Great Britain and its Constitution. The families of Byles, of Mather and of Belcher, from whom he had the honour of descending, have figured high in the annals of America and have been distinguished for their learning and integrity, their rank and reputation, and they were so happy as to retain that character till the last wanton Rebellion against the parent state levelled all distinction and trampled loyalty beneath her successful feet. In 1768, to his pecuniary loss, he relinquished with reluctance a large congregation of Protestant Dissenters in New London, Connecticut, and, from principles of conscience, conformed to the Church of England, notwithstanding that his venerable father, the Rev. Mather Byles (q.v.), a loyal subject of the King, remained a Dissenter from motives of equal sincerity. During the same year he sailed for England, where he received Holy Orders from Dr. Terrick, Bishop of London, and was appointed Rector of Christ Church, Boston, and a missionary of the Society of the Gospel in Foreign Parts. The University of Oxford honoured him with an honorary diploma for Doctor of Divinity. Having deviated from the ecclesiastical system of his ancestors and of his country-men, he lost much of his influence and popularity and was obliged at the evacuation of Boston to accompany the British troops to Halifax, Nova Scotia, where he and his wife and seven children were in great distress. (A.O. 13/43 ; A.O. 13/102.)

On July 5, 1784, in evidence in London in support of his claim for the loss of his property, he repeated most of the above facts, adding that at the commencement of the rebellion he repeatedly exhorted his congre-gation to be steadfast in their loyalty to the King. At Halifax he was chaplain to the Garrison and for a year to the Marines. His son was assistant secretary in 1784 to Major-General John Campbell, commander-in-chief in Nova Scotia. He was granted £30 for his expenses back to Halifax. (A.O. 12/100, f. 338 ; T. 50/8.)

The schedule of his property includes land at Springfield and Gran-ville, Massachusetts, and several bonds from different persons, named therein. His furniture was confiscated and sold. (A.O. 13/43.) He claimed £1,275 4s. for the loss of his property and was allowed £120 and £100 per annum for the loss during the war of his income as Rector of Christ Church. (A.O. 12/109.)

In addition to certificates to the loyalty of this clergyman from Sir William Pepperell, James Putnam, Harrison Gray, junior, and Ben-jamin Hallowell, there is one from the well-known Connecticut divine, the Rev. Samuel Peters, dated June 12, 1784, in which he says that from his early days he had known him. While he was a dissenting minister at New London, he considered him a loyal subject of the Crown and after his conformity to the Church of England and his appointment to Christ Church, Boston, by the Bishop of London, he distinguished himself as a faithful friend and subject both to Church and State by his superior learning and exemplary conduct. His father had set his son a bright and shining example in learning, piety and loyalty. (A.O. 13/43.)

Bishop Charles Inglis, of Nova Scotia, refers in a letter of March 18, 1789, to the Archbishop of Canterbury to his (the Bishop's) action in setting aside a former appointment of Dr. Byles, because of his encourage-ment of Dr. John Calef (q.v.) in aspersing the Bishop's character. (*Archives of Canada ; Corresp. of Bishop Inglis*, Series M., vol. 914, p. 144.)

This distinguished loyalist was born January 12, 1734-5. He graduated at Harvard College in 1751 and took the degree of M.A. there in 1754 and the same degree at Yale College in 1757. From 1755 to 1757 he was Librarian at Harvard College and resigned to accept the pastorate of the Congregational Church at New London. While acting as chaplain at Halifax he was curate of the historic Church of St. Paul's. In May 1789 he was appointed rector of Trinity Church, St. John, New Bruns-wick, where his congregation consisted mainly of loyalist refugees from

America, and where he died, March 12, 1814. (A. W. H. Eaton, in *New England Hist. & Gen. Reg.*, April 1915, pp. 101-117.)

His portrait is in the possession of the American Antiquarian Society.

Refs. : Appleton, *op. cit.* ; Stark, *op. cit. ; Loyalists' Claims, op. cit.*, p. 191.

PATRICK BYRNE

settled in Boston in 1774 as a trader, on his own property, and returned in March, 1775, to England, whence he sailed in a few months to South Carolina. Here he was seized with a " dangerous disorder " and was advised to go northward as the only hope of his recovery. Accordingly, he sailed for New York and thence to Philadelphia. The rebellion, however, spread so rapidly that before he recovered health all intercourse with Great Britain was stopped, and he was obliged to turn himself to industry to secure the remains of his wasted stock. All his endeavours were thwarted by fines and every other species of compulsion and cruelty until the landing of General Howe at the Head of Elk. Rumours having been spread afloat of the intentions of Congress to imprison every Tory able to bear arms, he crossed the Delaware in the night and got to Egg Harbour, where he embarked as a passenger on a schooner bound for St. Eustatia. As soon as this vessel put to sea, Patrick Byrne with the assistance of two of the crew and a loyalist passenger, took possession of the vessel by confining the master and compelling the rest of the crew to assist in taking her to New York, where she and her cargo of flour and biscuits were sold for £1,700. This money was promised to the captors by the Admiralty Court at New York, but was afterwards refused and Byrne and the others put on board a man of war. On application to Commodore Hotham, Byrne and the loyalist were released. Here follows a long account of his attempts to recover the promised share of the prize money in London. (A.O. 13/43.)

This petition omits two important facts in an earlier petition to the Admiralty, dated June 18, 1778, in which he says that he was pressed into the Congress service on a vessel for eight months, and that the above schooner, named *Speedwell*, commanded by Abraham Outten, was the property of a rebel. On arriving in the Downs from America, he was pressed and detained on H.M.S. *Medway* until orders came for his release. (*Adm. Sec. In Letters*, 3885.)

DR. JOHN CALEF

served King George II in the capacity of surgeon in the navy and army during the wars in America. At the end of the war with France [in 1763] he was chosen a member of the House of Representatives of Massachusetts. On the requisition of the King to rescind a circular letter, published by a

former House, he voted for the legal authority of Great Britain in 1768*
and by this action lost the confidence of the people and much of his profession as a physician and surgeon.   During the rebellion he was arraigned,
tried and abused by the " outrageous mob " several times.   In June, 1775,
the Provincial Congress took from him a ship of 300 tons burden, which
had been lately built for him in partnership with a gentleman [Joseph
Parker] in London, together with the cargo, valued at £4,200 sterling,
and converted her rigging, etc., to the use of the " Rebel Navy."   During
the three following years he " suffered almost every persecution that
vindictive malice could invent, upon his refusal to carry arms against his
Sovereign, his House having several times been fired into, by night, and
himself threatened with Execution at his own Door, to prevent which,
he fled to Penobscot ; with which country he had been acquainted many
years, where finding the people well affected to Government, he sail'd
for Halifax to make known to Your Majesty's Servants their Disposition,
to explain the Importance of that Country, and in their name to solicit
Protection."   On the passage he had the misfortune to be met by a
privateer from Halifax, which captured his vessel, and took all his effects
and papers.   He was present during the operations of the British forces
at Penobscot and was by General Francis MacLean appointed Inspector
and justice of the peace over the inhabitants and superintendent of the
Indian tribes of Penobscot.   He prays for compensation for the loss of
his property, over £9,000, and for the establishment of his appointments
at Penobscot.   His wife and ten children he left to the mercy of the rebels.
(A.O. 13/73.)

On June 25, 1775, Dr. John Calef presented a memorial to the Provincial Congress at Watertown, praying for permission to sail his ship
laden with provisions from Danvers to Penobscot, where, according to
Captain James Buck, most of the inhabitants had lived for some time on
fish, while many families had eaten neither bread nor meal for many
months.   The request was refused by the Congress on June 29, as being
" inconsistent with the best interest of the colony."   (A.O. 13/73.)

Captain Henry Mowat (q.v.), in his letter to Lord George Germain,
dated from H.M.S. Albany, May 9, 1780, introduced Dr. Calef as one of
the first loyalists who were most useful to General MacLean, as the most
equal to the task of working reformation in the minds of the people in
America.   So conspicuous a change had he effected in the inhabitants by
his unwearied pains and understanding of them, since his appointment as
inspector, that had he not been an eye-witness he could not easily have
believed it.   He laments that the Bostonians are allowed to dominate the
naval position, through the slowness of H.M.S. Albany and Nautilus,
which failed to capture a new American ship, the Protector, of 28 guns.
Captain Mowat laments further his inability to protect the coast, and this
unhappy position has been his ever since Lord Howe removed him from

* See page 58.   Dr. Calef craved forgiveness in a public notice, dated October
3, 1774, for his rescinding vote on June 30, 1768 (Publications of Colonial Soc. of Mass.,
viii, 97).

the *Milford*. Dr. Calef is well qualified to give an account of affairs.
(*Ib.*)

Peter Frye (*q.v.*), in a certificate dated December 20, 1780, states
that on June 30, 1768, he was a member of the House of Representatives
when a requisition was made by the King to rescind a circular letter published by a former House.* After the mob burnt his (Frye's) house in
1774 he removed to Ipswich and was there a neighbour of Dr. Calef, who
was a firm and steady supporter of Government often at the hazard of his
life, and was a witness of the damage done to his (Dr. Calef's) house by
balls shot into it, as well as of other acts of violence and cruelty too many
to recite. Dr. Calef was known before the fateful day of June 30, 1768,
as a physician and surgeon of repute, with a large and extensive practice
for many miles around Ipswich. (*Ib.*)

Thomas Goldthwait (*q.v.*), commander of Fort Pownall, Penobscot,
states in two certificates, dated London, December 20, 1780, and October
16, 1781, that in the year 1745 he was a passenger in the *Massachusetts*
frigate† to Boston from Louisburg after the expedition against that French
stronghold, and that Dr. Calef was then the surgeon on board. The
doctor was afterwards employed as surgeon in the Provincial service against
Canada. He was ever a firm loyalist. (*Ib.*)

According to a letter from Governor Hutchinson to the Earl of Dartmouth, dated Boston, December 30, 1772, Dr. John Calef, a man of good
character and a loyalist, was about to sail for England as an agent for
the settlers in the eastern parts of Massachusetts, to solicit a confirmation
of the grants made to them by the General Court. The Governor could
not give him any encouragement, but said that he thought this business
would end in a separation of that territory from the rest of the province.‡
(Copy in *Ib.*)

Captain John Macdonald, of the 84th Foot, in a certificate dated
London, February 20, 1782, says that at the end of March, 1779, Dr.
Calef came in a small boat at great risk to his life, both from rebels and
the dangers of the sea, from Penobscot to Annapolis Royal, where he was
then stationed with two companies of his regiment. The object of the

* See page 58.
† The Rev. Samuel Fayerweather, a loyalist, was chaplain on board this frigate.
‡ October 9, 1772, the settlers of Deer Island authorised Dr. Calef to act as
their agent in presenting a petition to the King for a grant of this Island. The
petition has sixty signatures (*Earl of Dartmouth MSS., op. cit.*, ii, 99, 185–6.). A
similar petition was submitted by the settlers of Southern Fox Island, November 25,
1772. (*Ib.*, p. 108.) A memorial was presented to the King by Dr. Calef in October,
1772, on behalf of the proprietors of twelve townships lying in the territory of
Sagadahock. (*Ib.*, pp. 103, 104.). Dr. Calef wrote from Ipswich, February 1, 1775,
to Sir Francis Bernard an account of his visit to Sagadahock and Deer and Fox Islands,
where he found a great increase in the number of the settlers, who desire a separate
government from Massachusetts. (*Ib.*, p. 264.) Sir Francis Bernard, in a letter to
Lord Dartmouth, dated April 18, 1775, urges the scheme of forming Sagadahock
into a separate province ; the population is not less than 20,000 and it would be a
resort for the persecuted loyalists of New England. (*Ib.*, p. 290.)

doctor's dangerous passage was to communicate to his Majesty's officers the desire of a great part of the inhabitants of the eastern county of Massachusetts to remain under the British Government and to recommend the establishment of a post there, which would much conduce to the King's service. This he urged in the strongest terms to Captain Henry Mowat (q.v.), of H.M.S. *Albany*, then in the harbour of Annapolis Royal, and to Captain Macdonald himself, in ignorance of the intentions of Government to send an expedition there. These two officers advised Dr. Calef to return to Penobscot, to prepare the minds of the people for any eventuality, while they communicated his reports to Brigadier-General Francis Maclean, who, on arriving at Penobscot,* found that the doctor had been most useful and had executed his trust with fidelity. The General appointed him inspector and commissary, chief justice of the peace for the county, overseer of the works, and superintendent of the Indians. On May 9, 1780, Dr. Calef left for England as a deputation from the inhabitants, to lay their state before the King and to pray for the establishment of civil government. (*Ib.*)

A long statement, dated May 9, 1788, from Joseph Parker, junior, late of Hertford, England, but now of Mettingham, near Bungay, England, on behalf of Dr. Calef, concerns the loss of a vessel belonging in part to Dr. Calef. The best materials were used in the construction, and the sails, rigging, etc., were sent out by Parker and were equal to those supplied to the East India Company. The vessel was, in fact, superior to most of those built in America. Parker made a deposition on June 4, 1788, that one Robert Calef (a kinsman of Dr. John Calef, and an insurance broker in London in 1783) had been master of Parker's ship, the *London Packet*, and was resident in Boston in or shortly before 1778. With these papers are several printed policies of insurance of six vessels of Joseph Parker, trading between England and Massachusetts in 1774-5, with their names and those of their masters. (*Ib.*)

Dr. Calef was " regularly introduced to the medical Arts " and was surgeon of a provincial ship of war [the *Massachusetts*] at the reduction of Louisburg in 1745. In the war commencing in 1756 he was surgeon of a provincial regiment under Colonel Jonathan Bayley, and served under Generals Lord Loudoun and Amherst for five years. At the end of this war he settled down at his native place, Ipswich, in the medical profession. In 1773 the inhabitants of Penobscot delegated him to go to England to solicit the royal approbation of the grant of thirteen townships by the General Assembly of Massachusetts in 1763, lying to the eastward of Penobscot River. Lord Dartmouth informed him that nothing could be done immediately as to these grants, but that the application would be considered in due time. Dr. Calef returned to Penobscot and carried out Lord Dartmouth's injunctions to keep the people quiet. He travelled eight times through the country, confirming the people in their loyalty, and by his influence prevented them from joining in the rebellion. He

* Dr. Calef wrote *The Siege of Penobscot by the Rebels in* 1779, published in 1781 and reprinted in the *Magazine of History* (extra number 11, 1910).

was frequently called upon to bear arms by leaders of the rebellion and in February, 1779, he was threatened with execution at his own door. In this perilous position he was obliged to abandon his wife and ten children to the mercy of the rebels at Ipswich, and went to Penobscot, where he found the inhabitants firm for Government. Here follows an account of his voyage to Nova Scotia and of his appointments at Penobscot and of his voyage to England to prevail upon the King to separate Penobscot into a province independent of Massachusetts. Before leaving England he exacted a promise that this would be done. He begs to be confirmed in his appointment as inspector of the woods of the district of Sagadahock, which would be a happy mark of his Majesty's favour to the only one of the seventeen loyal voters of 1768 who has not received any token of the King's approbation, and thereby enable him to collect his scattered family from among the rebels and settle down with them in peace at Penobscot, of which domestic happiness he has been a stranger for more than thirteen years. (A.O. 13/73.)

In 1784 he was in England and gave evidence in support of his claim for compensation. The Commissioners having seen with their own eyes so much poverty mixed with so much loyalty and spirit in Dr. Calef, allowed him £50 to discharge his small debts and to pay for his passage back to New Brunswick, where he was appointed surgeon to the garrison at St. John, August 25, 1784. (A.O. 12/101, f. 45 ; T. 50/8.) He was awarded compensation to the amount of £2,400 from his claim of £9,880 18s. and £100 per annum for the loss of his income during the war. (A.O. 12/109.)

During his residence at St. John, this loyalist was accused of spreading a scandalous report of the alleged criminal connection of the Bishop of Nova Scotia (Dr. Charles Inglis) with a woman of ill-fame in that town, named Crage, in the summer of 1788. The Bishop states that Samuel Hake, a loyalist from New York and the real author of this slander, and the Rev. Samuel Peters, a rival of the Bishop, had fabricated a number of falsehoods against him in London. In a letter to the Archbishop of Canterbury in 1789 the Bishop describes Dr. Calef as a " weak enthusiastical man," a warm patron of the Countess of Huntingdon's preachers at St. John, and as greatly offended because the Bishop would not ordain one of these men. The doctor had been represented to the Bishop as a man who would " alternately pray and whims with Methodists, get drunk, and blaspheme like an atheist." The Bishop absolves Peters from being a party in this audacious slander, though he considered him as one of the fabricators of the falsehoods published in London, and though actuated by the keenest malice against the Bishop. Dr. Calef when threatened with an action for slander recanted and said he spoke only in a " ludicruous way," without any design to injure the Bishop's reputation. (*Archives of Canada; Correspondence of Bishop Charles Inglis*, 1775-1791, Series *M*, vol. 914, pp. 131-152).

Dr. John Calef was the son of Robert Calef, clothier, of Ipswich, Massachusetts, where he was born, August 30, 1726, and grandson of Robert

Calef, author of the satire on witchcraft, *More Wonders of the Invisible World*. He died at St. Andrews, New Brunswick, October 23, 1812. (*Acadiensis*, vii, 261-273.) The Friendly Society of St. Andrews, founded in 1803, included among its first members Dr. Calef, Robert Pagan, John Campbell, Christopher Hatch, Thomas Wyer, John Dunn and Daniel McMaster, all loyalists. (*Acadiensis*, vii, 187-192).

His family Bible, containing the names and the dates of the births of his children by his second marriage, and some of his old furniture, are, or were, in the possession of Mr. George Mowat, of Beech Hill, St. Andrews, New Brunswick.

According to an anonymous letter to the Commissioners of American Claims, Dr. Calef had been exerting himself to get into the rebel service and had placed his sons in it. (With the Oliver papers in A.O. 13/48.)

References : Sabine, *op. cit.* ; Force, *American Archives*, Series IV, vol. iv, p. 663 ; *The Frontier Missionary, op. cit.*, p. 173 ; *American MSS. in Royal Inst., op. cit.*, ii, 118 ; iii, 407, 420 ; *Loyalists' Claims, op. cit.*, pp. 173-4 ; *Judges of New Brunswick, op. cit.*, p. 128.

PATRICK CALLAHAN

This steadfast loyalist removed in 1782 with his family to the British lines at Penobscot, where he bought a small lot of land and built a wooden house. In April, 1786, he was living at St. Andrews, New Brunswick. (A.O. 13/22.)

REBECCA CALLAHAN

the widow and sole heir of Charles Callahan, of Pownalborough, Maine, who, after suffering great abuse, was expelled in June, 1777, from the province. From April 23, 1778, he commanded H.M. sloop, *General Gage*, on the coasts of Nova Scotia. He afterwards served as a pilot in the Royal Navy and lost his life in H.M.S. *North*,* on the passage from Cape Breton to his own ship in Penobscot Bay in December, 1779. Within a few months of her husband's expulsion Rebecca Callahan herself was turned out of her home by rebels, and soon afterwards was pursued from place to place with warrants for imprisonment, but by the help of friends and by hiding herself in woods and barns she eluded her enemies and eventually fled to Nova Scotia. All the Callahan property is stated to have been confiscated and sold,† including what is described in the inventory as his elegant house and furniture, as well as farming stock and utensils. With the memorial of Rebecca Callahan is an affidavit of John McNamara, late of Pownalborough, declaring the truth of the schedule of the Callahan property, and another from the Rev. Jacob Bailey, formerly Episcopal minister

* H.M.S. *North* took part in Sir George Collier's signal defeat of the American fleet in Penobscot Bay in August, 1779. She was lost on the voyage from Spanish River to Halifax in January, 1780, with Captain Selby and most of the crew. (*American MSS. in Royal Inst., op. cit.*, ii, 19, 83.)

† The property was not, however, confiscated.

at that place and himself a loyalist refugee, to the same effect. (A.O. 13/97 ; A.O. 13/107 ; A.O. 12/10, ff. 351-3.)

The Rev. Jacob Bailey (whose warden Charles Callahan had been at Pownalborough) wrote on April 11, 1787, to the Commissioners from Annapolis Royal, testifying to her loyalty and good character and to her intention not to return to a country where she had received so much cruel treatment. (A.O. 13/50.) He had already given evidence before the Commissioners in support of her claim on October 17, 1786, and added that Charles Callahan was an Irishman and a mariner, and that a brig was being prepared for him at Penobscot at the time of his death. (A.O. 12/10, ff. 354-9.)

She received £150 compensation from her claim of £1,110, for the loss of her personal property, the real estate not having been confiscated. (A.O. 12/61, f. 44 ; A.O. 12/109.)

In spite of her former resolution not to return to America, she ended her days at Pownalborough.

References : *The Frontier Missionary, op. cit.*, pp. 176, 327–9 ; *Ontario Archives, op. cit.*, pp. 745–7 ; *Colls. of N. Scotia Hist. Soc.*, xiii, 31–3.

SARAH CALLAHAR (or KELEHAR, KELHIER)

was comfortably settled at Boston, where her husband, Daniel, was employed in the Commissary General's department early in the Revolution. He left Boston at the evacuation by the British troops and died in New York. She was living at Halifax, Nova Scotia, in 1786. (A.O. 13/26.)

MAJOR ALEXANDER CAMPBELL

was a merchant in Boston before joining, on April 19, 1774, General Robert Pigott's brigade as a volunteer and loyalist. He served at Bunker Hill as a volunteer and there received seven wounds. Upon recovering his health, he was ordered with the army to the southward. At the evacuation of Boston by the British forces his wife, Mary, and family embarked in a sloop (his own property) and sailed for Halifax, thence to New York, but they were captured by an American privateer. Andrew Mitchell, formerly a merchant at New York, was also captured on board the sloop.

Such were the zeal and loyalty of Campbell that he volunteered to make the hazardous journey to North Carolina with a company of ninety men, raised by himself, with a view to enlisting the numerous body of his own countrymen, the Highland emigrants, in support of Government. For this purpose he provided a cargo of necessary articles to the value of between £1,500 and £2,000, all of which was captured in 1776. He died on the expedition from Jamaica to the Spanish Main.

The claim of his widow, Mary Campbell, for the loss of his property in Boston was disallowed for want of satisfactory proof of loss. (A.O. 12/109.) This property was bought in 1793 by John Walker. (Suffolk County Recs., Lib. 175, p. 106.)

According to a certificate of Major-General William Erskine, dated May 7, 1786, Major Campbell was serving with the " Royal South American Rangers"* at the time of his death at Black River on the expedition to the Spanish Main. He joined the British army at the commencement of the American rebellion, having been an officer on half-pay residing at Boston. He behaved with great spirit at Bunker Hill. On returning from the expedition to Cape Fear River, North Carolina, General Erskine took him into his own family and found him very useful in patrol duty and in gaining intelligence of the situation of the enemy. (A.O. 13/73.)

Governor Archibald Campbell, of Jamaica, in a letter, dated Jamaica, December 18, 1782, says that the 100 men of Odell's American Rangers were not sent to the Spanish Main in pursuit of fresh conquests, but merely to protect British settlers and the friendly Indians from annihilation by the Spaniards. The consequences fully justified this measure ; the settlers on the shore were re-established in peace, the enemy's projects discomfited, their troops and stores captured, and the detachment actually returned to Jamaica without the loss of a man. (*American MSS. in Royal Inst., op cit.*, iii. 267.) The Governor was evidently unaware of the death of Major Campbell.

His brother was Patrick Campbell, formerly of Adam Street in the Adelphi, London, afterwards of Ballird(?), in Perthshire, and, at the time of his death, of Achalader in the same county.

WILLIAM CAMPBELL

was born in Cowal in Argyllshire and emigrated to Massachusetts in 1768, settling at Worcester, where he carried on a business as merchant in partnership with Andrew Duncan, a compatriot and loyalist from Glasgow. He was obliged to escape to Boston in May, 1775, after enduring persecutions and insults from mobs and committees and compulsory hard labour, and left behind over £2,000 worth of goods and debts. His partner had married an American lady and did not, therefore, wish to leave Worcester, though he was subjected to insults and was obliged to subsist on the remainder of the stock-in-trade. Campbell was living at Halifax, Nova Scotia, in 1786 (A.O. 13/24), but later removed to St. John, New Brunswick, where he was for twenty years Mayor, and where he died in 1823 at the age of 82. (Sabine, *op. cit.*)

Andrew Duncan died in 1787, leaving a widow, Sally L. Duncan. (Recs. of Worcester County Registry of Probate, Case 17,926, Series A ; Ex inform. Mr. Arthur S. Houghton.)

REV. HENRY CANER (Plate IX)

had been in Holy Orders in the Church of England in America for upwards of 45 years, thirty of which as Rector of King's Chapel, Boston,

---

* The Loyal American Rangers (Odell's American Rangers) were raised as a loyalist corps early in 1780 by Major William Odell. Alexander Campbell was appointed on February 19, 1780, Major and Commandant of the corps.

where his Majesty's Governors and other officers of the Crown attended public worship. Until the unhappy rebellion he was always well respected by persons of all religious denominations in the town. In consequence of his attachment to the Crown and his own sincere endeavours to support in public and private his Majesty's Government he became obnoxious to the rebels. After sharing in the dangers and hardships of the siege of Boston he was obliged, at the evacuation of that town by the British troops, precipitately to leave his home without being able to bring away any of his effects. Not only his house, library and furniture, but also several bonds and notes, amounting to £2,000 sterling, were left. (A.O. 13/73.) With his memorials is a long list of his books, nearly 1,000 in number, besides two closets full of bound books and valuable pamphlets, and a list of wines, a fine harpsichord, a handsome chaise, elegant furniture, his portrait by Smibert, and a painting of the Last Supper* and other pictures.

In evidence Dr. Caner stated that his family consisted of a niece† and one servant. He could not accept preferment in the Church in England because of his failing eyesight and advanced age. The Commissioners in their decision alluded to his eminence in America and expressed a wish to recommend him for preferment in the Church, but he declined for the reasons stated above. (A.O. 12/105, f. 56.) He claimed £3,900, for the loss of his property and was granted £900. His claim of £200 per annum for the suspension of his income during the war was granted. (A.O. 12/109). A pension of £100 was granted to him until his death. (A.O. 459/7; A.O. 459/11; T. 50/6.)

Governor Hutchinson, in a certificate dated April 11, 1778, said of Dr. Caner that he was for many years considered as of the first reputation and character among the Episcopal clergy of Massachusetts and that he was the author of several very sensible publications in favour of the authority of Parliament, which were greatly applauded. (A.O. 13/73.)

A demand was exhibited in September, 1781, by Thomas Bulfinch and James Jvers for the sum of £1,500 for three sets of silver Communion vessels said to have been carried off by Dr. Caner from King's Chapel, Boston, a demand which was not allowed as not being well supported agreeable to the resolutions of the Commonwealth. (A.O. 12/81, f. 72.) This ardent loyalist carried away the royal plate presented to King's Chapel by William and Mary, George II and George III, rather than it should be desecrated by the " rebels." (E. Alfred Jones, *Old Silver Vessels of the American Churches*, 1913, p. 59.)

Several of his letters on Church matters are preserved in the Library of Fulham Palace. In 1761 and again in 1767 he appealed for a resident Bishop in America. The address (now at Lambeth Palace) to George III from the Episcopal clergy of Massachusetts, including Dr. Caner, assem-

* Charles Paxton (*q.v.*) in a letter dated October 20, 1784, says that this picture was sent as a present to Dr. Caner by Mr. Trecothick, who suggested that the wardens and vestry might buy it from Dr. Caner and put it up in the Chapel, but a vote of the congregation could never be obtained for that purpose (A.O. 13/49).

† Sarah Gore, wife of John Gore, of Boston. (A.O. 13/73.)

bled at Boston in January, 1761, praying for the appointment of Bishops in America, is endorsed by Secker, Archbishop of Canterbury, that it was not thought proper to present it to the King, as the request for Bishops was deemed premature. (A. W. Rowden, *The Primates of the four Georges*, 1916, pp 280-5).

William Knox, Under-Secretary of State for the American Department, suggested Dr. Caner as the first Bishop of the new colony of Penobscot. (Governor Hutchinson's *Diary*, ii, 290-1.)

The Rev. Henry Caner, born about 1700, was the son of Henry Caner, a master builder and carpenter, hailing from Long Ashton in Somersetshire, who was connected with the enlargement of King's Chapel, Boston, in 1713-5, and who in 1717 removed to New Haven to superintend the erection of the first hall for Yale College. This loyalist graduated at Yale College in the class of 1724. For a time he was a school teacher at Fairfield, Connecticut, and in his spare time studied divinity under the Rev. Samuel Johnson. Having been ordained in England, he returned as a missionary at Fairfield, where he ministered for nearly twenty years and was the most popular preacher in the Church of England in Connecticut. In 1747 he began his long and successful ministry at King's Chapel, Boston, where he was highly respected for his high character and superior intellectual gifts. (Dexter, *Biog. Sketches of Grads. of Yale College*, 1885, pp. 296-9.) He received the degree of M.A. in 1735 and that of D.D. in 1766, both by diploma from the University of Oxford.

This pious ecclesiastic with High Church and Tory leanings, a scholar and a gentleman, died at Long Ashton early in 1793. By his will he left a legacy to Sarah Gore (widow of John Gore, of Boston), who lived with him. His portrait, by Smibert, left behind at Boston, was engraved by Peter Pelham in 1750.

A scurrilous verse in a ballad of 1774 is published in the *New Eng. Hist. Gen. Mag.*, xiii, 132.

References : Hawks and Perry, *Doc. Hist. of Prot. Epis. Church in U.S.A.*, Nos. 4-9 ; *Annals of King's Chapel, op. cit. ;* Stark, *op. cit.*, pp. 346-9 ; *Loyalists' Claims, op. cit.*, pp. 272-4 ; *Publications of Colonial Soc. of Mass.*, x, 67-71.

MARGARET CAVARLEY

was the widow of Anthony Cavarley, steward to the Royal Naval Hospital at Boston, who, during the war with France in North America, held a similar appointment at Louisburg. He died in 1776 at Halifax, Nova Scotia, whither he had accompanied the British troops at the evacuation of Boston in March, 1776. She was at Halifax at the end of 1785, when her claim was rejected. (A.O. 13/26.)

ANDREW CAZNEAU

was always a true and faithful subject of the King and did everything in his power to suppress the unhappy political dissensions. During the blockade of Boston he bore arms for the relief of the garrison and for the protection of the town. In July, 1776, he sailed for Halifax, and thence to Staten Island, where he remained until New York fell into the hands of the British. At New York he took up arms for the relief of the garrison and the defence of the city. In August, 1780, he received a commission as Marshal of the Vice-Admiralty Court at Newport, Rhode Island, an appointment which was terminated by the evacuation of that place in October following, when he was immediately appointed Judge of the Vice-Admiralty Court in Bermuda, and a member of His Majesty's Council for that island.* Here he remained until May 6, 1783. With his memorial is a schedule of his losses in property, including his large brick house in Queen Street, Boston, adjoining the New Court House. He was also part owner of a large house in Milk Street, formerly in the occupation of Lady Hazelrigg, inherited from his loyalist brother, William Cazneau, who died in 1776; and also part owner of a house near the Mill Creek in Boston, devised by his grandfather, Captain James Scutt,† to him and his brothers and sisters. He claimed for eight years' loss of practice in his profession as an attorney, at the rate of £150 a year. (A.O. 13/97). His estate was declared forfeited, November 28, 1780. (A.O. 12/82.)

This gentleman of character, talents and virtue, as Sabine describes him, returned to Boston in 1788, and died at Roxbury, Massachusetts, in 1792. His wife, Hannah, was a daughter of John Hammock, of Boston, merchant, and sister of Sarah Leonard, wife of Daniel Leonard (*q.v.*).

SHADRACH CHACE

was born in America in 1749, and on October 19, 1777, was appointed Ensign in the Loyal New Englanders. In July, 1781, he joined the 3rd Battalion of De Lancey's Brigade, in the same rank. (Ind. 5605-6.) He is named in the Banishment Act of Massachusetts.

On February 5, 1792, he married Martha Evens, at Somerset, Bristol County, Massachussetts. (W.O. 42/C9.) He died, January 22, 1830, at St. John, New Brunswick, where his grant of land, dated September 14, 1784, is recorded in Book A. (Sabine, *op cit.*)

Richard Holland (*q.v.*) and Levi Chace were Lieutenants in the Loyal New Englanders.

DANIEL CHAMIER

In a letter of July 27, 1776, to Anthony Chamier, dated Staten Island, New York, he says that the little army of British heroes continues to be very healthy and in high spirits. Lord Howe had arrived and made many alterations, greatly for the better, in the disposal of the fleet.

* Daniel Leonard (*q.v.*) (his brother-in-law), was appointed Chief Justice of Bermuda in 1781, and William Browne (*q.v.*) was Governor.

† Peace Casno [Cazneau] and Martha Scutt were married in 1737. Captain James Scutt, a mariner, mentions in his will, 1766, his wife, Elizabeth, his daughter, Mary Cazneau, deceased, and his grandson, Andrew Cazneau.

The brothers [Howe] are as one man. After mentioning operations of the British naval force against the American batteries about New York, he says that Colonel Patterson, Adjutant General, on his way to New York under a flag of truce, told him that General Washington's headquarters made a brilliant appearance, particularly in the great profusion of ribands which distinguished the American Regiments. Seven transports from Scotland had just arrived, bringing the Highlanders, very healthy, young, and of good appearance. (C.O. 5/154, f. 171.)

Chamier emigrated early in life to America and resided for several years at Baltimore, Maryland. In August, 1768, he was appointed deputy-surveyor and searcher in the Customs at Boston. On arriving there he found the inhabitants in a state of such violent opposition to the Acts of the British Parliament as to compel the Commissioners of Customs and their officers to seek refuge in Castle William; but he, upon receiving his commission from the Board of Customs, proceeded to execute the duties of his office, and continued to discharge his duty in that perilous and critical situation with zeal and fidelity. In 1770 he was appointed the principal in this office* and acted as such until the Spring of 1772, when severe illness obliged him in October to remove to Charlestown, South Carolina. In the summer of 1775 he removed to Savannah, Georgia, but finding that place not safe for loyalists he sailed to St. Augustine, East Florida, in which expensive place he remained for a few years in the expectation of the success of the British arms, until fevers compelled him to seek recovery in his native country. On the passage he was captured and taken to Newburyport, Massachusetts, and there kept a prisoner for nearly twelve months. (A.O. 13/73.)

He was appointed Commissary of Stores, Provisions and Forage for the British forces at St. Augustine, September 25, 1777. (Ib.)

James Simpson, formerly Attorney-General of South Carolina, in a certificate dated November 23, 1786, states that in 1774-5 he was well acquainted with Chamier at Charlestown, where he conducted himself as a faithful and loyal subject and openly declared his opposition to the revolutionary measures, and was consequently threatened with such violence as to compel him to leave. A certificate of Robert Alexander, loyalist lawyer of Maryland, dated November 27, 1786, says that he had been long acquainted with Chamier in Maryland. He met him in New York in the summer of 1781, after his release from imprisonment by exchange. (Ib.)

His original instructions to search under Writs of Assistance, dated October 19, 1770, at Boston, are signed by Charles Paxton, William Burch and Henry Hulton, three of the Commissioners of Customs. (Ib.)

On June 13 and 16, 1783, he gave evidence in London in support of his claim, and reiterated a part of his memorials, adding that he was born in Ireland, and that he arrived in England in September, 1781.

---

* His original commission is in A.O. 13/73.

Rev. Henry Caner

PLATE IX

PLATE X

John Chandler

(A.O. 12/99, f. 324.) He was granted £160 per annum for the loss of his official income during the Revolution. (A.O. 12/109.)

Daniel Chamier was probably the son of Daniel Chamier, born in 1722, who emigrated to America in 1753, and who lived in Maryland as Sheriff of Baltimore County from 1767, and later at New York, as Auditor and Comptroller of Accounts. He died in 1778, leaving a widow, Achsah. A pedigree of this old French Protestant family was printed under the authority of Somerset Herald, August 31, 1855. (Courthorpe, *Daniel Chamier and His Descendants ; Memoir of Daniel Chamier, Minister of the Reformed Church*, 1852 ; Lart, *Huguenot Pedigrees*, 1924, i, 25.)

Thomas Jones, the loyalist author of the History of New York, makes serious charges against Chamier in his conduct as Commissary, but Jones's judgments must be received with caution. (Vol. I, pp. 129–141.) Accounts of Chamier as Commissary-General are in T. 64/118.

Daniel Chamier died in London, probably in 1791, and his estate was administered to Judith Des Champs, his cousin-german.

References : *American MSS. in Royal Inst., op. cit.*, i, 33, 83, 92, 102 ; *Maryland Hist. Mag.*, iv, 284–6 ; Force, *American Archives*, Series IV, vol. iv, pp. 318, 337, 833 ; *Maryland Archives*, iv, 307 ; xiv, 429, 474 ; xxi, 265, 270, 372.

GARDNER CHANDLER

His confiscated estate was sold for £569 8s. 9d., and the claims against it were £829 10s. (A.O. 12/82.) He recanted later, and remained in Massachusetts. He was the son of John Chandler (*q.v.*). (Stark, *op. cit.*, p. 390.)

JOHN CHANDLER (Plate x)

In consequence of his loyalty to his King and attachment to the British Government, he suffered the greatest indignities and insults from the rebellious Americans, and was threatened with the deprivation of his liberty unless he would sacrifice his loyalty and renounce the Worcester Protest,* which he had promoted and signed, and adopt in its stead " a very treasonable league and covenant." To save himself from a very ignominious death he fled to Boston in November, 1774, leaving a beloved wife and sixteen children to the mercy of the rebels. Four sons at the risk of their lives soon afterwards escaped to Boston, while his eldest son [John] was confined to his house, and his second son [Clark] was imprisoned in the common gaol at Worcester. He was for many years a member of His Majesty's Council for Massachusetts, Colonel of Militia, Judge of Probate and a Magistrate for the county of Worcester, and as such considered himself as under stronger obligations to use his influence for quieting the minds of his countrymen and inducing them to pay a proper submission to the laws and authority of Great Britain, than if he had been in a private station. The penalty of his loyalty was the hostility

* See Appendix.

F

of the people. He received no support from his estate since September, 1774. (A.O. 13/73.)

John Chandler was shipwrecked and nearly lost his life on a voyage which he was obliged to take for the recovery of his health, presumably after arriving at Halifax, Nova Scotia. His income from his real and personal estate, acquired by his own honest and honourable industry, amounted to over £1,300 a year. (*Ib.*)

In another memorial he says that he brought forward the Worcester Protest against the rebellion, and was supported by the principal people of the town of Worcester, and that to render it more effectual he and his loyal associates caused it to be entered on the town records and published in the newspapers. A mob, drawn from all the neighbouring towns, seized him, and in order to save himself from immediate death he was obliged to renounce the Protest and subscribe to " a very treasonable league and covenant." He sailed from Halifax with three sons, and arrived in England in July, 1776. These sons afterwards accompanied the army to New York, and did military duty or otherwise performed loyal services. (*Ib.*)

In a fourth memorial, dated Halifax, Nova Scotia, May 1, 1787, he expresses his desire to remain there with his children, having two sons there, and a daughter married to James Putnam (*q.v.*). One of these sons served in the Quartermaster-General's department for several years, and is so infirm as to be incapacitated from active life and is dependent upon his father for support. (*Ib.*)

With these memorials are many certificates and affidavits to John Chandler's loyalty, including one from Colonel Abijah Willard (*q.v.*) (who had known him for more than forty years as a distinguished loyalist and an eminent public man, who enrolled himself in a company of Associated Loyalists at Boston and cheerfully did military duty in defence of the town) and another from Joshua Upham, (*q.v.*), who was an eye-witness of the scene in 1774 when about 5,000 people assembled in Worcester to prevent the sitting of the Court of Common Pleas, and to stop the administration of His Majesty's Government. John Chandler and a few other loyalists were led in triumph through the mob and compelled to submit to the insolence and humiliating terms of violent and distracted men. Chandler was of one of the first families in Massachusetts and possessed of a very large landed estate. (*Ib.*)

With the Chandler papers are schedules of his real estate, with a full description, and the names of previous owners and other details ; several certificates as to the sale of his confiscated property, except his mansion house and certain other property assigned by the State to his wife, Mary Chandler, for her support during her natural life ; a list of the purchasers of his confiscated estate, with the prices realised and a list of creditors and his protest against some of the claims ; and an inventory of his personal property. (*Ib.*)

From his claim of £11,067 13s. for his confiscated property, he received £7,221 as compensation from the British Government. (A.O. 12/109.)

Other references are in A.O. 12/105, f. 122; A.O. 12/82; A.O. 13/83.

This eminent loyalist died in London, September 20, 1800, and was buried in Paddington churchyard, where also his son, Rufus (*q.v.*), was buried. His son, William, was a second lieutenant in the Loyal Associated Volunteers of Boston under Francis Green (*q.v.*). Another son was Gardner (*q.v.*).

His portrait is in the possession of the American Antiquarian Society, Worcester, Massachusetts.

References : Sabine, *op. cit. ; Mrs. Lucretia (Chandler) Bancroft, a letter to her daughter, Mrs. Gherardi*, by A. McFarland Davis, in *Proc. of Amer. Ant. Soc. of Worcester*, October, 1900 ; *American MSS. in Royal Inst., op. cit.*, iv, 327 ; *Loyalists' Claims, op. cit.*, 335–6 ; Stark, *op. cit.*, 388–92. *Lawful Money*, 1778 and 1779, by A. McFarland Davis, in *New Eng. Hist. & Gen. Reg.*, April, 1903 ; Ex inform. Miss Elizabeth H. Chandler ; *John Chandler and a few of his Descendants*, by Chandler Bullock, 1922 ; *The Loyalist Side of the Amer. Revolution*, by Chandler Bullock, 1925.

RUFUS CHANDLER

son of John Chandler (*q.v.*), was bred to the profession of the law, and was well established in practice at Worcester, which town he was obliged to leave in September, 1774, for Boston. He was one of the signatories to the Worcester Protest. At Boston, and later at New York, he served in the Associated Loyalists. On June 2, 1783, he was appointed one of the commissioners for examining the claims of loyalists applying for passages from New York. (A.O. 13/73; A.O. 12/100, f. 198.) With his memorials is a schedule of his professional income in 1773–4.

He claimed at the rate of £287 per annum for the loss of his income during the war, and was allowed £240, and a pension of £120. (A.O. 12/109.)

Rufus Chandler sailed for Nova Scotia in October, 1786, in the hope of finding scope for his professional abilities, but that province was already overcrowded with refugee lawyers, and he eventually returned to England, where he died in London, October 11, 1824, and was buried in his father's vault in Paddington churchyard. In his will he left all his real estate to his daughter and only child, Eliza Putnam Vose, of Augusta, Maine, and portraits and sketches of himself and his wife to his kinsman, James Putnam. (Erskine, 346.) He graduated at Harvard College in 1766.

His father-in-law was James Putnam (*q.v.*).

EBER CHASE

See p. 84.

JAMES CHASE

was born at Freehold, Massachusetts, and was living there at the beginning of the rebellion. He joined the British Army at Rhode Island in

1778 and lived at Lloyd's Neck, New York, until the end of the war.
His father, George Chase, commanded the militia before the Revolution,
and as a loyalist embodied men in support of the Crown and was imprisoned.
James Chase claimed for 275 acres of land and for one-sixth of the sloop
King Fisher, lost on Long Island during the war. (A.O. 12/11, ff. 66–8 ;
A.O. 13/50.) His claim for the sloop was disallowed, having been em-
ployed in advantageous trade during war. (A.O. 12/61, f. 66.)

He settled at Maugerville, New Brunswick, and his grant of land
there, dated September 3, 1784, is recorded in Book 2.

George Chase (1719-84), his father, was an innkeeper at Assonet
village, and was a large landowner and an enterprising and useful man, a
selectman, assessor and treasurer, of Freetown (*New Eng. Hist. and Gen.
Reg.*, xix, 325–6.) He and his son, George, were voted for trial as Tories,
May 31, 1777. (*Hist. of Freetown*, p. 23.) The name of George Chase
appears in a list of officers commissioned for the Second Regiment of
Militia in Bristol County in 1762 as Lieutenant in Captain James Winslow's (First Freetown) Company in Colonel Gilbert's Regiment. In
July, 1771, his name is recorded as Captain in the First Freetown Company
of the regiment of Colonel Thomas Gilbert (*q.v.*). (Archives of Mass.,
Muster Rolls, vol. 99, pp. 53, 417.) He is described with Jail Hathaway
as Captain in Colonel Thomas Gilbert's battalion of Tories. (*Hist. of
Freetown*, p. 74.)

Reference : *Ontario Archives, op. cit.*, p. 302.

PELEG CHASE

of Swansea. For his loyalty he was confined as a prisoner from April 13,
1778, until the Peace, for refusing to take the oath of allegiance to the
State of Massachusetts. (A.O. 13/24.)

WILLIAM AND EBER CHASE

They claimed jointly for the sloop *Warren*, lost in Rhode Island in,
1778. Their memorial is dated Swansea, Massachusetts, April 10, 1786.
Their claim was rejected. (A.O. 13/24.)

WARD CHIPMAN (Plates xi and xii)

was born in Massachusetts, a counsellor at law, and ever a faithful subject
of the King previous to hostilities against Great Britain. In September,
1774, he was active in assisting to defend the house of Jonathan Sewall
(*q.v.*), Attorney General of Massachusetts, at Cambridge, with whom he
lived, against a violent attack by a mob, and was obliged to flee to Boston
for protection. Here he remained in the practice of his profession and
was thereby afforded a good livelihood of £400 a year, with the fairest
prospects from his connections and interests, of rising to lucrative and
honourable situations in the profession, only to be lost at the evacuation

Ward Chipman, Senior

PLATE XI

PLATE XII   Ward Chipman, Junior

of the place by the British. In 1777 he was appointed Deputy Muster Master General of the Provincial forces in America, and held this laborious office until the end of the war. (A.O. 13/50 ; A.O. 13/73 ; A.O. 12/11, ff.171–3, 179–80.)

Notwithstanding his estimates of his income, the Commissioners disallowed his claim of £400 per annum. (A.O. 12/61, f.90.)

According to a certificate of George Duncan Ludlow, he procured a licence for Ward Chipman to practise in the Supreme Court of New York while he held his office of Deputy Muster Master General. (A.O. 13/73.)

The original vellum document, appointing him as Registrar and Scribe of the Admiralty Court of Rhode Island, April, 1779, was sold by auction at Sotheby's, July 18, 1928.

His father was John Chipman, lawyer, of Massachusetts, and the date of his birth, July 30, 1754. He was sent to Harvard College, the *alma mater* of his father and grandfather, where he graduated in 1770, and studied law under Jonathan Sewall (*q.v.*) and Daniel Leonard (*q.v.*). Having sought an asylum with thousands of other loyalists in New Brunswick, he settled there and was admitted one of the eleven barristers and attorneys of New Brunswick, all exiles from the American Colonies. At the age of thirty he was appointed Solicitor General of that colony. Chipman was counsel for the celebrated Benedict Arnold in a slander case against Munson Hoyt. He was selected as counsel for the British Government under the treaty between the United States and Great Britain in 1794, and argued his case with great ability before the Commissioners appointed to determine what river was precisely intended under the St. Croix River in the Peace Treaty of 1783. The original Chipman and Barclay papers concerning the boundary are in the possession of Maine Historical Society. This lawyer was an unsuccessful candidate for the vacant post of British Consul at Boston, but was compensated by his elevation to the Bench of the Supreme Court of New Brunswick. One of his last public duties was in the capacity of agent for Great Britain in the Treaty of Ghent. His son, Ward Chipman,* an ardent loyalist as a boy and the fourth generation in the direct line to be educated at Harvard College, achieved distinction as Speaker of the House of Assembly and Chief Justice of New Brunswick.

Ward Chipman died as President and Commander-in-Chief of New Brunswick, February 9, 1824.

Portraits of father and son, both painted by Gilbert Stuart at Boston about 1808, are in the possession of Mrs. John Chipman Gray, of Boston, Massachusetts.

References : F.O. 5 ; H.O. 42/2 ; Ind. 5605-6 ; A.O. 13/83 ; Sabine, *op. cit.* ; *Judges of New Brunswick, op. cit.* ; *American MSS. in Royal Inst., op. cit.,* iv., 329, 406 ; Stark, *op. cit.,* 431–3 ; Burrage, *Maine in the North Eastern Boundary Controversy,* 1919 ; Rives, *Correspondence of Thomas Barclay.*

* E. Alfred Jones, *American Members of the Inns of Court,* pp. 48–9.

JAMES MILLER CHURCH

was the only son of Dr. Benjamin Church, who from being a violent Whig
turned over to the loyalists.   For his own loyalty he was left without
dependence at an early period of his life, just as he had begun to study
physic and surgery under his father.   During the war he was granted an
appointment as surgeon's mate and ensign to the West Middlesex Militia
in England.   (A.O. 13/73 ; A.O. 12/99, f.132.)
    He and his two sisters, Sarah Weld and Hannah Kirkby, petitioned
for support, after their mother's death.   (A.O. 13/73.)   The three jointly
claimed £3,450 for the loss of their property in Massachusetts and were
awarded £500.   (A.O. 12/109.)   He received a pension of £12 10s. until
October, 1831.   (T. 50/28.)
    He was born in 1759.   His sister, Sarah, born in 1761, married
Benjamin Weld, a loyalist refugee ; and his sister, Hannah, born in 1764,
married William Kirkby, a London merchant.   (J. A. Church, *Descendants
of Richard Church of Plymouth*, 1913.)
    James Miller Church was appointed ensign in the Royal Westminster
(3rd) Regiment of Middlesex Militia, July 25, 1794 ; Lieutenant, March 12,
1795 ; surgeon's mate in July, 1795 ; and surgeon, December 25, 1796.
He retired April 18, 1817, and was residing at Brentford (Army Lists.)

SARAH CHURCH

was the widow of Dr. Benjamin Church and mother of James Miller
Church (*q.v.*).   In her memorial she states that her husband, " in consequence of certain services," rendered by him to Government, was apprehended in September, 1775, by the rebels and thrown into Norwich gaol
in Connecticut and thence removed to a gaol in Boston, where he was
confined for a great part of the time in a dungeon and denied intercourse
with his friends and refused provisions.   General Howe, commander-in-
chief of the British Army in America, having been informed of the wretched
condition of Dr. Church, sent one Henry, a surgeon and a prisoner, to be
exchanged, and this arrangement was approved by the Provincial Council,
but the mob, with General [William] Heath at their head, prevented the
exchange, and caused Church to be removed from the cartel vessel and
re-committed to gaol.   Not content with casting him into prison, the
mob broke open his house and pillaged or destroyed all the contents,
without leaving even a change of clothes for his wife and children, or even
a bed to lie on.   The only property which she was able to recover was a
small quantity of silver plate, barely sufficient to pay for her passage to
England.   Permission was refused her for the direct passage to England
and she was obliged to travel first to France.   (A.O. 13/73 ; C.O. 5/116.)
    From a copy of an extract from a letter from Thomas Brown to Wil-
liam Perry, of Hereford, dated Halifax, May 16, 1782, it would seem
that Dr. Benjamin Church was put on board a small schooner which
Captain Smethwick bought of Jo. Clark and sailed from Boston in

February, 1778, bound for the West Indies, and was lost at sea. A number of other vessels sailing at the same time foundered at sea. One man only was saved and brought back an account of the melancholy disaster. (A.O. 13/73.)

With the memorial is a schedule of the property of Sarah Church. (A.O. 13/73.) Sarah Church received a loyalist pension of £150 a year until her death, August 8, 1788. (T. 50/6 ; T. 50/10.)

Mr. Sparhawk, in his evidence in support of her claim, stated that her husband was a spy. (A.O. 12/105, f. 57.)

The history of Dr. Church in the early days of the Revolution has been often told and need not be repeated here. (Force, *American Archives*, Series IV, vol. iii, pp. 958, 1481–2.) Some letters from him as one of the Sons of Liberty are in the Wilkes Correspondence in the British Museum. (Addl. MSS., 30870.)

His father, Benjamin Church, would seem to have had loyalist tendencies. In his will of November 18, 1780, he bequeathed £5 and the remains of his library to this son, if alive (for alas ! he is now absent, having been cruelly banished from his country, and whether living or dead, God only knows). This bequest to go to James Miller Church, in the event of the death of Dr. Benjamin Church.

LIEUTENANT GIDEON CLARK

Having exerted himself in many ways to uphold the Constitution and Government of Great Britain, and having from the first rise of the political dissensions opposed the measures pursued by Congress, he was subjected to insults and imprisonment. He gave every aid in forwarding his Majesty's service and in rescuing seamen and soldiers from imprisonment by the rebels, as well as performing certain secret services. With this memorial, dated Northampton, Massachusetts, March 28, 1786, is a certificate from subscribers, who from their long acquaintance with him, attest the truth of his memorial, and is signed on their behalf by Colonel Stoddard. There is also a certificate of the following five loyalists, of Northampton, dated March, 1786, appointing Justus Wright (*q.v.*) their attorney in prosecuting their claims for compensation : Gideon Clark, Aaron Wright, junior, Ebenezer Putney, Selah Wright and Hains Kingsley, (A.O. 13/80.)

In his will, dated February 20, 1814, and proved April 5, 1814, he is described as yeoman, of Westhampton, Massachusetts. He mentions his wife, Esther, his eldest son, Levi, his son Gideon, and several daughters.

REV. WILLIAM CLARK (Plate XIII)

was in December, 1768, ordained by the Bishop of London, and in the same year appointed a missionary of the Society for the Propagation of the Gospel, at Dedham (where his income was derived from an endowment

by Samuel Coburn or Colburn *) and Stoughton.† As a warm and
affectionate friend to the British Government in the Colonies, steadily
attached to the English Constitution in Church and State, he continued
in the peaceable discharge of his duty without meddling in political
affairs, and on the whole lived quietly except for occasional threats, until
May, 1777, when, for recommending a distressed loyalist (who was
almost murdered and driven by the mob out of Dedham) to the humanity
of a gentleman in another county, and for harbouring a loyalist who had
been driven out of Boston, he himself was the victim of the same " merciless rabble," and was arrested and ordered to attend for trial at Boston
on June 12. Although he was denied the benefit of counsel for his
defence, and subjected to many other disadvantages, he believes he would
have been acquitted of the charge of being an enemy to his native country,
but at the close of the trial he was required to make a full declaration of
his affection to American Independence and a renunciation of his allegiance
to the Crown. Having conscientiously and solemnly refused, he was
condemned to transportation as a felon to the West Indies or some part
of Europe, and his property ordered to be confiscated. He was accordingly put on board a guardship and was kept a prisoner for about a year,
until released upon production of a medical certificate, when he was
allowed to go within the British lines in Rhode Island. Here a testimonial
was raised for his benefit at Newport, July 14, 1778, and a list of subscribers with the amounts is appended. In a long and melancholy letter
of November 10, 1780, from London to the Rev. T. B. Chandler‡ (whom
he addressed as the respected head of the American clergy) he says that
a murmur prevailed among many of the inhabitants of Newport against
the burden of the loyalist refugees, because of the scarcity of the necessaries of life, which were not obtainable even for money, except for the
troops. Never can he now think without tears of the melancholy scenes
of that time. Friends advised him to take sail for England, where the
loyalists were encouraged and protected, and where he might live comfortably until the restoration of peace. With infinite reluctance he left
his wife (for a short time, as he had hoped) and his native shores. On
arriving in England he was surprised to find himself much blamed for his

---

* Details of this endowment are in a letter from the Rev. William Clark, December
8, 1783. (A.O. 13/73.). Samuel Coburn, yeoman, of Dedham, left by will in 1756
money towards building a church at this place and an acre of land as a site. After
the death of his mother, the whole of his estate was directed to be applied to building
a church, or towards paying a preacher to maintain the public worship of the Church
of England in Dedham. (Ex inform. Mr. Francis H. Bigelow.)

† Stoughton Church was closed in 1777 and never permanently re-opened.

‡ This venerable and respected clergyman and loyalist exile was warmly recommended by his brother clergy in America as the first Bishop of Nova Scotia. A
recommendation to this effect, signed by the Rev. Charles Inglis (who became the
first Bishop of that province) and by sixteen other New York clergy, was sent to Sir
Guy Carleton, commander-in-chief of the British army in America, March 26, 1783.
(E. Alfred Jones, *The Loyalists of New Jersey*, 1927, pp. 41-3.)

imprudence in coming, and was recommended to return to America. Alas ! what tennis balls of fortune were the unhappy loyalists. After a pathetic recital of his sufferings for lack of money, in spite of his frugality, with nothing to save him from hunger and cold through the ensuing winter, and nothing to be gained by returning to America, where he would perish, he states that his wife had perished in Rhode Island from the want of the necessaries of life, as did his only child, an infant. If, after all, he must perish amidst plenty, God's will be done. This letter was followed on the 27th by one from the Rev. T. B. Chandler to the Treasury, supporting in the strongest manner the unhappy exile's appeal for relief ; the poor man had been deprived of speech and hearing by the severities inflicted upon him by the revolutionists. Benjamin Thompson (later known as Count Rumford) (*q.v.*), who was at that time in the office of the Secretary of State for the American Department, also appealed to the Treasury in a letter of November 30 to grant him an allowance. " £40 or £50 a year (he says) would be Mexico and Peru to a man in such deplorable circumstances." (A.O. 13/73.) He was subsequently granted a pension of £60, upon his own application, supported by Samuel Porter, his former schoolmate (*q.v.*). (A.O. 12/99, f.53.)

The Rev. William Clark arrived in Nova Scotia in June, 1786, and settled at Digby. In a letter of May 21, 1787, he declares his intention not to return to the United States, the land of his nativity, although so near to it. (A.O. 13/102.) According to his letter of December 4, 1788, he had gone to Digby to enjoy a retired and quiet residence among his own countrymen and fellow sufferers for loyalty, and that he might do some good in life, which he could not do in England. His infirmities compelled him to remain dependent upon the benevolence of Government. (A.O. 13/85) Some criticism appears to have been made on his being a loyalist pensioner, for in his letter of May 21, 1787, to the Rev. Samuel Peters he says that he (Peters) knows him as a man of honour and spirit who would sooner die than abuse the favour of Government. Were he inclined to go and live among the revolters in the United States, his generous heart and honesty would tell the Government so, and he would resign his pension. As to the scandalous report, of which he and other loyalists in Nova Scotia are suspected, his heart recoils at the ungenerous baseness and meanness of it. Such insinuations are the work of Congress men, who will receive the reward of their wages in due time. If any act of disloyalty can be proved against him by positive evidence, he will consent to be hanged on the next tree or gibbet. (A.O. 13/102.)

Notwithstanding his declaration that he had no intention of removing permanently to the United States, the Rev. Samuel Peters, acting as his attorney in London, asked for permission for him and his sickly wife to remove from Digby to a warmer climate. (A.O. 13/73.) The request was granted and his pension was paid to him until his death in November, 1815 [at Quincy, Massachusetts]. (T. 50/7 ; T. 50/25.)

The sum of £30 was paid to him as compensation for the loss of his property, and he received £50 per annum for the loss of his ministerial income during the war. (A.O. 12/109.)

In a letter he says that "never man lived more peaceably and quiet ; never man meddled with politics, or was a better friend to civil and religious liberty " than he himself. But he attributed his persecution to the fact that he received a small salary from the Society for the Propagation of the Gospel, in London. *Hinc illæ lachrymæ*. (*Proc. of Mass. Hist. Soc.*, 2nd Ser., xii, 153.)

This loyalist was the son of the Rev. Peter Clark, of Danvers, Massachusetts, and graduated at Harvard College in 1759 ; he was ordained in London in 1768. His portrait is at the Dedham Historical Society Library.

References : *The Frontier Missionary, op. cit. ;* Worthington, *Hist. of Dedham,* 1837 ; *Ontario Archives, op. cit.,* p. 1,248 ; *Loyalists' Claims, op. cit.,* pp. 121–2.

ISAAC WINSLOW CLARKE

In November, 1773, when he and his brother Jonathan were appointed two of the consignees of the East India Company's teas sent to Boston,[*] they were obliged by the outrages of the people to abandon their business and to retire to Castle William in Boston Harbour, to the total stoppage and ruin of their commerce from that time until the spring of 1775, when they went to Quebec to engage in business. When the city of Quebec was threatened by the Americans, the two brothers embarked with their merchandise for Great Britain. In March, 1776, he and his brother were appointed Assistant Commissaries of the British Army in Quebec. (A.O. 13/97.)

These two loyalists were the sons of Richard Clarke (*q.v.*). Isaac Winslow Clarke's wife, Anne, daughter of John Powell (*q.v.*) wrote an account of a journey from Detroit to Montreal in 1789 ; she died in 1792. He died, July 7, 1822, at Cape Chat in the Gulf of St. Lawrence, aged 77, and was buried with military honours in the Protestant Burial Ground at Montreal. Three of his children, Richard, Susanna and Margaret, received grants from the Compassionate Fund after his death. (W.O. 25/3089.)

JONATHAN CLARKE

was a son of Richard Clarke (*q.v.*) and a brother of Isaac Winslow Clarke (*q.v.*). His letter to Elisha Hutchinson from Quebec, September 24, 1775, is in the British Museum (Egerton MSS., 2659, f.172.) See Governor Hutchinson's *Diary*, i, 540.

* A letter on the subject of the tea from their brother-in-law, John Singleton Copley, December 1, 1773, has been published (*Letters and Papers of J. S. Copley and Henry Pelham,* 1739–1776 (1914) pp. 211–3.)

RICHARD CLARKE, BENJAMIN FANEUIL, JUNIOR, THOMAS AND ELISHA HUTCHINSON

In 1773 they were appointed agents of the East India Company in Boston for selling their teas. By the faithful discharge of their duties and by their known principles of loyalty and veneration for the British Government, they became peculiarly obnoxious to the machinations of the leaders of the American Rebellion and consequently sustained great sufferings and losses from the rage of the misguided people. Some time before the arrival of the teas in Boston, many menaces and some violent outrages were perpetrated to deter them from discharging their trust, and under these difficulties they petitioned the Governor and Council for aid and support. But notwithstanding all the endeavours of Governor Hutchinson to support them, they were unhappily disappointed in their expectations, their petition having been dismissed by the Council in such circumstances as greatly encouraged the factious party in Boston and the province. They were determined, even in the face of increasing difficulties and dangers, to fulfil the trust reposed in them, if protection for their persons could be assured. They now betook themselves to Castle William and soon afterwards the teas were destroyed. The design of the faction having been accomplished, they might reasonably have expected permission to return to their families without molestation, but so unrelenting was the rage against them for their loyalty and fidelity that they were obliged to remain for many months in the Castle, separated from their distressed families and exposed to the inclemency of a very severe winter, and destitute of the conveniences and comforts to which they had been always accustomed. After nearly a year's separation from their homes, they returned to Boston, then in occupation by General Gage [in March, 1774]. (A.O. 13/73.)

A similar memorial was presented to Lord George Germain, dated August 4, 1777, in which they pray for some mark of the royal favour, the grant made to them being insufficient for their support and inadequate to their sufferings and the rank in life which they had sustained. (*Ib.*)

RICHARD CLARKE (Plate xiv)

was a native and merchant of Boston. In 1773 he and his two sons, Isaac Winslow Clarke and Jonathan (*q.v.*), were appointed consignees of the East India Company's teas.* For many years before 1773 he had been engaged in a lucrative commerce by which he was enabled to support and educate in a reputable manner ten children, all of whom lived with him and were maintained by him until they arrived at the age of 21, and that he was enabled by the profits of his trade not only to support so large a family but also had a prospect of making a considerable addition to his

---

* Francis Rotch (*q.v.*), was an owner of the ship *Dartmouth*, which carried a cargo of this tea.

estate by his appointment from the East India Company.* (A.O. 13/73.) With this memorial is an account of his notes, bonds, debts, a schedule of his losses ; a letter, dated January 28, 1789, regarding his losses ; and a letter from one Dwight, dated Belcher Town, September 19, 1785, concerning Richard Clarke's property there, with a list of his lands sold at vendue and the names of the purchasers and the prices.

In his letter to the Treasury, dated October 24, 1777, he says that his son-in-law, John Singleton Copley, the artist, was in Italy at the outbreak of the American rebellion and consequently Mrs. Copley was under the necessity of removing from Boston to England. Copley was the owner of considerable real estate in Boston, but derived no benefit from it during the rebellion and is not so well established as a portrait painter in England as to be able to support his family except in the most frugal manner, a condition of affairs which obliged Richard Clarke to do all he could towards their subsistence. (A.O. 13/73.)

This loyalist at the age of 72 gave evidence in London in support of his claim and stated that his agency for the tea was worth £150 a year. (A.O. 12/105, f. 58.)

His claim of £4,925 for his losses in the rebellion was disallowed for want of satisfactory proof of loss. (A.O. 12/109.) His pension was raised from £80 to £150 in 1785. (T. 50/6 ; T. 50/9.) The Boston estate of Clarke was bought by Elizabeth Broomfield. (Suffolk County Recs., Lib. 151, p. 136.)

Richard Clarke, who graduated at Harvard College in 1729, and married Elizabeth Winslow in 1733, died in 1795 at the house of his son-in-law, John Singleton Copley, in Leicester Square, London. Copley had married in 1769 Clarke's daughter, Susanna (Sukey) Farnum. A family group of Richard Clarke, painted by Copley,† is in the possession of Copley Amory, Esq., of Boston. Two relics of the Clarke family are still preserved, namely, a silver tankard by John Coney, of Boston, engraved with the arms of Clarke, of Salford, Warwickshire, baronet, which was given to the North Church at Boston by Elizabeth Cabot, a sister of Richard Clarke ; and a silver basin, by the same maker and engraved with the same arms, which was bequeathed in 1728 to the Old South Church in Boston by Mary Saltonstall, wife of Governor Salstonstall and widow of William Clarke, an ancestor of this loyalist. (E. Alfred Jones, *Old Silver Vessels of the American Churches*, 1913, pp. 57, 58, 433.)

References : Drake, *Tea Leaves ;* Sabine, *op. cit. ;* Stark, *op. cit.*, pp. 405–9 ; *Publications of Colonial Soc. of Mass.*, viii, 78–90.

* For his papers regarding the tea, see *Publications of Colonial Soc. of Mass.*, viii, 78–90.

† Richard Clarke is seen seated with one of the Copley children on his knee ; Copley stands behind him ; on the right of Mrs. Copley is her son, the future Lord Lyndhurst, and on her left is her little daughter ; the girl standing, Margaret, married Gardiner Greene.

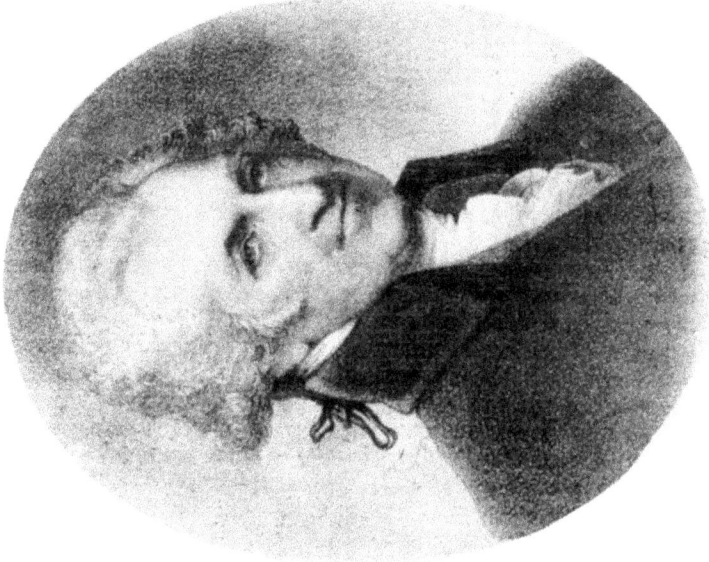

Dr. James Lloyd

PLATE XIII   Rev. William Clark

PLATE XIV

Richard Clarke and Family

ISAAC CLEMENS

was born in Boston and settled there as an engraver, silversmith and watchmaker about six months before the Revolution. He joined the Associated Loyalists at Boston and served until the evacuation of that town by the British troops, when he sailed to Halifax and thence to New York, where he was on constant military duty for about four years without pay or rations. Anxious to quell the unnatural rebellion, he distressed, harassed and perplexed the rebels by counterfeiting their bills of paper currency to the amount of over two million pounds sterling, which was circulated among them, and in this work he was encouraged and countenanced by many officers of the army and others in New York, for which he received no satisfaction other than the hope and pleasure of having distressed and confused the rebels.* (A.O. 13/73; A.O. 13/97; A.O. 12/100, f. 263.)

According to a certificate of Andrew Cazneau (*q.v.*), dated April 7, 1784, he (Cazneau) boarded at the house of William Hill, in New York, a brother-in-law of Clemens, who was a firm loyalist and was engaged in counterfeiting the American paper money. A certificate of Captain Caleb Wheaton (*q.v.*), confirms his success in counterfeiting this money. (A.O. 13/73.)

JEREMIAH COFFIN

At the commencement of the political disturbances, he with many other loyal inhabitants of Falmouth (now Portland), Maine, made ineffectual application to General Gage for a naval ship to be sent to Falmouth to maintain peace and order. This application having been known publicly, he soon became exposed to popular resentment, and in order to escape from taking a compulsory part on the side of the revolters, he sought a place of retreat in the British West Indies, in the hope that British Government would soon be re-established in America. He was born in 1750 and was the son of Dr. Nathaniel Coffin (*q.v.*). (A.O. 13/73.)

* General Sir Guy Carleton, in a letter, dated New York, July 24, 1783, to the President of Congress, states that he had given orders to facilitate the detection and imprisonment of counterfeitors or passers of Morris's notes within the garrison at New York. (C.O. 5/110, f. 333.). The General also wrote to Lord North on the same subject, August 1, 1783. (*Ib.*, f. 329.). With one Power, an American printer, William May, a native of Woodstock, Connecticut, and M.A. of an American College, was tried by court martial in August, 1783, for making and passing counterfeit currency, known as Morris's notes. The court had doubts as to the complicity of these two men, but Sir Guy Carleton ordered May to be banished as an infamous cheat, whose offence was aggravated by his superior education and by the rumour that he was in Holy Orders and that he had served as Chaplain in the American army. These notes and bills were sent to Elias Boudinot (C.O. 5/111, ff. 25–6, 291.).

JOHN COFFIN

In 1774, when the inhabitants of Boston refused to accommodate the British troops with quarters, he surrendered his distillery and sugar house as barracks for them. For this loyal action he was regarded as an enemy to America, and quitted Boston (his native place) in July, 1775, for Quebec, accompanied by his wife and eleven children. During the siege of Quebec by the Americans in December, 1775, he bore arms in the loyal militia. (A.O. 13/50; A.O. 12/11, ff. 177–180.)

Lieutenant-Colonel Henry Caldwell, commanding the loyal militia in Quebec, states in a certificate that John Coffin distinguished himself during the siege; and Brigadier-General Allan McLean, in a letter of July 27, 1776, speaks highly of Coffin's services and ascribes to his particular attention and exertions the repulse of Montgomery's force of Americans. (A.O. 12/11, ff. 181–190.)

The schedule of his losses of property at Boston include a distillery and wharf, and his brig, *Dispatch*, detained at Lisbon by the British Consul on suspicion of being the property of an American rebel in the winter of 1775. This vessel was afterwards released but was captured by an American privateer and re-taken by a British ship. He also lost a schooner, *Neptune*, which was sold by the master, Thomas Fraser, in the West Indies. He produced deeds and a long account of his property in Boston, including a share of a sugar house in Essex Street, inherited by his wife, Isabella, from her father [Thomas Child, distiller and sugar baker]. (A.O. 12/11, ff. 177–190.) Copies of the judgment, confiscating his estate, and copies of the three conveyances of part of his confiscated property, besides copies of other papers, are in A.O. 13/50.

He claimed £4,368 11s. for the loss of his property and was allowed £1,510. (A.O. 12/61, ff. 79–80; A.O. 12/109.)

John Coffin was Inspector of Police for the town and suburbs of Quebec.

In a testimonial from Lord Dorchester, Governor of Quebec, dated Quebec, May 28, 1787, he says that ever since his arrival there, Coffin had proved himself a zealous citizen. During the siege of Quebec his behaviour was such as to deserve applause, particularly by his vigilance, coolness and fortitude on December 31, 1775, as one of the militia guard in the preservation of Pres de Ville against the attack of Montgomery on that post. (A.O. 13/50.)

This ardent loyalist was a member of a conspicuous Boston family, distinguished for its services to the Crown in the Revolution. He was the third son of William and Ann Coffin and was born on August 19, 1729. He died at Quebec, September 28, 1808, leaving several sons who became prominent in the public service of Canada. (Stark, *op. cit.*, pp. 243–6.)

JONATHAN PERRIE COFFIN

was the fifth son of Nathaniel Coffin, of Boston, and signed the loyal address to George III (see Appendix). He was admitted to the Inner Temple, March 28, 1787, and migrated to the Middle Temple, July 20, 1796. His brothers were the distinguished loyalist officers, General John Coffin, and Admiral Sir Isaac Coffin. (Stark, *op. cit.*, pp. 233–46; E. Alfred Jones, *American Members of the Inns of Court*, 1924, pp. 50–1.) Another brother was William Coffin (see Appendix).

DR. NATHANIEL COFFIN

Mr. Hallowell, in evidence on behalf of his widow, Elizabeth, on June 19 and 25, 1783, stated that her husband was a loyalist pensioner, formerly Deputy Cashier in the Customs, who died in October, 1780. She was granted a pension of £40 per annum. (A.O. 12/99, f. 332.)

This Customs officer was a physician at Falmouth (now Portland) in Maine. His name, with that of his son, Jeremiah (*q.v.*), appears frequently in the Index of the Registry of Deeds of Cumberland county, Maine, indicating that they did large business in real estate. (Ex inform. Mr. Arthur S. Noyes.)

JAMES COLLINGE (or COLLINS)

settled on the River Penobscot about 1763 and was in quiet possession of 100 acres of land. On the arrival of British troops to occupy Penobscot, General MacLean issued a proclamation, requiring all loyal subjects to repair to the Royal Standard, with a promise of protection. As a British subject by birth, and a loyalist in principle, he repaired thereto and repeated his oath of allegiance to the King. Soon afterwards he was employed on important services for the General, and thereby rendered himself so obnoxious to the people that they deprived him of his farm and property. With his memorial is a list of his effects. Brigadier-General John Campbell granted him on June 21, 1781, a small tract of land to settle upon at Penobscot. (A.O. 13/73.)

At the evacuation of Penobscot he went to St. Andrews, New Brunswick, thence to Halifax and England, where he visited relations at Bacup, Lancashire. He expressed a wish in his evidence on June 8, 1786, to return to St. Andrews, where he had four sons. (A.O. 12/101, f. 324.)

From his claim of £518 for his property he was awarded £200. (A.O. 12/109.) He received a pension of £16 until 1804, which was probably the date of his death. (T. 50/11 ; A.O. 461/19.)

His name as James Collins is recorded as the owner of property at St. Andrews, in the Index of Charlotte County, New Brunswick.

ALEXANDER CONSTABLE

was an Englishman and a distiller at Boston, who assisted Colonel Joseph Goreham in 1775 to raise the Royal Fencible Americans, in which he received a commission as Lieutenant. He served at the battle of Bunker Hill. In consequence of disappointment in promotion he soon embarked for England, where he was introduced to Lord George Germain, and was given letters of recommendation to General Sir William Howe in America. Having returned to America he served as a volunteer with General Leslie in New Jersey and was wounded. For his good conduct he was promoted Captain in the 2nd battalion of De Lancey's Brigade* in 1777. He was now ordered to Georgia and sailed thither with his wife, Jane. On the passage they were taken prisoners and carried to Charlestown, South Carolina. Here he was kept for eighteen months, loaded with 40 pounds weight of iron. By his zeal and sufferings in the loyalist cause, he endeared himself to the loyalists of Charlestown, who offered to raise a regiment of 500 men to be commanded by him. Before accepting this offer, he deemed the approval of the King absolutely necessary. A memorial was accordingly drawn up by him, and his wife was to have taken it to London. She sailed from Charlestown on October 5 in the *Mary and Charlotte* transport, which sprang a leak a few leagues out. The distress and anxiety of the people on board increased until November 1, when the exhausted crew, overcome by continual fatigue and labour, declared the impossibility of keeping the ship any longer afloat. In this deplorable condition, in momentary expectation of being suddenly buried in the waves, gracious Providence was pleased to interpose for her deliverance by sending H.M.S. *Hydra* to the relief of the transport, and under the active and humane attention of her commander, all the passengers and crew were saved. One memorial is prefaced with a recital of the most severe afflictions and distresses which she suffered during her husband's imprisonment and while she herself was a prisoner at Charlestown. (A.O. 13/73.)

In a printed copy of his marriage certificate he is described as a brewer and bachelor, of Portsmouth, England, and his wife, Jane Ogilvie, as a spinster, of Gosport, where the marriage was solemnized, August, 28, 1772, in the Parochial Chapel. (*Ib.*) One Blurton stated that Captain Constable was a Scotch gentleman. (A.O. 12/99, f. 310.)

Three certificates, from Major General A. Leslie, Colonel Nisbet Balfour and Captain Alexander Shaw, testify to his loyalty and services. That of the last officer states that his well-known attachment to Government " brought upon him the bitterest enmity of an ungenerous enemy

---

* Captain Constable was tried by court martial on April 30, 1778, for quitting redoubt No. 7 contrary to orders, for absenting himself for several hours, and for falsely alarming the outposts during the night. He was found guilty of the two first charges and was cashiered, but was re-instated later on account of his previous good character. (*Orderly Book of De Lancey's Brigade*, 1917, pp. 66, 67.)

and the cruelest hardships easily in the power of civilised malice to invent."
(A.O. 13/73.)

The memorial of the loyal inhabitants of South Carolina, September 12, 1780, offering to subscribe towards raising a regiment for Captain Constable, is signed by 100 names. (*Ib.* and A.O. 12/46, ff. 314–33.)

With the Constable papers in A.O. 13/73 is the first page of *The Royal South-Carolina Gazette*, for June 30, 1780, which contains a letter to the printers from " A Loyal Englishman," contrasting the forbearance of Captain Constable with the cruel conduct of " that lawless Tyrant Rutledge* . . . " towards the Captain for fifteen months. There is also a letter from Constable himself, containing an account of the treatment (during his own imprisonment) of William Tweed, John Dewar, and Andrew Groundwater, as follows : In January, 1779, on his passage from New York to Savannah on Colonel Archibald Campbell's expedition, the transport entered St. Helena's Sound through the master's ignorance and was captured by Daniel Dessausure, of Beaufort Island, a pirate without even the pretence of a rebel commission. Captain Constable was at first a prisoner on parole at Beaufort, but was taken later to Charlestown, where he remained until January 30 without parole. On January 27, he delivered a letter addressed to the commanding officers of the British forces in Georgia, to a loyalist named William Tweed, who was bound for that province. Tweed and his companions, William Remington, John Dewar, and Andrew Groundwater, were captured on the 30th by a militia guard and sent to Charlestown and the letter taken from Tweed. Captain Constable was consequently apprehended and confined in " a loathsome dungeon," denied all intercourse with his wife or friends and daily insulted by militia men and certain officers, namely, William Doughty, Hopton Pinckney, William Burrows, and Captain Alexander Moultrie. Later he was removed to the common gaol in Charlestown and loaded with irons. Tweed and his comrades were tried for sedition, before Thomas Heyward† and John Mathews‡ as Judges, the jurors being Samuel Legare, foreman, William Somersall, James Wakefield, Edward Trescot, William Cunnington, James Henry Butler, John Spicega, Basil Laneau, George Redhammer, Samuel Butler, John Baddely, James Ballantine and Joseph Kimmel. Remington turned informer. Tweed and Groundwater were convicted and hanged. Rutledge, without trial or any evidence, ordered Tweed's wife, daughter, and son-in-law, to be confined in gaol for many months, and then shipped them off, on a vague report that they were incendiaries. Captain Constable was accused of encouraging them in a wild plot to destroy Charlestown, and was therefore chained to the floor and not allowed to buy food to supplement his daily allowance of water and rice. On the approach of General Prevost he was

* John Rutledge, a member of the Middle Temple and the future Chief Justice of the United States.

† Thomas Heyward, a member of the Middle Temple, and a signatory to the Declaration of Independence.

‡ John Mathews, a member of the same Inn, and Governor of South Carolina.

loaded with four pairs of irons, one of them being of uncommon size and specially made for him. After Prevost's retreat, Captain Constable was kept on board a prison schooner for two months, and in trying to escape was captured and sent back to gaol, where he was again stapled to the floor and exposed to the weather in a garret during the most sickly months. He fell ill and was refused a doctor at his own expense and denied food sent by his friends. On the news of the approach of General Sir Henry Clinton and his troops, he was treated better, and was at last released on May 12, 1780. There follows a statement by Robert Johnston that Captain Constable did not break his parole by sending the letter by Tweed, who left Charlestown on January 27, and was captured at Hilton Head, 100 miles away, on the 30th, whereas the parole was signed before Major George Turner on the 30th. The foundation for the charge was that the letter was dated the 31st, which was a most unaccountable mistake. Then Charles Ramadge certified that he, as commissary of prisoners, tendered a parole to Captain Constable when he was brought from Beaufort to Charlestown, but he refused to sign it. A note states that Captain McDonald confirms the facts that the letter was dispatched on the 27th and that no parole was given until the night of the 30th.

Colonel Charles Pinckney had qualms of conscience at the decision to execute Tweed and Groundwater, as expressed in his letter to General Moultrie. (McCrady, *Hist. of S. Carolina in the Revolution*, 1775–1780, pp. 345–7.)

Captain Alexander Constable survived his release from prison only a few months, having died in October, 1780.

Jane Constable's claim of £400 was disallowed. (A.O. 12/109.) She was put on the pension list as an officer's widow. (Ind. 8229.)

Reference : *Loyalists' Claims, op. cit.*, pp. 319–20.

ROBERT COOK

was born in America and lived at Wrentham. He served as a private soldier in 1745–6 in Governor Shirley's provincial regiment. From 1755 until 1761 he served the King as a soldier, the latter part of the time as Lieutenant in the regiment of Colonel Richard Saltonstall (*q.v.*). In 1775 he collected 25 loyalists to suppress the mobs and riots, and for his loyalty he was imprisoned and persecuted until June, 1775, when he escaped to the British troops at Boston, leaving a wife and thirteen children. From August 14, 1776, until March 18, 1777, he was in command of a company in the Queen's American Rangers, commanded by Lieutenant-Colonel Robert Rogers. In these different stations he did all he could to serve His Majesty and now in the decline of life he prays for relief. (A.O. 13/2 ; A.O. 13/107.)

Captain William Fowler, in his certificate of May 27, 1779, states that Sir William Howe thanked Robert Cook for his services as a good officer in the Queen's American Rangers and promised that he should be provided for in one of the new corps. (A.O. 13/107.)

In A.O. 13/137 is a list of his farm stock. He got a military allowance of £50 a year from 1787.

Robert Cook was the son of Cornelius and Eunice Cook and was born July 4, 1729, at Westborough. He married in 1749 Sarah, daughter of Samuel and Dorothy Crosby. (Westborough and Shrewsbury Vital Records.) In 1756 he was impressed or enlisted to serve under Lieutenant Colonel Thwing, but was reported as not having joined the regiment. He served as a private in Captain Slocumb's company in Colonel Williams's Regiment, April 14 to November 21, 1758; as sergeant in this company, April 2 to December 29, 1759; and as Lieutenant in Captain John Nixon's company, April 18 to December 7, 1761. (Record Index to Muster Rolls Series, 1710–74.) He returned from New Brunswick, where he had lived for a few years after the Revolutionary War, and settled at Ward (now Auburn) in Massachusetts, and there died in 1797. (Ex inform. Mr. Daniel S. Farrington.)

JOSEPH COOKSON

In 1772 he was appointed a clerk in the Customs Office in Boston. He served at Bunker Hill and as one of the Associated Loyalists during the blockade of Boston. Dependent upon him in 1784 was his poor, aged and infirm mother, the widow of a master and commander in the Royal Navy, who had been in the service for 45 years. (A.O. 13/73.)

Cookson returned to England in 1776 and became an ensign in the English militia during the American Revolution. (A.O. 13/79.)

The Commissioners condemned his claim for compensation as preposterous, his salary having been continued to him in England, and declared that he was not an American, and if he was, he was no sufferer by the war. (A.O. 12/101, f. 90.)

MICHAEL COOMBES

was born at Marblehead and was educated in the principles of the Church of England and early taught to be obedient to the laws and the Constitution of Great Britain. At the risk of his life and fortune he supplied the British garrison at Boston in November, 1774, with a cargo of boards and timber. On returning from Jamaica in September, 1775, with a cargo of rum and sugar, his own property, he put into Martha's Vineyard, where he was detained for some time by contrary winds. The committee of that quarter ordered him into Dartmouth with his ship, to prevent him from sailing to Boston, and put in there on 19th of that month. In May, 1776, he was compelled by the committee to sell a part of his cargo for the use of their army, for paper money. The remainder of the cargo he was able to hide in a store a few miles up Dartmouth River, where it remained in safety until General Grey with a detachment of British troops went against Dartmouth, and his ship and goods were wholly destroyed by fire, after being secreted for nearly three years, during which time he was severely persecuted for his steady attachment to the mother country, and was confined to his own house for eighteen months for refusing to take the oath of fidelity to the thirteen States. At last, in September, 1779, to avoid violence and outrage, he was obliged to leave his wife and family to the mercy of committees and in the night escaped in a small boat to Penobscot, where he landed on October 29. Failing to find employment there, he took passage with Captain Henry Mowat (*q.v.*) to Halifax, and thence to New York, where he landed in March, 1780. During that summer he served in the merchant service. On March 12, 1781, his ship was destroyed in a gale. (A.O. 12/99, f. 179; A.O. 13/73.)

The ship destroyed at Dartmouth was the *Sally* [named after his wife], built at Lynn, Massachusetts, in 1773. (A.O. 13/73.) A schedule of his losses is with his memorials, as well as copies of certificates from Samuel Curwen (*q.v.*) and Peter Frye (*q.v*), testifying to his industry and loyalty, and a certificate from the Rev. Joshua Wingate Weeks (*q.v*) that Coombes, a loyalist who acted from principle, was a member of his Church at Marblehead and for refusing to bear arms against the King he was apprehended and tried in the same court as Weekes, but was acquitted of the charges of crimes against the State. (*Ib.*).

He claimed £1,545 for his losses and was awarded £210 and a pension of £40. (A.O. 12/109; A.O. 13/87.)

For some years after the war, Michael Coombes commanded a ship in the trade from London to Spain and Portugal (A.O. 13/137), but he returned to America later and died at Marblehead, February 16, 1806, aged 75.

From a copy of the appraisement of the estate in 1764 and of the will of his father, Joshua Coombes, it would seem that Michael Coombes inherited property at Marblehead. By a resolve of the General Court, February 20, 1782, a part of his estate was assigned to his wife, Sarah. (A.O. 12/82, f. 10.)

JOHN COPPINGER

was born in Ireland and in 1752 emigrated to Boston, where he had a chocolate factory, and was compelled to quit that place because of the decided part which he took against the malcontents on behalf of his King and the British Government. Soon afterwards he sailed on a voyage to Quebec as master of the *Lovely Kitty* and arrived there just before the attack by the Americans under Montgomery and Benedict Arnold. In consequence of the scarcity of soldiers to defend Quebec, he and his crew were detained to help the garrison. He was obliged to sell his vessel. His health was permanently impaired by his exertions during the siege, and subsequently lost the use of his limbs, having been turned out of the two London hospitals, Guy's and the London, as incurable. With his memorial is a certificate from H. T. Cramahé, Lieutenant Governor of Quebec, testifying to the truth of the statement that Coppinger and his crew were detained to assist in the defence of Quebec. (A.O. 13/73; A.O. 13/97; A.O. 12/101, f. 28.)

Coppinger received a pension of £15 from 1784 to October, 1786. (T. 50/8; T. 50/9.)

LETITIA COPPINGER

a spinster, left Boston at the evacuation by the British troops and sailed for Halifax. On the passage she was shipwrecked near Cape Cod and was taken prisoner by the rebels, who stripped her of her property, to the value of £500, taking even the buckles from her shoes. She eventually got to Canso. (A.O. 13/73.)

HANNAH CORDIS

For many years she was the owner and keeper of the British Coffee House in [King Street], Boston, which she devoted entirely for the entertainment of officers of H.M. Navy and Army, from their first arrival in Boston until the evacuation. In consequence, the House was wholly deserted by the inhabitants during that time. She left a considerable estate in Boston and the country, and is now in low circumstances in England and incapable, from her age and infirmities, to procure any support. (A.O. 13/73.)

Governor Hutchinson, in his certificate of October 15, 1777, says that she was a woman of good character and that her house was the resort of persons well affected to Government. (*Ib.*)

The British Coffee House was the scene of the attack made by John Robinson on James Otis, and from its balcony Thomas Boulton (*q.v.*) read his burlesque. Here also was held the " Monday Evening Club," which met to discuss politics and which included Harrison Gray, the elder (*q.v.*) and other worthies. Likewise the " Fire Club," which included James Boutineau, Benjamin Faneuil, Samuel Fitch, Thomas Flucker and Harrison Gray, all loyalists. It is frequently mentioned in the Diary of John Rowe. (*Proc. of Mass. Hist. Soc.*, 2nd. Ser. x, 11–108.) For a " double bowl punch," 20 shillings was charged by Mrs. Cordis in 1767 and 30 shillings for a bottle of Madeira. (*Ib.*)

She was the second wife and widow of Cord Cordis,* of Boston, yeoman, whom she (as Hannah, widow of Elnathan Jones) married, October 2, 1740, and whose will of July 23, 1772, mentions three sons, Thomas, John and Joseph, and two daughters, Sarah Wheelwright and Catherine Hoyland, as well as his wife, Hannah. He died at Concord, Massachusetts, July 29, 1772 ; she died in London in 1779.

THOMAS COULSON

He was settled at Falmouth (now Portland), Maine, and was ever a true and loyal subject.

In 1775 he finished building a three-decked ship and purchased a cargo of timber for her. The sails and rigging came from Bristol (England) a few days after the time fixed by Congress for the non-importation of British goods, and the Committee of Falmouth resolved

* *Annals of King's Chapel, op. cit.*, ii, 120.

that they should be returned to Bristol, whereupon he applied to Admiral Graves for assistance and for protection for rigging his ship, Captain Mowat (*q.v.*) going ashore for this purpose. A mob from the eastern parts, headed by Brigadier Samuel Thompson, lay in ambush until an opportunity occurred to seize Captain Mowat and take his ship, *Canso.** The Captain was seized but was set at liberty by the intervention of inhabitants of Falmouth. The mob, however, increased in such numbers, and being incensed at the release of Mowat, could no longer be awed by authority and immediately took possession of Coulson's mansion house and store and sacked the latter of English dry goods and hardware.† Depredations were made on his boats by others. (From a certificate signed by Enoch Ilsley, Joseph Noyes, Lemuel Weeks and Nathaniel Coffin, in A.O. 13/73.)

In April, 1775, he was violently driven away with his family and obliged to seek the protection of the British troops at Boston. All his convertible property was seized and converted for the use of the American army, while his house and stores were burnt in the destruction of Falmouth by Captain Henry Mowat (*q.v.*). He left America in August, 1775, and sailed for England, where, having been reduced to indigence, he was obliged to resume his former occupation as a mariner and go to sea for the maintenance of his large family. With this memorial is a schedule of his real property at Falmouth. (A.O. 13/73.)

He went to Falmouth as a master mariner and settled there. On November 27, 1769, he married Dorcas Coffin, daughter of Dr. Nathaniel Coffin (*q.v.*).

Thomas Coulson died at Bristol in April, 1787 (leaving a widow and seven young children) and was buried at St. Augustine's in that city, under the name of Colston. His executors claimed £1,899 for the loss of his American property and were awarded £750. (A.O. 12/109.) In his will he mentions his parents, John and Elizabeth Coulson; his brother, Francis; his brother-in-law, Jeremiah Coffin (*q.v.*); his eldest son, John; and his wife, Dorcas.

References: *Mass. Archives*, vol. 164, pp. 133, 134, 211, 334, 337, 381, 382; vol. 199, p. 71; J. P. Baxter, *Doc. Hist. of Maine*, vol. xv, p. 60; Ex inform. Miss Ethel P. Hall.

* Another version of this episode has been published. Thompson and 50 armed men (each wearing a sprig of spruce in his hat and carrying a spruce pole with a green top for a standard) seized Mowat with the surgeon of his ship and the Rev. John Wiswall (*q.v.*), who were taking a walk on Sandy Point. As soon as Hogg, master of the *Canso*, heard of the capture, he wrote to Colonel Freeman that if these three prisoners were not released within an hour or two, he would reduce Falmouth to ashes. Thompson's action was done in opposition to the wishes of the Committee of Correspondence of Falmouth and he was rebuked by the Provincial Congress. (Force, *American Archives*, Series IV, vol. ii, pp. 552–5, 585–7; vol. iii, pp. 1169–70.)

† See *New Eng. Hist. & Gen. Reg.*, xxvii, 256–6.

THOMAS COURTNEY

was eligibly situated as a merchant tailor in Boston and left there with the British troops in March, 1776, for Halifax, and thence to New York, where he resided for four years. From New York he sailed for Charlestown, South Carolina, and remained until the evacuation of that province by the British in 1782. His next place of abode was St. Augustine, East Florida, where he bought a house. From this place he sailed to Shelburne, Nova Scotia, with the object of settling there, and after spending £5,000 in building houses, warehouses, wharfs and mills, he was at last reduced to the necessity of removing to Halifax in that province. At the age of 68 he arrived in England, to seek relief. (A.O. 12/3, ff. 36–42 ; A.O. 13/98.)

His name is appended to the petition of 106 loyalists to Parliament, stating that for several reasons they could not put in their claims within the time specified. It was signed by six other Massachusetts loyalists, William Hill, John Hill, William Warden, Justus Wright, George Spooner and Edward Dougherty. (A.O. 13/98.)

Thomas, Richard and James Courtney, of Boston, removed to Shelburne, where they built largely, but owing to the decline of this loyalist settlement, Richard went to Charleston, South Carolina, and James to Wilmington, North Carolina (Sabine, *op. cit.*)

Reference : *American MSS. in Royal Inst., op. cit.*, iii, 266.

WILLIAM COWPER

With his papers is a list of losses in property sustained by him in consequence of his loyalty. This property passed into his possession on his marriage to Hannah Evans (formerly Hannah Shilcock) at Trinity Church, Boston, on January 14, 1776, who was the widow of William Evans, silk dyer, of Marlborough Street, Boston. There are also copies of conveyances of property to William Evans in 1769, and bonds due to Evans. (A.O. 13/97.)

JAMES CRAIGE

a native of New England, who at an early period of the political dissensions took an open and active part in support of His Majesty's Government and thereby rendered himself so obnoxious as to make it necessary for him in March, 1775, to flee for safety to Boston. He remained with the British army throughout the war, serving for a considerable time as master carpenter in the Quartermaster General's Department and often doing military duty. His estate was confiscated and sold and included a farm in Oakham (a deed of gift from his father), where he lived. (A.O. 13/97.)

In evidence on April 19, 1786, at Halifax, he stated that in 1774 he opposed the choosing of county delegates and prevented the town of Oakham from doing so. (A.O. 12/10, ff. 127–9.)

Timothy Ruggles (*q.v.*) says in an affidavit that Craige was personally known to him for many years before the rebellion, and was considered a staunch loyalist. (A.O. 13/50.)

He claimed £339 as compensation for the confiscation of his property and was awarded £230. (A.O. 12/61, f. 20 ; A.O. 12/109.)

In an affidavit he is described as Captain James Craige, formerly of Oakham, wheelwright. (A.O. 13/50 ; A.O. 12/10, ff. 125–6.)

This loyalist was the son of Captain James Craige, of Lexington, Massachusetts, who removed to Oakham in 1750, and was born May 7, 1729. He married Mary Holton in 1751. He was a popular and prominent man in Oakham and was selectman and town clerk. Before the Revolution he was a captain in the militia. His brother, Joseph, did not share his political views. Captain Craige settled at Annapolis in Nova Scotia and died, April 9, 1806 ; his widow died March 20, 1809. (Ex inform. Mr. Henry P. Wright, of New Haven.)

References : Sabine, *op. cit.* ; *Ontario Archives, op. cit.,* pp. 588–9.

MARGARET CRAWFORD

was the widow of James Crawford, merchant, of Boston, who took an active part in opposing the rebellion with all his might, interest and influence. Those inhabitants who traded with him were warned publicly that they would be deemed enemies of America. He died in 1777, leaving her with six children. (A.O. 13/50.)

She was a native of Ireland and emigrated to America young. James Crawford followed the British troops and served as a volunteer in New York, Philadelphia and New Jersey, and died at New York in 1778 (1777 is stated above). The names of three children include that of a daughter, Martha, wife of George Thomas, a loyalist, who served in the King's American Regiment, and who was living at Shelburne in 1786. She was at this place in 1783. (A.O. 12/10, ff. 254–5.) Her claim of £250 was met with an allowance of £50 for her furniture. (A.O. 12/61, f. 30 ; A.O. 12/109.)

James Crawford's Boston estate was bought by L. Webber. (Suffolk County Recs., Lib. 177, pp. 185–6.)

Reference : *Ontario Archives, op. cit.,* pp. 138–9.

WILLIAM CRAWFORD

was an Irishman and emigrated to Massachusetts with his father, John Crawford, and mother, settling at Shrewsbury as a farmer. In January, 1778, he went within the British lines, having escaped from confinement on a guardship, to which he had been condemned and sentenced for loyalty. He served under the Quartermaster General and in the Barrack department. In 1787 he was settled at Kingston, New Brunswick. (A.O. 12/11, ff. 17–20 ; A.O. 13/50.)

According to a certificate, dated Shrewsbury, September 14, 1778, and signed by Captain Ebenezer Ingalsbe, this loyalist had paid ten (?) pounds as a fine for neglecting to march when drafted, agreeable to order and a resolve of the General Court of September 7, 1778. (A.O. 13/50.)

According to the valuation of his property made on behalf of the State, as a loyalist absentee, in April, 1779, it was worth £3,242 10s. (A.O. 13/97.) He claimed £320 for his property and was granted £191. (A.O. 12/61, f. 57 ; A.O. 12/109.)

A list of the names and ages of his eight children is in A.O. 13/97.

William Crawford was granted a town lot at St. John, New Brunswick in 1784 (Grant Book B), and on January 9, 1787, he was granted 190 acres in King's County, New Brunswick. (Grant Book A.) (Ex inform. Mr. R. W. L. Tibbits.)

Reference : *American MSS. in Royal Inst., op. cit.,* iv, 372.

WILLIAM CROSS

For two years before the rebellion he had carried on the trade of bookbinder and stationer at Boston, his annual profits being £150. From April 29, 1775, he was entirely deprived of carrying on his trade. He joined a volunteer company in Boston and served until the evacuation of the town, when he accompanied the British troops to Halifax and thence to New York, where he was present at the taking of that city by the British in September, 1776. He served as a volunteer at New York until May, 1777. (A.O. 13/24.)

This loyalist settled at Digby and afterwards at Annapolis, in Nova Scotia, where he was appointed in 1790 stationer to the Royal Artillery Department and where he was town clerk. He married a daughter of Andrew Ritchie, senior (*q.v.*), and died in August, 1834. (Calnek and Savary, *Hist. of the County of Annapolis,* pp. 175, 176, 573–580.)

ANNE AND ELIZABETH CUMMING

were milliners, of Boston, whose property was forfeited on account of their loyalty. (A.O. 12/82.) Their name appears as Cummins in the list of loyalists who left Boston with the British army in March, 1776. (Stark, *op. cit*, p. 134.)

ARCHIBALD CUNNINGHAM

This prosperous Scotsman of Boston joined the Loyal North British Volunteers in 1775. A schedule of his property shows that he was a general merchant. The Rev. William Walter, in a letter to the Commissioners, April 18, 1786, says that he knew him at Boston and later at New York and Shelburne, and ever esteemed him as perfect in his loyalty, amiable in his private character, and a very valuable citizen. (A.O. 13/24.)

Cunningham was treasurer of the Scots Charitable Society, instituted at Boston in 1657, and took away all the books of the Society to

New York. Of the 27 members of the Society in 1775, 20 were banished for loyalty. In 1775 the funds amounted to £900 in lawful money. Governor John Hancock would seem to have had an eye on these funds. (*American MSS. in Royal Inst., op. cit.*, iv., 232, 241.)

He was a prominent freemason and a member of the North Church in Boston. About the end of the war he sought refuge at Shelburne, Nova Scotia, and was Clerk of the Peace and Register of Probate there. (Stark, *op. cit*, p. 451.)

This Scotsman married Lydia Scott at Boston, April 3, 1766. His second wife was named Huldah. He died February 10, 1829, and was buried in the Presbyterian graveyard at Shelburne.

SAMUEL CURWEN (Plate xv)

The following is a copy of his memorial :

That your petitioner was forced to abandon his house & dwelling by the repeated menaces of the people for the few days he remained among them after the unhappy rencounter at Lexington ; who reproached as Tories & persons disaffected to their cause who did not join in accusing the K's troops as aggressors, were for supporting Law & order, & for forbearing future violences ; among wch number your petitioner was one— Taking refuge aboard a vessell bound to Philadelphia he arrived yre hoping to find a security from outrage & indignity, but in this he was mistaken, for tho' that city had during former wars shown an aversion to military Levies & arrangements, & in the late dispute, hitherto, a singular moderation, at this period the political phrenzy there had risen to an equal heigth with New England— And your Petitioner was soon informed yt that city would prove no refuge to him, even by those friends from whose protection He vainly expected safety— That the only condition of his continuing there was a public renunciation of his principles, acknowledging his errors & promising future obedience to the new assumed powers ; Loth to be held up to the public in so disgraceful & mortifying a view, & confess a well known falsehood, he took the only alternative in his power ; all comunication to the northward being forbidden by the city comittee of safety & inspection, lest Genl Gages troops at Boston should be supplied with bread & provisions, & by land no letters but such as were allowed by their state inquisitors could be sent, & travelling was become impracticable, he took shipping again, & after a series of dangers in a very tedious voyage arrived in London, where & in the country he has resided, subsisting whilst his own stock lasted on that, & since, on the state bounty— having lately received overtures from some of his townsmen since the peace to return, & the sad derangement of his affairs arising from the grievous burthens imposed by the new State, & the bad management of those to whom he comitted his* makes him wish to attempt to revisit his native country of NE : but the advices of his friends rendring it doubtful wether he can consistent with his safety &

* A word is missing here.

comfort pass the short remainder of his days being not far below threescore years & ten, the assigned period of human life, he proposes to retreat to Nova Scotia, or one of the royal colonies if he cannot obtain a desired resettlemt on the forementioned terms, He therefore humbly prays liberty to appoint an agent to receive the usual allowance hitherto continued to him, for so long a time hereafter as shall be judged proper. (A.O. 13/100.)

Endorsed :

Granted July the 6th 1784

In his evidence in London he stated that he was a merchant at Salem, also Collector of the Import Duties, a Justice of the Peace and Deputy Judge of the Admiralty Court. By the Revolution he lost property to the amount of £6,000. He was granted a pension of £100. (A.O. 12/105, f. 123.) He signed the memorial from 29 distressed loyalists from Massachusetts in England, praying for relief. (A.O. 13/46.)

His Journal and Letters, edited by G. A. Ward in 1864, are important for an account of his life in England throughout the American Revolution and for his letters to and from other loyalists.

When the news of Curwen's arrival at Boston from his exile in England reached his wife, she had " an hysterick fit." Curwen had written from London to a friend at Salem that if his wife should " obstinately resolve to live and die at Salem ... it is my express and peremptory order, command, and injunction on my heirs that on no consideration her dead body be entombed with my late niece [Sarah Curwen, who died in 1773] or any of my family, being unwilling that her dust should be mixed with that of a family to which she bore enmity ; and I should be not a little deranged in the Resurrection morning to find Abigail Curwen [his wife] starting up by my side ... and be put out of sorts at a season so solemn and important is too mortifying a thought to indulge." (*Holyoke Diaries,* 1709–1856, ed. by George Francis Dow, 1911, p. 111.)

Samuel Curwen died at Salem in 1802, aged 86. His pastel portrait by Benjamin Blythe, 1772, is in the Essex Institute, Salem.

Reference : Stark, *op. cit.,* pp. 246–254.

EBENEZER CUTLER

of Groton was an importer of English goods and was possessed of a good estate. For continuing in his business after the Non-Importation agreement, he was overtaken by a mob on the journey home from Boston and was carried back there and carted through the streets. For this insult and injury he commenced a suit at law against the ringleaders of the mob, but from the disposition of the people at that time, no jury would agree upon a verdict. In September, 1774, he left home to avoid a mob that was coming against him. In trying to escape to Boston in April, 1775, he was captured and insulted and abused, and after his release the political resentment was continued against him, so much so that he escaped to

Portsmouth, New Hampshire, and thence to H.M.S. *Scarborough* and to Boston, where he immediately joined the Associated Loyalists. He served with the army until 1778, when he sailed for England. In the hope of being useful he returned to New York and joined a company of loyalists, and afterwards did military duty in South Carolina. In 1781 he had a store on Long Island, New York, when he was called upon to go with a detachment of dragoons to the east end of the Island to take a number of rebel officers concealed there. This business was successfully accomplished through his assistance, and for his part in it he incurred the bitter resentment of the inhabitants and was obliged to quit. (A.O. 13/50 ; A.O. 13/73 ; A.O. 12/11, ff. 223–8.)

Governor Hutchinson, in a certificate of May 23, 1778, states that Ebenezer Cutler was abused in newspapers as one of the chief obstructors of the confederacy against the importation of British goods. (A.O. 13/73.)

His brother, Jonas Cutler, was his partner at Groton and died in 1781. His brother Zaccheus Cutler, a loyalist (A.O. 12/104, f. 62 ; T. 50/6), did military duty as Lieutenant in New Hampshire and was lost at sea on the passage from London to South Carolina in 1780. His eldest brother, Elisha, was always friendly to the Americans. A description of the Cutler property is appended. (A.O. 12/11, ff. 229–235.)

Ebenezer Cutler claimed £4,028 and was allowed £301. He was granted a loyalist pension. (A.O. 12/61, f. 98 ; A.O. 12/105, f. 59 ; A.O. 12/109.)

His father was Ebenezer Cutler, of Weston, Massachusetts. By his first wife, Miriam, daughter of James Eager (*q.v.*), this loyalist had a son, Ebenezer, born in 1765, who was obliged to leave Harvard College shortly after the outbreak of war. Against his name in the College Register the word " Traitor " is said to have been added, though he was a mere boy at the time.*

This loyalist settled at Annapolis, Nova Scotia, and died there in 1831.

References : Force, *Amer. Archives*, Ser. IV., vol. ii., p. 632 ; *Ontario Archives, op. cit.*, pp. 1285–8.

NATHANIEL DABNEY

was pleasantly situated in Salem in the several businesses of apothecary, druggist and grocer, in all of which he had been regularly educated. His clear annual profit was at least £400 sterling, with a prospect of an increasing income. He had an estate, and moneys out on interest, to the amount of £4,000. Having resolutely dissented from the rebellious measures, he was constantly insulted, threatened and harassed (notwithstanding all possible prudence), and for more than two years he was in a continued state of duress, and even the most necessary utensils of his business were wrested from him, on the pretence of satisfying mulcts and penalties for not joining and personally assisting the rebel forces. At

* This register is not now extant.

length he was obliged to escape from Salem, leaving his wife and family, and eventually arrived in England. (A.O. 13/44.)

His large bell-metal mortar with pestle, weighing nearly 60 pounds, was ordered to be sold, November 4, 1776, at a public " outcry," to satisfy a fine and charges for not serving on the jury at the Maritime Court at Salem on June 17, 1776. A warrant was issued, summoning him to attend before Judge Timothy Pickering, junior, at the Court at Salem on September 21, 1776, to show forth his reasons for not serving on the jury at the Admiralty Court on June 24, 1776, to try and condemn all vessels investing the American coast and brought into either of the counties of Suffolk, Middlesex or Essex, Massachusetts. (A.O. 13/44.)

His pension of £70 was continued to him. (A.O. 12/105, f. 60.) He was doubtless the Dr. Daubeny, of Salem, to whom Samuel Curwen (*q.v.*) wrote in London on January 3, 1778. (Curwen, *Diary, op. cit.*). He apologized later for signing the address to Governor Hutchinson and was declared to be treated as a real friend to America. (Force, *op. cit.*, Ser. IV., vol. ii., p. 852.)

ISAAC DA COSTA

In 1745 he was present at the defence of Annapolis Royal in Nova Scotia and served as a volunteer at the siege of Louisburg in the same year. Governor Shirley afterwards gave him a commission in the train of artillery under Colonel Gridley.* He likewise held a commission in the batteaux service under Colonel John Bradstreet, and in 1755 he served as captain in Colonel Williams's† regiment, which was almost cut off in the memorable battle between General Johnson and Count Dieskau. From 1758 to 1764 he was master in the Navy Yard at Halifax, Nova Scotia. He afterwards contracted to build the fortress at Annapolis Royal. In 1774 he was possessed of an estate in New England, returning him an annual income of £200, and in the same year inherited £4,000 from his father. He returned to Boston from England in January, 1778, and was immediately taken into custody as a loyalist. Having refused to take the test oaths he was cast into prison and banished on a French vessel and landed in England, June 27, 1778. (A.O. 13/44 ; A.O. 13/79.)

With his memorial is a copy of a letter from Joshua Davis (who married his sister, Martha da Costa), dated Boston, September 12, 1774, stating that this loyalist's father died July 13, 1774, leaving a will, in which he directed Isaac da Costa and others to act as executors. As to political affairs in Boston, Joshua Davis is unable to describe or paint them, even if he had the pencil of the most eminent painter, as they are in the most distressed and confused situation imaginable. The inhabitants are

* Colonel Jeremiah Gridley, a distinguished American soldier in the Colonial period and during the Revolutionary War.

† Colonel Ephraim Williams, at the head of the Massachusetts troops, was killed near Lake George, September 8, 1755, in the expedition against Crown Point, commanded by Sir William Johnson, when Dieskau was defeated.

really in a state of captivity, all trade and commerce having been cut off by the unjust and cruel Port Bill and other Acts of Parliament. Boston is no better than a garrison town and is filled with a number of red coated " murderthers." This very day a man was shot for desertion, such are the terrible laws of arms. These dreadful times will (he is afraid) end in bloodshed and slaughter, as the people are determined not to give up their liberties and privileges to such tyrannical and oppressive measures.

Additional facts in his career are given by Isaac da Costa in his evidence on May 6, 1783, namely, that from 1768 to 1778 he was resident in England and Holland, trying to recover his estate in Holland. His wife was a woman of some property. He was the owner of real property called Needham in Massachusetts, for which he paid £1,300 sterling in 1762, and the rents from which, amounting to over £200 per annum, were remitted to him by his father until the rebellion. He was also the owner of 22,000 acres of land in Nova Scotia. He was in prison for fourteen months for debt until March, 1783. (A.O. 12/99, f. 218.)

Colonel Joseph Goreham (q.v.) in a certificate, dated April 24, 1783, states that Isaac da Costa was known to him for many years and was always looked upon as a man of property. (A.O. 13/44.)

Isaac da Costa was suggested as a member of the expedition for the discovery of the north-west passage. (Page 11.)

John da Costa, his father, was a mason in Boston and in his will (dated May 13, 1769, and proved July 19, 1774) bequeathed property to his six children.

THOMAS DANFORTH

In his memorial he states that his first ancestor in America settled in 1635 at Cambridge, Massachusetts, and was a gentleman of considerable fortune. Three of the early Governors or Lieutenant Governors of the province were of his family and all his other ancestors to his father were clergymen of respectable characters. His father [Samuel Danforth] was early advanced to the first places of rank and honour and was a member of the General Assembly for almost half a century. For more than thirty years he was a member of the Provincial Council and was President for many years. At the alteration of the form of provincial government and appointment of the Council by the King, he was persuaded that his example would be good if he continued as President, though he had intended to retire on account of his advanced age, on the understanding that this son would succeed him as a member of the Council and in his other offices of Judge of Probate and Judge of the Court of Common Pleas. The public disorders now increased and the mob compelled Samuel Danforth to resign from the Council and he retired to a lonely village, away from his family and friends, where he languished and died [in 1777]. Meanwhile his house was taken by the American army as a barrack. After taking the degree of Master of Arts at Harvard, Thomas Danforth continued his studies in law for several years at the College, under the direction of one of the Judges of the Supreme Court, and also acted as a tutor, particularly as assistant to the Professor of Mathematics and Natural Philosophy,* and was soon chosen a Fellow of the College. At the end of 1769 he left the College and was admitted to the Bar of Massachusetts. In his legal career he laboured under great difficulties in consequence of his opposition to the " prevailing madness " and of his conspicuous position in the county and in Charlestown, which was a town particularly fanatical and rebellious. He ceased practice in 1772. Thomas Danforth now went into Boston to avoid insult and injury from mobs and on the requisition of General Gage did duty during the blockade by patrolling the streets every third night as Lieutenant in the volunteer company of Colonel Abijah Willard (q.v.). This duty he performed until ill-health compelled him to retire. He was a justice of the peace and was appointed during the blockade of Boston, temporary Registrar of the Vice-Admiralty Court for the four New England provinces, the former holder of this office under Thomas Bernard having joined the rebels. All the records of this Court from the first settlement of New England were [in 1783] in his possession in London.

For several years before the war, when it was evidently the design of a set of desperate people in Boston to bring on a rebellion, a society was held at Cambridge consisting of his father [who graduated at Harvard College in 1715] and other gentlemen, to which he himself was admitted while at Harvard College, with the object of supporting the constitution and laws of the province and thereby incurred the resentment of those plotters of the destruction of the constitution. He is unwilling to relate particular circumstances to demonstrate the reality of his attachment to his professed principles as a loyalist or to show the flattering consequences he might probably have obtained by conforming to the political wishes of Mr. Adams at Paris and Mr. Dana at St. Petersburg, who were formerly his intimate friends and brother barristers, and of Mr. Lovell, his schoolmaster, now a member of Congress, and of others of equal consequence. His loyalty arose from natural temper, from education and from expectations. Having devoted his life to the age of nearly thirty in preparing himself for future usefulness, he now finds himself in his fortieth year banished from his native land under pain of death to a distant country [England], where he has not the most remote family connection, nor scarcely an acquaintance who is not in the same circumstances—cut off from his profession and from every hope of importance in life and in a great degree deprived of social enjoyments, and where, unknowing and unknown, he is unable to procure common comforts and conveniences in a station much superior to that of a menial servant without the assistance of Government.

In 1773 Danforth was promised by Lord Dartmouth the first vacancy in a suitable office in America, particularly that of Attorney General of Massachusetts was proposed to him, but he declined the offer because of his inexperience and of his particular friendship with the holder of that

* John Winthrop was Hollis Professor of Mathematics and Natural Philosophy, 1738–79.

office [Jonathan Sewall]. The Secretaryship of the province was also promised him upon a vacancy occurring. (A.O. 13/44.)

Certificates to his loyalty from Harrison Gray, Thomas Flucker and Lieutenant Governor Thomas Oliver are in A.O. 13/79. Affidavits of no interest are in A.O. 13/83 and A.O. 13/85.

This loyalist claimed compensation at the rate of £100 a year for the loss of his professional income during the war and was allowed that amount. (A.O. 12/109.) He was granted a pension of £50 until his death in 1820. (A.O. 459/7 ; T. 50/46.)

Thomas Danforth was born September 1, 1744, graduated at Harvard College in 1762 and died in London.

His elder brother, Samuel Danforth, physician (Harvard, 1758), was also a loyalist, and was at first treated harshly by the Whigs, but the scarcity of medical men in Boston enabled him to live down the early opposition to his loyal principles. (Sabine, *op. cit.*) He became President of the Massachusetts Medical Society, who have his portrait, painted by Gilbert Stuart about 1809.

References : Sabine, *op. cit.* ; *Earl of Dartmouth MSS., op. cit.,* ii, 156, 176, 184, 468 ; Stark, *op. cit.,* pp. 126, 134, 138 ; *Loyalists' Claims, op. cit.,* p. 26.

SAMUEL DASHWOOD

His goods were forcibly removed from his warehouse in Boston by a body of armed men, on instructions from Sir William Howe, early in March, 1776, to prevent them from falling into the hands of the rebels. Isabella Welch, widow, and Hannah Durant, wife of Ephraim Durant, were witnesses of the removal. (A.O. 13/44.)

Joshua Loring (*q.v.*) said that Dashwood's claim for compensation was unjust and that he was ever looked upon as unfriendly to the cause of Great Britain and as an impudent, troublesome and notorious rebel. (*Ib.*)

Note of a question to be asked of him by the Commissioners : Was he not in debt to his merchants before April 19, 1775, and why did he not sell his goods between that date and the evacuation of Boston by the British troops in March, 1776, when he might have made a remittance in public bills at 17½ per cent. discount ? Surely this was a good time to pay his debts in England if he had been so disposed, but the fact is that he sent what money he had into the country by his wife, and kept his goods for the rebels. (*Ib.*)

There are memorials and several documents relating to his claim for the alleged loss of his goods. (*Ib.* and Treas. I, f. 622.)

His claim of £2,758 10s. was disallowed. (A.O. 12/109.)

Samuel Dashwood had lived at Boston for thirty years and had served under Admiral Sir Peter Warren at Louisburg in 1745. He returned to the United States. (*Loyalists' Claims, op. cit.,* pp. 337-8.)

Samuel Curwen   PLATE XV

PLATE XVI

Mrs. Benjamin Davis

BENJAMIN DAVIS, SENIOR

In 1769 and 1770 he was in partnership with his brother, Edward, as a merchant in Boston, and in consequence of his refusal to sign the Non-Importation agreement they dissolved partnership. In 1774 his own warehouse was transformed into a barrack for the British soldiers and was destroyed by fire, together with the wharf on which it stood. He lost a whaling sloop which docked at Salem in 1775 and was not allowed to sail for Boston. After serving in the Associated Loyalists, he accompanied the British troops from Boston to Halifax in March, 1776, and thence to New York. His vessel separated from the main fleet in a gale and was captured by the Americans. Davis himself was sent to Boston and put into gaol, with orders that he was to be kept alone and not allowed visitors except in the presence of gaolers, and not to be permitted writing materials or a candle. In this condition he remained from July 26, 1776, to June 4, 1777, faring hard and obliged to support his son, Benjamin, and a negro servant, taken prisoners at the same time. He was finally exchanged and travelled by land from Boston to New York, a distance of about 300 miles, penniless. His expenses in gaol and on the journey amounted to £200. Congress and the State legislatures having denied encouragement to the loyalists to return to their homes, and deeming it unsafe to return to Boston (as one of the proscribed persons) he was under the disagreeable necessity at the evacuation of New York to seek an asylum at Shelburne, Nova Scotia. With his memorial is a schedule of his losses and a list of personal property. (A.O. 13/50; A.O. 12/10, ff. 204-212.)

His claim of £4,865 13s. was met by compensation to the amount of £300. (A.O. 12/61, f. 27; A.O. 12/109.)

Benjamin Davis, his son, was in London in 1784, and wrote two letters to the Commissioners, dated May 10 and 13, in support of his father's claim, adding that he had been with his father through the whole war and was an eye witness of his sufferings. (A.O. 13/137.)

Benjamin Davis, the elder, married (as his second wife) Anstis or Anstace, daughter of Stephen Greenleaf, last Sheriff of Suffolk County, Massachusetts, under the Crown, whose portrait is in the possession of Miss Ellen S. Bulfinch. Her portrait by Copley is in the Brooklyn Museum, New York. (Plate XVI.) Her sister, Abigail, was the wife of Martin Howard (q.v.). His third wife was Alice Whipple.

He was the second son of Dr. William Davis, was educated at Boston Latin School, and was a member of the Sandemanian Church in Boston (see p. 23). With his son, Benjamin, he was in exile at Shelburne, Nova Scotia, and settled as merchant. He died at Boston, September 14, 1805, aged 77. (H. H. Edes in *Publications of Colonial Soc. of Mass.* vi, 109-130.)

Reference : *Ontario Archives, op. cit.*, pp. 637-8.

JOHN DAVIS

was born in England and taken as a child by his parents to Boston.   Here
he was the Clerk of Christ Church,* and storekeeper to Aaron Davis and
Company, merchants, and also owner of freehold and leasehold estate in
Providence, which was confiscated.   He was strongly solicited to enter
the American service and was promised great preferment therein.   Having
resisted these temptations he was put into prison at Cambridge.   Upon
his release he went into Boston and joined the Associated Loyalists under
Timothy Ruggles (*q.v.*).   Davis was captured with several others in July,
1775, in an attempt to procure hay for the British in Boston, and was
offered a commission in the American army, but with just abhorrence
peremptorily refused it.   He appears to have sailed for England soon
afterwards, and there got into a little business, which proved a failure,
and he was cast into the King's Bench Prison for debt. (A.O. 13/44 ;
A.O. 13/96.)

The Commissioners regarded his ownership of property as " moon-
shine " and refused him an allowance, on the ground that he had produced
no proof of ownership or of personal loyalty. (A.O. 12/100, f. 272.)

DEBLOIS

In A.O. 13/96 is a joint memorial of Gilbert and Lewis Deblois, late
of Boston, now of London and Peckham, and of Stephen Deblois, George
Deblois, senior, and George Deblois, junior, late of Salem and Newburyport, and now of Halifax, Nova Scotia, concerning their joint business at
New York from November, 1776, to October, 1783, and to the capture
of the ship *Martha* and cargo by an American privateer, re-captured by
H.M.S. *Rainbow*, and condemned under the Prohibitory Act.

GEORGE DEBLOIS, SENIOR

was born at Oxford in England and settled at Salem as a merchant and
importer of British goods.   For several years he was warden and treasurer
of St. Peter's Church, Salem.   As early as the Stamp Act and on various
other occasions his firm attachment to the British Constitution and
government was manifested.   Some time before the commencement of
open hostilities he could seldom walk the streets without suffering insults
from the violent republicans.   Immediately after the skirmish at Lexington
he and other loyalists were called upon to take up arms against Great
Britain, a demand which he resolutely refused.   Fearing violence because
of this refusal he embarked for Nova Scotia on April 28, 1775, accompanied
by his wife and two children, taking with him a small part of his furniture.
He remained at Halifax until June, 1777, when he sailed with his family
to New York, and there joined the Independent Company of Massachusetts

* The records of Christ Church shew that he was offered or given this appointment, August 12, 1773.   (Ex inform. Mr. C. K. Bolton.)

Volunteers, in which he did military duty during nearly four years' residence there. In this same year he, with George Deblois, junior, and Gilbert and Lewis Deblois, formerly of Boston, but then in England, and his brother, Stephen Deblois, then at Rhode Island, started a business in New York as importers of English goods, under his control and that of George Deblois, junior. In 1778 a cargo of goods for their store, to the value of over £6,700, was shipped from London in the *Martha* *and on the passage was captured by H.M.S. *Rainbow* and taken to Halifax, Nova Scotia, and condemned as lawful prize, although the property of loyal British subjects and destined for the needs of the British garrison and loyal inhabitants in New York. This loss was so great that the firm were unable to retrieve their financial affairs. In April, 1778, they suffered another heavy loss by the capture of the sloop *Hawke*, with a cargo of goods, by the Americans. With this memorial is a schedule of the debts due to him and other losses. (A.O. 13/96; A.O. 12/10, ff. 11–15.)

According to his evidence at Halifax, Nova Scotia, on December 3, 1785, Gilbert Deblois emigrated to America in 1761. He not only made himself obnoxious at Salem by his support of Great Britain during the Stamp Act disturbances, but also by signing the addresses to Governors Hutchinson and Gage. Dr. John Prince, formerly of Salem, gave testimony to his character and loyalty. (A.O. 12/10, ff. 16–19.)

His claim of £1,811 11s. included debts of £1,062 10s. He was allowed £40. (A.O. 12/61, f. 3; A.O. 12/109.)

Samuel Curwen (*q.v.*) in his Diary mentions his visit to Oxford on May 6, 1777, and seeing Christ Church with the father of George Deblois.

Reference : *Ontario Archives, op. cit.*, pp. 491–3.

GEORGE DEBLOIS, JUNIOR

was the son of Lewis Deblois (*q.v.*) and was born at Boston. He settled at Newburyport as a merchant. After the skirmish of Lexington every able-bodied man in this place was called upon to enrol himself in the American army, but Deblois, having been from education and principle attached to the British Government, resolved to leave the country rather than submit to this demand. Accordingly, he embarked on April 25, 1775, for Nova Scotia and thence in December to New York, where he joined Governor Tryon's loyal militia and afterwards the Independent Company of Massachussetts Volunteers. He refers to his partnership in the above-mentioned business and to his losses therefrom. There is a list of book debts. He settled at Halifax, Nova Scotia, after the war. (A.O. 13/50; A.O. 13/96; A.O. 12/10, ff. 20–6).

He produced a certificate, dated October 20, 1777, signed by William Coffin, in proof of his membership of the above Massachusetts Volunteers. (A.O. 12/10, ff. 27–8.)

His claim for compensation amounted to £2,096 18s. 7d. (A.O. 12/61, f. 4.)

Reference : *Ontario Archives, op. cit.*, pp. 493–4.

* See above, under Deblois.

GILBERT DEBLOIS (Plate xvii)

was a merchant in Boston, where he had been settled for more than thirty years, and at Providence, Rhode Island. The total value of the goods imported by him during that period was nearly £200,000, which produced an annual profit of £1,200 sterling. He was ever an active loyalist, from the time of his opposition to the Non-Importation Agreement. In the trial of Captain Thomas Preston, of the 29th Regiment, he gave this officer particular aid in obtaining a fair and just trial. Deblois was appointed in 1774 agent for British transports at Boston and furnished them with necessaries and money. As such he became very obnoxious, having been held up in the Boston newspapers as an enemy to America, insulted day and night, and suffered in his property. He accompanied the British forces at the evacuation of Boston, with three of his young sons, leaving behind his wife and four children, and was proscribed. (A.O. 13/44.) He says in his statement of account that he apprehends the Common-wealth of Massachusetts will not be benefited greatly by the confiscation of his estates, inasmuch as a considerable part was invested in the hands of committees, who did not render an account satisfactory to the public, with the result that a proposal was made that the General Court should institute an enquiry into the conduct of these committees, but the affair was dropped. Furthermore, the charges on the sales were great. (*Ib.*)

With his memorial is the written testimony of Captain Thomas Preston, from Merrion Street, Dublin (undated), in which he says that Gilbert Deblois rendered him many services at Boston. When he was put into gaol for what was called the bloody massacre, Deblois got him valuable evidence and gave him the character of many of the men returned as jurors in his trial and was thereby enabled to have set aside most of those returned by the town, who were men of violent principles, and substituted for them men of moderate views from the country. On a deficiency of jurors, Deblois got himself put on the panel and was confined in gaol during the whole week of the trial, with the other jurors. By his attention and close examination he detected perjury in some of the evidence, but by his influence on the other jurors he was a great means in securing his (Captain Preston's) acquittal. Several anonymous letters were sent to Deblois, threatening him with destruction for his attachment to the British officers and loyalists. (*Ib.*)

The following remarks are made by this loyalist on the claims against his estate :

(*a*) Thomas Dawes. He denies that he owes him a penny.
(*b*) Estate of Captain Lewis Turner, deceased. The balance is in favour of Deblois himself.
(*c*) Dr. James Lloyd. Same remark.
(*d*) His son, Gilbert, for debts contracted by Mrs. Gilbert Deblois, senior, after the departure of her husband. She paid this debt.
(*e*) Estate of Edward Winter, deceased. The balance is in favour of Deblois.

(f) Estate of his father, Stephen Deblois, for £1,301 8s. His father assured him that he would never demand it unless forced by want.

Accounts are given, showing the balances. (*Ib.*)

His son, Francis Deblois [born in 1763], went to Boston in August, 1784, to collect debts and to try to recover the Deblois estate for the benefit of the family. He died, however, at Boston early in March, 1786. Gilbert Deblois himself, in response to the entreaties of his family, sailed later for Boston and wrote from there in 1787. (*Ib.*)

With his documents are copies of inventories of his goods at Boston and Providence ; many papers and letters relating to his property and losses ; and a list of book debts and notes of hand due to him. (*Ib.*) There is also a copy of the will of his father, Stephen Deblois (who died at Boston in 1778), dated August 10, 1777, by which he leaves to his two sons, Gilbert and Lewis (*q.v.*), only 5s. each, because (according to Gilbert) any larger legacies would be confiscated. (*Ib.*)

He was granted a pension of £100 from 1787. (A.O. 12/102, f. 98), and compensation £3,260 from his claim of £4,702 (A.O. 12/109.)

This loyalist was born, March 15, 1725, and by his marriage to Ann Coffin, daughter of William Coffin, became connected with several prominent Boston families. He was a great supporter of King's Chapel, Boston, where he was vestryman and warden. In 1789 he returned to Boston for the marriage of his son, Lewis. He died at Peckham, near London, November 27, 1791. (A. W. H. Eaton in *New England Hist. and Gen. Reg.* 1913.)

His portrait by Copley is in the possession of Mrs. C. H. Parker, of Boston.

LEWIS DEBLOIS

This merchant and stedfast loyalist, of Boston, in his memorials states that the loyalists of Boston were unaware until March 4, 1776, of General Howe's intention to evacuate that place, and therefore he was unable to remove all his goods in the short time available. These goods, according to an affidavit of his former apprentice, Jeremiah Fones Jenkins, of Boston, were confiscated. Lewis Deblois was appointed a fireward at Boston, November 14, 1775. (A.O. 13/44.)

Governor Hutchinson, in a certificate of June 3, 1777, testified to his loyalty and to his steady adherence to the Church of England (*Ib.*)

With his documents are several of his letters relating to his losses, including a thousand tons of shipping returned to Boston from South Carolina during the Stamp Act revolt ; a detailed account of the monthly amounts of the imports from Hayley and Hopkins of London, from February, 1770 to August, 1774, totalling £31,027 15s. 11d. ; and the appellants's case in their claim for the capture of their ship *Martha.* (Printed).

He claimed compensation for his losses, £2,378 16s. and was allowed

£1,233. (A.O. 12/109.) His pension of £100 was continued until 1800. (A.C. 12/105, f. 61 ; T. 50/6 ; A.O. 461/16.)

His brother was Gilbert Deblois (*q.v.*)

References : *Acadiensis,* ii, 193 and iii, 298 ; *Loyalists' Claims, op. cit.,* p. 288.

WILLIAM DICKERSON

of Marblehead. Nothing is stated in his claim of £275 for compensation, regarding his career. (A.O. 13/80.)

NATHANIEL DICKINSON

was a native of New England, settled on his own estate at Deerfield, and because of his activity in opposing the rebel measures he was severely treated by mobs, who tied him up to be hanged and often threatened his life. In April, 1775, he fled for protection to Boston. He received the thanks of General Howe for killing a rebel at Bunker Hill ; he remained with the British army throughout the war, serving in the Commissary General's department and frequently doing military duty and ever ready and willing to risk his life. For his loyalty he was named in the Banishment Act and his property confiscated and sold. His brother, Samuel, a warm loyalist, died at Deerfield, Massachusetts, in November, 1782, without a will. (A.O. 13/50 ; A. O. 12/10, ff. 188–195, 430–6.)

With these memorials is an inventory of his personal estate, confiscated and sold by public auction, December 17, 1776, and the prices realised ; several certificates relating to his property ; and a certified copy of the expenses of the Deerfield Committee of Correspondence in selling his property, amounting to £298 16s. and including £13 7s. paid to David Sexton for selling liquors at the auction. (A.O. 13/50.)

According to his letter to Colonel Abijah Willard, dated from Carleton, New Brunswick, February 3, 1784, he valued his property at £25,000 in Massachusetts currency. (*Ib.*)

In 1786 he went to Deerfield to try to recover possession of his estate but failed.

This loyalist claimed £18,750 and was allowed £1,145. (A.O. 12/109.) The property of his brother, Samuel, was in the possession of his sister [Hannah, wife of Colonel William Williams, a loyalist] and his claim for it was, therefore, disallowed. (A.O. 12/61, ff. 54–5.)

His grant of land in New Brunswick, September 14, 1784, is recorded in Book A at Fredericton.

Nathaniel Dickinson was the son of Samuel Dickinson and was born at Deerfield, October 7, 1734. (Sheldon, *Hist. of Deerfield,* ii, 713–4 ; Ex inform. Miss Emma S. Coleman.)

References : *American MSS. in Royal Inst., op. cit.,* iv, 15 ; *Ontario Archives, op. cit.,* pp. 218–221.

THOMAS DIXON

of Boston, married Katherine Wethered of that town at King's Chapel there, April 9, 1761. On September 25 of the same year he was appointed Lieutenant in Captain Benoni Danks's company in the Corps of Rangers under Major Joseph Goreham (*q.v.*) and accompanied the corps to Havana. He died at Westmoreland, New Brunswick, November 8, 1809. (W.O. 42/D22.)

JOSEPH DOMETT

was born at Boston and was liberally educated. From 1772 he was deputy comptroller of Customs at Falmouth (now Portland), Maine, and was obliged twice to take refuge on one of his Majesty's ships from the violence of the people. From 1776 to 1779 he was living in Boston, where he not only remained stedfast in his refusal to avail himself of advantages from his acquaintance with the leaders of the Revolution, including the services of a friend, a member of Congress, but did all in his power to further the interests of the British Government. At great risk he got an interview with General Campbell, a British prisoner at Concord, and offered him his services, and served General Riedesel and other officers of the Convention at Cambridge, by changing their money and by other services. His loyalty and sufferings and his readiness to serve the officers of the Convention at great risk to himself are confirmed in a long letter from General Riedesel to Lord George Germain, dated Cambridge, November 25, 1778. (A.O. 13/44.)

With his memorials is a copy of a resolve of the Massachusetts House of Assembly, June 4, 1779, proving his correspondence with the enemy ; and a long letter from his friend, Dr. Isaac Rand, dated Boston, February 26, 1781, relating to the doctor's efforts regarding Domett's property and stating that his (Dr. Rand's) brother, John Rand, had lost his life in H.M. frigate *Andromeda*, in the hurricane off Martinique, October 11, 1780.

In 1782 Joseph Domett and his wife were residing at Axminster, in England, surrounded by agreeable relations and friends, who endeavoured to make them happy. (From his letter to Sir William Pepperell, dated October 23, 1782.) (*Ib.*)

The Commissioners, having made enquiries as to his reasons for remaining in Boston from 1776 to 1779 and taking the oath of allegiance to America, discontinued his pension of £80, November 1, 1784. (A.O. 12/105, f. 33.) In a long letter dated December, 1784, he offers the explanation that he was suffering from paralysis, and the oath was extorted from him in his helpless condition, in violation of his loyal principles. (A.O. 13/44.) In consequence of the evidence on February 10, 1786, of several conspicuous loyalists in his favour, testifying that his conduct in remaining at Boston and taking the oath was due to his ill-health and to the threats of further persecution, the Commissioners revoked their former decision to discontinue his pension and granted him £40 a year as from

October 10, 1784, his wife having died in the meantime. (A.O. 12/101, f. 302.)

His father, Joseph Domett, in his will, dated April 14, 1762, directed that this loyalist should give his brother, George, £100, on account of the liberal education given him (Joseph) by his father. (From a copy of this will in A.O. 13/44.)

References : *The Frontier Missionary, op. cit.*, p. 330 ; *American MSS. in Royal Inst., op. cit.*, i, 445, 483 ; *Loyalists' Claims, op. cit.*, pp. 239–240 ; Egerton MSS., British Museum, 2659, f. 42.

EDWARD DOUGHERTY

of Boston, where he gained a comfortable livelihood. In September, 1775, he joined the Loyal Irish Volunteers at Boston, under the command of James Forrest (*q.v.*), and served until the evacuation of that town by the British troops, when he went to Halifax and thence to New York. Here he joined a volunteer company and endeavoured to carry on a little business. With his memorial is a schedule of his losses. (A.O. 13/44.)

A certificate of allegiance is signed by Governor William Tryon, of New York, January 24, 1777. Two certificates, signed by Captain Oliver Templeton, of the Loyal New York Volunteers, state that Dougherty joined his company, November 10, 1777, and served until May 11, 1782, while another certificate, signed by James Forrest, states that he joined the Loyal Irish Volunteers in September, 1775. (F.O. 4/1.) In his affidavit of April 12, 1790, Dougherty says that he joined the Associated Loyalists of Boston before joining the Loyal Irish Volunteers. (A.O. 13/98.)

He was granted £20 in 1787, apparently to return to Nova Scotia. (A.O. 12/102, f. 103.) He claimed £432 and was allowed £80. (A.O. 12/109.)

JONATHAN DOWSE

was the son of Joseph Dowse (*q.v.*) and was extra Surveyor and Searcher for the Ports of Salem and Marblehead. (A.O. 13/44.)

He received compensation for the loss of his official income during the war, at the rate of £50 per annum (A.O. 12/109), and was granted a pension of £20 until 1802. (A.O. 12/105, f. 35.) In September, 1788, he was living at Carmarthen in South Wales.

He was born July 22, 1739.

References : A.O. 13/83 ; A.O. 13/85 ; *Loyalists' Claims, op. cit.*, pp. 25–6.

JOSEPH DOWSE

Surveyor, Searcher and Landwaiter of the Customs at Salem. He was granted a pension of £60. (A.O. 12/105, f. 34.)

His three spinster daughters, Margaret, Catherine and Isabella

Dowse, petitioned on June 20, 1788, from Boston, Massachusetts, that the pension paid to their father, who died in 1785, and to their mother, since deceased, may be continued to them. (A.O. 13/44.) Their petition was granted and the pension was paid until their deaths. (A.O. 12/101, f. 235 ; A.O. 461/16 ; A.O. 463/23 ; T. 50/11 ; T. 50/22.)

A certificate from the Rev. Samuel Parker, rector of Trinity Church, Boston, dated June 18, 1788, states that Isabella Dowse, youngest daughter of Joseph Dowse, was baptized in this church, May 22, 1743, and that Mrs. Jane Dowse, widow of the said Joseph Dowse, died March 20, 1788, aged 78, and was buried in the family vault under this church. (A.O. 13/44.)

Joseph Dowse was married to Jane Steel at Boston, December 14, 1734. His son was Jonathan Dowse (q.v.)

MARGARET DRAPER

Her late husband, Richard Draper, who died June 5, 1774, was firmly attached to the British Government and detested all treasonable and seditious publications, and was from principles alone, regardless of the frowns of his countrymen and the loss of his business, a firm loyalist. Margaret Draper's grandfather, father and husband had been printers to the King from the first settlement of Massachusetts. General Gage having continued his favours, and she having an inclination for her late husband's business as a printer, she carried it on. Proclamations and every intelligence for the service of Government were published in her paper, the first newspaper printed in America.* Military law then prevailed, and she, a woman, timid and debilitated by the anguish of losing her worthy husband, admitted those pieces of information and remarks which rendered her extremely obnoxious to her countrymen, whose principles were perverted by rebellion and discontent. This was her situation when the short warning came for the evacuation of Boston by the British troops. Fear forbade her to tarry in a place where inflammatory disposition was then raging. The alternative was equally distressing, for by leaving America she was sacrificing that property which had supported her family in genteel independence. In England she sought an asylum, and with an only daughter, the companion of her flight, threw herself upon the protection of a Government remarkable for hospitality and justice. In her parental anguish for her tenderly educated daughter she petitioned that they, as exiles among strangers, may not be allowed to sink into destitution. (A.O. 13/44.)

With these documents is a schedule of her property, real and personal, including a new fount of letters by Caslon, which was bought by her late husband at the express request of Governor Hutchinson for the purpose of printing a new law book. The fount was not, however, unpacked, and was re-sold to Caslon for £20, at a loss of £46 9s. 4d.

* For an account of the Boston newspapers see the *Publications of Colonial Soc. of Mass.*, vol. 9.

The number of copies of her newspaper, *The Massachusetts Gazette or Boston Weekly News Letter*, printed weekly, was 1,550 or more. Her husband printed a quarter of the 60,000 to 70,000 copies of Ames's Almanack. (*Ib.*)

In A.O. 13/44 are several affidavits. One from James Whyte, a printer, of Boston, dated London, July 3, 1784, says, *inter alia*, that Draper was printer to Harvard College and that his new house in Newbury Street, Boston, was confiscated and sold to Richard Devens, Commissary General of Massachusetts. One from John Howe, printer, Halifax, Nova Scotia, dated May 6, 1785, says that after Draper's death he was employed by his widow to assist in carrying on his newspaper, of which 1,500 copies were printed weekly. A third, from John Murray, states that Draper's newspaper was the only paper [in Boston] which took a decided part in support of British authority, and that it was the only paper before and during the blockade of Boston which admitted and encouraged speculations in support of British authority, and for these reasons was voted to be burnt by the common hangman.

There are also accounts from John Boyle and two apprentices for conducting Mrs. Draper's business from May 19 to August 4, 1774. Boyle had been engaged in printing and binding certain books (mentioned) for Richard Draper from 1769 to 1774. In her comments on Boyle's claim for work done, she says that he entered her employ on May 19, 1774, but having been thwarted in his attempt to make her newspaper subservient to the party of rebellion, he left her on August 4 following. An account of Edward Draper, a former apprentice, was for work done in the Draper office from 1770 to 1775.

Several affidavits and certificates to the loyalty of Richard and Margaret Draper from General Gage, Colonel Nisbet Balfour, Chief Justice Peter Oliver, Daniel Leonard, Jonathan Sewall, Adino Paddock and Joseph Woodward, of Boston, are in A.O. 13/44.

She claimed compensation to the amount of £2,093, and was allowed £929. (A.O. 12/109.)

Margaret Draper is mentioned in the will of her husband, Richard Draper, dated November 8, 1766, and proved June 20, 1774, as is also his mother-in-law, Elizabeth Draper.

Her daughter, Margaret Draper, appealed for an increase of her mother's pension of £100, but was refused. (A.O. 12/105, f. 62.) This pension was paid until 1804. (A.O. 461/19 ; T. 50/11.)

JACOB DUITZ, OR DIZE

emigrated with his wife from Germany about 1754 and in 1759 enlisted at Fort Pownall. At the end of the war in 1763 he bought land at Penobscot and settled there as a farmer. (A.O. 13/44.) He was granted a pension of £20 a year as a deserving loyalist (A.O. 12/101, f. 77), and received compensation £300, less £7 for pension, from his claim of £300. (A.O. 12/109.)

Gilbert Deblois

PLATE XVII

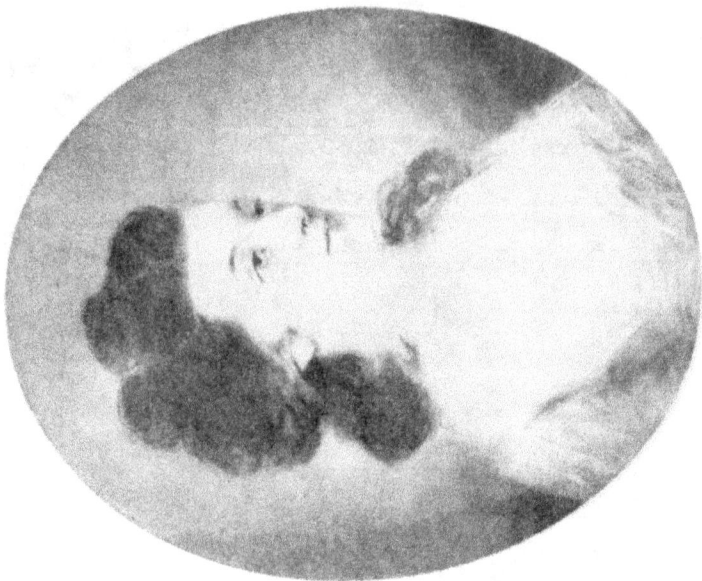

Philip Dumaresq and Mrs. Dumaresq

PLATE XVIII

OF MASSACHUSETTS

ELIZABETH DUMARESQ

At the beginning of the rebellion she lived at Boston with her brother [Philip] (*q.v.*), who was so reduced in circumstances by the rebellion as to be scarcely able to support his own family. She was therefore compelled, though born and educated in the style of a gentlewoman, to engage herself as a servant to a lady going to Grenada and remained with her until the capture of that Island, when she fled to England. As a loyalist her property in Eastern Massachusetts was lost to her. (A.O. 13/44.)

General H. S. Conway, in his letter to the Commissioners, dated March 20, 1783, says that she belongs to a family well known in the Island of Jersey. (*Ib.*)

In her letter to the Earl of Shelburne, dated September 14, 1782, she pictures her situation, without friends or money, as truly deplorable and her distresses more than she can describe. Her father's mother, Frances Carteret (she says), was a close relation of the late Earl of Granville, while she herself has the honour to be related to Lord Shelburne's first wife.* (*Ib.*)

Joseph Waldo (*q.v.*), writing to her from Bristol, April 11, 1783, says that her late father, Philip Dumaresq, had in 1771 a just claim to 1,500 acres of land in the Muscongus Patent, which his father, Cornelius Waldo, had granted to Philip Dumaresq† as an obligation for his expense in settling two townships. (*Ib.*)

Elizabeth Dumaresq was granted a pension of £30 a year in 1783. (A.O. 12/99, f. 134.)

She was born in 1730.

PHILIP DUMARESQ (Plate xviii)

was in flourishing business " in the commission way " at Boston before the Revolution, which reduced him from affluence to the necessity of taking refuge on a desolate island [at Abaco in the Bahamas], with his wife and a large family. Dumaresq left Boston in March 1776 for Nova Scotia, and in October sailed for New York, where he tarried until the evacuation of that city by the British, when he was appointed commissary to the loyalist refugees bound for Abaco. By great industry he had laid a foundation (as he had hoped) for the future support of his family, but all his labour of two years was blasted by the hurricane in September 1785. In an estimate of his losses he adds that he was a merchant in Boston and from 1769 agent for the principal merchants of the Island of Jersey and of the town of Southampton, England, for supplies for their fishery in Newfoundland and for spermaceti manufactures in America. He was one-third owner of the sloop *Dolphin* (Nathaniel Beaty, master) and likewise one-sixth owner of the brig *Industry*, of which George Erving

* The Earl of Shelburne married (i), in 1765, Lady Sophia Carteret, daughter of John (Carteret), Earl Granville. (G.E.C. *Peerage*.)

† Presumably Philip Dumaresq, President of the Council and Collector of Customs in Cape Breton. (See p. 60.)

was one-third owner. He was also owner of the schooner *General Howe*, which was destroyed by order of Governor Tryon. (A.O. 13/59.)

His wife, Rebecca, was granted £470 for the loss of her property. (A.O. 12/109.)

Philip Dumaresq, second son of Philip Dumaresq, captain in Colonel Waldo's Regiment at Louisburg in 1745, was born at Boston in 1737 and was sent to England for his education. He returned to America as *aide-de-camp* to the Earl of Dunmore, successively Governor of New York and Virginia. He left the army and was married in 1763 at King's Chapel, Boston, to Rebecca, daughter of Dr. Sylvester Gardiner (*q.v.*). (Foote, *Annals of King's Chapel, Boston*, ii, 362–3.) In 1789 he was appointed Receiver General of the Bahamas and in 1792 Searcher of the Customs there; he died at Nassau, New Providence, in the Bahamas, September 28, 1800. A miniature portrait of this loyalist and a crayon portrait of his wife, Rebecca, by Copley are the property of Rebecca Dumaresq's great-great-granddaughter, Mrs. Austin Wadsworth, of Boston.

His son, Philip, served as a volunteer in the Royal Navy from 1793 and had risen to the rank of Captain before his death by drowning in 1807. He was at the celebrated battle of the Nile in 1798, for which he received the gold medal, as did the officer of Bostonian birth, Admiral Sir Benjamin Hallowell-Carew.

Reference : *American MSS. in Royal Inst., op. cit.*, ii, 308 ; iv, 42, 272–3, 283.

DANIEL DUNBAR

of Halifax, Massachusetts, gentleman, was from infancy loyal to the King and the British Government. He was in the service of his King at Fort William Henry in 1755 and at the reduction of Quebec in 1759. In 1774 he was a Second Lieutenant in the militia at Halifax, his place of residence. Early in 1775 he suffered much persecution, having been put on a sharp rail and on another occasion driven about forty miles from his habitation, until he was obliged to seek refuge in Boston. At the evacuation of Boston he sailed for Halifax, Nova Scotia, and on the passage from that place to New York he was taken prisoner by the Americans. Upon his release he went to Newport, Rhode Island, and thence to Newtown, Long Island, where he married in 1779 or 1780 Naomi Hallett, a widow. Here he took care of a farm and kept a ferry boat to carry British soldiers and other passengers to and from New York. Having saved some money by his industry, he bought in January 1782 a lot of land in Maiden Lane, New York, for £1,200, from Robert Bayard. His wife declined to go to Nova Scotia at the evacuation of New York by the British and consequently he moved in 1784 into that city, where he bought and sold lumber. His land and house in New York were confiscated in 1784. (A.O. 13/44.)

With his petition, dated November 27, 1789, are documents regarding his confiscated property. (*Ib.*) Dunbar was granted compensation, £1,000, from his claim of £1,726. (A.O. 12/109.)

JOHN DUNN

was for many years a master mariner, in Boston, under various owners of vessels, including Colborn Barrell (*q.v.*). During the siege of Boston in June 1775 he removed with his wife to Quebec, in the hope of finding employment to support his family. His wife died there during the siege. He came to Bristol, England, in December 1776. A certificate to his loyalty is signed by the following loyalists : the Rev. John Troutbeck, John and George Erving, Gilbert and Lewis Deblois, Thomas Hutchinson, Richard Clarke and Colborn Barrell. He was granted a pension of £50. (A.O. 13/44 ; A.O. 12/105, f. 63.)

John Dunn married Rebecca Arno at Boston, November 3, 1763.

CYNTHIA DWIGHT

She and her late husband, Sereno Edwards Dwight, and one child, set sail with their father, Timothy Dwight (see below) in April, 1776, for West Florida, where they arrived in August. Her husband was employed as surgeon in the British forces for two and a half years and assisted in taking Fort Panmure. Finding danger about them, they, with their two children and a party, started in June, 1781, on a journey overland across the wilderness, without a guide or compass, and arrived in Georgia at the end of November, she being pregnant, and the whole time with no shelter but the Heavens and no bed but the earth. The party, pursued by savages on the whole journey, endured every distress in crossing wide and rapid rivers, into the violent waters of which their horses were obliged to plunge. After arriving at Savannah, she and her children were seized with smallpox. At this capital of Georgia her husband was appointed surgeon's mate to the King's American Regiment. In August, 1782, they removed to Long Island, New York. He went to Port Roseway (Shelburne), Nova Scotia, and on the passage to New England was lost at sea in October, 1783. (A.O. 13/80.)

In his original memorial, dated April 21, 1783, Sereno Edwards Dwight states his loyalty and sufferings in bringing his wife and family over 1,500 miles from West Florida. (*American MSS. in Royal Inst., op. cit.*, iv, 43.) He was put on half-pay as Ensign in the King's American Regiment. (Ind. 5475.)

JONATHAN DWIGHT

Having been educated to the highest veneration for order and constitutional liberty and the strictest loyalty to his King and the British Empire, he opposed the violent measures of the revolutionary party, even at the risk of personal safety. In April, 1776, he left with his father, Timothy Dwight, on the voyage to Natchez. In consequence of his assistance to Henry Edwin Stanhope and Gregory, both loyalists, in escaping from Northampton gaol (Massachusetts) to their vessel at Middletown, Connecticut, he was taken prisoner with his father. Upon the advice of his father he returned to Northampton from the Mississippi, and arrived there (after imprisonment on the voyage at Jamaica) in 1779. He remained at Northampton and maintained his loyalty. In 1782 about twenty head of cattle were seized from him, on suspicion of being intended for the British troops in New York. (A.O. 13/80.)

The truth of the above memorial is certified by Theodore Dwight, of Northampton, March 28, 1786. (*Ib.*)

One Jonathan Dwight died September 5, 1831, aged 88.

MARY DWIGHT

was the widow of Timothy Dwight, of Northampton, who for his zeal and loyalty was deprived of all his public offices, and who suffered much persecution, including actual confinement, between 1774 and 1776. At length he endeavoured to escape from these evils by attempting to found a new settlement on the Mississippi, and formed a considerable company for that purpose.* He had actually embarked at Middletown, in Connecticut, when his vessel was stopped and he was arrested on suspicion of having assisted Stanhope and Gregory, who had been loyalist prisoners in Northampton, in escaping. After four months' detention he sailed to Natchez and took possession of a plantation, which he cultivated and improved until his death there [June 10], 1777, soon after which the jurisdiction of this territory was usurped by the Congress and all his title to his estate was lost. Meanwhile, she, at her mansion at Northampton, suffered every evil that misguided zeal, vulgar ignorance and virulence could dictate. She was not only denied the common intercourse and civil offices of her friends, but was compelled to pay heavy contributions and military mulcts. At other times her children and domestics were pressed into the American service, and on refusal were disarmed and imprisoned. She suffered " great devastation of property." (A.O. 13/80.)

A certificate to the truth of this memorial is signed by Jonathan and Cynthia Dwight (*q.v.*), Northampton, March 28, 1786. (*Ib.*)

Timothy Dwight was the only surviving son of Colonel Timothy Dwight, of Northampton, and was born May 27, 1726. He graduated at Yale College in 1744, and afterwards settled as a merchant at Northampton, where he became Registrar of Probate for Hampshire County in 1748. In 1758 he succeeded his father as Judge of the Court of Common Pleas ; was selectman, 1769–74 ; town recorder, 1760–75 ; and was for several years representative in the General Court, as well as Major of Militia. His wife, Mary, who was the daughter of the Rev. Jonathan Edwards, died at Northampton February 28, 1807, aged 73. His eldest son was President of Yale College. (Dexter, *Biogs. of Graduates of Yale College.*)

* An account of General Phineas Lyman's Mississippi adventure is in C. W. Alvord's *The Mississippi Valley in British Politics*, 1917.

GEORGE DYMOND

of Boston, commanded in 1774 the armed schooner *Sophia*, and, as sole water-guard in the service of the Customs, transported soldiers from Castle William to Salem for the protection of the Commissioners and other Customs officers, and safely conducted the revenue chest of money from Boston to Salem, in defiance of the rebels. He commanded this vessel until 1776. On the voyage to England he was taken prisoner and carried to Philadelphia, and after enduring great fatigue he obtained, with difficulty, a parole for New York. His valuable tract of land in New Hampshire, granted to him in 1772 when he was living there, was confiscated. His private fortune was expended during the war and his health shattered. (A.O. 13/44; A.O. 13/109; A.O. 12/99, f. 82.)

JAMES EAGER.

was born in New England and lived at Northborough, where he "opposed from the beginning the unlawful measures which brought on the American War," and thereby rendered himself obnoxious to the rebels, who in 1776 committed him to gaol. Early in 1777 he escaped to New York and there served in the Commissary General's department and often did military duty in a volunteer company.

With his papers is a copy of the order for the confiscation of his property, with a description. (A.O. 13/102.) The total of claims against his property amounted to £3 1s. 9d. and the proceeds of sale to £131 7s. 4d., the balance going to the State. (A.O. 12/82; A.O. 12/83.) His name, with that of John Eager, appears in the muster roll of loyalists in the county of Annapolis, Nova Scotia, in June, 1784, (Savary, *Hist. of the County of Annapolis, Supplement,* p. 109.)

JOSIAH EDSON

of Bridgwater, was rendered obnoxious to the seditious by his acceptance of the appointment of Mandamus Councillor in August, 1774, and was soon afterwards compelled by the popular frenzy to leave his home and family and take refuge in the British garrison at Boston. His estate and effects were soon seized by the town committee of Bridgwater and every possible method was taken effectually to ruin his interests and to harass and distress his family. Having been reduced to poverty he was obliged to appeal to General Gage for support, and was granted £100, and a similar amount was allowed later by General Sir William Howe. He accompanied the British army to Halifax in March, 1776, and thence to New York. (A.O. 13/44.)

Governor Hutchinson, in his certificate dated May 24, 1779, says that he had known this loyalist for over twenty years in Massachusetts, and that he was for a great part of that time a member of the House of Representatives. Although he was one of the seventeen "rescinders" * he

* See page 58.

was chosen a representative again.   The Governor always esteemed him as a man of great integrity and a friend to Government on principle.   (*Ib.*)

In a letter dated from New York, March 9, 1779, to Chief Justice Peter Oliver, enclosing a memorial, Josiah Edson says that he has but one son, who lived on his farm, which he was obliged to hire with the stock for three years by the town committee, who in 1778 took it from him, sold the personal estate and leased out the real property to others, excepting one-third allowed to his (Josiah Edson's) wife.   This son, together with the latter's eldest son, a boy of about 17, was often called upon to do military service for the Americans, and obliged to pay fines or go to gaol.   Josiah Edson's son died at Windham, Connecticut, in March, 1779.   (*Ib.*)

The claims against the estate amounted to £165 0s. 1d. and the proceeds from the sale to £563 3s. 7d., the balance going to the State.   (A.O., 12/82.)

Josiah Edson graduated at Harvard College in 1730 and was a member of the Ancient and Honourable Artillery Company of Massachusetts from 1747 and commanded the Bridgwater regiment from 1772. (Roberts, *History of that Company*, ii, 44.)

He died in New York in 1779 or 1780.

Sabine, *op. cit.*

THOMAS EDWARDS

was born in Boston, and at the outbreak of the war was living in Connecticut.   He joined the British army in 1775, and served as a commissary throughout the war.   His losses were £3,000.   He went to Nova Scotia in 1785.   (A.O. 12/101, f. 206.)

This loyalist married, in 1758, Mary Johonnot, daughter of Andrew Johonnot, of Boston, and niece of Peter Johonnot.   He was in business at Middletown, Connecticut, and died in London.   His wife died in Boston in 1792.   (Stark, *op. cit.*, p. 411.)

GEORGE ELLISON

had " very great property " in Kennebec, and was offered a Captain's commission in the American service.   Having refused this commission, he was threatened with violence, and was obliged to flee to Boston, leaving his wife, Tamar, and family and property to the mercy of the rebels.   He joined the 4th Regiment as a volunteer at Boston, and died from wounds during the war.   His widow was taken into the family of General Gage for twelve months, and was living at Windsor, Nova Scotia, in 1786.   (A.O. 13/25.)

JOHN EMERSON

was born in New England, and lived at Worcester, where he took an early and decided part on the side of the Crown, so much so that he became obnoxious, and was obliged, in December, 1774, to discharge his men and forsake his business as a house carpenter and joiner. In March, 1775, he was repeatedly pressed by committees and leading men of the faction to accept a commission in the American army; but he refused. Having fled to Boston, he was introduced to General Gage, to whom he gave all the intelligence in his power, and was encouraged to remain there in the hope of a speedy suppression of the rebellion. He joined the Associated Loyalists in Boston, and took up arms in defence of the town during the blockade. He was entrusted with despatches from the British head-quarters in Boston to Earl Percy, then covering the retreat of the troops from Concord. At New York, whither he had accompanied the British troops in 1776, he joined the Quartermaster-General's department and served at the taking of Long Island. In June, 1777, he accompanied the army in charge of the provision train to the Head of Elk, and thence to Philadelphia, where he remained until the evacuation. From New York he went as an officer on board a private ship of war on a cruise against the enemy, and was afterwards shipwrecked and sent to the West Indies, where he suffered almost incredible hardships. He arrived in England in October, 1781, destitute and his health wrecked. John Emerson was in Canada in 1787 and 1788, his wife, Elizabeth, being in London. (A.O. 13/44; A.O. 13/45; A.O. 12/99, f. 208.) His claim was £260, and the allowance £100. (A.O. 12/109.)

WILLIAM ISHAM EPPES

During the blockade of Boston he served, at the age of 15, in the Associated Loyalists under Colonel Abijah Willard (*q.v.*), and left with the British troops at the evacuation. At New York he enrolled in, and did duty with, the Associated Volunteers of Massachusetts for the defence of the city, and remained there until October 19, 1778. In February, 1779, he went as a volunteer on H.M. frigate *Arethusa*, on a cruise with Captain Charles Holmes Everitt, his particular acquaintance. This vessel* was wrecked on the coast of France in March, and he was a prisoner in France for nine months. After his release he was appointed purser of the *Scourge* sloop, and served as such until the end of the war.

This young loyalist was born at Salem, and at the outbreak of war he was " learning a profession superior to what most young men of his country could boast of," and was serving his time as an apothecary and chemist with Dr. Sylvester Gardiner (*q.v.*), who had promised to give him the practice in due course. (A.O. 13/44; A.O. 12/100, f. 92.)

According to a certificate of Admiral Clark Gayton, R.N., Mrs. Abigail Gardiner, the mother of this loyalist, was a niece of the Admiral's former wife. (A.O. 13/44.) She was the second wife of Dr. Gardiner (*q.v.*), her former husband being William Eppes. (Stark, *op. cit.*, p. 314.) This loyalist's sister, Abigail, married Richard Routh (*q.v.*).

* See Clowes, *Hist. of the Royal Navy*, iv, 24.

I

GEORGE ERVING

In his memorial of June 26, 1776, he says that the Boston Port Bill of 1774 was by its operation a punishment to the innocent and a reward to the guilty. The tradesmen and other inferior persons, who were the chief agents in the outrages, found themselves more at their ease than they had ever been before, by having no work to do and being supported in idleness by the ill-timed contributions and benefactions of other colonies. By his support of Governor Hutchinson and the consignees of the tea, and by his acceptance of the appointment of Mandamus Councillor, he lost popularity and suffered loss in his business, which had produced him in 1774 net profits of £1,200 to £1,500 sterling a year. He was the owner of land in Dominica and property in the town of St. George's, Grenada, as well as expectations from his father of £12,000 to £15,000. By his marriage, in 1775, to the daughter of Isaac Royall (q.v.), he acquired part of the sugar plantation in Surinam and the reversion of the Royall estate in Massachusetts. After the skirmish at Lexington on April 19, 1775, and the consequent blockade of Boston, George Erving was totally separated from his customers and debtors, to the serious depreciation of his trade. When, in 1779, the combined fleets of France and Spain were in the English Channel, and an invasion of England hourly expected, he wrote to Lord George Germain offering, in case of emergency, to raise 100 men and to put himself under the orders of the Commander-in-Chief. The Dutch war having broken out in December, 1780, and all communication cut off between Holland and Surinam, he lost the last retreat of his fortunes. Thus, banished from his own country and stripped of the greatest part of his property, he had no other resort than to submit his case to the compassion of the British Government. (A.O. 13/44.)

In a long memorial, dated February 1, 1786, George Erving expresses his mortification at the favour shown to the American rebels, in contrast to the neglect of the loyalists who had hazarded everything and lost all in maintaining their fidelity to the King and British Government. " To the former, who were in declared rebellion against the Government, whose Country was made the Theatre of a long desultory War, a peace hath been granted in which their Independency hath been fully acknowledg'd and by which they are not only left in quiet possession of their Estates & properties, but have in effect the Estates & properties of the poor Loyalists ceded & guaranteed to them : Superadded to this Compensations have been made in various instances, and to a very great amount, to those very Rebels, for the ravage, waste & damage done to their [the loyalists'] Estates & properties, and in many Cases unavoidably so, during the War, as the Commanders in Chief, and others who have been the Channels of this bounty can pronounce. The reason given for these humiliating concessions was, the expediency of a peace. And, to remove the chief obstacle that seem'd to stand in the way of this blessing vizt. the providing for the Loyalists, it was urg'd that it would be far less expensive to Gov^t. to grant full restitution to them, than to raise fresh Millions for prosecuting an unavailing War, which seem'd to meet the general wish and concurrence of the Nation. If the Gov^t. found it necessary to make peace with the American States, and to accomplish it, was induced to grant them the property of the Loyalists, without even consulting them ; or, what is the same thing, was not in a condition to insist on the repeal of all proscriptive and confiscating Laws pass'd against them in the several States, or make any provision whatever for them, it must be presum'd that the Honor of Gov^t. is engaged to indemnify her suffering friends for these Sacrifices. . . ." George Erving goes on to picture in flowery language the awfulness of banishment from his native land, standing next to the sentence of death. Convicts, loving their country, prefer to return from transportation and risk the certain death awaiting them if detected. "What (he says) may be suppos'd to be the feelings & sufferings of y^r Memorialist [George Erving], cut off as he is from a State of Affluence and in the full career of prosperity ; sent into perpetual Exile, his Estate and Effects confiscated, and at last thrown into a state of narrow and precarious dependance upon the Government for which all this hath been suffer'd ? To the Loyalists who have come to this Country [England], there seems to have been a great inequality in the distribution of the favors of Gov^t some thro' importunity alone, some by friends and some by a happy manner of telling their story, and setting forth their own worth & consequence, have been br'ot into particular notice and handsomely provided for, whilst many of real merit, merely from modesty and reserve have been wholly neglected." Later he qualifies this alleged partiality by saying that it was unavoidable in the abundance of claims. He maintains that the Massachusetts Loyalists, " for reasons needless to recount at present," have the first claims on the benevolence of Government, especially those called " Notorious Conspirators," who are under perpetual proscription. The claims of these two classes should not be treated on an equal footing, contrary to the Act of Parliament, for to the " Notorious Conspirators " the door of their country is perpetually shut, while to others permission is given by an Act passed in 1784 to return and re-possess their estates that are not confiscated. After referring at length to the scheme for compensation, Erving says that the claimants for real estate have one great advantage over those claiming for personal property. Under the Confiscation Act of Massachusetts, 1779, it is provided that all debts due to any of the citizens of the United States from any of the " Notorious Conspirators " shall be paid out of their respective estates. This held out a prospect of relief to many, especially to him. But in 1784, an Act was passed in Massachusetts, in violation of the Definitive Treaty of Peace (which solemnly stipulated that there shall be no confiscation of property thereafter), which ordains that all personal estates of loyalists who sought the protection of Great Britain since October, 1774, shall be deemed to have been confiscated, the operation of which was that he, having considerable demands to discharge in America, was deprived of the means of doing so, according to the first Act. According to the fourth article of the Treaty it is expressly agreed that the creditors on either side shall meet with no lawful impediment to recovery of the full value in sterling of all *bona fide* debts.   This article seems on the part of America to be " tortur'd into a meaning almost contrary to what it expresses."   The " Notorious Conspirators," who by the Massachusetts Act are deemed to be outlaws, are deprived from all benefits under this article.   According to the sixth article of the Treaty it was agreed that after the ratification of the Treaty, all loyalists' estates, not already confiscated and sold, should be restored to the rightful owners.   Thus he claimed, in behalf of his wife, for the remainder of the estate of her father, Isaac Royall, at Medford.   Having sent orders to his attorney at Boston to demand immediate possession of this estate, he was informed that the State had granted a lease of it for a number of years.   Rather than break faith with the lessor, the State preferred to break public faith, and in plain violation of the Treaty of Peace, an Act was passed by the Legislature of Massachusetts in 1784, declaring that all such estates of loyalist absentees as have been mort-gaged by the State shall be considered as confiscated, saving only the right of redemption in the legal claimants, upon paying and discharging such mortgage.   He was therefore unable to get possession until April, 1787. George Erving concludes his long and spirited account of his losses by roundly accusing the British Government for neglecting to make any adequate protest against these violations of the Treaty, or to remon-strate against the repeated indignities or to defend the poor American loyalists who had sought refuge under the wings of Government from the " relentless malice of their countrymen." (A.O. 13/137.)

In his inventory of the estates of Isaac Royall he says that all the furniture and family pictures in the mansion house at Medford were sold by public auction and the proceeds paid into the State Treasury.   The garden contained the best collection of fruit trees and plants in Massa-chusetts. (A.O. 13/44.)

According to his long version of the affair of the brig, *Industry*, it was seized in August, 1775, and condemned by the officers of the Cus-toms, to gratify their resentment against Admiral Graves, whose authority clashed with theirs.   This ship and cargo were bought by George Erving and others. (*Ib.*)

In A.O. 13/45 are a list of his debtors and the amounts due ; an inventory of the goods left in his store ; a long statement of his losses since April, 1775 ; and his letter of July 25, 1789, regarding his suit at law against the Rev. Samuel Peters, the loyalist divine of Connecticut, executor of Dr. Thomas Moffatt, for the recovery of money due to his late father, John Erving.   There are also references to his half of 3,000 acres of land in New Hampshire, granted to his brother, William Erving,* for his military services in the war with the French in America, half of

---

* William Erving was also a loyalist, but returned to America after the Revo-lution and became a citizen of the United States (in the case of George Erving, in A.O. 12/73, ff. 179–192).

Thomas Flucker

PLATE XIX

PLATE XX

John Erving

which had been given by William to him (George) and the other half to his brother, John.

George Erving was granted compensation £455 from his claim of £5,839. (A.O. 12/109); and a pension of £200 until his death in 1805. (T. 50/6; A.O. 462/20.)

Other references to this loyalist are in A.O. 12/73, ff. 179–192, where there is a long inventory of his property; A.O. 12/105, ff. 3–4, 8; and A.O. 12/107, ff. 48–9.

He was a younger brother of John Erving (*q.v.*), and graduated at Harvard College in 1757, and died in London. (Stark, *op. cit.*, pp. 298–9; *Loyalists' Claims, op. cit.*, p. 306.) A man of this name, from Boston, took the degree of M.A. at Glasgow University in 1762.

One of his documents in A.O. 13/45 is sealed with arms (damaged). The crest is a wheel, and the motto : *Sub Sole Sub Umbra Virens.**

* This is said to be the motto of Bonshaw in Scotland, from whom the Erving family claim descent.

JOHN ERVING (Plate xx)

By accepting the appointment by mandamus to a seat in the Council of Massachusetts in June, 1774, he was regarded by the disaffected as a traitor to his country, and whosoever could most distress him in his person or estate had most merit with the multitude. (A.O. 13/44.) By the Boston Port Bill he suffered great losses in his foreign trade. The details of his losses include two brigs, *Harmony* and *Comfort*; effects in the Island of St. Croix; two rope-walks and warehouses in Boston; and other property. (A.O. 13/45.) He complains that his brother-in-law, James Bowdoin, had injured the Erving property by his procrastination in settling the affairs of the estate. (A.O. 12/105, ff. 3–4, 8.) From his claim of £1,500 he was allowed £100, less £8 10s. for pension. (A.O. 12/109.) His pension of £200 was increased to £300, and was paid until his death, July 17, 1816. (T. 50/6; T. 50/25.)

This loyalist was the elder son of Hon. George Erving, Member of the Council of Massachusetts (died in 1786), and the brother of George Erving(*q.v.*); he graduated at Harvard College in 1747, and died at Bath, England. His wife, Maria Catherina, a daughter of Governor Shirley, of Massachusetts, and sister of Elizabeth Hutchinson (*q.v.*), died a few months previously. (Stark, *op. cit.*, pp. 298–9; *Loyalists' Claims, op. cit.*, pp. 305–6.)

His portrait, by Blackburn, is in the possession of Mrs. Hamilton Hoppin, of New York.

An account of the Erving family is in *Proc. of Hist. Soc. of Mass.*, 2nd Ser., V, 9–16.

PETER ETTER

was born in Berne, Switzerland, in 1715, and emigrated to America in 1737, settling, in 1752, as a weaver at Braintree [now Quincy], Massachusetts. He " took a decided part in support of the Antient and legal

Constitution of the Colonies," and consequently became obnoxious to the rebellious faction and was compelled to seek the protection of the British Army in Boston in 1775. His three adult sons joined the British Army, one of whom died. Six weaving frames, with all his tools for silk, cotton, thread and worsted and other appliances were left behind at Braintree. This Swiss loyalist was an exile at Halifax, Nova Scotia, in 1786. (A.O. 13/50; A.O. 13/107; A.O. 12/10, ff. 301–8; A.O. 12/61, f. 38.) He was allowed £70 from his claim of £1,015 6s. (A.O. 12/109.) John Müller and Timothy Noonan, presumably loyalist exiles, in a certificate dated Halifax, December 5, 1783, testified to their knowledge of Peter Etter's property. (A.O. 13/107.)

His son, Peter, was a watchmaker at Halifax, Nova Scotia, in 1786. (A.O. 13/107.) Another son, Franklin Germanus, described as a gentleman, was born in America about 1752; married Elizabeth Cleverly at Christ Church, Braintree (Quincy), February 28, 1775; joined the British Army, October 26, 1777, was promoted lieutenant in the Loyal Nova Scotia Volunteers, December 25, 1780; and died September 28, 1828, at Chester, Nova Scotia, where he was buried in the Presbyterian burial ground. (Ind. 5604–5–6; W.O. 42/E5.)

Reference: *Ontario Archives, op. cit.*, pp. 686–7.

BENJAMIN FANEUIL

an agent in Boston of the East India Company, was one of the consignees of the celebrated tea, and, after suffering insults from the mob, with them took shelter, in November, 1773, at Castle William, in Boston Harbour, where he spent a long and severe winter until August, 1774. With his memorial is a list of his bonds. (A.O. 13/45; A.O. 12/105, f. 64.) In a letter of November 15, 1773, to his friend, Frank Waton (?), he gives an account of the affairs connected with the tea. (C.O. 5/133.)

Benjamin Faneuil died at Bristol, England, in February, 1787, leaving a widow, Jane, who was granted a loyalist pension of £80 until 1799. (A.O. 12/102, f. 68; A.O. 461/16; T. 50/11.) By his will of October 2, 1784, proved May 16, 1787, he left legacies to his wife, to his brother Peter [a loyalist], and to his sister, Mary Bethune, wife of George Bethune, of Boston (Major 211). His wife was the daughter of Addington Davenport. (Stark, *op. cit.*, p. 232.)

Loyalist Claims, op. cit., pp. 234–5.

WILFRED FISHER

is mentioned in A.O. 12/83, f. 1.

SAMUEL FITCH

He was appointed Advocate-General of Massachusetts upon the resignation of Jonathan Sewall (*q.v.*) in November, 1769. "Having been led from the course of his reading to the particular study of the principles and history of the British constitution, he early imbibed a strong pre-dilection in favour of a system of government which he considered as the most perfect that human wisdom had ever adopted. . . ." During the blockade of Boston he joined the Associated Loyalists under Adino Paddock (q.v.). This lawyer claims to have been the only one who stepped forth, in response to the order of the Court, to defend the Custom House officer indicted for murder. In one of his petitions he asserts that between 18,000 and 20,000 men fit to bear arms fled to Vermont from other States, to avoid the heavy taxes, and to escape from military duty during the Revolution, and there " found an asylum from their difficulties." He describes Henry Lloyd (q.v.) as his " near family connection." (Adm. 2/1057, ff. 494–5 ; A.O. 13/73 ; A.O. 13/83 ; A.O. 12/105, f. 90.)

In A.O. 13/45 are two anonymous letters, attacking Fitch's claim for compensation from the British Government and stating that the furniture which he alleges to have been lost in Boston was taken to Europe by a British warship, except what he sold at Halifax, Nova Scotia ; and that Dr. [James] Lloyd (q.v.) as a creditor had seized every shilling of the Fitch property. The second letter, by the same writer, alleges that Fitch's professional income never reached £1,000.

Samuel Fitch was the eldest child of Joseph and Anne Fitch, of Lebanon, Connecticut, where he was born, January 16, 1723–4. After leaving Yale College (class of 1742) he was appointed in June, 1746, a lieutenant in Captain William Whiting's company of foot in the intended expedition against Canada. In 1766 he received the honorary degree of M.A. from Harvard College. Colonel Eleazar Fitch, of Windham, Connecticut, a loyalist, was his brother, and Colonel William Fitch, of the 83rd Regiment of Foot, was his son. He occupied pew No. 60 in King's Chapel, Boston. (Annals of King's Chapel, op, cit., ii, 314 ; Dexter, Yale Biographies, i, 706.)

John Adams, in his diary for 1765, gives a pleasant account of a Club of young lawyers in Boston, founded by Samuel Fitch and others.

This lawyer died in exile in London, October 4, 1799, aged 75, and was buried in the graveyard of St. Mary's Church, Battersea, where also his wife, Elizabeth (née Lloyd, of Boston), was buried in February, 1800, aged 77. Before his death he had received £5,000 compensation from the British Government and £550 a year during the war for the loss of his professional income, as well as a pension of £260. (A.O. 12/109 ; T. 50/6 ; T. 50/8 ; A.O. 459/7 ; A.O. 461/16.)

THOMAS FLUCKER (Plate xix)

lived at Charlestown, where his house, with its furniture and silver plate, was destroyed in the fire of June, 1775, as was also his pew in the church there. He died February 15, 1783, leaving a widow, Hannah, a son, Thomas, then a Captain in the 86th Foot of the British army, and three unmarried daughters. His widow was granted a loyalist pension of £200 a year. (A.O. 13/45 ; A.O. 12/99, f. 109.)

With the memorial of Hannah Flucker is a long inventory of the Flucker estate; an original deed, dated June 1, 1773, of Sarah Waldo, widow of Samuel Waldo, son of Samuel Waldo, of Falmouth (Portland), Maine, for £3,777 2s. 6d. for her late husband's two-fifth share in the Muscongus Patent,* called the Owl's Head Neck; and a full history of this Patent, which was granted by Charles I to the first council of Plymouth, who in 1629 granted it to Beauchamp and Leverett. There is also an affidavit of Hannah Horwood, daughter of Thomas and Hannah Flucker [and widow of Captain James Urquhart, of the 14th Foot, who fought in the battle of Bunker Hill, and was town major in Boston], denouncing the unjust demand of General Henry Knox, her brother-in-law, against her father's estate. (A.O. 13/45.) Other Flucker references are in A.O. 13/137, and A.O. 12/105, f. 125.

In a memorial of Sarah Lyons Flucker, widow of Captain Thomas Flucker, dated Wells, Somerset, August 4, 1786, the death of her mother-in-law, Hannah Flucker, is stated to have occurred on December 28, 1785. In a letter, dated from Antigua, July 30, 1788, she prays for further leave of absence. (A.O. 13/73.)

Thomas Flucker was born at Charlestown in 1719, and was appointed Secretary of Massachusetts in 1770. His first wife was Judith Bowdoin, and his second was Hannah, daughter of General Samuel Waldo, and sister of Francis Waldo (q.v.). His daughter, Lucy, married Henry Knox, a General in the American army during the War of Independence, and Secretary at War in Washington's Administration. His son, Thomas, mentioned above, graduated at Harvard College in 1773, and served in the British army during the Revolution. (Stark, op. cit., pp. 402-4.) Copley's portrait of Thomas Flucker, the elder, is at Bowdoin College, Maine.

TIMOTHY FOLGER

lived formerly in Nantucket, and was at Dartmouth, Nova Scotia, in December, 1790. With Samuel Starbuck he was possessed of considerable property at Nantucket, particularly five whaling vessels, which suffered in the King's cause during the war. At the conclusion of the war he and Starbuck moved to Nova Scotia to carry on their whale fishing. The British Government, desirous of confining the whale fishery to the shores of Great Britain, these two loyalists declared their intention to remove there with their families, and petitioned for an annuity for the term of their lives. (Chatham Papers, Bdle. 220.)

JAMES FORREST

was born in Ireland, and in 1761 settled in Boston as a merchant, and became prosperous, his income being £800 to £1,000 a year. In 1775, he raised, at considerable personal expense, a company of 97 men and 5 lieu-

* See page 60.

tenants, called the Loyal Irish Volunteers,* which he commanded and did constant duty during the blockade of Boston. In 1776, in returning from the West Indies with a cargo of supplies for the army, he was captured by the Americans and put into prison in Philadelphia. Soon afterwards, the *Beverly* transport, with his family, furniture, account books and other valuable papers, foundered at sea between Halifax, Nova Scotia and New York. His family were saved by the exertions of Captain Jacobs, of the frigate *Amazon*. In 1777, having invested the remainder of his fortune in tea, his son took a cargo in the schooner *Resolution*, with a convoy, to Philadelphia, and met Lord Howe in H.M.S. *Eagle*, coming down the River Delaware, and was ordered by his Lordship to return with his vessel to New York. This vessel was run ashore and seized by the rebels and all his property lost, to the total ruin of James Forrest. His eldest son [Charles Frederick Forrest], after five years' service under Sir James Wallace, as midshipman and mate in six or seven engagements, lost an eye, and in 1785, was serving in the Russian Navy on the Caspian Sea. His son, James, served throughout the American War of Independence as Lieutenant in the 17th Foot of the British Army. (A.O. 12/74, ff. 319–324 ; A.O. 12/101, ff. 183, 273 ; A.O. 13/73 ; A.O. 13/100.)

He was part owner with Philip Dumaresq (*q.v.*) of the schooner *General Howe*.

EDWARD FOSTER

was born in Boston, and was a prosperous blacksmith and the owner of freehold property in Middle Street and Beer Lane. He was known as a friend to Government, and always made open profession of his loyalty, and was ready at all times to support it. For his loyalty he not only endangered his property but also his personal safety. When Boston light-house was destroyed by the rebels he voluntarily offered to repair it, and with the help of his workmen did so in two days. He left Boston at the evacuation by the British troops, and settled at Halifax in Nova Scotia. His estate is described (A.O. 13/50 ; A.O. 12/10, ff. 39-46 ; A.O. 12/61, f. 8 ; A.O. 12/81, f. 81.) He claimed £535, and was allowed £235. (A.O. 12/109.)

Edward Foster was a Sandemanian, and with other loyalist refugees introduced that faith into Halifax, where it flourished for many years.† In his long letter of May 1, 1782, to Robert Ferrier, he says : " But, alas ! that goodliest of all sights is no more to be seen at that place [the Sandemanian Church at Boston].‡ At this were I not waxed very gross in heart, mine eyes must flow with rivers of tears, whenever I think on the goodness of God manifested to his people in that place, and the ill returns made Him, whereby he has been provoked to remove the candle-stick out of his place ; and, oh ! what a large share of the guilt is charge-

---

* See Appendix.
† Ex inform. Mr. Harry Piers, of Halifax, a descendant.
‡ See page 23.

able on me . . ." (*Letters by Robert Sandeman, John Glas, etc.,* 1851, p. 130, *et. seq.*)

He died in 1786 in Nova Scotia (Sabine).

Reference : *Ontario Archives, op. cit.*, pp. 37–9.

JOHN FOWLER

of Stockbridge, yeoman, was " fully convinced as a Christian that his duty to his King must be performed by him to answer a good and just conscience," and publicly forbid all rebellious and riotous proceedings before his escape from home. He would seem to have been a son-in-law of Samuel Whelpley, of Stockbridge, who, in a letter of March 28, 1786, addresses Fowler and his wife as " Dear Son and Daughter." His property was valued by John Whitlock, of Stockbridge, probably a kinsman of Captain John Whitlock, of the Queen's Rangers. With his memorial is a certificate of the value of his property. In 1786, he was at Kingston, New Brunswick. (A.O. 13/50.) His compensation amounted to £145 from his claim of £426. (A.O. 12/109.)

LORING JOHN FRISWELL

was born in Boston, and from June, 1755 to 1758 served as a midshipman in H.M.S. *Sterling Castle*. In consequence of his knowledge of North America he was sent in 1758 to Lake George to serve under General Abercrombie, who granted him a captaincy in a company of " Batteaux and Rangers " which took part in the attack on Ticonderoga, serving afterwards under General Bradstreet against Frontenac on Lake Ontario. In 1759 he was present at the siege of Quebec in H.M.S. *Princess Amelia*, and commanded the flat-bottomed boats during the whole siege. In 1764 he was granted 3,000 acres of land on the River Bouquet, opposite the Isle of Valeur, on the western side of Lake Champlain. In 1768 he commanded H.M. *Packet* from St. John's [Prince Edward Island] to Nova Scotia, and was afterwards employed on the survey of the coasts of North America under Des Barres.

Friswell's elder brother, Andrew, was killed in 1759, under Wolfe, at the Falls of Montmorency, and his only surviving brother served in the Governor of Nova Scotia's Regiment [in 1778].

In May, 1778, he was a prisoner for debt in the Fleet Prison, and in January, 1782, in the Marshalsea Prison. (C.O. 5/116, f. 149 ; A.O. 13/54.)

One H. Tucker, in a letter to the Treasury, May 3, 1782, describes this man as Loring John Fraser, alias John Friswell, and as one of the greatest swindlers and forgers. Moreover, he took no part in the Revolution on the side of the Crown. (A.O. 13/54.)

PETER FRYE

for many years was a Judge of the Inferior Court of Common Pleas; Justice of the Peace; Register of the Probate Court; and acting Lieutenant-Colonel in the militia previous to the Revolution, all in the County of Essex. In 1768, he was a member of the House of Representatives, when he voted to rescind a vote of a former Assembly* "inviting the other provinces to elect members to meet in General Congress." In conse quence of this vote he was thrown out at the ensuing election. As a magistrate, in 1774, he dispersed a mob illegally assembled, and issued a warrant for the arrest of certain committee men. On the night of October 5, 1774, his house, furniture, books, silver and other valuables, as well as his warehouses, were destroyed by fire, presumably incendiary, and he, with his wife and children, who were in bed, with much difficulty escaped. Peter Frye settled afterwards in Ipswich, where he hoped to remain in peace, but his loyalty having rendered him obnoxious, he was obliged to flee in a small open boat to H.M.S. *Mermaid*, commanded by Captain Hawker, whom he accompanied on the expedition against Machias. This ship was lost in a gale, with British troops on board, early in 1779, near Egg Harbour. At the end of 1779, he arrived in England. With his memorial is an inventory of his personal property. (A.O. 13/45.)

Peter Frye claimed £842, and was allowed £650, less £6 10s. for his pension. His claim of £217 for the loss of his official income during the war was met by an allowance at the rate of £150 (A.O. 12/109); and he received a pension until his death early in 1820. (A.O. 459/7; A.O. 461/15; T. 50/6; T. 50/26.) Another reference to him is in A.O. 12/105, f. 65.

This loyalist was born in 1723 at Andover, Massachusetts, and settled at Salem. (*Loyalists' Claims, op. cit.*, pp. 224–5; *Journal of Samuel Curwen* (*q.v.*), p. 547.) He graduated at Harvard College in 1744, and died in January, 1820, in London. His son, Peter Pickman Frye, who was pardoned as a loyalist in 1777, was sentenced to be shot for desertion from the provincial forces, but was reprieved through the intercession of his grandmother, Mrs. Love Pickman. In September, 1778, he attempted to hang himself. (*Holyoke Diaries*, pp. 96, 99.)

THOMAS FULL

was a pilot under the Crown, at Boston. With his memorial is a schedule of his losses. (A.O. 13/50.)

ANTILL GALLOP

of Cambridge, High Sheriff of Middlesex County, was at Windsor, Nova Scotia, after the war. (A.O. 13/26.)

* See page 58.

WILLIAM GALLOP

was a master mariner and joint owner of vessels in Boston. For six months he was a pilot on H.M.S. *Greyhound*, and served in the same capacity on different privateers in the service of the British and did all he could to distress the rebels. In 1780 he settled at Penobscot, where he had a grant of two lots of land, and built a house. In April, 1784, he removed to St. Andrews, New Brunswick. (A.O. 13/50.)

JAMES GAMAGE

shopkeeper, of Boston, where he was born, claimed £95 5s., and was allowed £40. (A.O. 12/109.) He had a lot of land at Braintree through his wife, Elizabeth. He settled as a shopkeeper at Shelburne, Nova Scotia, where his neighbours were Thomas Full and James Selkrig. (A.O. 13/50; A.O. 12/10, ff. 244-6.)

Reference : *Ontario Archives, op. cit.*, pp. 655-6.

DR. SYLVESTER GARDINER (Plate xxi)

The following notes are from his printed and unprinted memorials of October 10, 1783. After a declaration of his loyalty he says that during the war with the French an express by way of Boston from General Amherst to Wolfe, then near Quebec, applied to him for assistance at Boston. He advised him to go to Governor Pownall, but the express refused, alleging that an unhappy difference subsisted between the General and the Governor. The doctor thereupon took the express to his (the doctor's) own vessel, and sailed with him to Kennebec, a passage of sixteen hours. By this service the express was enabled to reach Wolfe— the only one of three expresses which had started—and Wolfe was thus able to win his celebrated victory. On their arrival at Kennebec he wrote to Captain Howard, of Fort Western, desiring him to send his son (the only man whom the doctor knew in all the country capable of performing the service) with the messenger to Quebec. He likewise wrote to Captain Lethgow,* at Fort Halifax, to supply the party with stores. Both readily complied with his requests.

When he received directions to secure the River Kennebec against the designs of the French and to establish a post for Quebec on that river

---

* William Lithgow served as armourer at St. George's Fort, 1735–1740; as armourer and lieutenant, 1742; as lieutenant, 1746, and as captain, 1746–1748, mainly if not entirely at St. George's Fort. He served as captain at Richmond Fort and Fort Halifax from 1750 to 1767. As Colonel Lithgow he was at Fort Halifax in 1762–3, and reference is also found to him between 1767 and 1773 (ex inform. Mr. F. W. Cook, Secretary of Massachusetts). His deposition of June 6, 1767, describing his thirty years' knowledge of the Kennebec River, is in *New England Hist.-Gen. Reg.*, xxiv, 22–6.

PLATE XXI   Dr. Sylvester Gardiner and Mrs. Gardiner

PLATE XXII

General Timothy Ruggles

and thereby to render available the timber supplies to the eastward of it, Governor Shirley's court opposed the request on account of the expense, and the Governor sent for Dr. Gardiner, then chairman of the Kennebec Company,* and asked him whether that company would bear a part of the expense. The doctor finally brought the company to agree and to build one of the two necessary forts, on condition that he would advance the required sum, which he did. The company gave him their bond, which remained undischarged at the date of this memorial. Governor Shirley was thus able to persuade his court to secure the country against the French by building Fort Halifax, while the Kennebec Company built Fort Western. (A.O. 13/45 ; A.O. 13/73.)

With his memorial in A.O. 13/45 is a long list of his estates, and a long account of bonds and mortgages due to him, with the names of the debtors and the amounts. There is also a copy of a letter from his loyalist son-in-law, Oliver Whipple, of Portsmouth, New Hampshire, on the evasion in Massachusetts of the 5th and 6th articles of the provisional Treaty of Peace. Many loyalists (he says) in consequence of the treaty had attempted to return to America, but they were either seized and imprisoned or sent back with usage of severity.

Dr. Gardiner rendered conspicuous service to the wounded at Bunker Hill, and his carriages brought wounded British officers to their quarters in Boston from Charlestown.

In consequence of his loyalty he sacrificed a fortune of £40,000 sterling, the timber was plundered from his property, he was obliged by his necessities to sell his furniture in New York and his silver in London, and was reduced from affluence to poverty. One Benjamin Kent made a claim against his estate of £362 16s. to Robert Hallowell, Dr. Gardiner's son-in-law, and executor, which he verily believed was a most infamous transaction, and that there was not one person in Boston who was not of the same opinion. A tenant of Dr. Gardiner, Samuel Goodwin by name, claimed £258 17s. 10d. The executors of the doctor commenced a suit against the claimant for money due on a note of hand and a large balance due to his estate. But, perhaps, the most infamous claim was that for £1,589 18s. by Edward Welch, also a tenant, whose reason for making this claim was that he thought that Dr. Gardiner's property would be confiscated and imagined that the doctor would rather he (Welch) should have it than the State. This is the same man who, according to a letter of Dr. Gardiner's son, William, dated June 13, 1783, had been plundering the timber from the property. (A.O. 13/45.)

While the British Army was in occupation of Boston he obtained a judgment against the estate of Briggs Hallowell, which was set aside by resolve of the General Court, October 7, 1779. (A.O. 12/82.) A list of claims against his estate is in A.O. 12/81, f. 85. His property was

---

* Dr. Gardiner and other loyalists were among the signatories to the petition in 1752 of the proprietors of the Kennebec Tract that this tract may be formed into a separate country. With this petition is a list of papers sent by the proprietors. (British Museum, Addl. MSS. 15,488.)

valued at £43,000. He was granted an allowance of £150 a year. (A.O. 12/105, f. 9.)

Robert Hallowell (*q.v.*), an executor and legatee, commenting on the will of Dr. Gardiner, mentions the doctor's son, William, a loyalist, who died unmarried about April 1787 ; his daughter, Rebecca, wife of Philip Dumaresq (*q.v.*) ; his daughter, Abigail Whipple, who was strenuously attached to the British Government and her husband, Oliver Whipple, likewise a loyalist ; and his son, John Gardiner, whose wife and children were zealous loyalists. (A.O. 13/46.)

John Adams in 1771 went to Mr. Pitts to meet the Kennebec Company—Bowdoin, Dr. Gardiner, Hallowell and Pitts himself. There (he says) I shall hear philosophy and politics in perfection from Hallowell ; high flying, high church, high state from Dr. Gardiner ; sedate, cool moderation from Bowdoin ; and warm, honest, frank Whiggism from Pitts. Adams went home, having learned nothing. (Adams, *Works*, ii, 225.)

Dr. Sylvester Gardiner was a warden of King's Chapel, Boston, in 1756–60 and 1763–75. Many references to this eminent loyalist may be found in *Annals of King's Chapel*. He died at Newport, Rhode Island, August 8, 1786, aged 80.

His portrait by Copley and that of his second wife, Abigail, daughter of Colonel Benjamin Pickman, of Salem, and widow of William Eppes, and mother of William Isham Eppes (*q.v.*), are in the possession of Robert H. Gardiner, Esq., of Gardiner, Maine.

His third wife was Catherine, daughter of Colonel Thomas Goldthwait (*q.v.*) and niece of Henry Barnes (*q.v.*). She married, in 1789, William Powell, merchant, of Boston, who died about 1805 ; she died in 1830, aged 86.

References : T. 1/520, ff. 225–230 ; *The Frontier Missionary, op. cit.*, Appendix, pp. 290–3 ; *Loyalists' Claims, op. cit.*, p. 218 ; Stark, *op. cit.*, pp. 313–7 ; *Proc. of Mass. Hist. Soc.*, 2nd Ser., iii, 2–3.

SAMUEL GARNETT

His claim of £350 was disallowed (A.O. 12/109). He settled at St. Andrews, New Brunswick, where he was admitted a barrister-at-law in 1785, and received the appointments of Clerk of the Inferior Court of Common Pleas, Judge of the Probate Court for Charlotte County, and Master extraordinary of the Court of Chancery. In 1790 he sailed for England to press his claims for war service as an officer in the Provincial forces during the Revolution. He died in 1801 (*Judges of New Brunswick, op. cit.*, pp. 149–150.)

A loyalist of this name was a tailor and liquor dealer and was obliged to quit Boston in consequence of his loyalty. (A.O. 13/73 ; A.O. 12/105, f.126.)

Martin Gay

Dr. Samuel Stearns

PLATE XXIII

PLATE XXIV

Colonel Thomas Goldthwait

GEORGE GAY

of Bridgewater, shopkeeper and owner of considerable property, was called upon to take an active part in the rebellion, but avoided it by taking refuge among the Quakers at Dartmouth. Here he was discovered and was taken prisoner to Plymouth upon suspicion of giving intelligence to the British, and there detained for five months. In 1781 he was granted £40 by the British Government to take him to New York. (A.O. 13/73.)

MARTIN GAY (Plate xxiii)

was a prominent founder and copper smith in Boston, and esteemed and respected by his fellow citizens. He was part owner of the sloop, *Polly* (Samuel White, master), which was captured in November, 1775, on returning from Nova Scotia to Boston with a cargo of wood and provisions for the British garrison besieged in Boston. He and Jabez Hatch were taken prisoners. By his industry he had saved £7,000 sterling. With his memorial is General Sir William Howe's appointment of him as a fire ward, November 14, 1775, and an inventory of his property, which included clock bells, brass andirons and sets of brass capitals for clock cases. (A.O. 13/50.) During his exile, his wife, Ruth, was permitted by the General Court one-third part of his estate and the remainder of his furniture, as well as the use of his tools. (A.O. 12/82.) A long account of his property is in A.O. 12/10, ff.103–112. He was allowed £1,130 from his claim of £2,850. (A.O. 12/109.)

Martin Gay was the son of the Rev. Ebenezer and Jerusha Gay and was born at Hingham, Massachusetts, in 1726. He was a member of the Ancient and Honourable Artillery Company of Massachusetts in 1761, lieutenant in 1770 and captain in 1772. He returned to Boston in 1792 and died in 1809 (Roberts, *Hist. of the A. & H.A.C.*, ii, 106; Stark, *op. cit.*, pp. 321–5).

His portrait was engraved by Elson from a pastel, for the Colonial Society of Massachusetts.

References: A.O. 12/102, f. 168; A.O. 13/87; *Ontario Archives, op. cit.*, pp. 568–571; *Publications of Colonial Soc. of Mass.*, iii, 379–400.
Ex inform. Mr. Martin Gay and Mr. E. Howard Gay.

FREDERICK WILLIAM GEYER

By resolve of the General Court, July 6, 1781, it was determined to refrain from proceeding with the libel against his house and land at Wheeler's Point, Boston. (A.O. 12/82.) A list of claims was made against his estate. (A.O. 12/81, f.83; A.O. 12/83, f.1.) He lived after the war with his family at Boston, as a British subject, in the house in Summer Street, formerly his own, which had been confiscated. Every one had shown him the utmost friendship and civility since returning there (Anstey's Report, in A.O. 12/81, ff.40–3).

He was named in the Banishment Act, but returned to Boston and was naturalized as a citizen of Massachusetts in 1789 and resumed business. He died at Walpole, New Hampshire, in 1803 (Sabine, *op. cit.* ; Stark, *op. cit.*, pp. 350–1.)

His grandson was Captain Frederick Marryat, the well-known novelist.

SAMUEL GILBERT

was born at Taunton, Massachusetts, the son of Nathan Gilbert, and lived at Berkeley, Bristol County. He served at the reduction of Cape Breton (*i.e.*, at the siege of Louisburg) and in 1755 commanded a company of Massachusetts troops in the reduction of the Acadians in Nova Scotia. In 1774 he associated with about 300 loyalists of Bristol County, under his brother, Colonel Thomas Gilbert (*q.v.*), for the purpose of keeping peace and order. In April, 1775, a few days before the battle of Lexington, these loyalists were overpowered by a large body of armed rebels, and he was struck by a firelock and lost the sight of one eye. One-third of his property was set off by the State for the use of his wife. With his memorial is a schedule of, and other papers relating to, his property. He settled at Annapolis, Nova Scotia. (A.O. 13/50; A.O. 12/10, ff.337–345.) The sum of £1,195 was allowed to him from his claim of £2,896 1s. (A.O. 12/109.)

Samuel Gilbert was a lieutenant-captain in Captain Daniel Hill's company at the eastward from December 5, 1748, to June 13, 1749 (Muster Rolls Series.)

According to Sabine he returned from Nova Scotia and settled in Massachusetts.

THOMAS GILBERT

was born in Taunton, Massachusetts, and early in life was engaged in His Majesty's service, in command of a company of Massachusetts forces in the siege of Louisburg in 1745. In 1755 he served as Lieutenant Colonel of provincial forces under Timothy Ruggles (*q.v.*) in the attempt against Crown Point and after the battle succeeded Colonel Williams (who was killed on that day) in command of the regiment. In 1760 he removed to Freetown, Bristol County, where he purchased an estate and was a resident there at the commencement of the rebellion. For fifteen years he was a member of the General Assembly and was active in opposing all measures against Great Britain. He was also a Colonel of militia and a justice of the peace. In 1774 at the request of General Gage, he took command of 300 loyalists in Bristol County, armed for the purpose of keeping the neighbourhood in subjection to the King's authority. Within a few days of the affair of Lexington, he found that he was soon to be attacked by the whole of the malcontents in his part of the country and wrote to the Governor for assistance and in reply he received assurance that 300 of His Majesty's troops should be sent by way of Newport. In his absence at Newport, whither he had gone to enquire the reason for the delay in the arrival of the promised troops, his house was beset on April 9, 1775, by a large number of men, estimated at 2,500, who apprehended all the loyalists and plundered his house. In this dangerous situation he sought refuge on board H.M.S. *Rose* and later reached Boston with three sons. He eventually settled at Conway, Nova Scotia, with his wife, three sons, one daughter and six grandchildren. With his memorial is a schedule of his estate and papers regarding the confiscation of his property. (A.O. 13/50; A.O. 12/10, ff.131–147.)

He told his sons on May 4, 1775, to die by the sword rather than be hanged as rebels, which would be their fate if they joined the Americans (Force, *Am. Archives*, Ser. IV., Vol. II., p. 508.)

His son was Thomas Gilbert (*q.v.*) His brother was Samuel Gilbert (*q.v.*)

The Colonial services of this loyalist were as follows. In August, 1748, he was sentinel in Captain Thomas Buckminster's company of volunteers. In 1761 he was captain in the second Brookfield company in Colonel Murray's regiment. From March 27, to December 17, 1755, he was Lieutenant Colonel in Colonel Timothy Ruggles's Crown Point expedition. His name appears as Colonel of the Bristol County militia in 1762, 1767, 1769, 1771, and 1773–4 (Muster Rolls Series.)

Sabine in his account states that Colonel Gilbert died about 1796 on the River St. John, aged about 82.

He claimed £11,012, and was allowed £3,830 (A.O. 12/109.)

Ontario Archives, op. cit., pp. 589–90, 592–3.

THOMAS GILBERT, THE YOUNGER

was the son of Colonel Thomas Gilbert (*q.v.*) and was born at Berkeley, Bristol County. Early in life he served as a militia officer and was Major of the 2nd Regiment in that county. He was one of the 300 loyalists of this county who were apprehended in 1775. From May, 1776 to February 24, 1779, he served as master of a transport vessel and was captured by an American privateer and taken in irons to Hartford gaol in Connecticut. He settled at Digby, Nova Scotia. (A.O. 13/24.)

He was appointed second lieutenant in Captain French's Berkeley company in his father's militia regiment and was promoted second major in 1771 (Muster Rolls Series.)

LEMUEL GODDARD

of Plymouth took a decisive part as a loyalist early in the struggle, and was obliged to quit in April, 1775, and flee to Nova Scotia, where he joined the British service and served until the peace. His wife and five small children were brutally treated and plundered of their clothes at Plymouth. He was at Shelburne, Nova Scotia, in 1786. (A.O. 13/24.)

SAMUEL GOLDSBURY

was the son of John Goldsbery (Goldsbury) and his wife, Eunice, of Wrentham, and was a loyalist from the outbreak of the rebellion. He was a lieutenant in the Associated Loyalists in Boston until the evacuation of that place by the British, when he sailed for Nova Scotia and New York. Here he served as a volunteer at the battle of Brooklyn, and was appointed a captain in the second company of the Loyal Associated Refugees commanded by Colonel Edmund Fanning, January 17, 1779. At the evacuation of Rhode Island by the British troops, he was commissioned to raise a company for the corps of Major Upham (q.v.) which defended Lloyd's Neck on Long Island, New York, against an attack by a detachment of French forces, and afterwards served at the reduction of New London under Benedict Arnold. Samuel Goldsbury also served on the British sloop, *Savage*, with a party of loyalists under his command on an expedition to Martha's Vineyard. Upon the evacuation of New York in 1783, he went to Nova Scotia, where he was granted a plantation. (A.O. 13/45; A.O. 13/73; A.O. 12/102, f.151.) According to a letter dated from London, February 4, 1790, he was destitute and his wife insane in America, with several young children. (A.O. 13/137.) He died August 20, 1815. (Ind.: 5606.)

HENRY GOLDTHWAIT

was a merchant at Penobscot. At the siege of Fort George, Penobscot, by the rebels, he was taken prisoner and stripped even of the clothes on his back, and his goods plundered. The rebels having been defeated he escaped from captivity and pursued them with a party of loyalists, until a ball wounded him. He was appointed deputy commissary of refugees at Penobscot, but was obliged by his wound to resign, and he sailed for England, December 24, 1781. (A.O. 13/73; A.O. 12/99, f.263.) His father, in a letter dated December 2, 1788, stated that he (Henry) had quitted his business in London and was in Guernsey, apparently trying to obtain a military appointment. (A.O. 13/84.)

He was born in 1759 and was the son of Colonel Thomas Goldthwait (q.v.) and his second wife, Catherine Barnes. He was married in England to Sarah Winch, of Bampton, Oxfordshire, and, in 1793 was an Ensign in the Independent Company of Invalids and in 1795, lieutenant in the Royal Garrison Battalion, being put on half pay in 1796. He died at sea in 1800 (Chamberlain, *Doc. Hist. of Chelsea, Mass.*, 1908; Stark, *op. cit.* pp. 360–1.)

In 1789 Henry Goldthwait was appointed waiter and searcher in the Customs at Turks Island (A.O. 13/45).

CAPTAIN PHILIP GOLDTHWAIT

was born in Boston. In 1759 he commanded the sloop, *Industry*, at the siege of Quebec, and in 1760 served in the Ordnance. He commanded

Harrison Gray

PLATE XXV

PLATE XXVI

John Gray

H.M. schooner, *Neptune*, in 1775, and was ordered by his brother, Major Joseph Goldthwait, barrack-master at Boston, to sail to eastern Massachusetts to purchase wood and provisions for the British troops, but was captured on March 2, 1776. General Sullivan ill-treated him as a prisoner, and put him into irons before committing him to Fort Kittery. Once again he was captured and sent to Pownallborough gaol, whence he escaped on August 3, 1778, with James McMaster (*q.v.*) and another loyalist, and they put to sea in an open boat, and after beating about for three days they were taken up by Admiral Sir George Collier. He afterwards commanded the *Rainbow* on an expedition to Machias and was taken prisoner by an American privateer, but was released by Collier, under whom and Admiral Arbuthnot he acted as pilot in several ships of the Royal Navy. (A.O. 13/73 ; A.O. 13/84.)

His brother, Major Joseph Goldthwait, having died at New York* on October 3, 1779, he (Philip) bought in 1780 a commission for 1,000 guineas in the Band of Gentlemen Pensioners, producing an annual income of £65 to £70, and an annuity of £70 on the life of the Earl of Chesterfield, from money recovered from the estate of his deceased brother. His brother, Samuel, arrived in England from America and proceeded against him for the greater part of the money from Joseph's estate, and consequently Philip was obliged to sell his above commission in 1784 for £650. He appears to have met with various misfortunes in trade in England, and to have been very extravagant since his arrival there in 1780. (A.O. 13/73 ; A.O. 13/84 ; A.O. 12/99, f.308 ; A.O. 12/102, ff.90, 213.) His claim of £2,700 was disallowed. (A.O. 12/109.)

His father, Joseph Goldthwait ; his brothers, Joseph†, Samuel (a merchant at Newport, Rhode Island), and Dr. Michael B.‡ ; his uncles, Ezekiel and Colonel Thomas Goldthwait (*q.v.*) ; and his cousins, Thomas and Henry Goldthwait (*q.v.*), were all loyalists.

Philip Goldthwait was born in 1733 (Chamberlain, *Doc. Hist. of Chelsea, Mass.*)

Loyalists' Claims, op. cit., p. 196.

COLONEL THOMAS GOLDTHWAIT (Plate xxiv)

was appointed in 1763 in command of Fort Pownall, Penobscot (built in 1759), with the rank of Colonel in the army, on the recommendation of General Amherst. This fort was destroyed in 1775 by Colonel Cargill and his party. He was for several years Superintendent of Indian affairs— an office of which he was deprived by the General Assembly in 1770 because of his attachment to the Crown and the British Government. He was likewise Secretary at War of Massachusetts. On May 2, 1769, he was appointed an officer of the Customs at Penobscot and the original

---

* He was buried in St. Paul's Church (A.O. 13/84).

† See Appendix.

‡ He was surgeon's mate in the Military Hospital in New York, and died during the war, leaving a widow, Abigail (*Am. MSS. in Royal Inst., op. cit.,* ii, 348 ; iii, 236.)

appointment on parchment, signed by Charles Paxton (*q.v.*), William Burch (*q.v.*), Henry Hulton (*q.v.*) and J. Temple, Commissioners of the Customs in North America, is in A.O. 13/84, together with several papers relating to his property and certificates to his loyalty and services. On his large landed property at Penobscot, 25,000 acres in extent, he was a considerable breeder of horses. (A.O. 12/101, f. 280; A.O. 12/105, f. 11.)

From his claim of £6,338 he was allowed £1,820, and was compensated at the rate of £200 a year for the loss of his income as an officer of the Crown during the war. (A.O. 12/109.) He was also granted a loyalist pension of £100 until his death. (A.O. 459/7; A.O. 461/16; T.50/6.)

Colonel Goldthwait gave information to the Commissioners that Mr. Conyers, a relation of the Penn family, had told his (the Colonel's) son that Lady Juliana Penn had gone to Paris to negotiate with Dr. Franklin for the recovery of the Penn property in America. Mr. Conyers added that no application would be made to the British Government for compensation for this confiscated property, as Lady Juliana was "a rebel to all intents and purposes, and that if her wishes or the wishes of her family could have availed, the Americans had succeeded long before they did." (A.O. 13/85.)

This loyalist was the son of Captain John Goldthwait and his wife, Jane Halsey, and was born in Boston in 1717-8. He married (i), in 1742, Esther, daughter of Colonel Epes Sargent; and (ii), Catherine Barnes, sister of Henry Barnes (*q.v.*). His daughter, Catherine, by his first marriage, was adopted by Henry Barnes and married in 1784, Dr. Sylvester Gardiner (*q.v.*) and two years later, as a widow, she married William Powell, merchant, of Boston. Thomas Goldthwait, merchant, selectman, and representative to the General Court, was a man of ability and of unbounded enterprise. He died at Walthamstow, Essex, August 31, 1799, his wife having predeceased him, December 16, 1796. (Chamberlain, *Doc. Hist. of Chelsea, Mass.*, 1908, ii, 602-9.) His portrait by Copley is in the possession of Dr. John T. Bowen, of Boston.

Loyalists' Claims, op. cit., pp. 264-6; Stark, *op. cit.*, pp. 356-8.

THOMAS GOLDTHWAIT, THE YOUNGER

In A.O. 13/84 is a long statement of his services and an autobiographical sketch of his career In 1759 and 1760 he accompanied his father, Colonel Thomas Goldthwait (*q.v.*) as Paymaster of the troops sent by the New England provinces to assist General Amherst against Crown Point and other French forts. In June, 1770, he was appointed first Lieutenant of Fort Pownall, Penobscot, with the rank of Major in the army. In 1794 he returned to America from England and remained there until December, 1811. On the return voyage to England he was taken by a French privateer and was stripped of all his personal property. This privateer having been chased by an English armed ship, Thomas Goldthwait and four others were put into a small boat and turned adrift in the Channel well towards France. By the merciful intervention of Providence, favourable winds washed the boat ashore near Weymouth. His only nephew and only surviving heir of the family served nearly twenty years in the Royal Navy and died in its service.

He was a merchant at Penobscot, where his property and Fort Pownall were destroyed by the rebels. He escaped to the West Indies and thence to England in 1777. (A.O. 13/73.) Compensation, £740, was granted to him from his claim of £1,385 and a loyalist pension. In 1821, he was granted £30 to relieve his distressed condition. (A.O. 12/105, ff. 11, 66 ; A.O. 12/109.)

His brother was Henry Goldthwait (q.v.).

For more detailed particulars of Thomas Goldthwait, the younger, see Chamberlain, *Doc. Hist. of Chelsea, Mass.*, 1908.

JANE GORDON

was the widow of Alexander Gordon, merchant, of Boston, who left four sons and a daughter. After her husband's death she instilled into the minds of her young children " sentiments of unalterable attachment to their Sovereign and adherence to the British Government." For practical proof of her loyalty she adduces the fact that she purchased an ensigncy in the 65th Foot for her eldest son, who was afterwards a Lieutenant of Light Infantry in that regiment at Boston. During the siege of Boston two other sons likewise went into the British army, their commissions having been purchased by her. By her attention to the British officers wounded at Bunker Hill she incurred the hostility of the Americans. She was heir to considerable property in Georgia by the death of an uncle. She left Boston for Nova Scotia and England in 1775 and eventually settled in Edinburgh, where she and her daughter were reduced " from a once happy, easy, and comfortable situation [in America], to the distressing state of uncertainty and dependence." (A.O. 13/96.)

In her memorial, dated Edinburgh, November 4, 1777, Jane Gordon states that her eldest and youngest sons were then in the British army. Her second son was an apprentice to a merchant at Charlestown, South Carolina, and, to avoid serving in the military forces of the rebels, escaped to the woods, where he remained for several days and nights until he got away in a warship. (A.O. 13/73.) In a letter of February 14, 1786, she states that her son, Hugh, "meets with many disapointments, tho' he is cleaver and industrious." (A.O. 13/96.)

She died in June, 1789, at No. 19, Princes Street, Edinburgh. (A.O. 13/137.)

May 3, 1765, Jane Gordon of Boston, widow, was appointed to administer the insolvent estate of her late husband, Alexander Gordon, late of Boston, merchant. The births of their children recorded at Boston are as follows :—George, born August 6, 1755 ; Alexander, born April 21, 1757 ; Annabella, born April 27, 1758 ; and Hugh Mackay, born September 18, 1759.

The following are the commissions of the three sons in the British army :—

George, Ensign, January 12, 1770 ; Leiutenant, August 2, 1775 ; and Captain, December 16, 1778, all in the 65th Foot ; and Lieutenant-Colonel, 29th Light Dragoons, March 16, 1798.

Alexander was commissioned Lieutenant in the 2nd Foot, November 6, 1778. He was drowned in the Bay of Inverness, Scotland, January 19, 1834, and is described as Captain in this regiment. (*Gent. Mag.*)

Hugh Mackay, who had served as a volunteer under General Sir William Howe in 1775-6, was commissioned Lieutenant in the 16th Foot, April 27, 1778, and Lieutenant-Colonel in the same regiment, January 18, 1798. He was promoted Colonel, April 25, 1808, and Major-General, June 4, 1811. He died in 1823. His portrait, painted by Opie, was engraved by Barney.

Jane Gordon was the daughter of Mrs. Mackay, of King Street, Boston, and sister of the second wife of James Murray (*q.v.*).

JOHN GORE

was for 38 years a colour merchant and painter in Boston and served as an officer in the militia before the Revolution. During the blockade of Boston he served in the police. With his memorial is a schedule of his property and a list of notes of hand. (A.O. 13/73.) He returned to Boston and was naturalised. (A.O. 12/81, f. 38 ; A.O. 12/82 ; A.O. 12/105, f. 127 ; A.O. 13/96.) This loyalist was born in 1718 and in 1758 was appointed a Lieutenant in the Ancient and Honourable Artillery Company of Massachusetts ; he was pardoned by the legislature in 1787 and died at Boston, January 15, 1796. (Roberts, *Hist. of Ancient and Honourable Artillery Co.*, ii, 25 ; Stark, *op. cit.*) His son was Hon. Christopher Gore, Governor of Massachusetts, 1809-10.

COLONEL JOSEPH GOREHAM

This member of the Massachusetts family of this name, born about 1728, was put on half-pay at the end of the American War in 1783 and remained as such until his death, July 20, 1790. (Ind. 5605 ; W.O. 24/750 ; W.O. 25/3096.)

He had served in the army since 1745 and was present at the sieges of Louisburg, Quebec and Havana. He was appointed Major of a Corps of Rangers in America, August 2, 1760, promoted Major Commandant, September 25, 1761 ; and Lieutenant-Colonel of Foot, May 25, 1772. (*Earl of Dartmouth MSS.*, *op. cit.*, ii, 249 ; *Amer. MSS. in Roy. Inst.*, *op. cit.*, i, 3.)

Colonel Goreham was a member of the Council of Nova Scotia from 1766 and was Lieutenant-Governor of Placentia from 1775. (*Amer. MSS. in Roy. Inst.*, *op. cit.*, iii, 31.) During the American War of Independence he was Lieutenant-Colonel Commandant of the Royal Fencible

Americans,* a loyalist regiment which served mostly in Nova Scotia. In July, 1777, a court martial was ordered on him, to investigate the charges of Major Thomas Batt on the "debilitated state" of the regiment. (*Ib.*, i, 122-3) and exception was taken to some of his proceedings regarding clothing for his regiment. (*Ib.*, 156–9, 172, 371, 380.) In a letter to General Sir Henry Clinton, June 18, 1780, he complains of the "virulent, unjust & groundless representations" made against him. (*Ib.*, ii, 140.) He was mortified that because he held provincial rank only, he was passed over for the command of all the troops in Nova Scotia, on the death of Brigadier-General Maclean in May, 1781. (*Ib.*, ii, 288, 300.) ·

Reference : *Nova Scotia Archives*, 1869, p. 232.

THE GOULD FAMILY

John, Samuel and Elizabeth Gould, were minors in 1776, when they accompanied their guardian, the Rev. John Troutbeck (*q.v.*) to England. Their trustee, Dr. William Lee Perkins (*q.v.*) claimed on their behalf for property at Boston, lost or destroyed, of which there is a schedule. John Gould became a surgeon's mate in the British forces [and was granted a diploma of membership of the Corporation of Surgeons of England, May 3, 1781]. Samuel Gould was a merchant and Elizabeth Gould married George Henry Monk [Major of the Loyal Nova Scotia Volunteers]. Each was granted a loyalist allowance of £100 a year. (A.O. 13/50 ; A.O. 13/73 ; A.O. 13/92 ; A.O. 12/105, f.115.)

They were the children of John and Elizabeth (Wentworth) Gould, who were married in 1758. (*Annals of King's Chapel, op. cit.*, ii, 122.) Their aunt, Sarah Gould, married the above Rev. John Troutbeck.

HARRISON GRAY, THE ELDER (Plate xxv)

With his petition and memorial, proclaiming his loyalty and mentioning his appointments as Treasurer and Receiver-General of Massachusetts since 1753 and as a Mandamus Councillor, is a schedule of his losses. These include three houses in Boston, of which he obtained legal possession in 1775 by virtue of a judgment of the court against John Hancock, a judgment which was set aside by an Act of the State of Massachusetts. There is also a list of bonds due to him and the names of the debtors, one of whom was James Otis for £38 5s. 4d. The sum of £2,655 16s. 9d. was due to him by loyalist refugees in England. (A.O. 13/45 ; A.O. 13/73.) There was no mortgage on his estate. (A.O. 12/82.) A list of claims against his estate is in A.O. 12/81, f. 82. This eminent loyalist claimed £8,151 for the loss of his property and was allowed £2,037 and at the rate of £400 for the loss of his official income during the war. His pension was £200. (A.O. 12/105, f.128 ; A.O. 12/109.)

Harrison Gray was a member of the "Monday Evening Club" (with the Adamses, Otises, and other worthies) which met weekly to

* *Colls. of New Brunswick Hist. Soc.*, No. 5, p. 217.

discuss politics at the British Coffee House, kept by Hannah Cordis (*q.v.*).
He was satirized under the name of " Scribblerius Fribble " in Mercy
Warren's play, *The Group*, in 1775. He died in 1794. For his property,
see *Publications of Colonial Soc. of Mass.*, xiv, 320–350.

In evidence in London he claimed to have been the author of the
pamphlet, *The Two Congresses Cut Up*. (*Loyalists' Claims, op. cit.*,
pp. 104–5.)

His portrait by Copley is in the possession of William A. Otis, Esq.
His son was the loyalist of the same name (*q.v.*).

References : Adams, *Works*, ii, 163, 260, x, 193 ; Stark, *op. cit.*, pp. 334–6.

HARRISON GRAY, THE YOUNGER

In two long letters, dated May 30, 1789, and March 21, 1790, he
laments his pathetic condition on the reduction of his pension, the recent
death of his wife and the long and sad illness of his lovely daughter.
(A.O. 13/137.) He was deputy Treasurer of Massachusetts under his
father, Harrison Gray (*q.v.*), for thirteen years. (A.O. 13/73.) He claimed
£50 ; and was allowed £50. (A.O. 12/109 ; A.O. 12/105, f.128 ; *Loyalists'
Claims, op. cit.*, pp. 233–4.)

JOHN GRAY (Plate xxvi)

brother of Harrison Gray, the elder (*q.v.*), was a ropemaker in Boston,
where he remained throughout the blockade and supplied the Royal
Navy with cordage as usual, though all the other ropemakers had quitted
the town from fear of being compelled to do so. (A.O. 13/73 ; A.O.
12/105, f. 129.) One John Gray claimed £486 and was allowed £100.
(A.O. 12/109.)

His portrait by Copley is in the possession of descendants.

JOHN GRAY, THE YOUNGER

son of Harrison Gray, the elder (*q.v.*), was apprenticed to Mr. Otis.*
As one of the Associated Loyalists of Boston he did military duty before
the evacuation of the town by the British. He embarked for Ireland
[in 1775] in his brother's brigantine, to obtain provisions and on the
return voyage he was captured within six hours' sail of Boston. (A.O.
13/45 ; A.O. 13/73.) Stark, *op. cit.*, p. 336.

LEWIS GRAY

merchant, of Boston, served in the Loyal Associated Volunteers. With
his memorial is an estimate of his losses and many papers relating to his
property. (A.O. 13/45 ; A.O. 13/75.) As a loyalist refugee in England

* Probably James Otis, the lawyer, or his brother, Samuel Allyne Otis, who had
married Elizabeth, daughter of Harrison Gray.

he served in a temporary post in Lord North's administration. (A.O. 13/73.) The sum of £462 was allowed him from his claim of £3,597. (A.O. 12/109.)

FRANCIS GREEN

a native of Boston, was descended from "ancestors emigrated from Great Britain at the settlement of New England, who (in an honorable succession in public stations in America) have transmitted to him the principles of loyalty to the Crown, and affection to the Nation." He served as an officer for ten years in the 40th Regiment of Foot,* at Louisburg, in Canada, at Martinique and Havana, and upon his retirement from this regiment he settled as a merchant in Boston in 1765. Early in the Revolution he exerted himself to promote reconciliation with, and to prevent a political separation from, the mother country ; nevertheless he " experienced in the months of June and July, 1774, the greatest and most public personal indignities, was twice assaulted by the Republicans of Connecticut, and mobb'd in the towns of Norwich and Wyndham." In town meetings he publicly exerted himself to discourage and abolish committees of correspondence and to promote as an act of justice an agreement to pay for the tea destroyed. To the effects of the blockade of Boston he imputed " a melancholy & irreparable breach in his family of the most delicate & affecting nature."† (A.O. 13/45 ; A.O. 13/73.)

On November 1, 1775, Francis Green was appointed Captain of the third company of Loyal Associated Volunteers of Boston, with Ebenezer Spooner and Josiah Jones (q.v.) as lieutenants and Abraham Savage (q.v.), William Chandler‡ and Nathaniel Coffin as second lieutenants. The original appointment is in A.O. 13/45.

In the course of the war, Green and Philip Dumaresq (q.v.) as joint owners fitted up the war vessel *Tryon*, of 16 guns and 72 men, with George Sibbles as master, and this vessel achieved considerable success against the Americans in sundry encounters. In one sanguinary engagement, on Christmas Day in 1779, the *Tryon* endeavoured to recapture the *Thorn*, formerly of the Royal Navy, and Sibbles was mortally wounded and many officers and men were killed, and the *Thorn* disabled. Benjamin Bradford (q.v.) was injured in trying to capture this vessel.

Francis Green was also active in equipping, in conjunction with George Leonard (q.v.), the ship *Oliver Cromwell*, captured from the Americans and renamed the *Restoration* (Harry Hatch, master). He equipped at his own expense, in 1780, the armed sloop *Carleton*, of 12 guns, as a unit for the refugee fleet under George Leonard. This vessel was afterwards wrecked on the passage to South Carolina. (A.O. 13/45 ;

---

* His commissions were : Ensign, July 2, 1755 ; and Lieutenant, September 30, 1761, until 1766. General Howe's original certificate to his gallantry during the war with the French is in A.O. 13/73.

† This melancholy event was the death of his first wife Susanna, on November 10, 1775.

‡ Son of John Chandler (q.v.).

A.O. 13/73; A.O. 13/79.) He was the author of a plan* to consolidate the force and number of the American loyalists and "to bring their usefulness into efficiency," by which means he contended that their application for compensation from the British Government would perhaps have been rendered unnecessary. (A.O. 13/45.) With his memorial are many papers relating to his property. (*Ib.*)

He was granted a pension of £100 until his death (A.O. 12/105, f.10; T.50/11; T.50/28), and was compensated £295 from his claim of £1,149. (A.O. 12/109.)

This staunch loyalist fled to Halifax with the British army in March, 1776, and thence to New York and England. In 1784 he was appointed High Sheriff of the important naval town of Halifax, Nova Scotia. Penelope Winslow wrote in April, 1785, that he enjoyed all the pomp of that pompous town and that anyone would by his style and state swear he was a born Halifaxian. (*Winslow Papers*, p. 288.)

Francis Green was the son of Benjamin Green, Secretary to the British forces at the siege of Louisburg in 1745, and later Treasurer, member, and President of the Council of Nova Scotia, who died in 1772. (Murdoch, *Hist. of N. Scotia*, 1866, ii. 505–6.) His son, Charles, was a deaf mute and was placed at Mr. Braidwood's School† in Edinburgh during his exile in England. The physical afflictions of this son created within him a strong desire to alleviate the unhappy lot of the deaf and dumb, and with this object he published anonymously in 1783 the pamphlet, *Vox Oculis Subjecta*. Upon returning to Massachusetts in 1797 he published various essays in the *Boston Palladium* and other newspapers in 1803–1805 upon the education of deaf mutes. He died at Medford, in that state, in 1809, at the age of 67, the last male branch of his family. His second wife, Harriet, was a daughter of David Mathews, last loyalist Mayor of New York. (Address of Hon. Samuel A. Green, printed in *Facts Relating to the History of Groton*, 1914.)

References : A.O. 13/100 ; *American MSS. in Royal Inst.*, *op. cit.*, ii, 437, 484 ; iii, 329 ; iv, 461 ; *Ontario Archives*, *op. cit*, pp. 1208–10 ; *Loyalists' Claims*, *op. cit.*, pp. 99–100 ; *Proc. of American Antiquarian Soc.*, April, 1900.

JONATHAN, EBENEZER AND ALEXANDER GREENLAW

These three loyalists (whose aged parents died about 1776) had lands on Deer Island, near Penobscot. They were all taken prisoners, with their brother Charles, by the "rebel brig *Pallas*," and treated with every indignity, so much so that Charles became insane. They were all settled at St. Andrews, New Brunswick, in 1786. (A.O. 13/50.) The three brothers claimed £657 1s., and were allowed £50 each. (A.O. 12/109.) According to Sabine, Jonathan died in 1818, aged 80 ; Ebenezer about 1810, aged 70 ; and Charles about 1810, aged 70, all at St. Andrews.

* There is no account of this plan in his papers.
† An account of Thomas Braidwood (1715–1806) is in the *Dict. of Nat. Biog.*

ANN GREENLEAF

was the widow of Charles Burrell, a surgeon in the Royal Navy, who with his eldest son was lost at sea in H.M.S. *Badger*.* She afterwards married Daniel Greenleaf, surgeon on H.M.S. *Adventure*, who served during the war with France. At the peace of 1763, she and her husband settled in Boston, where he died in 1777. Ann Greenleaf was of British birth and was a resolute loyalist, and at great hazard carried letters and intelligence to and from British officers who were prisoners in Massachusetts, notably Colonel Archibald Campbell and Colonel Philip Skene. Having been discovered by the rebels she was threatened with death. By the advice of Colonel Campbell she sailed for England, accompanied by her three children, mentioned in their father's will of July 22, 1776—Daniel, Silence and Eleanor—only to find all her friends dead and no help procurable in her distress. (A.O. 13/45; A.O. 13/73; A.O. 12/105, f. 104.) Her claim of £407 was disallowed. (A.O. 12/109.) Ann Greenleaf was granted a pension of £40 until her death in 1800. (A.O. 461/16; T. 50/11.)

SAMUEL GREENWOOD

was an American by birth and a mast-maker at Boston, who as a refugee carried on the same business later at Halifax, Nova Scotia. (A.O. 13/50; A.O. 12/10, ff. 36–8; A.O. 12/61, f. 7.) He is in *Ontario Archives*, *op. cit.*, p. 37.

BENJAMIN GRIDLEY

The son of Isaac Gridley was born at Boston, and graduated at Harvard College in 1751.

In 1774 he was commissioned a magistrate in Boston, and according to Lord Percy he was the only magistrate there who ventured to perform his onerous duties, which he executed in a spirited manner. A year later he was appointed a Judge of the Court of Common Pleas, going to his duty from his brick mansion house with an elegant cupola, after the manner of St. Paul's Cathedral, as it is described. Courted by the Whig party, Benjamin Gridley refused all their offers of favours with disdain. While the town of Boston was in the occupation of the British troops he served in the Associated Corps of Volunteers.

In his memorials of 1776, 1779 and 1782, this active loyalist maintains that he was for several years since 1765 a writer in the public papers of Boston in defence and support of the Royal Government, at his own expense, and his "lucubrations" were "a scourge to a numerous group of seditious Gazetteers and Pamphleteers who audaciously reviled King, Parliament, Ministry and Governors."

Always active in the suppression of disorders and defiance of the law,

---

* There are records of this ship until April, 1762, at which date Charles Burrell was surgeon (Navy Records).

Gridley on one occasion put the Mutiny Act in force, to put down those who attempted to induce by bribes and other means the British soldiers to desert.*

This loyalist barrister-at-law claims to have been the sole magistrate who dared to show his face and put the statute of mutiny into force in Boston in 1774 and 1775. He also imprisoned a traitor, who had led 700 armed men and forcibly attacked the mansion of a loyalist. He likewise prevented a revolt of the British troops under General Gage, and hindered the insurgents from entering Boston, thereby saving the garrison from the " jaws of impending fate."

Benjamin Gridley was the presiding judge when Harrison Gray recovered judgment for £942 11s. 8d. in the Court of Common Pleas at Boston in July, 1775, for damage against John Hancock, who was committed to gaol.

He left Boston with the British troops in March, 1776, and from Halifax sailed for England, where he was " enrolled as Volunteer in an American military corps in aid of ye Imperial Crown of England, at a time ye arms of France menaced an invasion." This was a loyalist corps formed by Sir William Pepperell, the distinguished exile from Massachusetts, shortly after the alliance had been sealed between France and America. (A.O. 13/45 ; A.O. 13/73.)

Thomas Flucker (q.v.), in his evidence in London, stated that Benjamin Gridley was a man of education, in small practice as a lawyer.

He appealed for a genteel employment after the war, but at his age it must be *otium cum dignitate*. The Commissioners reported that he had endeavoured to carry some of the British Acts of Parliament into effect with more zeal than any other magistrate. (A.O. 12/105, f. 67.)

Compensation—£100—was granted to him from his claim of £1,550. (A.O. 12/109.)

Reference : *Loyalists' Claims, op. cit.*, pp. 251–2

*Samuel Dyer was taken prisoner for endeavouring to persuade British soldiers at Boston to desert in 1774, at the instigation of Samuel Adams and Dr. Young, who, according to Dyer's deposition, employed him to collect shipwrights and carpenters together in certain taverns in Boston, at the expense of the Sons of Liberty, for the purpose of forming a mob whenever required at a minute's warning. Dyer himself was to have been one of the disguised party who destroyed the famous tea, but was prevented by sickness from attending. Samuel Adams in June, 1774, promised Dyer four pounds sterling for every soldier whom he prevailed upon to desert, and every deserter was promised a like sum or 300 acres of land. (C.O. 5/120, ff. 42c, 43.)

Samuel Mouat, mariner, declared on oath that John Short, merchant, near the Draw Bridge in Boston, had given a soldier four dollars and a suit of clothes for deserting from the British army ; that Colonel Meshech Weare, Judge of the Superior Court of New Hampshire, had in June or July, 1774, in Boston offered, in his (Mouat's) hearing, 303 acres of land to any soldier who would desert ; and that Colonel Weare offered one Kelly, then confined for debt at Amherst, his freedom and £150 sterling if he would head a regiment of armed men to attack the British troops in Boston. (C.O. 5/120, f. 42 d.)

John Adams said of him in 1769 that he possessed capacity, real sentiment, fancy, humour, judgment and observation; yet, he had no business of any kind, was in bed till ten in the morning, laughed, drank and frolicked, and neither studied nor practised his profession (quoted by Sabine).

DORCAS GRIFFITH

was the widow of Thomas Griffith, merchant, of Boston, her birthplace. With her widowed daughter, Sarah Hinson, she kept a shop for linen drapery and grocery on Hancock's Wharf in Boston.

Thomas Flucker (*q.v*), in evidence upon their claim, stated that these two women kept a huckster's shop and lived well. Dorcas Griffith was a common prostitute, and bred up her daughter in the same way. She was kept by the famous Hancock [John Hancock, first signer of the Declaration of Independence], and when he turned her off, she lived with Captain Johnston, of the Marines. On this evidence, the loyalist allowances of these women were discontinued on January 5, 1782 (A.O. 12/105, f. 103), as they " were not proper objects for the bounty of Government." (A.O. 12/100, f. 323), in spite of the certificates to their loyalty presented by General Gage, General Sir William Howe, and Sir William Pepperell. (A.O. 13/73.)

A certificate from Captain David Johnston, of the Royal Marines (presumably the officer mentioned by Flucker), late aide-de-camp to Earl Percy in America, states that having been wounded in the battle of Bunker Hill, he was taken to Boston, and must have died in the street had not Dorcas Griffith and her daughter taken him into their house. To their humanity he owed his life. (A.O. 13/73.)

Sarah Hinson wrote to one Roberts from Chelsea, January 18, 1784, appealing for support in her extreme poverty and that of her mother. (A.O. 13/44.)

EZEKIEL HALL

was a man of handsome fortune, and in 1786 was in reduced circumstances at Boston, Massachusetts, from his decisive defence of Great Britain. (A.O. 13/95.)

JAMES HALL

served as an officer in the Royal Navy in the Seven Years War, and at the peace of 1763 appears to have settled as a master mariner at Boston. He was master of the ship *Francis*, part owned by Francis Rotch (*q.v*), which carried a cargo of the celebrated tea from London to Boston in July, 1774, when the mob entered the ship and plundered or destroyed everything on board. The *Francis*, then a British transport, was wrecked in March, 1779, off the Isle of Wight on a passage from Ireland to London, and he and his wife narrowly escaped death by drowning. During the war James Hall served as master in the *Ardent*, of the Royal Navy, which was captured by the combined fleets of America and France in 1779.

Afterwards he was master of H.M.S. *Defence*, of 64 guns, and died as such at Portsmouth, England, in November, 1781. (A.O. 13/46.) His widow, Martha Hall, claimed £599, and was allowed £220. (A.O. 12/109.)

THOMAS HALL

is described as late of Billericay, and was presumably a loyalist. His widow was granted permission by the General Court, November 2, 1785, to sell her dower and buy estate. (A.O. 12/82.)

BENJAMIN HALLOWELL (Plate xxvii)

was appointed in March, 1764, Comptroller of the Port of Boston. In the riots on the passing of the Stamp Act he suffered from the fury of the populace and his newly-built house was damaged within and without, and part of his furniture destroyed.* The compensation offered by the House of Assembly was inadequate, owing to political opposition and prejudice, to cover the damages sustained. During nearly two years' absence in England his wife and children suffered repeated insults and abuses, and his daughter was in consequence deprived of her reason and died at the age of 15. He returned from England in September, 1770, as a Commissioner of Customs. With his memorial is a schedule of the lots of land granted on the Kennebec River by the Kennebec Company to his father, with the value thereof. There is also an inventory of the furniture left in his house in Boston in 1776, including a fine painting and a number of family pictures. (A.O. 13/46.)

Among other documents are a conveyance to him, September 14, 1767, by Briggs Hallowell, merchant, Bombay Hook, on the Kennebec River, of the sloop *Oliver Cromwell*, which was burnt by Captain Mowat (*q.v*) in the destruction of Falmouth (Portland), Maine, in 1775; Walter Logan's affidavit to the purchase of property on Jamaica Plain for Mary, wife of Benjamin Hallowell, in 1773; a list of deeds of his property; an extract from the will of his father, Benjamin Hallowell, January 25, 1773, leaving ship and mast yards to him; a list of bonds due to him; extracts from letters of his agent, William Foster, concerning his property; and several letters relating to the Hallowell and Kennebec properties. There are also his letter of November 18, 1785, stating that the cost of building houses of brick and wood in Boston before the war was one-fifth less than houses entirely of wood; an affidavit of Samuel and Bemslie Peters, dated July 6, 1789, that according to many letters received from America the value of lands in four New England States had fallen in price since 1774 from £8 to £2 an acre, and that purchasers could not be found; and also a list of the names of persons who had demanded money to be paid out of his estate, by order of the State, November, 1779, with his remarks thereon. (*Ib.*) A list of claims against his estate is in A.O. 12/81, ff. 95-7.

* See *Proc. of Mass. Hist. Soc.*, 2nd Ser., xvi, 110, *f.n.*

Benjamin Hallowell

PLATE XXVII

PLATE XXVIII

Robert Hallowell

In his interesting letter on conditions in Boston, dated September 5, 1774, he says that the passing of the Quebec Act* had had an amazing effect among the people by increasing their clamour and opposition to the mother country. (C.O. 5/175, f. 10.)

He was allowed £6,011 from his claim of £7,782, and was granted compensation at the rate of £500 a year for the loss of his official income during the war. He received a pension of £200 until his death. (A.O. 12/109; A.O. 459/7; A.O. 461/15–16; T. 50/9.)

His descendants recovered his confiscated estate by a law suit (Drake, *Roxbury*, p. 497; Drake, *Boston*, p. 686; *New England Hist. and Gen. Reg.*, xii, 72).

His brother was Robert Hallowell (*q.v.*). His eldest son was Nicholas Ward Boylston (*q.v.*) and another son became Admiral Sir Benjamin Hallowell Carew, Royal Navy.

Benjamin Hallowell died at Toronto, Canada, in 1799 (Stark, *op. cit.*, pp. 281–2).

His portrait is in the possession of Henry G. Vaughan, Esq., M.F.H., Norfolk Hunt, Hallowell, Maine.

REBECCA HALLOWELL

widow of Benjamin Hallowell, of Boston, and mother of Benjamin and Robert Hallowell (*q.v.*). In her memorial, dated London, March 13, 1784, she says that she left Boston at the evacuation by the British troops and was now aged nearly 86. Her mansion house in Boston was let to Samuel Adams by the State of Massachusetts immediately after her departure in March, 1776, and was occupied by him until August, 1784, when he left it in a ruinous condition. It was afterwards let to Joseph Coolidge. According to an extract from the will of her husband, dated January 25, 1773, he left property to his daughter, Rebecca, wife of Captain Thomas Bishop, who died childless; to his son, Samuel, since dead; to his sons, Benjamin and Robert; to his daughter, Sarah, wife of Samuel Vaughan;† and to Ann, wife of Captain Paston Gould. (A.O. 13/46.)

Her claim of £1,763 was disallowed. (A.O. 12/109; A.O. 12/105, f. 105.)

ROBERT HALLOWELL (Plate xxviii)

was appointed in June, 1768, deputy Comptroller of the Port of Boston under his brother Benjamin (*q.v.*), who was then Comptroller, and who was obliged by the insurrectionists to leave. In 1770 he received the

---

* The Quebec Act of 1774, an important measure in the history of religious liberty, excited great indignation among the Puritans of New England and the Whigs in England, as the Roman Catholic religion, the faith of the great majority of the inhabitants of Canada, was virtually established by this measure. (Lecky, *Hist. of Eng. in the Eighteenth Century*, iii, 399.)

† Samuel and Sarah Vaughan were the parents of William Vaughan, merchant and author. (*Dict. of Nat. Biog.*)

appointment of Collector of Customs at Piscataqua and later in the same
year that of Comptroller at Boston. During all the scenes of anarchy
and confusion prevailing in Boston he persevered in executing his official
duties with unshaken fidelity, often at the risk of his life. In consequence
of the Boston Port Act he removed in June, 1774, with other Customs
officials, to Plymouth, a small fishing town, and continued there in a very
disagreeable state until April, 1775, the date of the battle of Lexington,
when he fled to Boston, leaving all his papers and effects behind. (A.O.
13/46.)

With his memorials is an account of money received by Robert
Hallowell from seizures between 1771 and 1773 ; and his letter, dated
April 26, 1787, requesting leave to sail for Boston to settle the affairs of his
father-in-law, Dr. Sylvester Gardiner (*q.v.*), and to preserve the remaining
part of his brother's property. He had returned before December 8, 1788,
the date of another letter of no interest. (*Ib.* and A.O. 13/85.)

Robert Hallowell claimed £886 10s. and was allowed £450. He
was granted compensation at the rate of £450 a year for the loss of his
official income during the war and a pension of £220 until his death.
(A.O. 12/109 ; A.O. 12/105, f. 36 ; A.O. 459/7 ; T. 50/6 ; T. 50/45.)
A list of claims against his estate is in A.O. 12/81, f. 98. He died at
Gardiner, in Maine, in April, 1818. (Stark, *op. cit.*, p. 281.)

His portrait by Gilbert Stuart is in the possession of Robert H.
Gardiner, Esq., of Gardiner, Maine.

Reference : *Loyalists' Claims, op. cit.*, p. 232.

RICHARD ACKLOM HARRISON

succeeded his father [Joseph Harrison] as Collector of Customs at Boston
in June, 1773. He " found it necessary as an executive officer to act with
the utmost caution and delicacy to avoid furnishing the leaders of opposition with any just pretence for impeding the collection of the revenue and
the due execution of the laws of trade, yet notwithstanding all this cir-
cumspection he often found himself in the most embarassed & perilous
situation & sometimes his life in imminent danger . . ." He left
Boston for England in 1774. His father as Collector, assisted by this son,
his deputy, seized in June, 1768, John Hancock's sloop, *Liberty*, and this
son was knocked down and dragged along the street by the hair of his head
and otherwise ill-treated.* Among his losses was his library of 700 volumes
and an astronomical quadrant which had belonged to the great astronomer,
Halley, who had made many of his observations by it. (A.O. 13/46 ;
A.O. 12/105, f. 131.)

A contemporary account of the outrage by the mob on Benjamin
Hallowell, Comptroller of Customs, Joseph Harrison, Collector, Richard
Acklom Harrison, son of the Collector, and Thomas Irving, Inspector of

* For the assault upon him in 1768 see the *Acts of the Privy Council, Colonial*,
printed 1912, v, 246–265 ; and Stark, *op. cit.*, pp. 319–321.

Customs, for seizing the sloop *Liberty* in 1768, when the red flag was hoisted at the Liberty pole by the Sons of Liberty on June 14, is in T. 1/465, together with several documents and copies of papers relating to this affair and to conditions in Boston.

On April 21, 1775, he dined in London with Governor Hutchinson, who says in his diary that he thinks that Harrison's father had been private secretary to Lord Rockingham, presumably before his Custom's appointment in America. He appears to have been appointed Collector of Customs at Hull about 1783.

Richard Acklom Harrison claimed £1,887 and was allowed £350. For the loss of his official income during the war he claimed £1,240 and was allowed at the rate of £1,100 per annum. He was granted a pension of £361 until his death in November, 1813. (A.O. 12/109; A.O. 459/7; T. 50/44.) Administration of his goods was granted to his sister, Elizabeth Harrison, spinster and only next of kin, December 4, 1813. He is described as a bachelor, late of Kingston-upon-Hull.

LIEUTENANT WILLIAM HASWELL

was for thirty-four years in His Majesty's service, and for twenty-seven years was a Lieutenant in the Royal Navy. From 1765 he resided at Nantasket. He was taken prisoner with his wife, a son and daughter, on October 28, 1775, and removed to Hingham. Although confined in the town of Hingham he succeeded in giving intelligence to the Commander of the British fleet off Boston. When the fleet and transports had left Boston at the evacuation, he heard on March 26, 1776, that the Americans had planned to send down five fire rafts to destroy the whole British fleet in Nantasket Road, and he sent Joseph Jones, a fisherman, of Hingham, with a warning to the British officers, and he verily believes that this intelligence saved the fleet and transports from destruction. During his imprisonment in Hingham he received many lucrative offers from Congress to command an American fleet, but as a loyalist he rejected such offers. He was a prisoner in this town for two years and at Abington for six months (A.O. 13/46.)

With the above memorial are an account of his property lost in consequence of his loyalty, including land at Falmouth, Maine, inherited by his wife, Rachel Woodward, from her father and grandfather, Ebenezer and Smith Woodward; many papers relating to his property and certificates to his loyalty; and a certificate from Samuel Thaxter and others, of Boston, dated April 26, 1787, confirming his statements regarding his imprisonment, and adding that he was sent to Halifax, Nova Scotia, and there exchanged for one Philip Duval, or Deval, captain of the American privateer, *Rattlesnake*. On his property at Nantasket, a fortification was erected upon a hill by order of Congress.

William Haswell confirmed the above statements in his memorial, before the Commissioners on February 10, 1786. Here, however, 1763 is the date given of his settlement at Nantasket. (A.O. 12/101, f. 298.)

By order in Council he was one of the Lieutenants superannuated. His allowance of £50 was, nevertheless, continued. (A.O. 13/85.) He claimed £2,037 and was allowed £430, less £4 10s. for pension. (A.O. 12/109.) A pension of £40 was granted to him from 1784 until his death in 1805. (T. 50/8 ; A.O. 462/20.)

Administration of his estate was made July 12, 1805, by his widow, Rachel. He is described as late of Newport in the county of York (England) and a superannuated Captain on half-pay in the Royal Navy.

Early in 1776 he and his family were ordered from Hingham (whither he had removed from Nantasket) into a town away from the coast, as his presence in a place bordering on Boston harbour might be dangerous and might enable him to correspond with officers of the Royal Navy. (Force, *Am. Archives*, Ser. IV, Vol. IV, p. 1282.)

CAPTAIN HAWES HATCH

was born about 1750, and served seven years in the Provincial forces in the war. In December, 1782, he was promoted Captain in the Prince of Wales's American Volunteers, having been transferred from De Lancey's Brigade, and was on half-pay until 1804. (Ind. 5605–6.)

He was a brother of Captain Christopher Hatch. He died at Lebanon, New Hampshire, in 1807. (Sabine, *op. cit.*)

NATHANIEL HATCH

of Dorchester, a member of his Majesty's Council for the province ; a Justice of the Peace ; Colonel of Militia ; Judge of the Court of Common Pleas for Suffolk County ; Clerk of the Superior Court ; and Deputy Judge of the Vice-Admiralty Court. He claims to have been the only magistrate who attended and protected one of the consignees of the celebrated tea from violence until the mob had dispersed. He had two pews, one in Trinity Church in Boston and the other in Dorchester Meeting House. With his memorials is a schedule of his property, and a letter, dated October 18, 1783, regarding his property at Belchertown, ten miles from Hadley in Connecticut. (A.O. 13/46.)

His widow, Elizabeth, in an undated memorial, states that her husband had ended his life by his own hands, apparently on July 10, 1784, from dejection of spirits and his losses by the Revolution. She mentions her daughters, Jane, Mary and Susannah. (*Ibid.*) On July 22, 1784, John Nichols, in evidence in her behalf, stated that she was destitute of the means of support and confirmed her account of the suicide of her husband. She was granted £100 per annum. (A.O. 12/101, f. 7.) Dr. Peter Oliver records that Colonel Hatch cut his throat at Pangbourne, near Reading, in England, soon after a cheerful dinner (in Governor Hutchinson's *Diary*, ii, 409.)

There is a list of claims against his estate in A.O. 12/81, ff. 99–100, and he is mentioned in A.O. 12/105, f. 132. His widow claimed £2,605 and was allowed £1,400 (A.O. 12/109), and was granted a pension of £100 until 1805. (A.O. 462/20; T. 50/8.)

His son was Paxton Hatch (*q.v.*).

Nathaniel Hatch, who was the son of Colonel Estes Hatch, one of the heroes of the Louisburg expedition, graduated at Harvard College in 1742. (Stark, *op. cit.*, pp. 429–30.)

PAXTON HATCH

son of Nathaniel Hatch (*q.v.*), was sent to Philadelphia College for his education in 1772, and was there at the outbreak of the war. He was frequently urged to join the American army, and with most of his companions in the College was promised promotion. For his refusal to forsake his loyalty he suffered great reproaches and insults, and his supplies and the common necessaries of life were cut off. At length, and with much difficulty, he obtained leave to go to Boston, and thence to England. He was granted a pension of £80. (A.O. 13/46; A.O. 12/105, f. 116.)

According to the College records he entered in May, 1775, and was of the class of 1780.

JOSIAH HENEY

of Penobscot, bore arms, and was settled as a carpenter at Halifax, Nova Scotia, in 1785. (A.O. 13/26.)

JOHN HICKS

printer and part owner, with Nathaniel Mills (*q.v.*), of the *Massachusetts Gazette and Post-Boy*. (A.O. 13/96.)

JOHN HILDING

was formerly a private in the 42nd Foot, whose discharge from the army was purchased by his wife, Jane, a Scotswoman, widow of James McDonald, soldier in the 42nd Foot. He settled in Boston about 1766 as a shoemaker and publican. He joined Burgoyne's army at Stillwater, in Colonel Skene's company, and was taken prisoner. He was sent on the prison ship in Boston harbour for refusing to take up arms for America. In an attempt, nine weeks later, to capture this ship, John Hilding and his accomplices, one Armstrong, John Irwin and James Jackson, were discovered and executed. Mrs. Katherine McGennis, in a certificate, states that she was a witness of the execution of Hilding in Boston. Jane Hilding afterwards went to New York, and there built a house in Broadway. She was in London in 1788, when she wrote the memorials from which the above account is taken. She was granted a pension of £20 from 1788. (A.O. 13/46; A.O. 13/100; A.O. 12/102, f. 140.)

JOHN HILL

With his memorials of 1789 and 1790 are certificates to his loyalty
from Governor Franklin of New Jersey. (A.O. 13/46.)

THOMAS HILL

claimed £56 and was allowed £20. (A.O. 12/109.)

WILLIAM HILL

was born at Boston, and was a baker there. He offered his free services
as baker for the garrison, and acted as such for the 14th Regiment. At
the trial of Captain Preston in 1774 he was chosen a juryman, and thereafter incurred the resentment of the people ; was threatened with death,
frequently insulted, and his house tarred. (A.O. 13/50 ; A.O. 12/10,
ff. 34–5.) Strong certificates to his character and loyalty were given
him by General Leslie and others. He was granted a pension of £25.
(A.O. 12/102, f. 160.) His claim for furniture at Boston was withdrawn,
as his house was in possession of his mother. (A.O. 12/61, f. 6.) He
claimed £300, and was allowed £150. (A.O. 12/109.) He sought
refuge at Shelburne, Nova Scotia, and was coroner there. (A.O. 13/46.)

References : Sabine, *op. cit.,* ; *Ontario Archives, op. cit.,* p. 495.

JOHN HILT

was born in Boston, the son and heir of John Hilt, a volunteer in the
French War. He left America " twenty-one years ago " (evidently before
the Revolution). His undated memorial is endorsed : " Very impertinent
Gentleman." (A.O. 13/46.)

RICHARD HOLLAND

was born in America about 1742, and in May or June, 1783, was
married at Hampstead, New York, to Jane Bailey, spinster, of Jamaica,
New York. He appears to have died at Jamaica, having been a half-pay
officer of the Loyal New Englanders. (W.O. 42/H20 ; Ind. 5605.)

This loyalist was appointed in 1771 instructor to the tribe of
" Churches Indians," at Wottuppa in Freetown, Bristol County, and held
that office until September 1, 1776. Previously he had been a schoolmaster in Boston under the Society for the Propagation of the Gospel.
In May, 1778, he acted as guide with the 22nd Regiment through the
towns of Bristol and Warren, Rhode Island, and in the same month he
was a guide on an expedition to the Fall River, Freetown, under Major
Edmond Eyre, of the 54th Regiment. (A.O. 13/50.)

The above memorial is dated St. John, New Brunswick, February 6,
1786. According to Sabine, he was a grantee of St. John, and settled

on the coast at Dipper Harbour, where he was alive in 1843. This latter statement is in conflict with the above official note on the date of his birth. Sabine also states that his father-in-law was Josiah Dean, of Taunton, Massachusetts, who died there in 1773, intestate.

The commissions of Richard Holland in loyalist regiments are as follows : Lieutenant, Loyal New Englanders, June 1, 1777 ; Ensign, Queen's Rangers, February, 1779 ; and Lieutenant, Queen's Rangers, August, 1780. One Joseph N. or W. Holland was enlisted by him as a volunteer in the Loyal New Englanders, and was doubtless a family connection.

BENJAMIN MULBERRY HOLMES

His original commission, dated June 1, 1775, from General Gage, as Captain (with the rank of Major) of a company of foot to do duty at the North Battery, Boston, belonging to the militia regiment of Colonel John Erving, junior, and his original appointment by General Howe as a fire-ward, November 14, 1775, are in C.O. 5/754. There is a list of claims against his estate in A.O. 12/81, ff. 112-3. He is in A.O. 12/10, ff. 296–300, and *Ontario Archives, op. cit.*, p. 154.

JOSEPH HOOPER

son of Robert Hooper, one of the Mandamus Councillors, a manufacturer of cordage and a merchant in Marblehead, distinguished himself early in the Revolution as a loyalist by drawing up and procuring the signatures of the most respectable inhabitants of Marblehead to a protest against the proceedings of the disaffected, which was the first protest ever published in America. He exerted himself by every means in his power in support of the Crown. When a detachment of the 64th Foot was stationed at Marblehead to execute the Boston Port Bill he was active in procuring quarters for the troops. Three attempts were made to burn his house after the withdrawal of these troops. He claims to have been the only person in Marblehead who did not in some measure comply with the dictates of the disaffected. Death was the probable consequence of his refusal to sign the public recantation within a few days, but fortunately his father had a ship ready to sail for Spain, and in order to preserve his allegiance to the Crown inviolate, he seized the opportunity to join this vessel, leaving a wife (within one month of child-birth) and two children, who were soon afterwards turned out of his house and property, and were obliged to seek shelter with her mother at Newburyport. Joseph Hooper's elegant mansion house was built by him only eighteen months before his flight from home, and contained a library of about 500 volumes, more than 350 ounces of silver plate, and a quantity of wines and liquors. By the death of his wife's parents at Newburyport he became possessed of her father's estate there, she being the only child. (A.O. 13/46.)

With this long memorial is a schedule of his property and some letters. According to one letter, dated March 9, 1789, he had started a paper mill at Bungay in Suffolk, which was now completely finished, but he was unable to proceed further from want of capital. It would seem from other letters that his father had succeeded in recovering his (Joseph Hooper's) property at Marblehead.

He claimed £9,160, and was allowed £2,302. (A.O. 12/109.) He was arrested for debt in 1786, and was obliged to assign a part of his loyalist's pension in payment. (A.O. 12/105, f. 133; A.O. 13/137.)

Joseph Hooper was the son of Robert Hooper, popularly known as "King Hooper," from his wealth and hospitality, and graduated at Harvard College in 1763. He married in 1766, Mary, daughter of Benjamin and Lucy Harris, of Newburyport. The address from the inhabitants of Marblehead to Governor Hutchinson in 1774 was signed by five members of the Hooper family. (Stark, *op. cit.*, pp. 223–4.) This loyalist died at the age of sixty-nine, at Bungay, and was buried at Holy Trinity Church, August 31, 1812.

References: *Ontario Archives, op. cit.*, pp. 1146–9; *Loyalists' Claims, op. cit.*, pp. 69–70.

MARTIN HOWARD (Plate XXIX)

Chief Justice of North Carolina. His mutilated letter from New York to Charles Mellish, September 12, 1777, concerning his affairs is in A.O. 13/41. He died November 24, 1781, and his loyalist pension was continued to his widow, Abigail. (T. 50/7; A.O. 461/16; A.O. 461/17; C.O. 5/176, f. 15.)

In her letter, dated from Boston, Massachusetts, January 18, 1785, his daughter, Anne Howard (by his first wife), states that she had failed to recover any of her father's property there. (A.O. 13/46.) Mr. Inman gave evidence for her on May 13, 1785, and stated that she had gone to Boston in June, 1783, in the hope of recovering her father's property. She had failed to get a farthing's worth of it in January, 1785, the date of her letter to Inman. (A.O. 12/101, f. 209.)

The memorial of Mrs. and Miss Howard shows that they had lost property in America valued at £3,329 8s. 6d. (A.O. 13/96.) Their petition of December 13, 1788, praying for the continuance of their loyalist pension of £50, is in A.O. 13/120.

One writer says of him that he had no superior, if an equal, in the Colonial judiciary of North Carolina. Most historians have dealt unjustly with his memory. Although a loyalist, he seems to have acted from conscientious motives, and was highly respected by the legal profession, including those of the opposite political faith.*

There is a long account of him in the *Publications of the Colonial Soc. of Mass.*, vi, 384–402. His second wife, Abigail, was the daughter of

* Marshall De L. Haywood, *Gov. William Tryon and his Administration in N. Carolina*, 1903, pp. 49–50, 96, 99.

Stephen Greenleaf, and died in 1801 ; her sister, Anstis, was the wife of Benjamin Davis (*q.v.*). He died in Chelsea (London), and was buried at St. Luke's Church. His daughter, Anne, married Andrew Spooner (*q.v.*).

Chief Justice Howard's portrait, by Copley, hangs in the Social Law Library at Boston.

HENRY HOWE

was born in and lived at Weston as a farmer. After refusing to join the American forces, and having been threatened with death, he escaped from home and eventually reached New York. There he served on board privateers and later in armed boats. There are several certificates to his loyalty and services. (A.O. 13/46 ; A.O. 13/96.)

HENRY HULTON

was Plantation Clerk to the Commissioners of the Board of Customs in London until 1767, when he was appointed one of the Commissioners of Customs in America. He also held the appointment of Principal Receiver of the Rents for Greenwich Hospital, in America. His home was at Brookline, near Boston. With his memorial are many papers relating to his property and his claims for compensation. (A.O. 13/46.) He claimed £1,820, and was allowed £1,550. His claim for the loss of his official income during the war was allowed at the rate of £500 a year (A.O. 12/109), and a pension was granted to him until his death. (A.O. 459/7 ; T. 50/9.) A list of claims against his estate is in A.O. 12/81, ff. 92-3. Other references to him are in A.O. 12/99, f. 261 ; A.O. 13/85, and A.O. 12/82.

Henry Hulton was the son of John Hulton, of Chester, and according to the inscription on his monument in the Church at Andover, in Hampshire, he was married [September 20, 1766, at St. Anne's, Soho] to Elizabeth, eldest daughter of Isaac Preston, of Beeston St. Lawrence, in Norfolk, and died February 14, 1791, aged 59 ; his wife died April 16, 1805. His eldest son, Thomas, who appears to have been born in America, was created a baronet in 1815 and took the maternal name of Preston.

His maiden sister, Ann Hulton, lived with him in America until 1775, and her letters written during her life there are of great interest. (*Letters of a Loyalist Lady*, 1927.)

SAMUEL HUNT

emigrated from Woolwich, the place of his nativity, to America during the war with the French, and settled and married in Boston. Afterwards he lived for seven years at Plymouth until 1773, when he was appointed a tidesman in the Custom House. He took the oath of allegiance to the State of Massachusetts. Having spent all his money, and being anxious

to get away, he went on board a rebel vessel, in the hope that this vessel
might be captured by the British, which accordingly happened in October,
1781, and he returned to Woolwich, where he worked as a labourer in the
" Royal Laboratory."   Confirmation of his loyalty is taken from the
order of the Committee of Correspondence of Plymouth to Thomas
Mayhew, justice of the peace, February 11, 1778, that Samuel Hunt and
others (named) were suspected of being inimical to the United States,
and requesting him, in accordance with the Act for prescribing and establishing an oath of fidelity and allegiance, to proceed immediately against
those loyalists.   The Commissioners refused Hunt compensation or a
loyalist allowance because he had taken the highly improper course of
taking the oath to the Americans without any necessity, but on the
testimony of Hallowell that he was a good Customs officer and a man of
good character, he was granted £10 to go to America, May 26, 1783.
(A.O. 13/46 ; A.O. 12/99, f. 255.)

WILLIAM HUNTER

was a Scotsman who settled in Boston in 1767 as an auctioneer.   Early in
the Rebellion he became exceedingly obnoxious to the revolutionary party
as a loyalist.   He was one of the Loyal North British Volunteers in Boston
before the evacuation of the town by the British.   From Boston he went
to Halifax and thence to New York, where he fitted out a vessel with a
cargo of provisions and liquors bound for the Chesapeake with the object
of supplying the British army.   On the voyage from New York to Quebec
he had the misfortune to be captured by an American privateer, and his
property, worth £1,200 sterling, taken.   This Scotsman subsequently
served as a lieutenant in a privateer, which foundered at sea and all on
board perished.   His widow, Dunbar Hunter, was granted £20 to enable
her to return to her native country, Scotland, and from 1786 a pension
of £20.   (A.O. 13/46 ; A.O. 13/137 ; A.O. 12/100, f. 57 ; A.O. 12/101,
f. 365.)   Her claim of £1,219 was disallowed.   (A.O. 12/109.)

MATTHEW HUTCHINS

was born in London and educated at Christ's Hospital.   In 1762 he was
apprenticed to George Erving (q.v.), of Boston.   He left that place with
the British troops in March, 1776, for Nova Scotia, and in 1786 he was
engaged in a public office at Shelburne.   (A.O. 13/50 ; A/O 13/96 ; A.O.
12/10, ff. 85-8 ; A.O. 12/105, f. 68.)   He was compensated £80 from his
claim of £150.   (A.O. 12/109.)
    This loyalist was the son of William and Elizabeth Hutchins and was
admitted to Christ's Hospital * in 1747 from the parish of St. Anne, Westminster.   He was discharged October 19, 1762, and was bound to serve
George Erving for seven years.   (Ex inform. Mr. William Lempriere,

* Christ's Hospital, a famous educational and charitable foundation, dating from
1552, originally in the City of London and now at Horsham

deputy clerk of Christ's Hospital.) In 1770 he married Dorcas Harris at Boston.

ELIAKIM HUTCHINSON

was a Judge of the Court of Common Pleas and a Mandamus Councillor, and died in the winter of 1775, leaving a widow, Elizabeth Hutchinson (*q.v.*), and a son, William (*q.v.*). He had graduated at Harvard College in 1730 and was a warden of King's Chapel, Boston, in 1743.

The documents (A.O. 13/46) relating to this loyalist are as follows :—

An inventory of his personal property, which includes 534 ounces of wrought silver plate and other objects, denoting luxury and prosperity; and a list of household goods sold by his widow at Halifax, Nova Scotia, May 30, 1776.

A paper showing that his wife, Elizabeth, was the daughter of William Shirley, Governor of Massachusetts, and that at the time of his death he left issue : Elizabeth (died in 1782), who married the Rev. East Apthorp, sometime Rector of Christ Church, Cambridge, Massachusetts, and afterwards Vicar of Croydon, near London (the burial-place of Governor Hutchinson) ; a son, William (*q.v.*) ; Frances, a spinster ; and Catherine, a spinster, who died in London in 1777. There is also a list of the names of seven children of the Rev. East Apthorp—Frances, Grizzel, Elizabeth, Anne, Harriet, Frederick and Susannah.

A great number of documents relating to Eliakim Hutchinson's estate.

There is a list of claims against his estate in A.O. 12/81, ff. 86-8, and another reference in A.O. 12/105, f. 134.

In A.O. 13/94 is a copy of the probate of the will of William Hutchinson, dated December 23, 1721 ; and papers relating to his estate. His wife, Elizabeth, is mentioned. She was the daughter of Thomas Brinley. (Stark, *op. cit.*, p. 396.)

ELIZABETH HUTCHINSON

was the widow of Eliakim Hutchinson (*q.v.*) and was a refugee in England. With her son, William (*q.v.*), she claimed £12,120 and was allowed £5,609. (A.O. 12/109.) According to a memorial of her daughter, Frances Hutchinson, dated March 24, 1790, she had died a few days previously.

ELISHA HUTCHINSON

son of Governor Hutchinson (*q.v.*), was granted compensation with his brother, Thomas, to the amount of £2,575 (A.O. 12/109), and received a loyalist pension of £150 (reduced later to £100) until April, 1824. (A.O. 12/105, f. 69 ; T. 50/6 ; T. 50/27.) A list of claims against his estate is in A.O. 12/81, f. 94.

The most interesting paper of this loyalist is the manuscript diary of his life in England as a refugee from June, 1774, to 1782 (British Museum,

Egerton MSS. 2669). Portions of the diary have been published with that of his father, but much of interest has been left out.

Elisha Hutchinson graduated at Harvard College in 1762, and with his brother, Thomas, was one of the consignees of the famous tea in 1773. He accompanied his father to England in 1774 and died there at Tutbury in 1824. His wife, Mary, was the daugher of Colonel George Watson, of Plymouth, Massachusetts, and died at Birmingham in 1803. (Sabine, *op. cit.* ; Stark, *op. cit.*, p. 177 ; *Loyalists' Claims, op. cit.*, p. 19.)

It was to this loyalist that Peter Oliver, the younger (*q.v.*), addressed a letter from Boston, December 7, 1775, in which he says that " Your wife [Mary] braves it out : by the last accounts from her in Sep.ᵗ she is President of a Club composed of 8 ladies. They meet over a tea table once or twice a week, in opposition to the Rebells. They keep up their spirits strangely. . . ." (Published in *Diary* of Governor Hutchinson, i, 581.)

FOSTER HUTCHINSON

He declares that he never disguised his political principles and nevertheless he was happy in possessing the confidence and esteem of the major part of the people who differed politically from him. He was a Judge of the Supreme Court of Massachusetts and Judge of Probate for the County of Suffolk. In July, 1774, when almost every person refused to accommodate them, he surrendered a store for the use of British soldiers as barracks. He accepted the appointment of mandamus councillor, though conscious he would forfeit esteem and render himself obnoxious. With his memorials are a schedule of his property and a statement of claim. Accompanied by his wife and nine children, eight of whom were females, he sailed with the British army for Halifax in March, 1776. (A.O. 13/50 ; A.O. 13/96 ; A.O. 13/137 ; A.O. 12/10, ff. 148-155 ; A.O. 12/105, f. 37.)

He was allowed compensation, £510, from his claim of £784 2s. (A.O. 12/109), and was granted a pension until his death (A.O. 459/7 ; A.O. 461/16 ; T. 50/6 ; T. 50/11.) A number of claims was made against his estate. (A.O. 12/81, f. 91.)

This loyalist graduated at Harvard College in 1743 and was a brother of Governor Hutchinson. He died, April 8, 1799, at Halifax, Nova Scotia, where his son of the same name was a Judge of the Supreme Court (*Ontario Archives, op. cit.*, pp. 97-8 ; Stark, *op. cit.*, pp. 177-8 ; *Proc. of Mass. Hist. Soc.*, 2nd Ser., xvi, 112-120.)

FRANCES HUTCHINSON

daughter of Eliakim and Elizabeth Hutchinson (*q.v.*), in a letter announced the death of her mother in March, 1790, and prayed for a continuance of her pension, which was granted as from 1789 (A.O. 13/46).

MATTHEW HUTCHINSON

was granted a loyalist pension of £24 from 1789 to 1803 (A.O. 461/19).

GOVERNOR THOMAS HUTCHINSON (Frontispiece)

There are no petitions or memorials of the Governor. In A.O. 13/46 there is a copy of his will and a schedule of his property, with a list of bonds and notes of hand due to him and an inventory of his personal property at Milton.

He mentions in his diary (ii, 85) that his personal goods and those of his sons were divided between Dr. Cooper* and Mr. Lothrop,† the latter of whom lived in his house. Deborah Cushing, wife of Thomas Cushing, a member of the Continental Congress, was granted the use of the Governor's furniture at Milton, December 27, 1775. (Force, *Amer. Archives*, Ser. IV, Vol. IV, pp. 1244, 1360.)

Chief Justice Peter Oliver (*q.v.*) wrote to the Governor's son, Elisha, October 25, 1783, that he (the Governor) had sold his Conanicut lands in Rhode Island to Governor Whipple some years before and had bought them back again later. He had let the farms on these lands at rentals yielding 3 per cent. (A.O. 13/79.)

His original will is in London (Somerset House : Collins 319). He left his estate to his sons, Thomas and Elisha, and his daughter, Sarah, wife of Peter Oliver (*q.v.*).

An affidavit of Henry Ward, Secretary of State of Rhode Island, certifies that the Governor's confiscated farm, of over 640 acres, in Jamestown, valued at 38 dollars an acre, lawful silver money, had been assigned by the General Assembly in May, 1781, as part payment of the arrears of pay due to the officers and men of Colonel Angell's Regiment. (A.O. 13/46.) Among the Colonial Records of Rhode Island is a volume entitled " Israel Angell, 1740-1832, Colonel of the 2nd Rhode Island Regiment," which contains letters of Colonel Angell concerning the lands set off for the Regiment. There are several references in these records to the confiscated property of Governor Hutchinson in the vicinity of Jamestown.‡

There are copies of the Governor's letters in C.O. 5/246. In one, dated Boston, January 22, 1771, on the political disorders in the Colonies, he declares that every Act of Parliament carried into execution in the Colonies had tended to strengthen Government. A firm persuasion that Parliament is determined to maintain its supreme authority is all that is needed. As a measure of discipline, kept as a rod over them and as security for good behaviour, he suggests that Maine and the country east of it, might be made into a separate province ; New Hampshire to be annexed to Massachusetts, or separate the country east of Penobscot and annex it to Nova Scotia.

In a letter dated August, 1771, he refers to the Otis-Robinson affair.

* The Rev. Dr. Samuel Cooper, of Boston.
† The Rev. John Lothrop.
‡ Ex inform. Mr. Herbert O. Brigham, State Record Commissioner.

In the last letter, dated July 3, 1773, he says that the Whig leaders in Boston have openly declared that they have taken no political step without advice and direction from England.

Two papers concerning his property are in A.O. 13/46. The first is a certificate, dated August 3, 1784, that the proceeds of the sale of his confiscated estates in Boston, Dorchester, Milton and Braintree, amounted to £5,563 10s. 2d., lawful money, and that the claims against his estate, allowed by the Judge of Probate, amounted to £1,046 4s 4d., lawful money, leaving a balance of £4,517 5s. 10d., lawful money, equal to £3,387 19s. 4d., sterling, which had been paid into the treasury of the Commonwealth.

The second is a letter from his son, Thomas, dated August 2, 1788, regarding claims of £1,046 4s. 4d. against the Governor's estate, in which he states that he verily believes they are fraudulent, for the reason that on the Governor's departure from Massachusetts, he made him his attorney and gave him a list of his debts, which he discharged. Although he remained for 18 months after his father, and although it was generally known that he was his attorney, yet no demand was ever made to him. At the most there could not be £20. due for trifling matters.

A list of claims against his estate is in A.O. 12/81, ff. 89-90.

During his exile in London, Governor Hutchinson wrote many letters of interest to the Earl of Hardwicke, his hospitable host on many occasions, and these are preserved in the British Museum. (Addl. MSS. 35427.)

The following summary has been made from the more interesting of these letters on American affairs :—

In a letter of November 2, 1774, he says that he had more than once resisted the demands of a mob and would have been tarred and feathered before he would have submitted to them, but in the case of the Councillors who have resigned they all lived in the country outside Boston, and they would have been obliged to quit their families and business, which would be too great a virtue in the present age. He refers in a letter of November 21 to the enthusiastic spirit spreading through Massachusetts for rebellion.

He says that one sensible gentleman wrote that the true reason why the people go to such lengths without terror is because never anything which has been threatened from England has yet been executed, and therefore they rely upon it that no other thing ever will be. (Letter, January 5, 1775.)

He had flattered himself that the Americans would not involve themselves in civil war, but he was now proved to be wrong in his conjectures. (June 14, 1775.)

The New Yorkers are laughing at Lord Chatham's plan and are ridiculing it in their newspapers. (June 17, 1775.)

Several New England families had arrived in London who could stand the siege of Boston no longer. Many more would have come if they could have brought anything with them for their support in England ; if they must starve, they say it is as well to starve at home as abroad. Among the refugees was Jonathan Sewall (*q.v.*), who had seen the whole of the action at Charlestown and thinks that 1,000 British troops were disabled before the entrenchment was forced and that less than 500 remained to drive more than 5,000 over Charlestown Neck.

One of the Commissioners of the Customs at Boston, who had formerly commanded a war vessel in the provincial service,* advised Admiral Shuldham to place his vessels otherwise than he did in the action at Charlestown, but he refused. The Commissioner proved to be right. The Admiral was mortified and came to blows with the Commissioner, who said that Shuldham drew his sword, which he took from him. (Letter of September 22, 1775.)

He refers to Lord Hardwicke's opinion, expressed last winter, that the Americans were more determined and would make a stronger resistance than was generally expected. The Governor says that whereas 10,000 troops would have suppressed the rebellion then, 30,000 would be required to effect it now. (Letter of October 18, 1775.)

Governor Hutchinson, in his letter of October 21, expresses the opinion that if the Americans took Canada, it may possibly be advisable to let the French King retake it and keep it, especially if he would exchange it for Guadaloupe.

He hopes that the Hessians would go up the Delaware River and humble the modern Babylon of Philadelphia, which Penn designed to resemble the ancient Babylon. The new Babylon, he thinks, will now share the fate of the old. (Letter of July 19, 1776.)

The war ought to be carried on without lenity. There was no way to conquer except by distressing the enemy, whether by white men or copper coloured, is immaterial. Carleton, British Commander-in-chief, restrains the Indians from attacking the frontier of New York and New England. If he (Carleton) imagines that men capable of such an unprovoked rebellion can be conquered by lenity and kindness, he (Hutchinson) will have no great opinion of his judgment. (Letter of September 26, 1776.)

In a letter of August 23, 1779, to Lord Hardwicke, he deplores the lack of the spirit of 1588 in England, when ships were fitted out by private persons and sent to join the Royal Navy and when men of rank and influence rode out along the sea coast, alarming the people and encouraging them to exertions. Now, there is an astonishing unconcernedness, which put him in mind of one of the characteristics of Englishmen, that they are more disposed to fight with each other in a civil war than to fight a foreign invader. Old as he is, he wishes he could be employed.

(See Hosmer's *Life of Governor Thomas Hutchinson*, 1896.)

THOMAS HUTCHINSON

eldest son of Governor Hutchinson (*q.v.*), was a Boston merchant and, with his brother Elisha (*q.v.*), was one of the consignees of the famous tea. In

---

* Benjamin Hallowell (*q.v.*) in early life had commanded an armed vessel and in the war with the French commanded the province twenty-gun ship, *King George*.

the joint memorial of these brothers they plead the many faithful services of their father and mention their own losses by the rebellion. With it are papers concerning the Hutchinson property. (A.O. 13/46.) Several letters written by him from Boston in 1774-5 to his brother, Elisha, in London are in the British Museum (Egerton MSS. 2559). In one of these, dated November 20, 1774, he appears to think that the people are determined to make a bold stand. Some other letters, regarding the tea, are with the same MSS.

In his memorial, dated from Orleans in France, July 28, 1787, he describes himself as the former Judge of the Common Pleas in the County of Suffolk, Massachusetts. (A.O. 13/46; A.O. 12/105, f. 37.)

He claimed £14,148 18s. and was allowed £6,025, less £65 for pension, and was compensated at the rate of £40 per annum for the loss of his official income during the war. (A.O. 12/109.) He was granted a pension until his death. (A.O. 459/7; T. 50/6; T. 50/11; T. 50/28; T. 50/43.) In his will he mentions his three sons, Thomas, Andrew, and the Rev. William Hutchinson. Thomas was admitted to the Middle Temple in 1792.*

This loyalist graduated at Harvard College in 1758. His wife, Sarah, was the daughter of Lieutenant Governor Andrew Oliver; she died in 1802. He died in 1811 and both were buried in Heavitree churchyard, Devonshire. (A.O. 12/105, f. 70; Stark, *op. cit.*, pp. 175-7; *Loyalists' Claims, op. cit.*, p. 9.)

WILLIAM HUTCHINSON

only surviving son of Eliakim and Elizabeth Hutchinson (*q.v.*), was appointed in 1767 a member of the Council and Receiver General and Treasurer for the Bahamas, and in 1775 a member of the Council for the Island of Dominica. On the voyage to Europe in 1776 his vessel was captured by an American privateer and he was detained a prisoner for ten months. Some time after his release he accompanied his maternal uncle, Major-General Thomas Shirley [son of William Shirley, Governor of Massachusetts], to the Leeward Islands and in 1781 he served as aide-de-camp, in the rank of Lieutenant-Colonel, and was present at the siege of Brimstone Hill,† in the Island of St. Christopher, until February 13, 1782. (A.O. 13/46.) With this petition is his memorial of November 19, 1778, and an order permitting him, as a prisoner of war, with a young lad, Thomas Shirley [probably his cousin], to proceed to Newport, Rhode Island, September 20, 1776. (A.O. 13/46.) There is also a long certificate of his uncle, the above General Shirley, Governor of the Leeward and Carribee Islands, stating, *inter alia*, that William Hutchinson had threatened Gould, Speaker of the House of Assembly of the Bahamas,

* E. Alfred Jones, *American Members of the Inns of Court*, 1924.

† The siege by the French of Brimstone Hill, St. Kitts, began in January, 1782, and General Fraser capitulated on February 12 following (Fortescue, *Hist. of the British Army*, iii, 407–8.)

for expressing himself in the highest terms of praise and approbation of the Americans in the Revolutionary war. This certificate is sealed with the Shirley arms : Paly of six or and azure a canton ermine. Crest— The head of a Saracen. Motto—Pro Rege & Republica. (A.O. 13/46.)

There is also an abstract of William Hutchinson's title to lands in Massachusetts, inherited from his great-grandfather, Richard Hutchinson, and his wife, Mary, and from his grandfather, Eliakim Hutchinson. This loyalist graduated at Harvard College in 1762.

References : A.O. 12/75, f. 29 ; A.O. 12/99, f. 282 ; C.O. 5/116, f. 237.

HENDERSON INCHES

was the owner of a rope walk and hemp house in Boston, of which possession was taken by the British troops. His widow, Elizabeth Inches, claimed compensation for this property in 1784. (A.O. 13/75.)

He was the son of Thomas Inches, a Scotsman, settled in Boston (Foote, *op. cit.*, ii, 119), and is mentioned in Rowe's Diary (*Proc. of Mass. Hist. Soc.*, 2nd Ser., Vol. X).

DAVID INGERSOLL

This loyalist was born September 26, 1742, and graduated at Yale College in 1761. At the conclusion of his studies in law he was admitted to the bar of Berkshire County, Massachusetts, in 1765, and settled at Great Barrington. Here he was in extensive practice, a justice of the peace, a member of the House of Representatives, and a captain of an independent company of militia with the rank of Major.

According to Thomas Flucker (*q.v.*), Ingersoll was at first a political follower of Adams and Otis, but that having been beaten in an electoral contest by one Roberts, a rebel, he changed his opinion and went over to the loyalists. Flucker seems to have entertained a grudge against Ingersoll, for he goes on to express surprise that he should receive so large an allowance as £200 a year when other loyalists with infinitely greater claims on the bounty of Government were granted only a half of that sum. Furthermore, Ingersoll had only come over to England for amusement, " to see old England and had at that time no idea of Boston being evacuated." (A.O. 12/105, ff. 136, 150.)

Another hostile witness was Pownall,* who hinted at some information he had received, and concluded with the expression, " It's well if he don't get hanged." Unfortunately, Pownall's evidence makes no explicit charge against Ingersoll (*Ib.*).

Whatever the opinion of Flucker and Pownall may have been, David Ingersoll had evinced his loyalty as early as 1774 by signing the address to Governor Hutchinson and was named in the Banishment Act of 1778.

* Presumably Thomas Pownall, formerly Governor of Massachusetts.

Another act in support of the Crown was in signing the loyal address to George III by loyalists of Massachusetts in 1779. (C.O. 5/7.) In his original memorial to the Earl of Dartmouth, dated February 7, 1775, he narrates in detail the attack on his house at Great Barrington in the early morning of August 2 previous, when he was compelled by the mob to endure the indignity of riding out fifteen miles to Canaan, where he was forced to sign a declaration under a "Liberty pole" (*Earl of Dartmouth MSS., op. cit.*, ii, 267), a violence which was in general condemned by the inhabitants in the county. (Force, *op. cit.*, i, 724–5.)

There are several letters regarding his losses in the Revolution in A.O. 13/47. His claim of £712 was disallowed. (A.O. 12/109.)

The Commissioners of American Claims were satisfied with Ingersoll's loyalty, despite the hostile evidence of Flucker and Pownall, and were particularly gratified by his act of loyalty to the throne of England by joining the English militia as lieutenant in the East Norfolk Militia, February 8, 1779,* and rising to the rank of Major at critical moments in the history of the country.

A witness to his loyalty was the Rev. Samuel Peters, the prominent Connecticut loyalist, who told the Commissioners that Ingersoll was very serviceable to the Church of England in Massachusetts in a dispute (not mentioned in detail) between that Church and the Dissenters (*i.e.*, the Congregationalists), and consequently he had many enemies among the " New England dissenters." The reverend gentleman mentioned that Ingersoll was known as a " forehanded " man in Massachusetts, *i.e.*, a rich man.

In 1783 and for several years afterwards he was residing at Thetford, where he was married in St. Cuthbert's Church on June 17, 1783, to Frances Rebecca Ryley of the parish of St. Peter in that borough.

He died November 10, 1796, at Hopton House, near Thetford, leaving a widow and three children.

In a letter from his friend, Gideon Bostwick, dated Great Barrington, January 12, 1784, giving news of Ingersoll's brothers and sisters, relations and former neighbours, including the truly loyal Major Stoddard,† of Pitts-field, mention is made that his (Ingersoll's) estate had not been confiscated, but it had been inventoried at about £800 and debts to £1,500. Although the Definitive Treaty of Peace had been known for some time in America it had not yet been published. Loyalists were thereby permitted to return to America, but so little was the Treaty regarded that insults and gross abuses had been inflicted upon those loyalists who had presumed to return. Ingersoll himself wrote to the Commissioners, from Thetford, March 6, 1787, stating that John Vandasen and Timothy Younglove, his former neighbours at Great Barrington, advanced him about £70 currency to enable him to go to England. He gave them his account books, bonds and notes, with a letter of attorney to collect all sums due to him and,

* At this date the militia was embodied in the regular army, but was disembodied shortly before 1783.

† Israel Stoddard (see Sabine, *op. cit.*).

Martin Howard

PLATE XXIX

PLATE XXX

John Joy

after reimbursing themselves, to remit the remainder to him, but he has never heard from them. The rogues appear to have imposed upon his estate, for he never owed £1,500. There are also other letters upon his affairs. (A.O. 13/74.)

References: Taylor, *Hist. of Great Barrington*, 1882, pp. 240, *et seq*. *Gent. Magazine*, vol. 66, p. 971 ; *Ipswich Journal*, November 19, 1796, and July 1, 1797. Ex inform. Mrs. O. W. Lane, of Great Barrington.

GEORGE INMAN

Contrary to the wishes of his father, Ralph Inman, he joined the British Army as a volunteer, and served as an officer during the Revolution in five campaigns. For two years before the peace he was employed on the recruiting service in England. In consequence of his perseverance in those constitutional principles of British liberty, which, in his opinion, were the most honourable and permanent security of American freedom, he was cut off from the kindred advantage of blood and from the inheritance of a fortune. (A.O. 13/37 ; A.O. 13/75.) According to a letter from his father, dated Cambridge, Massachusetts, June 30, 1783, he (the father) was severely punished for his son George's act in joining the British army, though it was done without his approbation at a time when his assistance and company would have been " a cordial " to him (the father). (A.O. 13/75.)

Sir William Pepperell stated that Ralph Inman was neutral in the rebellion and that George Inman was entitled to property in St. Eustatia in right of his wife.* (A.O. 12/99, f. 317.)

George Inman was born December 3, 1755, and entered Harvard College in 1768, taking the degree of B.A. in 1772. Upon taking his degree at Harvard, his father " made the genteelest entertainment " ever seen by John Rowe, the merchant, of Boston ; 347 ladies and gentlemen dined, and such an entertainment had not been made in New England before on any occasion. It was followed by a ball. (Rowe's Diary, in *Proc. of Mass. Hist. Soc.*, 2nd Ser., x, 43.) The Inman House at Cambridge is illustrated in Drake's *Hist. Mansions and Highways around Boston*, 1899. His commissions in the British army were as follows : Ensign in the 17th Foot, August 28, 1776 ; and Lieutenant in the 26th Foot, June 29, 1778 ; he died on military service in Grenada in 1789.

His interesting Journal, in the possession of the Cambridge (Massachusetts) Historical Society, contains a list of the engagements in which he served in the American War, beginning with Bunker Hill, including Brandywine and Germantown, and ending with the Battle of Monmouth, and the names of many loyalist refugees whom he met in England. The Journal has been published in the *Pennsylvania Mag. of Hist. & Biog.*, vii and xliv. (Ex inform. Mrs. Silvio Gozzaldi.)

* Mary, daughter of Bernard and Susannah (Riché) Badger, of Philadelphia.

M

JOHN INMAN

a clerk in the office of John Rowe, merchant, Boston, was granted a loyalist allowance of £100. (A.O. 13/47.) George Inman (*q.v.*) in his Journal, under date of September 17, 1783, states that John Inman had arrived in Boston the previous month, but was not suffered to land, and was sent off to Rhode Island. His loyalty was not suspect, but he did not appear to have exerted himself in the cause of government. (A.O. 12/105, f. 71.)

WILLIAM JACKSON

was born in Boston, and was a merchant there. He defied the Non-Importation agreement and openly imported goods, with the consequence that he incurred the hostility of the mob and the destruction of his property. At the evacuation of the town by the British he sailed to Nova Scotia, and on the passage he was captured by American privateers and taken to Portsmouth in New Hampshire, whence he was forced to walk to Boston in mud and mire up to his knees, suffering abuse and acts of inhumanity on the long journey. Having reached Boston he was cast into prison and detained 126 days. With his memorials is a certificate of Governor Hutchinson, testifying to Jackson's defiance of the Non-Importation agreement. (A.O. 13/47.) He had great property in land and personalty before the great fire of 1760 at Boston. Between that date and 1774 he had saved by industry and thrift about £6,000 sterling. Having sufficient to live upon he was refused an allowance. (A.O. 12/99, f. 309.) He was allowed £200 from his claim of £524. (A.O. 12/109.) A list of claims against his estate is in A.O. 12/81, f. 103. He died in England in 1810, aged 79. (Sabine, *op. cit.*)

Printed handbills were issued, desiring the Sons and Daughters of Liberty to refrain from buying anything from William Jackson, because of his audacious intention to continue the importation of British goods. (*Publications of the Colonial Soc. of Mass.*, viii, 99.) He was accused during the siege of Boston of misappropriating goods of Cyrus Baldwin, a patriot absentee. (*Proc. of Mass. Hist. Soc.*, 2nd Ser., xvi, 20.)

ROBERT JARVIS

was born in Boston and was in business there as a wine merchant. During the blockade he served in the Associated Loyalists by patrolling the streets and maintaining order at night. He left with the British troops at the evacuation of Boston, leaving his family behind. After suffering cruel usage and oppression his family were obliged to leave the town for New York. His eldest son, Philip, at the age of 20, was forced into the rebel service, but escaped at the first opportunity and got on board a vessel bound for France. This vessel was captured by a British cruiser and taken to the West Indies, where he was soon released and eventually got to England. Robert Jarvis then sent this son to New York to earn his own livelihood, but on the passage he was captured by the Americans and kept a prisoner for nine months in the Island of Guadaloupe. A younger son, born in 1764, was sent in 1778 to a merchant at Charlestown, South Carolina, who was murdered just before the evacuation of that place by the British, and the boy was obliged to join him in England. One Thomas Parker owed Robert Jarvis £100 and four years' interest on a bond, but absconded during the blockade of Boston, and Jarvis attached his estate as security. Parker returned later to Boston and sued Mrs. Jarvis for illegal attachment of his estate as security, and succeeded in obtaining a verdict for £160 damages and £20 for charges. With his memorial is a schedule of his property and two letters from Christopher Gore, of Boston, December 28, 1785, and May 26, 1787, referring to his unsuccessful attempts to obtain payment of the debts due to Jarvis, and stating that pleas were made to actions brought by loyalists for the recovery of debts that these debts were confiscated by the laws and were now the property of the commonwealth. The resolve, suspending payment of interest on debts due to loyalists, had been repealed, but little is to be expected from a jury who will decide the question of interest. The names of the debtors are given in Gore's second letter. In a letter from Jarvis to the Commissioners, dated September 24, 1787, he says that John Rowe,* of Boston, while pretending to be his great friend, took possession of his house in Purchase Street from Mrs. Jarvis by paying the money due on the Parker case, mentioned above, and offering to re-convey it to him (Jarvis) at the peace. In this letter he refers again to his property at length and includes a list of his debtors. According to a copy of a writ (here) to the sheriff of Suffolk County, Massachusetts, dated August 21, 1778, orders were given to arrest Robert Jarvis and commit him to gaol until he satisfied the debt incurred by him to John Rowe for the money paid for his own house. (A.O. 13/47; A.O. 13/74.) Jarvis signed the address to George III (see Appendix) and was allowed £45 from his claim of £780. (A.O. 12/109.) The Commissioners stated that he well deserved his allowance of £60. (A.O. 12/105, f. 135.) He died at Highgate, now a part of London, September 20, 1788, leaving a widow, Lydia, a son, Philip, and three other children. (A.O. 13/47.) His widow received a pension of £30 until 1799. (A.O. 461/16; T. 50/11.)

Reference: Sabine, *op. cit.*

DR. JOHN JEFFRIES

After taking his degrees at Harvard College [graduated in 1763] he applied himself to medical studies under an eminent physician, and went to England for a more complete course of medical knowledge. Having returned to Boston, he started practice as a physician and surgeon, and was employed not only in Boston but also in remote parts of Massachusetts

* The great merchant, whose diary is mentioned on page 177.

in extraordinary cases of surgery for nine years before the war. In May, 1774, he was appointed physician and surgeon to the Almshouse in Boston, improved as a town and provincial hospital. In the summer of 1775 the Governors of this Hospital were moving the sick, with a design to secure his abilities in the American army, and in consequence of his refusal to accompany them he was subjected to great difficulties and loss of income. After the battles of Lexington and Bunker Hill he attended the wounded and sick officers and men, and accompanied the British army on the evacuation of Boston. He remained at Halifax, Nova Scotia, for three years, attending the sick and wounded soldiers, both American and English, until February, 1779, when he was deprived of his appointment and he set sail for England. Here he remained for five months, until appointed Surgeon to the General Hospital in New York,* where he met General Sir Henry Clinton, Commander-in-Chief, who took him to South Carolina. He served at the siege of Charlestown in May, 1780, and later in the garrison at Savannah. In November, 1780, he embarked for England in the transport *Two Sisters*, and lost all his books, a vellum scabbard of his silver-mounted hanger, his silver spurs and gold laced hat, and remained there for the remainder of the war. During his residence in London he was " generally employed in attending on his countrymen, who from difference of climate, chagrin, and various circumstances, are very frequently disordered, and at the same time unable to reward the services of his profession."

Dr. Jeffries was the owner of houses, lands and wharfs in Boston and property elsewhere in Massachusetts and in New Hampshire, confiscated in March, 1782. He was also the owner of pew No. 67, in King's Chapel, Boston (*Annals of King's Chapel, op. cit.*). He received more applications for apprentices than he could admit, and received £100 a year as admission fee from his apprentices. His wife died of grief during or soon after the war. His father, David Jeffries, Treasurer of Massachusetts, was warmly attached to the American cause. (A.O. 13/47; A.O. 13/74; A.O. 12/99, f. 303.)

John Gore, a Governor of the Hospital at Boston, certified to Dr. Jeffries' loyal services to the Hospital (A.O. 13/74). Adino Paddock (*q.v.*), his friend from youth, in an affidavit, dated March 15, 1787, states that Dr. Jeffries suffered in his profession after giving evidence in the Supreme Court in favour of Captain Preston and the British soldiers in the " Boston Massacre " case, and that he was intended to be the sole heir of his great-uncle, John Jeffries, a Boston loyalist, who had brought him up and educated him. Fearing that his estate might be seized by the State if bequeathed to him, a loyalist, his great-uncle left it to the father of Dr. Jeffries. (*Ib.*)

Dr. Jeffries claimed compensation, £6,015 and was allowed £500. He was compensated at the rate of £320 a year for the loss of his pro-

* The date of this appointment is August 4, 1779. He passed the usual examination at Surgeon's Hall in London before sailing. (*Amer. MSS. in Roy. Inst., op. cit.*, ii, 4.)

fessional income during the war. (A.O. 12/109.) He received a loyalist pension of £80 until 1790, when it was increased to £100 and was paid until his death. (A.O. 459/7–8 ; T. 50/8 ; T. 50/45.) A list of the claims against his estate is in A.O. 12/81, f. 104.

Dr. Jeffries sold his commission in the Military Hospital, New York, in March, 1781, for £800, on the ground, apparently, that he had been refused leave of absence to settle his private affairs. It was sold without the knowledge of General Sir Henry Clinton, and was the first sale of an army surgeon's commission. Clinton was directed to make enquiries into the matter and to put a stop to such sales, as they might establish a precedent highly detrimental to efficiency by the introduction of improper persons into the military hospitals. (*Amer. MSS. in Roy. Inst., op. cit.,* ii, 262, 266.)

In 1765 this loyalist delivered a course of lectures on anatomy in Boston, thus ante-dating by 16 years Dr. John Warren, hitherto regarded as the first medical lecturer in Massachusetts (Ex inform. Mr. Albert Matthews).

Dr. John Jeffries is remembered for his crossing of the Straits of Dover in a balloon from London with Blanchard in January, 1785. An engraving was made of this great event, the first crossing by air, with Dr. Jeffries' portrait in it.

He received the degree of M.D. from Marischal College (now the University of), Aberdeen, in 1769. He died at Boston, September 16, 1819.

Sabine, *op. cit.,* ; *Amer. MSS. in Roy. Inst., op. cit.,* i, 265, 280–1, 370, 371, 394 ; Stark, *op. cit.,* 394–5.

JOHN JERVIS

was a merchant in Boston from about 1762, and suffered much for his loyalty. According to his memorial, his marriage was dissolved by Congress, and his wife, who was much younger than himself, was married publicly to another man, well knowing that he (John Jervis), her legal husband, was alive. He escaped from Boston in an open boat to Halifax, Nova Scotia. He was in London in 1789. (A.O. 13/47 ; A.O. 12/99, f. 243.) His claim of £1,240 was disallowed. (A.O. 12/109.) He received a pension until 1804. (A.O. 461/19 ; T. 50/11.)

PETER JOHONNOT

distiller, of Boston, as a loyal subject, ever revered the supreme legislative authority of Great Britain and did all he could to avert the war. He signed all the addresses, protests and associations of the loyalists, and personally attended all public meetings of the revolutionary party and openly protested against every measure which tended to the subversion of government. Peter Johonnot left Boston with the British troops in March, 1776, and went to England, where he remained until his death in London in August, 1809, at the age of 79. His large house and gardens in Boston were sold·by auction by order of the State, and were bought by a friend for the moderate sum of £225 sterling, and he expresses the hope that he might regain possession of the property for the same sum. His partner in one distillery in Boston and a store for the sale of West India goods was Ebenezer Seaver, his brother-in-law, whose deposition, dated Boston, November 14, 1783, gives details of the profits and other particulars of the business. The debts due to Peter Johonnot amounted to £5,000 sterling (A.O. 13/74.) He claimed £225 and was allowed that sum, less £2 10s. for his pension. (A.O. 12/109.) His pension of £100 was paid until his death. (A.O. 12/105, f. 137; T. 50/6.) A list of claims against his estate is in A.O. 12/81. He was a signatory to the address to George III (see Appendix).

This loyalist was the son of Zachariah Johonnot, of Boston, a descendant of French Huguenots, and married Katherine Dudley in 1750. (Stark, *op. cit.*, p. 410.)

Peter Johonnot in his will, dated December 22, 1804, and proved September 14, 1809, made bequests to his brother, Gabriel Johonnot; to his nephew, Samuel Cooper Johonnot, son of the said Gabriel; to his brother-in-law, Ebenezer Seaver; to Rebecca Coudon, of Massachusetts; and to Nathaniel Coffin, Collector of Customs in St. Kitts. (Loveday, 696.)

References : Sabine, *op. cit.*; *Loyalists' Claims, op. cit.*, p. 238.

COLONEL ELISHA JONES

a man of ample fortune, a member of the General Assembly and a justice of the peace, of Weston, died in 1775 at Boston, whither he had fled for safety. Several certificates to his loyalty, signed by Generals Gage and Howe and others, with papers relating to the confiscation of his property and descriptions of his lands, are in A.O. 13/47, 13/50 and 13/74. He left eleven sons who were loyalists, eight of whom served with His Majesty's troops and the others in divers ways in rescuing prisoners and giving intelligence. (A.O. 13/47.)

Colonel Jones was born at Weston in 1710, the son of Josiah and Abigail Jones, and married in 1733 Mary, daughter of Nathaniel and Lydia Allen, of Weston. His wife died in 1751 and he died in Boston, February 13, 1775. His only daughter, Mary (who married (i) the Rev. Asa Dunbar, and (ii) Joseph Minot), helped her brother, Josiah (*q.v.*), to escape fron Concord gaol by bringing him in food some files with which he filed away the window bars. Another loyalist, one Hicks, of Plymouth, escaped with him.

The names of his eleven sons, with particulars of their services in the Revolution are given below, under Nathan, Elisha, Israel, Daniel, Elias, Josiah, Ephraim, Simeon, Stephen, Jonas, and Charles.

References : Bond, Genealogies of families of Watertown, Waltham and Weston; *Boston Transcript*, article by Edmund Hudson, June 27, 1917; L. Chadwick, *Ontarian Families*, 1894, i, 167–180; *Ontario Archives, op. cit.*, pp. 751–4, 820–1, 911–2 and 917.

NATHAN JONES

was a Lieutenant-Colonel of militia, and had a handsome fortune. He appears to have settled for a time at Penobscot. (A.O. 13/47.) He is claimed as a loyalist by his loyalist brothers (A.O. 13/47), but this claim is disputed. He was born in 1734 and finally settled at Goldsbury in Maine.

ELISHA JONES

was a captain of militia and had a good estate at Pittsfield, in Berkshire County. He was taken prisoner in 1775 by the rebels and taken to Great Barrington gaol for refusing to join them. He escaped and got to New York and thence to Boston, where he joined the British Army. At the evacuation he accompanied the army to Nova Scotia and New York, and was there employed as a commissary to the Royal Artillery. He died at New York just before the evacuation by the British, leaving a wife, Mehitable, three sons and three daughters. (A.O. 12/10, ff. 373–380, 410–1 ; A.O. 13/50.) With this memorial of his widow are an inventory of his personal estate, conveyances of his property at Pittsfield, and a schedule of his confiscated lands.

Elisha Jones was born in 1737 and married Mehitable Upham. His descendants settled at Sissibo, now Weymouth, Nova Scotia.

ISRAEL JONES [1738–1825]

remained on his own farm. (A.O. 13/47.)

DANIEL JONES [1740–1786]

was Chief Judge of the Inferior Court of Common Pleas in New Hampshire, and was confined to his farm by the rebels in 1781. (A.O. 13/47.) He graduated at Harvard College in 1759 (A.B. 1769 and A.M.) and died at Hinsdale, New Hampshire.

ELIAS JONES [1742–1823]

was for many years a deputy sheriff, and was confined by the rebels to his farm in Massachusetts. (A.O. 13/47.)

JOSIAH JONES [born in 1744]

was an attorney at law in New Hampshire, and was obliged in consequence of his loyalty to seek shelter. (A.O. 13/47.) His sister, Mary, helped him to escape from Concord gaol (see p. 182). He settled as a lawyer at Sissibo, now Weymouth, Nova Scotia.

A loyalist of this name proceeded to Nova Scotia, May 30, 1775, by the sloop, *Polly* (Ephraim Jones, master), to obtain oats and straw for the British troops (Force, *Amer. Archives*, Ser. IV., Vol. II, p. 901.) This sloop was captured, and Josiah Jones was committed to Concord gaol. (*Ib.*, Vol. II, p. 1399.)

EPHRAIM JONES [1750–1812]

was settled in Massachusetts and was obliged to quit his home. He joined the Canadian army. (A.O. 13/47.) He settled after the war in Augusta, near Prescott, Upper Canada.

A loyalist of this name was a farmer at East Hoosack in Berkshire County, where he was taken prisoner. He escaped to Canada and joined Burgoyne's army, in which he acted as commissary and served in that capacity until the end of the war. (A.O. 13/75.)

SIMEON JONES [1751–1823]

lived in Cheshire County, New Hampshire, and for his active loyalty was obliged to leave his estate there and sacrifice his profitable office of clerk of the Inferior Court and flee to New York in 1776. He served in arms for the remainder of the war, first in Wentworth's Volunteers, and from February 25, 1781, as Lieutenant in the King's American Dragoons. His original commission is in W.O. 42/J11. He was married on August 13, 1786, at Trinity Church, Boston, Massachusetts, to Sarah, daughter of Dr. Thomas Williams, of Roxbury, Massachusetts. (W.O. 42/J11 ; Ind : 5606 ; A.O. 13/25 ; A.O. 13/47 ; A.O. 13/50.) He settled at Sissibo, now Weymouth, Nova Scotia.

STEPHEN JONES [1754–1830]

had just completed his education at Harvard College in 1775 and served in the Associated Loyalists of Boston, in Wentworth's Volunteers and as cornet in the King's American Dragoons. (A.O. 12/10, ff. 360–372, 389, 412, 441 ; A.O. 13/47 ; A.O. 13/50.) He settled at Sissibo (Weymouth), Nova Scotia. He took the degrees af A.B. and A.M. at Harvard in 1807.

JONAS JONES [born in 1756]

left Weston in disguise after the battle of Lexington and was captured, but had the good fortune to escape to Boston, where he joined the British Army on April 21, 1775. While scattering proclamations issued by General Gage in Massachusetts he was taken prisoner and confined for eighteen months. He escaped through the woods into Canada and nearly perished from his thirty days' exposure in the wilderness. For three months he served in obtaining intelligence in New York, Massachusetts and New Hampshire. After serving in Burgoyne's army with great applause and approbation he was sent into Canada and by Burgoyne's warm recommendation for his gallantry was granted a commission as ensign in the 20th Regiment of Foot. He was present in eleven actions, and among the acts of bravery was his successful defence, though severely wounded, against an attack by an American privateer while he was carrying dispatches. He was put on half-pay as Lieutenant in this regiment. (A.O. 13/47 ; A.O. 13/50 ; A.O. 13/74.) He married and died in London.

CHARLES JONES [born in 1760]

was at Harvard College at the commencement of the Revolutionary war. He joined Wentworth's Volunteers in 1777, at the age of seventeen, and in January, 1780, was promoted cornet in the Queen's American Rangers. He was killed in action in Virginia. (A.O. 13/47; A.O. 13/50.)

JOHN JONES

of Hallowell, Lincoln County [Maine], merchant and land surveyor, was imprisoned for loyalty and escaped to Canada by land. He was afterwards engaged in carrying dispatches from General Campbell at Penobscot to General Haldimand in Quebec and elsewhere. At the evacuation of Penobscot, where he had settled as a merchant, he joined the settlement of loyalists at Passamaquoddy. With this memorial is a schedule of his losses and a certificate from Richard Kidston (his former neighbour and presumably a loyalist), merchant, of Halifax, Nova Scotia. (A.O. 13/75.)

WILLIAM JONES AND WILLIAM HORTON

According to their undated joint memorial, William Jones in 1774 sent from Swansea, South Wales, in the brig *Townsend*, a cargo of merchandise to Falmouth (Portland), Maine, and William Horton, a Quaker, went as super cargo and factor, with the intention of settling there. Here he carried on a store for eight months. The brig returned to Swansea with a cargo and was sent out again to Falmouth in 1775 with more goods. Horton was requested by a mob of over 1,500 in 1775 to sign the protest against the British Government, which was alleged to be making use of means to bring the Americans into abject slavery, and to declare that he would with his life and fortune oppose such measures. He refused and sought refuge in the night on board Jones's brig, but before she could sail, the people of Falmouth took possession of her and all the persons on board. But she escaped during the night, and the loyal Quaker landed in Swansea in July, 1775. He appears to have settled later at Coalbrookdale, Shropshire. (A.O. 13/74.)

William Jones was a considerable merchant at Swansea between 1770 and 1790, and was the owner of coal mines. (Ex inform. Mr. D. Rhys Phillips, of Swansea.)

JOHN JOY (Plate xxx)

In 1759 he left a large and profitable business as a master builder and owner of great property in Boston and joined the expedition to Quebec, and was in command of eighty artificers, whom he had enlisted. After the surrender of Quebec, 125 French artificers were added to his command, and he was presented with a commission by the commander-in-chief as a mark of approbation of his conduct. Early in the Revolution this loyalist was employed as assistant engineer to the British troops under General Gage, who spoke warmly in person in London in support of his claim, adding that Joy did many things which others had refused to do. His real estate was worth £5,000. (A.O. 13/47; A.O. 13/137; A.O. 12/105, f.12.). His son was Michael Joy (q.v.). Governor Hutchinson, in a long letter dated June 15, 1778, recommended John Joy, Adino Paddock (q.v.) and Gore to the notice of the Commissioners, and stated that they had sustained commissions in the militia or provincial troops before the Revolution, which, besides their general fair characters, gave them influence. (A.O. 13/97.) Joy claimed £6,990, and was allowed £2,750, less £33 10s. for pension. (A.O. 12/109.) He was granted a pension until his death in 1804. (A.O. 461/19; T. 50/6.) A list of claims against his estate is in A.O. 12/81, f.102. He joined the Ancient and Honourable Artillery Company of Massachusetts in 1755. (Roberts, History of that Company, ii, 75.)

John Joy was born at Hingham, Massachusetts, in 1727, and married Sarah Homer; he died in London in 1804, and was buried in Bunhill Fields burial ground. His sons, Dr. John Joy and Benjamin Joy, were also loyalists. (Ex inform. Mrs. C. H. Joy; Stark, op. cit., pp. 412-3.)

His portrait, painted in London about 1780, is in the possession of Mr. Benjamin Joy, his great-great-grandson, who is also the owner of a portrait of his son, John, by Joseph Badger (1708-65), at the age of seven. See page 210.

MICHAEL JOY

son of John Joy (q.v.), accompanied his father to England as a loyalist refugee, and was granted an allowance of £100 a year. A continuance of his loyalist pension was refused, December 7, 1789. (A.O. 13/74; A.O. 13/137; A.O. 12/105, f.72.) He was born in 1754 and graduated at Harvard College in 1771. He married Susan, daughter of Joseph Hall, of Liverpool, and in 1812 bought Hartham Park, in Wiltshire, where he died in 1825.

EDWARD KEIGHTLEY, or Keighley

of Boston, was one of the Associated Volunteers who left with the British troops in March, 1776. His vessel was separated from the convoy and captured by American privateers. He was taken prisoner and forced to walk from Portsmouth, New Hampshire, to Boston, and there kept a prisoner until April, 1777. In 1785 he was at Halifax, Nova Scotia. (A.O. 13/26; A.O. 12/83, f.1.)

THOMAS KNIGHT

According to his memorial, dated Leicester, England, October 29, 1777, he had been "a strenuous opposer of the principles of those pretended sons of liberty in Boston, from the time of the passing of the Stamps Act to his being oblig'd to leave that place in the year 1775." His ropewalk was destroyed for the purposes of the British Army; while other parts of his valuable property were sacrificed to the " resentment of the rebels, his implacable enemies in Boston." His much beloved wife and small four children he suspects are still there, and " daily exposed to the insults and outrage of Persons of abandoned principles," which has brought him to an unhappy condition of mind, " almost inexpressible." Governor Hutchinson, who knew him personally, gave him a certificate of loyalty and of his membership of a company of cadets which attended upon the Governor. (A.O. 13/74.) His property, worth nearly £5,000, was confiscated. He was granted a pension of £60. (A.O. 12/105, f.1.)

WILLIAM LATTA

was a trader in Taunton, and the list of his books would seem to indicate a man of good education. With this list are several deeds of his property. (A.O. 13/51.) He was confined in gaol for refusing to join the American army, and upon his release he performed many kind offices for the British prisoners of war in Massachusetts. Later he was sent to a prison ship and detained for about six months (A.O. 13/91.) In A.O. 13/91 are the following three copies of documents : a libel, March 26, 1780, referring to the sale of his confiscated property; an order of August 4, 1777, requiring James Williams, sheriff of Bristol County, to convey Latta, then in his custody, to the Massachusetts Board of War, to be by them sent on board a guardship or otherwise secured, to await transportation ; and an order to the same sheriff to search for and apprehend this loyalist and Job Smith, Robert Caldwell, Abiel Smith and Abijah Hodges, all of Taunton, who had been endeavouring since April 19, 1775, " to counteract the united struggles of this & ye United States for the preservation of their Liberties and privileges"

William Latta claimed £375 14s. and was allowed £150. (A.O. 12/109.) He was at Lochwinnoch in County Renfrew, Scotland, in 1784. (A.O. 13/91.)

References : A.O. 12/10, f. 288 ; *Ontario Archives, op. cit.*, pp. 663-4.

HENRY LAUGHTON

was an importer of English goods, at Boston, and was part owner, with William Bollan, of ironworks at Taunton, Massachusetts. He was prosperous and able to educate and support his large family in a respectable manner. All his available iron was placed at the disposal of the British forces for the defence of Boston, where he supplied buildings sufficient to accommodate a whole regiment. With this memorial, dated from High-gate, near London, March 20, 1784, is the original appointment of this loyalist as a fireward at Boston, November 14, 1775 ; and the articles of agreement for leasing his Griffin's Wharf, Boston, for the use of the British military, for nine months, October 10, 1774. (A.O. 13/91.) A letter from Laughton, November 21, 1782, embodies most of the above memorial. (A.O. 13/74.)

Sir William Pepperell, in evidence, November 16, 1784, on behalf of his two children, John and Mary Laughton, stated that Henry Laughton had died on October 8, previously, and that his son, John, had been brought up as an apothecary and had recently served as surgeon's mate on an East Indian ship. This son was granted a loyalist pension of £25. He was drowned, June 28, 1786. (A.O. 12/101, ff.133, 362.) Mary Laughton received a pension of £25 from 1784 to 1800. (A.O. 12/101, f.133; T. 50/8; A.O. 461/16.)

John Joy, in letters of February 29, 1788, and May 5, 1789, states that Mary Laughton had gone to America to recover a legacy left by an uncle, but had failed. (A.O. 13/74.)

Reference: A.O. 13/137; A.O. 12/82.

JOHN LAWLESS

A copy of his long letter, addressed to his wife, Mehitable Lawless, at Salem, Massachusetts, and dated September 13, 1782, begins as follows:

My Best, My only Love
   To Hitty

In it he refers to the calumnies made to her that he was exceedingly gay and happy in England and totally indifferent whether he saw her or Salem ever again. He protests his abiding affections in ardent expressions. Since parting from her, happiness and contentment have been strangers to him. On his arrival in England he found that his father, two uncles and a sister had died, and that his eldest brother had since died. His father within a year of the death of his wife (John Lawless's mother) had married again to a woman with two children by a former husband, and had one son by this marriage, to whom his father had left his whole fortune of about £18,000. His father's wife had industriously propagated a report to his father that he (John Lawless) had joined the American service and been killed. With this letter he sent his wife a miniature, presumably of himself, in a shagreen case. He wished to be remembered to her cousins, Easter and Mrs. Ropes and to Samuel Flag, to whom he hopes to send a few new good songs, selected purposely for his refined taste and delicate ear. (A.O. 13/47.)

The above letter was written in answer to one from his wife, dated July 25 [1782], beginning "My best Friend," and expressing the hope that he will be able to return to America and promising to endeavour to obtain leave for his admission. (Ib.)

There are a letter from John Lawless to the Commissioners protesting against the shameful and unmerited attack on his character and conduct; and a memorial in which he says that his wife had since married another man, and the marriage authorised, and that both had actually recovered by a suit at law the whole of his property in America. (A.O. 13/47.) The intention of marriage between Mehitable Lawless and John Templeman of Boston was filed at Salem, March 1, 1783. (Salem Marriage Records.)

In A.O. 13/74 are the following papers of John Lawless : (i) A memorial, showing how he was hospitable to the British officers imprisoned at Concord, and how he repeatedly refused to take up arms for the Americans or to pay fines, for which actions he became obnoxious and was persecuted. At considerable risk he sought the protection of the British at Rhode Island in May, 1777. (ii) Certificates of Sir William Erskine, Baronet, Quartermaster-General, dated from Concord gaol, March 15, 1777, testifying to John Lawless's great attention to him. (iii) Certificates to his loyalty from Peter Frye (*q.v.*) and others. (iv) Order dated December 4, 1776, from the military officers, selectmen and committee of correspondence of Salem, ordering him to hold himself in readiness to serve for a term not exceeding three months, when called upon to reinforce the Continental army, pursuant to an act of the General Court of Massachusetts, entitled " An Act for providing a reinforcement to the American Army." (v) A certificate of William Coffin, junior, dated New York, October 20, 1777, that John Lawless was at that time a volunteer in Captain Willard's Company of Massachusetts Volunteers for the defence of New York. (vi) Two letters and a petition dated in 1782, on his distressed condition.

Thomas Flucker (*q.v.*) and Mr. Fisher, in evidence, stated that Lawless had married a lady of some fortune and had used her very ill and left her. Samuel Curwen (*q.v.*) described him as a Irishman and fortune hunter. The Commissioners agreed that he was an adventurer who had exaggerated his condition as a man of property. Nevertheless they thought him worthy of a commission in a marching regiment or in the Marines. (A.O. 12/105, ff.13, 25.) His claim of £7,500 was disallowed. (A.O. 12/109.) He signed the address to George III. (See Appendix.)

Mehitable Lawless, his wife, inherited property from her father, Samuel Bacon, of Salem. Her brother, Samuel Bacon, entered the American service and died January 29, 1777. In his will dated August 14, 1776, and proved June 2, 1777, he mentions his sister, the said Mehitable Lawless ; his brother, Josiah Bacon ; and Catherine, daughter of John and Mehitable Lawless. John Templeman, of Boston [second husband of Mehitable Lawless] was a surety to the bond of administration (Docket 1225 at Salem).

RICHARD LECHMERE

was of Taunton and was a Mandamus Councillor. In his memorials dated from England, June 7, 1778, and October 1, 1783, he states that he left Boston at the evacuation by the British with his wife and six children, bound for Nova Scotia, in a small ship crowded with nearly 100 persons, exclusive of the crew, without provisions or necessary stores, and from the beginning until the end of March they experienced " every species of indelicacy and illconvenience." He left Halifax for England in May, 1776. (A.O. 13/47 ; A.O. 13/74.)

With his memorials are many papers and letters. There is the original deed for his Pew No. 43 in Christ Church,* Cambridge, Massachusetts, dated April 19, 1762, and signed and sealed by Henry Vassall, the Rev. East Apthorp, Ralph Inman, David Phips (q.v.) and John Vassall (q.v.), with Charles Pelham as witness. Accompanying this document is the original deed of the sale of a pew [No. 82] in King's Chapel, Boston, by Nicholas Lechmere to Richard Lechmere, dated July 1, 1771. (A.O. 13/47.)

Among other papers is a copy of the account of the sale of his real estate at Cambridge, sold to Mr. Cabot ; and of his confiscated mansion house and distillery at Boston, sold to Mungo Mackay ; and details and plans of some of his estate in Massachusetts. (Ib.)

A letter from Thomas Ivers of Boston in April, 1784, regarding some of Richard Lechmere's property in Boston, states that Dr. Bulfinch took his chariot and used it and that the Rev. Dr. [Samuel] Cooper was given his chaise by the committee of sequestration. There is a copy of a long letter from Chambers Russell, dated Boston, February 12, 1787, written for Richard Lechmere's attorney, Mr. Lowell, on the difficulties in recovering debts due to him and stating that his confiscated lands cannot be restored to him. (Ib.)

His personal estate included a tree of his father's family in colours.

His losses amounted to over £8,000, exclusive of lands, and his property was the first to be destroyed in the Revolution. He was the treasurer of the Muscongus Patent† and was Naval Agent in Boston.

His son was apprenticed to one Thomas Russell and his brother-in-law was Jonathan Simpson (q.v.), who married his sister. His son Thomas received £100 towards the expense of fitting him out as a writer in the West Indies (A.O. 12/105, f. 139), and was probably the loyalist of this name who was a Cornet in the King's American Dragoons, on half pay until December, 1816 (Ind. 5606).

Letters of Richard Lechmere, written from Boston in 1774 to his London agents, Lane, Son and Fraser, show clearly the state of feeling in Boston at the time. (Proc. of Mass. Hist. Soc., 2nd Ser., xvi, 285–290.) This son of Thomas Lechmere, Surveyor General of the Customs for the Northern District of America, died December 16, 1813, aged 87 ; his widow, Mary, daughter of Lieutenant Governor Spencer Phips, and sister of David Phipps (q.v.), died February 19, 1815, aged 89 ; and his daughter, Margaret, died September 5, 1819, and all were buried in Bristol Cathedral, where there is a mural tablet to their memory. Commemorated on the same tablet are Thomas Lechmere, of The Circus, Bath, who died July 5, 1830 ; and his wife, Mary, who died September 25, 1816

There is a list of claims against the estate of Richard Lechmere which was not mortgaged. (A.O. 12/81, f. 109 ; A.O. 12/82.) He was granted a pension of £200 from 1782 until his death. (T. 50/6 ; T. 50/24 ;

* A plan of the pews with the names of the " Tory Proprietors " about 1770 is illustrated in a booklet on the Church by Mr. S. F. Batchelder, 1893.

† See page 60.

A.O. 461/17.) He claimed £7,529 11s. and was awarded £3,050. (A.O. 12/109.)

Mary, daughter of Richard Lechmere, was married to James Russell, a loyalist from Massachusetts (son of James Russell of Charlestown, and nephew of Judge Chambers Russell), at St. Peter's Church, Bristol, in 1780. Nicholas Lechmere, his loyalist brother, was a Customs Officer at Newport, Rhode Island.

Reference : Spark, *op. cit.* pp. 413-4, 453.

HENRY LEDDEL

was an Englishman who went to America young and was settled as a merchant at Boston from 1745 until the evacuation of the town by the British troops in 1776, except for two years spent with the army. He was commissioned in 1756 by Shirley, Governor of Massachusetts, as Secretary to Major-General Winslow, Commander-in-chief of the Provincial forces, and was afterwards Muster Master General to these forces. In 1757 he was taken prisoner by the French and Indians at Fort William Henry on Lake George.

Henry Leddel took his silver plate with him from Boston in 1776 to Halifax, and thence to New York, where he acted as first clerk to Coffin and Anderson, contractors to the British army. With his memorials are an account of his losses and an affidavit of James Barrick (*q.v.*) and his wife, Susannah, dated Exeter, England, March 20, 1786, that this loyalist had married their sister. (A.O. 13/47.)

He claimed £1,025 and was allowed £80. (A.O. 12/109.) He received a pension of £20 from 1784 to 1806. (T. 50/8 ; A.O. 462/21.) He married Elizabeth Barrick at Boston, January 19, 1745-6, and was a member of King's Chapel, Boston. (*Annals of King's Chapel, op. cit.*) Thomas Leddel (*q.v.*) was probably his brother.

THOMAS LEDDEL

was born in England and emigrated young to Boston, where he was settled as a merchant before 1775. He left with the British troops for Halifax and New York and at the latter place became clerk to Coffin and Anderson. He was granted a pension of £20. (A.O. 12/101, f. 78.) He was probably a brother of Henry Leddel (*q.v.*).

DANIEL LEONARD (Plate xxxi)

In his memorial are interesting details of his career in Massachusetts before the war. His father, Ephraim Leonard, and uncle were Judges of the Court. He studied law under Samuel White, barrister, Speaker of the Assembly and member of His Majesty's Council, whose daughter [Anna] he married, and to whose extensive legal practice he succeeded, together with the office of King's attorney for the county of Bristol. For the first four years of his practice he resided with his father at Mansfield and later removed to Taunton, where he maintains that before the Revolution he attended sixteen courts and transacted more business as attorney and counsellor than any other member of the profession in Massachusetts. At Taunton he improved his house by erecting a brick wall with "Chinese railing" in front and a flight of steps of Connecticut stone. (A.O. 13/47.)

With the above memorial is a copy of a conveyance of a piece of land to him by Ephraim Leonard, of Norton, Bristol County, dated May 12, 1762. In this memorial he mentions Colonel George Leonard, attorney-at-law [his cousin]; and Dr. William Baylies, both of whom married daughters* of the above Hon. Samuel White and his wife, Prudence. He also mentions Anna White Leonard (his daughter by his first marriage to Anna White), who had since married John Smith Esquire, junior, of the Island of Antigua.

Daniel Leonard gives an account of unjust judgments against his estate as an absentee loyalist, including one for £6 13s. 10d. by Seth Padelford, who served his clerkship with him, who was introduced by him to the bar as an attorney and who at the end of his term of clerkship gave him (Leonard) a promissory note for £81, which was the balance due for expenditure on his education and which is still due. Padelford also obtained for himself and his clients and relations property which had cost him (Leonard) over £1,000 sterling, for less than half its value. A copy of Padelford's bond is here. Mentioned also in this memorial are Seth Williams (q.v.) and Job Williams, loyalist refugees from Taunton. Daniel Leonard took with him to England a great number of deeds and other papers of clients, which he returned afterwards to Colonel George Leonard.

The following are summaries of letters and papers in A.O. 13/74.

(i) Henry Hulton (q.v.), in letters, dated August 5 and 6, 1779, to Sir Grey Cooper, states that Daniel Leonard was one of several gentlemen of the law who applied for the appointment of Solicitor to the Customs on the death of David Lisle. He had no personal knowledge of Leonard, but having been informed that he was the author of *Massachusettensis†*, the Commissioners of Customs appointed him to hold the office until confirmed by the home government.

(ii) A memorandum of Lord George Germain, dated July 4, 1780, adds that the appointment of Solicitor to the Customs was given to Leonard as a reward for his services in America and that since his arrival in England he had made himself very useful to government by his literary publications.

(iii) Copy of an extract from a letter from Lieutenant Governor Bruere to Lord George Germain, dated Bermuda, December 12, 1780, upon the chaotic condition of the Island and expressing the hope that

* Experience was married to Colonel George Leonard, and Bathsheba to Dr. Baylies.

† The replies of John Adams to these letters, under the pseudonym, Novanglus, are well known.

Francis Rotch

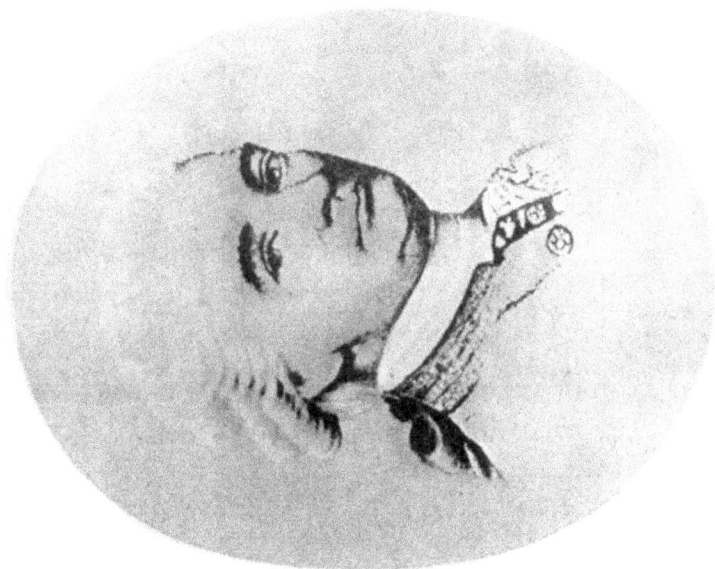

PLATE XXXI   Daniel Leonard

PLATE XXXII

Joshua Loring, the Elder

with the appointment of Daniel Leonard as Attorney General and member of the council and his presence on the spot, law and order will be established and the amazing trade in gunpowder and dry goods and the supply of over 1,000 vessels, mainly built in Bermuda, carried on by the Bermudians (in conjunction with St. Eustatia), with the Americans, will be crushed.

Another of Leonard's memorials states that he was appointed a member of His Majesty's Council of Massachusetts and was obliged to quit Taunton in 1774 by the outrages and threats of the mob, who had attacked his house and fired bullets into it. He sought shelter in Boston and there carried on his duties as member of the Council as far as was possible until the evacuation, when he accompanied the British troops to Nova Scotia. Here he was requested by Admiral Shuldham to act for the Crown in cases under the Prohibitory Act.

His letters of June 26 and 28, 1779, to Sir Grey Cooper, refer to his services as the author of *Massachusettensis* and to his services in England in a great variety of instances, unsolicited and unknown. His family connections in Bristol County were numerous and for many years he held the principal posts of honour and emolument there. He was educated to the law, had a very extensive practice and was possessed of a large patrimonial estate. For several years he was a representative in the General Assembly for Taunton, the principal town in the county. As soon as he discovered the real views and intentions of the leaders of the Assembly he opposed them to the utmost of his ability, within and without. On the day of the Lexington skirmish he offered his services as a combatant to General Gage and did duty on the night after the battle of Bunker Hill, and on several other occasions. As counsel for the Crown he attended all the prosecutions for violations of the Boston Port Bill. His large family were obliged from fear to leave their home at Taunton and follow him to Boston, the mob having forbidden the supply of provisions to them.

Two letters from Benjamin Thompson [Count Rumford], dated Whitehall, February 6 and August 10, 1781, relate to the appointment of Daniel Leonard as Chief Justice of Bermuda. [He was accompanied thither by his second cousin, William McKinstry (*q.v.*), and would be there in the time of William Browne (*q.v.*) as Governor.]

Daniel Leonard claimed £3,621, and was allowed £915 16s. Compensation at the rate of £500 per annum was granted to him for the loss of his official income during the war. (A.O. 12/109.)

He joined the Inner Temple in 1777,* and signed the loyal address to George III. (See Appendix.)

He graduated at Harvard College in 1760, and was Captain in the "Harvard Fencibles," a military company formed in 1757. His first wife, Anna White, whom he married April 2, 1767, died April 4, 1768. His second wife, Sarah Hammock, daughter of John Hammock, merchant, of Boston, whom he married in 1770, died on the passage from Bermuda to America in 1806, aged 78. Her sister, Hannah Hammock, married

* E. Alfred Jones, *American Members of the Inns of Court*, 1924.

N

Andrew Cazneau (*q.v.*) This eminent loyalist is said to be the "Beau Trumps" in Mercy Warren's *The Group*. He shot himself in London, June 27, 1829, aged 89. (Stark, *op. cit.*, pp. 325–332 ; Ralph Davol's *Two Men of Taunton*, 1912.) In his will, dated December 1, 1828, Daniel Leonard bequeathed property to his son, Charles, and his daughters, Anna White Smith, Sally Stewart, wife of John Stewart, and Harriet Leonard. His grandson, Leonard Stewart, doctor of medicine, was his executor.

References : A.O. 12/105, f. 39 ; *Letters of John Andrews*, 1772–6, ed. by Winthrop Sargent, 1866, p. 32 ; *Proc. of Mass. Hist Soc.*, 2nd Ser., vi, 251–7 ; *Loyalist Claims*, *op. cit.*, pp. 186–7 ; Fannie L. Koster's *Annals of the Leonard Family*, 1911.

GEORGE LEONARD

of Boston, fitted a fleet of seven armed vessels and three transports at his own expense for service with the British forces, and performed signal services himself with this fleet. For example, he accompanied the fleet to Martha's Vineyard and took and destroyed eleven American vessels. He induced the inhabitants of that island to furnish fresh provisions and fuel for the British garrison at Newport, Rhode Island, and the towns of Chilmark and Edgartown on Martha's Island voted unanimously to do so. (Treas. In Letters, 1/553.)

The names and other particulars of his vessels are as follows :

Frigate *Restoration*,* Harry Hatch, master, with 150 men and 20 nine pounders.

Sloop *General Prescot*, Harry Hatch, master, with 50 men and 10 nine and six pounders.

Schooner *Royal Charlotte*, Thomas Duggan, master, with 40 men and 10 six and four pounders.

Schooner *General Leslie*,† Thomas Dow, master, with 40 men and 10 four pounders.

Schooner *General Garth*, with 40 men and 10 four pounders.

Armed schooner *Hazard* and the sloops *George* and *Harriet*, with 60 men.

Transport brig *Lucy*, William Broad, master, and transport schooner *Sally*, Ambrose Cleaveland, master, with 9 men each.

Several armed boats.

A loyalist of this name was a Lieutenant in the Associated Loyalists of Boston. (See Appendix.)

A letter of Israel Mauduit, dated June 2, 1780, refers to the great services of George Leonard and his losses by the Revolution. (Treas. In Letters 1/553.)

With his memorials are several papers relating to his victualling the Associated Loyalists in Rhode Island in 1779 in his capacity of commissary of refugees, including detachments of the Loyal New Englanders ; an

* Francis Green (*q.v.*) claims to have helped in equipping this vessel.
† William McKinstry (*q.v.*) was a lieutenant on this vessel.

estimate of the losses sustained by him ; and many papers relating to the above vessels. (A.O. 13/51 ; A.O. 12/10, ff. 394–409, 438–9.)

He resigned his membership of the Board of Directors of the Associated Loyalists, September 10, 1782, and on October 5 he was granted an allowance of £200 a year. (*Am. MSS. in Royal Inst., op. cit.*, iii, 112, 138, 203.)

This loyalist sought refuge in New Brunswick at the end of the war and became prominent in public affairs, as a member of the Council for 36 years. He was born at Plymouth, Massachusetts, November 28, 1742, and died April 1, 1826, and was buried in the old burial ground at Sussex, King's County, New Brunswick, where there is a monument to his memory and that of his wife, Sarah, a native of Boston. (*Judges of New Brunswick, op. cit.*, pp. 2, 4, 133, 212, 229 ; Stark, *op. cit.*, p. 333.)

JOHN LEWIS

was appointed boatman at the Custom House, Boston, July 7, 1775. He left Boston with the British troops in March, 1776, for Nova Scotia, and thence to New York, where he bore arms as a volunteer in the Loyal Commissariat Volunteers, commanded by Major William Butler, who gave him a certificate of service. (A.O. 13/74.) He was at Halifax, Nova Scotia, in 1790. (A.O. 13/24.)

WILLIAM LEWIS

of Lynn, went to New York after the evacuation of Boston by the British troops, and there became a commander of two different privateers, one of which successfully saved the British transport *Russia Merchant*, carrying troops and stores. (A.O. 13/74.)

ANDREW LINEN

was an Irishman settled at Boston as a nurseryman and grocer in 1763, and joined the Associated Loyalists in 1775. During or after the war he settled on his own lands at Shelburne, Nova Scotia, where he was living in 1786. There is an affidavit, dated March 11, 1786, of John Harter, of Shelburne, formerly of Boston, and presumably a loyalist. (A.O. 13/51 ; A.O. 12/10, ff. 90–3.) He was allowed £40 from his claim of £350. (A.O. 12/109.)

ALEXANDER LINKLETER

was a trader in Boston and afterwards at Penobscot. He was at Halifax, Nova Scotia, in 1785. (A.O. 13/91.)

ZEBEDEE LINNEKIN

farmer, of St. George's, Maine, served as a pilot in British ships during the war. His memorial and claim, dated from St. Andrews, New Brunswick, March 24, 1786, are endorsed " rejected." (A.O. 13/51.) He was allowed £107 from his other claim of £389 18s. (A.O. 12/109.)

WARREN PITT LISLE

joined General Gage early in the Revolution, and apparently left Boston with the British troops in March, 1776. From July, 1783, to March, 1784, he lived in the island of Barbados. He died in 1788, leaving a widow and one child living in distressed circumstances in Canterbury Place, Lambeth, while his mother was in Barbados. (A.O. 13/47; A.O. 13/74; A.O. 12/102, f. 54.) He was allowed £900 from his claim of £1,425. (A.O. 12/109.)

He was the son of David Lisle,* a member of the Inner Temple and Solicitor to the Commissioners of American Customs, at Boston, who died in 1774 or early in 1775, leaving a wife, Jane, and this son and three daughters. One of these daughters married Samuel Lloyd (q.v.) The inventory of the personal property of David Lisle, who was succeeded by Daniel Leonard (q.v.), indicates a man of good circumstances, including as it does a quantity of silver ware (enumerated in detail), handsome furniture and valuable pictures and prints. (A.O. 13/47.)

HENRY LLOYD

was a principal merchant in Boston and agent to the contractors to the British troops. Accompanied by his family he left Boston with the British forces in March, 1776, for Halifax, Nova Scotia. (A.O. 13/47.)

With this memorial are certificates from General Gage and others, and many papers relating to his estate called the Manor of Queen's Village, Queen's County, Nassau Island (alias Long Island), New York, which he inherited from his father, Henry Lloyd, who died March 18, 1763, and whose will is dated March 3, 1763. This property passed to his father from the latter's wife, who had inherited it from a Mr. Ridgebell. Part of this confiscated property was in the possession of his nephew, John Lloyd, in 1784.

There is a copy of an extract from the will of his father, devising part of the above Queen's Village property among his four sons : Henry, this loyalist; John, of Stamford, Connecticut, merchant; Joseph, of Queen's Village Manor, yeoman; and James (q.v.), of Boston, physician.

John Lloyd, senior, of Queen's Village, in a letter to his brother, Dr. James Lloyd, dated August 29, 1784, states that he was then a tenant of his own son, John. There is also a letter from his nephew, John Broome, concerning his property, dated from New York, November 30, 1785.

Henry Lloyd claimed £10,162, and was allowed £3,300, less £40 for pension. (A.O. 12/109.)

In another memorial, dated April 14, 1788, he mentions that part of the compensation money was lodged at his bankers, Thomas Palmer and Hodgson, who had failed. In a long letter of the same date to his near family connection, Samuel Fitch (q.v.), he laments his sufferings and

* E. Alfred Jones, *American Members of the Inns of Court*, 1924.

distress at his advanced age by the bankruptcy of his bankers. (A.O. 13/74.)

William Hubbard, who was at St. John, New Brunswick, in 1788, had bought some timber from the Lloyd farm at Queen's Village. (A.O. 13/47.)

Henry Lloyd was a warden of King's Chapel, Boston, in 1756–7. (*Annals of King's Chapel, op. cit.*, ii, 155.) He was in Boston, Massachusetts, in October, 1785, and in London in February, 1787. According to Sabine he died in London late in 1795, or early in 1796.

Other references : A.O. 12/74, ff. 191–210 ; A.O. 13/137 ; Force, *Amer. Archives*, Ser. IV, vol. ii, pp. 1531–2.

DR. JAMES LLOYD (Plate xiii)

of Boston, physician, was owner or part owner of Queen's Village on Lloyd's Neck, Long Island, New York, and, according to Sir William Pepperell, was a loyalist, most forward and open and determined in his opposition to the rebellion, to a degree of imprudence (A.O. 12/75, ff. 9–28). He was imprisoned in 1774 or 1775 as a violent Tory, but appears to have remained in practice in Boston and was a Fellow of the Massachusetts Medical Society, incorporated in 1781 (A.O. 12/81, f. 43).

Abigail Adams in her letter of April 14, 1776, to her husband, John Adams, says that Dr. Lloyd and Dr. Miles Whitworth ought to be transported as Tories (Adams, *Letters*).

Dr. Lloyd died in 1810 at Boston, aged 82. (Sabine, *op. cit.*). He had served for two years at Guy's Hospital, London, and introduced improvements in surgery in Massachusetts in 1754 (*Proc. of Mass. Hist. Soc.*, 2nd Ser., I, 110.)

He was in possession of the Vassall family portraits, mentioned on a later page.

His brother was Henry Lloyd (*q.v.*)

The late Mr. Lawrence Park, in his admirable book (1926) on the pictures of Gilbert Stuart, declares that Dr. Lloyd in 1789 went to England to obtain compensation for his losses as a loyalist, but his application was refused unless he declared himself a British subject, which he declined to do. His portrait by Stuart was painted at Boston about 1808 and is in the possession of Mrs. Gordon Abbott, of Boston.

SAMUEL LLOYD

was appointed in September, 1767, a clerk in the office of the Secretary to the Commissioners of Customs at Boston and there married a young lady of small fortune, a daughter of David Lisle, solicitor to the Customs, and sister of Warren Pitt Lisle (*q.v.*) On the night of the battle of Lexington all their property was either seized or destroyed at their house outside Boston (A.O. 13/74.) In a letter dated from St. Omer in France, March 15, 1784, he says that by the hurricane in Barbados in October, 1780, he lost an income of nearly £400 a year and was consequently obliged for economical reasons to remove with his young family to St. Omer and there live on his small pension (A.O. 13/91).

JOSHUA LOCKE .

tidesman in the Customs at Philadelphia, claimed for land and a house at East Hoosuck (now Adams), in Berkshire County, and for a house in York township, [Maine], Massachusetts. He had been a lieutenant in the war ending in 1763 and during the Revolution carried despatches and served in the Commissary General's department (A.O. 13/51). At the end of the war he was appointed a weighing porter in the Port of London. He claimed £1,085 and was allowed £204 (A.O. 12/109) and received a military allowance of £30 from 1787 to 1810 (Ind : 5606).

WALTER LOGAN

In 1766 he was Comptroller of Customs at Perth Amboy, New Jersey, having gone from Roxbury, Massachusetts. His wife and family were banished from Roxbury on account of their loyalty and went to Needham, Massachusetts, where they left furniture in the houses of Eleazer Fuller and the Rev. Samuel West, who appear to have sheltered them. This Scotsman was the agent for the property of Governor Bernard (q.v.) in Massachusetts. He had shares in townships Nos. 2 and 5 in Penobscot Bay (A.O. 13/51). He settled in Scotland and was allowed £45 from his claim of £210, and at the rate of £80 for the loss of his official income during the war. His pension was £40. (A.O. 12/109.) Margaret, his wife, died in Edinburgh, October 13, 1841 (*Gent. Mag.*)

JOHN LONG

In 1774 he resided in Passamaquoddy and in 1779 removed to Fort George, Penobscot, where he commanded a privateer, owned by Robert Pagan (q.v.), Thomas Wyer and himself. On one cruise he was informed by prisoners that General Wadsworth* was in command of a large force of men at Camden, about thirty miles from Fort George, whereupon John Long landed fifteen men under his lieutenant, Stockden, who attacked Wadsworth and took him prisoner. With this memorial, dated from St. Andrews, New Brunswick, April 12, 1786, is a copy of an advertisement, July 22, 1779, offering a reward of 50 dollars for the capture of Long, who had escaped from custody (A.O. 13/51). (*Ontario Archives, op. cit.,* pp. 315-7.)

JOSHUA LORING, THE ELDER (Plate xxxii)

of Jamaica Plain, Roxbury, had been Captain in the Royal Navy and Commander of the naval ships on the Great Lakes ; Deputy Surveyor

* He was Colonel of a regiment of 365 men at Cambridge, Massachusetts, in February 1776. (*Mass. Soldiers and Sailors of Rev. War.*)

of the King's Woods in America ; Sheriff of the county of Suffolk ; and a member of the Council by writ of mandamus.   He left Boston in March, 1776, and went to England with despatches for Government and settled at Highgate, where he died, October 5, 1781, leaving a widow, Mary Loring [*née* Curtis]. (A.O. 13/74 ; A.O. 12/99, f. 198 ; A.O. 12/105, f. 107).

In his letter to John Blackburn in London, dated Boston, January 29, 1776, he comments on the lack of enterprise of the British Admiral in not sending cruisers to attack the American privateers which were capturing British ships (C.O. 5/40).

His four sons were Joshua (*q.v.*) ; Benjamin, a graduate of Harvard College, and a surgeon in the British forces in the American Revolution and a twin brother of Joshua ; Joseph Royall ; and John, both officers in the Royal Navy. His daughter, Hannah, was the wife of Joshua Winslow (*q.v.*)

Mr. Stark gives an account of the services of this loyalist in the war with the French in North America, and states that he declared to a friend on the morning of the battle of Lexington, "I have always eaten the King's bread, and I always intend to " (Stark, *op. cit.*, pp. 423–4).   In a letter (unpublished) to General Abercrombie in 1758 he expressed his regret that he had not carried out his duties satisfactorily (Lot 438, in sale of the Abercrombie papers, at Sotheby's, March 2, 1917).

His portrait hangs in the offices of the British and Foreign Bible Society in London.

His widow, in her memorial of December 13, 1783, states that her husband was repeatedly mobbed and ill-treated and was obliged to leave his home as early as August 31, 1774, and seek refuge in Boston.   In her letter of February 2, 1789, she says that her two sons, Joseph Royall and John, had nothing for their support at that time but their half-pay as Lieutenants in the Royal Navy.   With this letter is a schedule of the Loring property (A.O. 13/47).   His house was commandeered for use as a hospital by the Americans (Force, *op. cit.* Ser. IV., vol. ii, p. 1436.)

John Loring rose to the rank of Captain and served with distinction in the Royal Navy until his death in England, November 9, 1808.

The amount of compensation granted to Mrs. Mary Loring and her son, Joseph Royall, was £3,356, from her claim of £4,815 6s. (A.O. 12/109 ; T. 50/14).   She died in 1789.

Reference : *Loyalists' Claims, op. cit.*, pp. 13–14, 327–9.

JOSHUA LORING, THE YOUNGER

He had held a commission as Lieutenant in the 15th Regiment of Foot and served for several years in the army in North America.   For his military services he was granted 20,000 acres in New Hampshire. He resided at Dorchester, Massachusetts, and in 1775 bought the office of Sheriff of the County of Suffolk for the sum of £500 from the previous holder. He also held the office of Deputy Surveyor of Woods in North America. On April 19, 1775, he was obliged to abandon his home and with his wife and children fly for refuge to Boston, where the duties of his office of Sheriff in issuing proclamations brought upon him particular resentment, but nevertheless he continued in his duties, to the satisfaction of the Commander-in-Chief. Joshua Loring left Boston with the British army in March, 1776, and accompanied it to Halifax and New York, where he was appointed Commissary of Prisoners.

With his memorials are many of his letters and copies of official documents relating to the Loring property (F.O. 4/1; A.O. 13/47; A.O. 13/74; A.O. 12/81, ff. 107–8; A.O. 12/99, f. 198).

His military commissions were: Ensign in the army, July 11, 1761; Ensign in the 15th Foot, September 26, 1762, and Lieutenant in the same regiment, August 21, 1765. He retired in June, 1768. (Army Lists.)

On October 7, 1775, he was appointed sole auctioneer for Boston, for the disposal of property sold by order of his Majesty's Courts (Force, *op. cit.*, Ser. IV, vol. iii, p. 984).

According to a memorial of his widow, Elizabeth, announcing his death on September 18, 1789, at Englefield near Reading, he had " disdained the most flattering overtures from the disaffected party " in the Revolution. (A.O. 13/47.)

Captain Joshua Loring is said to have become rich by feeding the dead (in charging for the provisions of dead prisoners of war) and starving the living (Moore, *Diary of the American Rev.*, ii, 110). Elias Boudinot, the well-known American Commissary of Prisoners was, however, well satisfied with the treatment of prisoners in New York in February, 1778. (*Am. MSS. in R. Inst.*, *op. cit.*, i, 191), though Loring may have erred on the side of excessive economy in 1780 (*Ibid.* ii, 144). General S. Silliman, a prisoner of war of the British was well treated (T. Jones, *Hist. of New York in the Revolution*, i, 351). His wife's name was associated in a scandal with General Sir William Howe, Commander-in-Chief, whom she accompanied in the American campaigns. (*Ibid.*) Jones's observations must, however, be received with caution.

Many original documents relating to his duties as Commissary of Prisoners are in the Royal Institution.

He claimed £1,050 for the loss of his property and was granted £830. (A.O. 12/109.)

Joshua Loring at his death left a widow, Elizabeth, and five children, Eliza, John Wentworth, Henry Lloyd, William and Robert (Macham 550). His widow received a loyalist pension from 1789 until 1831 (T. 50/11, T. 50/28.) His elder son became Rear-Admiral Sir John Wentworth Loring.

BENJAMIN LOVELL

was born at Boston and had just taken his degree of B.A. at Harvard College [in 1774]. Ever firmly attached to the British Government, he was appointed in 1775 a conductor and clerk of stores in the Royal Artillery at Boston. General Gage having suspected him of sending the wrong ammunition to the Royal Artillery at Bunker Hill, under the influence of his brother [James Lovell], a member of Congress, discharged him from his offices. The Commissioners reported on his evidence on August 9, 1784, that they doubted from the way he had stated his case whether he wished well to Great Britain or not in the war and thought that perhaps he was one of the worst of enemies under the mask of friendship and it would be highly improper to recommend bounty to a man who had been dismissed under such suspicious circumstances (A.O. 12/10, f. 26).

Having received a liberal education and having no means of subsisting in America except by joining the rebels, and being willing to use every lawful means for his support, he accepted soon after his arrival in England in 1775 an appointment as tutor to the son of a gentleman of fortune and character. Upon the removal of his pupil to Geneva, Benjamin Lovell, in his anxiety to avoid being a burden to Government, accepted an engagement to instruct the children of a lady, whose death deprived him again of employment (A.O. 13/74).

In his letter of April 22, 1779, and his memorial of February 3, 1784, he states that he had intended taking orders in the Church of England after leaving Harvard and that he had resisted the attempts of his elder brother, the above James Lovell, to wean him from his loyalty and enter the American service. In 1779 he was appointed on the ordnance staff at Woolwich in England and served there until the peace (A.O. 13/74).

According to a certificate of General Gage, dated February 7, 1778, of which there is a copy in A.O. 13/74, the General acquitted him of any criminal offence in regard to Bunker Hill.

He was the eighth son of John Lovell,* headmaster of the Boston Latin School, a loyalist himself, who died in exile at Halifax, Nova Scotia, in 1778. On May 3, 1776, he was admitted to Lincoln's Inn,† but was not called to the English bar. According to Sabine, he was guilty of sending cannon balls of the wrong size to Bunker Hill and was a minister of the Gospel in England before his death in March, 1828.

His brother was John Lovell (*q.v.*).

JOHN LOVELL (Plate xxxiii)

No loyalist was more importunate in London than this Bostonian. In one petition he claims to have been distinguished for his loyalty and for his fidelity during the war. In another he states that after the evacuation of Boston by the British he was thrown into prison and kept, mostly in close confinement, for over three years for "asserting and maintaining the rights of Parliament." In a third he craves for compensation, consistent with the dignity of the King and the honour of the nation, on the ground apparently that it was the King and nation who "ordered and at first bound him to the measures he persued in America (by which he is

* John Lovell's portrait by Smibert is at Harvard University.
† E. Alfred Jones, *American Members of the Inns of Court*, 1924.

affraid he has unfortunately employ'd Seven Years of his life) as he hopes
such Grant will enable him to go to Halifax in the Ships that sails in a
few days, his Family Connections being there, and is more Convenient
if necessary for your Memorialist to make terms with the Americans 'on
the best of terms he can,' as Lord Shelborn has pleas'd to say he wisht
every American to do." (A.O. 13/43.)

Another petition contains his explanation for remaining in Boston
after the departure of the British troops. Remembering (he says) the
special Proclamation of the King, promising protection and encouragement
to his loyal subjects who should use their endeavours to quell the rebellion
and bring the disobedient into due submission he could not think it
becoming to leave Boston and preferred to remain there and make such
exertion as he hoped would merit his Majesty's approbation, in preference
to becoming a burden on the nation. (Ib.)

The following is from an anonymous statement of the case of John
Lovell, directed to Henry Strachey. He served an apprenticeship to a
merchant in Boston and at the expiry thereof he went as a clerk to Commodore Joshua Loring (q.v.) in which appointment he acquired a sufficient
sum of money to start a small business. After some years he failed, and
on making an unsuccessful demand on his former master and benefactor,
Loring, he went to England to lodge a complaint in the public offices
against him, but having failed to produce proof of his charges he returned
to Boston in very low circumstances and was obliged to seek the shelter
of his worthy father, the Master of the Grammar School, while his wife
returned to her friends. He remained dependent on his father for some
years and his conduct was frequently so ungovernable and outrageous as
to endanger the lives of the whole family, so much so that his father was
under the necessity of requesting the interposition of the magistrates,
with the result that he was committed to the public workhouse, where he
was an inmate for some time and there threatened frequently to take his
own life. At his father's intercession he was liberated. His character
was now such that he was generally avoided and for years he idled away
his time about the town without employment or visible means of support,
except such as he received from his father and friends. This was his mode
of life at the outbreak of the rebellion. During the siege of Boston he
joined the Associated Loyalists for the common defence of the town.
He also acted with Crean Brush in taking possession of certain merchants'
goods to prevent them from falling into the hands of the rebels. For this
duty John Lovell was apprehended after the British evacuation. He
might have escaped arrest if he had accompanied the British troops ; but
as he was a man of no weight or consideration with the rebels and possessed
of no property whatsoever, he was soon discharged for the offence of
assisting Brush, but his continuance in prison was due to his litigious
disposition and abuse of the leading men. This narrative was written
with a view to prevent imposition upon the British Government by a man
who rates his pretensions high and in bombastic language, who was always
of a low cast of character, indigent and worthless, and who was despised

even by his own brother, a member of Congress. In explanation of the certificates to the loyalty of Lovell by Sir William Pepperell and other distinguished loyalists, they were intended to secure for him a bare subsistence.

This anonymous statement, which was supported by Robert Auchmuty, Thomas Flucker and several other Boston loyalists, concludes with the assertion that " there is not a person who was in America about the time of the Blockade of Boston but what are sufficiently acquainted with the motives for General Cleaveland* being so zealous an advocate for Mr. L—— *but I forbear mentioning it.*" It is endorsed, " it is hop'd that this will be destroy'd after proper use is made." (A.O. 13/43.)

The original certificate of Sir William Pepperell, dated December 15, 1780, states that he was intimately acquainted with Lovell in Boston, where he bore the character of a very loyal subject. Harrison Gray, the elder, in his certificate, dated June 13, 1788, says that he came from a good family, that but few loyalists had suffered more for his firm attachment to the British Government and that he was now supported chiefly by the charity of the loyalists (A.O. 13/43.)

His long letter to Lord Hillsborough, December 15, 1781, concludes as follows : " I pray your Lordships answer to my application, for if you will not grant it, I must get it into Parliament in any way I can where I hope to find Friends tho' I am now as destetute of able support for that purpose as when I was to meet General Washington flusht with Success and left to defend my self not only against him, but an Act that might make even a Turkish Sulton blush." (A.O. 13/74.)

Lovell, in his letter of March 25, 1782, to John Robinson, Secretary to the Treasury, expresses his sense of his deception and ruin by the King and the late Parliament. He desired a pass to proceed to Ostend that he may depart honourably to the American Congress to seek that relief denied to him by the King and his ministers. He threatens to bring his case before Parliament if his application for compensation is not granted. (A.O. 13/74.)

The Commissioners remarked that Lovell's conduct and character were very singular. Although they had received many certificates to his loyalty they had also received many anonymous letters and likewise information from very good authority that he was a very undeserving man and of bad character. As he wished to return to America and was very troublesome and seemed almost insane, they thought that £30 well bestowed, upon condition that he removed himself from England (A.O. 12/99, f. 8).

There are many other papers in A.O. 13/43 ; A.O. 13/47 ; A.O.

---

* Samuel Cleaveland entered the ranks of the Royal Artillery in 1734 and rose to the rank of Colonel, October 30, 1775. He was promoted Major General, February 19, 1779, and Lieutenant General in 1787. According to Sparks, *American Biographies* (x, 153-4) he was responsible for the balls not filling the cannon at Bunker Hill.

13/74 ; A.O. 13/79 ; A.O. 12/102, f. 49 ; F.O. 4/1 ; H.O. Dom. 42/1 ; C.O. 5/754.

Other references are *Ontario Archives, op. cit.*, pp. 1139–40 ; *Loyalists' Claims, op. cit.*, pp. 65–6 ; *American MSS. in Roy. Inst., op. cit.*, ii, 13.

His brother was Benjamin Lovell (*q.v.*).

WILLIAM LUCE

was born at Boston and settled as a merchant at Elizabethtown, New Jersey, where he claims to have been the first man to oppose the rebels and where a gallows was erected in front of his door as a warning to him to refrain from active loyalty. In January 1776 he sailed for Jamaica in the West Indies and on the return voyage a year later he was captured. He afterwards acted as pilot and guide for the British on many expeditions. On February 19, 1777, he was appointed Captain in the King's militia volunteers. On July 2, 1781, he was given a warrant to raise a company of armed boatmen, which he commanded for 15 months. (A.O. 12/100, f. 347.) He claimed £1,425, and was allowed £1,272. (A.O. 12/109.)

Reference : *Loyalists' Claims, op. cit.*, pp. 313–4.

EDWARD LYDE

of Boston, merchant, was descended from reputable ancestors, as grandson of Governor Belcher, of Massachusetts, and was always able to appear in the character of a gentleman. He was a justice of the peace for Suffolk County. He fled from Boston to England in 1776 (A.O. 13/51 ; A.O. 13/74 ; A.O. 12/10, ff. 281–6). There are papers concerning the confiscation of his property in A.O. 13/51.

This loyalist was the son of Byfield Lyde and his wife, Sarah Belcher. His brother, Byfield Lyde, and his nephew, George Lyde (*q.v.*) were also loyalists. He died in New York in 1812, aged 87. (Stark, *op. cit.*, p. 447 ; A. W. H. Eaton, in *New England Hist. & Gen. Reg.*, Apr. 1915, p. 112.)

Reference : *Ontario Archives, op. cit.*, pp. 144–6.

GEORGE LYDE

was, in his own words, descended from one of the first families in Massachusetts and bred a gentleman and was for many years acting Collector of Customs at Falmouth (Portland), Maine, and deputy Receiver for Greenwich Hospital. Having experienced almost every species of persecution from the rebellious part of his countrymen for his unshaken loyalty to the best of sovereigns, he was at last banished and was ordered by the Committee of Correspondence to leave the town within a week from May 12, 1777. With another loyalist he secretly purchased from Thomas Ross (*q.v.*) a sloop named *St. Vincent*, with a cargo of timber bound for the West Indies, on the express condition that the vessel should sail for Halifax, Nova Scotia ; but the vessel not being ready to depart within the specified time for his enforced departure from Falmouth, he was obliged in the dead of night to steal away to a small island in the harbour with only one dwelling-place upon it. About a mile from this house was a cave in a mountain and there he remained in hiding for a week, fed by the good peasant. At length his sloop sailed and he was taken on board. Within a short distance of Halifax she was captured by H.M.S. *Scarborough* (Captain Andrew Barkley) and taken into that port and condemned and sold under the Prohibitory Act of 1776 at Halifax, June 28, 1777, notwithstanding the intercession of General Eyre Massey and others and in contradiction, as he conceived it to be, of the royal proclamation inviting loyalists to flee for safety to the royal standard and promising to protect their persons and property. A loyalist, he adds, who had fled from persecution should not be the victim of such confiscation of his vessel. Thus he suffered from both sides in the conflict. (A.O. 13/47; A.O. 13/74; A.O. 13/91.)

With his petitions is a certificate of Lieutenant Governor Thomas Oliver, stating that George Lyde's father married a daughter of Governor Belcher, of Massachusetts. There are also certificates from General Eyre Massey and Henry Newton, Collector of Customs at Halifax in 1780. (A.O. 13/74.)

His long and eloquent letter, dated London, October 22, 1782, pictures his wrongs and sufferings. What with the plunder of one side and the other in the Revolution he is left naked in the world as he was born. If compensation be impossible, he hopes he may have an appointment in the Royal Household, the army or navy or some other place. (A.O. 13/74.)

George Lyde claimed £600 and was allowed £80. His claim of £125 for the loss of his annual official income during the war was met by a grant at the rate of £100 per annum. (A.O. 12/109.) A pension of £50 was granted to him until his death. (A.O. 459/7; A.O. 461/15; T. 50/6.) With a schedule of his losses there is the deed of sale of the above sloop by Thomas Ross (*q.v.*), May 17, 1777. (A.O. 13/47.)

The Commissioners described him as "a stout young man" and recommended him for a commission in the army or marines or an appointment in the Customs. (A.O. 12/105, f. 40.)

He was the son of Byfield Lyde (a loyalist, of Boston, who died in exile at Halifax, Nova Scotia, in 1776) and his wife, Sarah, only daughter of Governor Belcher. His uncle was Edward Lyde (*q.v.*). A sister married Joseph Domett (*q.v.*). (Sabine, *op. cit.*; Stark, *op. cit.*, p. 447.)

JOHN LYMBURNER

was a yeoman, of Fort George, Penobscot, and was there in January, 1784. (A.O. 13/91.)

MATTHEW LYMBURNER

was a Scotsman who had settled at Majabigwaduce in 1770 and who affected to be neutral in the political disputes of the Revolution but in private was a loyalist. He settled at St. Andrews, New Brunswick. (A.O. 13/51.) He was allowed £60 from his claim of £395 11s. (A.O. 12/109.)

References : *Ontario Archives, op. cit.*, pp. 311-2 ; *Acadiensis*, vii, 229.

DONALD McALPIN

was born in Scotland and emigrated in 1757 to New Hampshire, settling finally in Boston, where he was a dancing master. He was in command of a military company during the war and was severely wounded. (A.O. 12/101, f. 39.)

WILLIAM McALPINE

For twenty years this Scotsman, who was born in 1731, had been a printer, bookbinder and stationer at Boston and had two printing presses constantly employed, with ten or twelve workmen. His sales were extensive and his trade flourishing. In Boston, the spirit of rebellion (he says) was fiercer than in any other part of America. Spies were placed to watch the words and actions of a Briton. The vilest of people were engaged in the despicable office of informer. Life and property having become insecure, associations of loyalists were formed to oppose persecution and lawless authority, and he joined the Loyal North British Volunteers, in which he served until the evacuation of Boston by the British. In his hurried departure he was obliged to leave all his property behind, worth £1,800 sterling. From Halifax, Nova Scotia, he sailed in 1777 for Greenock, Scotland, where he had the happiness of meeting his tenderly loved wife. He was born in the vicinity of Greenock and was educated there. With the help of Mr. Kincaid, his Majesty's printer for Scotland, he pursued his business as a printer in Greenock. (A.O. 13/47 ; A.O. 13/75.) With his petition is an original certificate with the autograph signatures of the magistrates, ministers, elders and principal merchants of Greenock, testifying to his personal worth. This is endorsed by John McAlpine, late Lieutenant in the 87th Foot, dated Edinburgh, August 29, 1787, declaring his knowledge of the loyalty and services of William McAlpine. (A.O. 13/47.) There is also an affidavit, dated January 8, 1784, of John Semple, of Glasgow, formerly a merchant in Boston and New York, that McAlpine ws a true loyalist and had served with him in the Loyal North British Volunteers in Boston ; and another affidavit, from James Henderson, of Glasgow, formerly a merchant and loyalist in Boston, testifying to his loyalty. (*Ib.*)

Three of his letters dated in 1785, 1786 and 1787, are of no interest. (*Ib.*) He claimed £850 and was allowed £600. (A.O. 12/109.)

He died at Greenock, July 20, 1788, leaving a widow and a mother-in-law, Elizabeth Glass.

Governor Hutchinson in an undated note says that if McAlpine had " not been well affected, it would have been remarked for the singularity of it, as differing from other Scotchmen in the Town, who were almost without exception good subjects." (A.O. 13/75.)

McAlpine was the sole printer of Ames's well-known Almanacks (first issued in 1726 in Boston) from 1766 until 1773. His printing works in 1768 were in Marlborough Street, "midway between the Governor's and Dr. Gardiner's." The author has a copy of *Two Discourses*, by the Rev. Samuel Hopkins, printed by McAlpine, 1758, which has the autograph of Lord Buchan.

WILLIAM McCLANING

mariner, Boston. (A.O. 13/75.)

GILBERT McCLURE

was a merchant and shipbuilder at Falmouth (Portland), Maine. On leaving that place he left his property in charge of Thomas Cumming, a loyalist. He was at Ayr, Scotland, in 1785. (A.O. 13/95.)

DR. WILLIAM McKINSTRY

a physician, was obliged to flee from his home at Taunton and seek safety at Boston in 1774, and there attended the wounded after the battle of Lexington. He died on board a transport at Nantasket in March, 1776, leaving a wife and eight children, the eldest of whom was William (*q.v.*). His wife and family proceeded to Halifax, Nova Scotia, and thence to New York and Rhode Island, where she and five children fell into the hands of the revolters at the evacuation by the British.

An inventory of the personal property of Dr. McKinstry is dated August 21, 1784, and signed by his widow, Priscilla, at Haverhill, Massachusetts [where she died in 1786]. With it is a copy of a deed of sale of property by Dr. McKinstry and his wife, Priscilla, June 9, 1775. (A.O., 13/47.)

The children were granted £500 from their claim of £661. (A.O. 12/109.)

Dr. William McKinstry was born October 8, 1732, and married in 1760 Priscilla, daughter of the Rev. Nathaniel Leonard, of Plymouth, Massachusetts, and had ten children. (Willis, *Genealogy of the McKinstry Family*, 1866, pp. 19–22.) Willis says here that Priscilla was a sister of Daniel Leonard (*q.v.*), but Sabine says she was a cousin and was "a finely educated and high-spirited woman of elegant manners," who "was compelled by a large collection of females to march round the *Liberty Pole*."

REV. WILLIAM McKINSTRY (Plate xxxiv)

was the eldest child of Dr. William McKinstry (*q.v.*) and was born in 1763. At the early age of 15 he served in the Associated Loyalists in Rhode Island and was in several actions. He was a Lieutenant in the armed sloop, *General Leslie* (see page 194), which was captured by the Americans, and he was taken prisoner in November, 1778. Upon his release, he sailed for England, and on the return voyage to America as a volunteer to join the

Associated Loyalists, he had the misfortune to lose his right hand in an engagement with an American privateer. In 1781 he accompanied his kinsman, Daniel Leonard (*q.v.*), to Bermuda. (A.O. 13/75.)

In a memorial dated April 29, 1789, praying for a continuation of his loyalist pension, he is described as the Rev. William McKinstry. (A.O. 13/47.) His pension of £50 was paid until his death [at Concord, New Hampshire, August 26, 1823, aged 61]. (A.O. 12/105, f. 73 ; T. 50/6 ; T. 50/27.)

In the long account in Sabine he is described as a graduate of Oxford, but his name is not in Foster's *Alumni Oxonienses*, nor is there any record of his being Rector of East Grinstead or Lingfield, as stated by Sabine.

His portrait by Samuel F. B. Morse, the inventor of the telegraph, is in the possession of the New Hampshire Historical Society.

JOHN MALCOLM

This loyalist Surveyor of Customs at Falmouth (Portland), Maine, served with honour in the long war in America between the French and British, and held three commissions as Captain. He appears to have been a mariner before his appointment to the Customs, having commanded twelve different merchant ships in various parts of the world. From Falmouth he fled to Boston and claims to have been the first man to be tarred and feathered in the Revolution. (A.O. 13/75 ; A.O. 13/79 ; A.O. 12/105, f. 141 ; *Earl of Dartmouth MSS.*, *op. cit.*, ii, 192, 263.)

In an interesting letter* of January 31, 1774, by Miss Ann Hulton, sister of Henry Hulton (*q.v.*), she describes the shocking treatment of this poor old man, who was stripped naked on one of the coldest nights in winter and his arm dislocated by the violence used in taking off his clothes. He was then tarred and feathered and dragged in a cart, followed by a mob of thousands, some beating him with clubs—a spectacle exhibited for about five hours. The poor old wretch behaved himself with great intrepidity through it all, and so far from complying with the demand to curse his masters of the Customs and the King and Governor, he cried aloud, " Curse all traitors." To all the threats of death by hanging he replied calmly that the mob could not hang him, for God was above the devil. So savage was the cruelty of the mob that the doctors had no hope of his recovery. He had fought under Governor Tryon against the Regulators in North Carolina.

A dispute occurred between John Malcolm and Francis Waldo (*q.v.*). (Gov. Hutchinson's *Diary*, ii, 100–1 ; Acts of the Privy Council, Colonial.)

Towards the end of the American War of Independence he was appointed an Ensign in an Independent Company of Invalids at Plymouth, England, and died there, November 23, 1788, leaving a widow and two children unprovided for. On April 1, 1791, his family were at Boston, Massachusetts, and appealed to be put on the Compassionate List for orphans of British officers. (W.O. 25/3101.)

* See page 167.

John Malcolm served as an Ensign under Colonel Waldo in the 2nd Massachusetts Regiment at Louisburg in 1745 and was captain of a vessel which carried despatches from Louisburg to Boston in the same year. (Stark, *op. cit.*, pp. 451–2 ; Diary of John Rowe, in *Proc. of Mass. Hist. Soc.*, 2nd Ser., x, 82.)

JAMES, PATRICK AND JOHN McMASTER

These three brothers were " natives of the county of Galloway, in Scotland, where their ancestors resided for a number of years with un-blemished reputations and unshaken loyalty." James emigrated in 1765 to Boston, followed by Patrick in 1767. John first settled at Portsmouth, New Hampshire, in 1768, and remained in America until 1772, when he left for London. They established a large and profitable business in these two towns as merchants and importers of British goods, having imported between the years 1769 and 1774 goods to the value of more than £15,000 per annum. From their high position as merchants, James and Patrick McMaster were strongly solicited early in the political disputes to join the rebels, but " from the honest principles of loyalty to their Sovereign & this country, & as bound by their allegiance they constantly rejected & opposed by every means & arguments in their power the insidious attempts of the disaffected." They refused to sign the Non-Importation agreement ; and were proscribed and " were many times in danger of their lives." Patrick suffered much for his loyalty and was threatened with tar and feathers, eventually seeking refuge at Castle William in Boston harbour. Here the brothers carried on their business as importers of British goods. In October 1770 they returned to Boston and were joyfully received by the inhabitants, who in general had agreed to abandon the scheme of non-importation. The whole town attributed the abandonment of this scheme to the steady resolution of these two loyalists. John and James are mentioned in the Banishment Act of New Hampshire, 1778. Patrick was enrolled a member of the Loyal North British Volunteers at Boston in 1775 and sought refuge at Halifax in 1776. James escaped from Portsmouth, New Hampshire, in H.M.S. *Rainbow* and settled at Shelburne, Nova Scotia. Their brother, Daniel, went to New Hampshire to recover debts due to the brothers and recovered £814 17s. due at Boston. (A.O. 13/51 ; A.O. 13/91 ; A.O. 12/11, ff. 23–31.)

In A.O. 13/51 is a long list of their debtors, with the amounts due.

Peter Mitchell, formerly the clerk of the McMasters at Portsmouth, New Hampshire, testified by certificate to their property there, dated Portsmouth, March 9, 1786. (A.O. 13/51.)

The recantation of James McMaster is in Force, *American Archives*, Ser. IV, vol. ii, p. 552.

Patrick McMaster had a lot at St. John, New Brunswick (*Acadiensis*, v, 309). He was drowned by the foundering of a schooner in the Bay of Fundy in 1797 (Murdoch, *Hist. of Nova Scotia*, iii, 167). Daniel,

o

who also had a lot at St. John, married the only daughter of the Rev. Samuel Andrews, an Episcopalian loyalist, of Connecticut (*Acadiensis*, vii, 209).

ARCHIBALD McNEILL

was a noted baker and flour merchant, of Boston, whose annual income from his business amounted to £500, and who was murdered by two Indians on his journey to settle on his granted lands on the River St. John in New Brunswick in July, 1784. His grandfather was Roland Houghton, of North Yarmouth, Casco Bay. There are several papers and affidavits concerning his property (A.O. 13/51 ; A.O. 13/91), and a list of claims against his estate (A.O. 12/81, f. 111). His widow, Elizabeth, and her five children, namely, Archibald, who was in the Island of Jamaica in 1787 ; Elzabeth Shoolbred, wife of David Shoolbred, merchant in Quebec in 1787 ; Sarah or Sally McNeill and Mary Walter, both in Quebec in 1787 ; and Nancy Hill, in the United States in 1787, were granted compensation £2,137 from their claim of £7,322 15s. (A.O. 12/61, ff. 77-8 ; A.O. 12/109.)

An account of the transaction of Archibald McNeill with John Fenton, of Charlestown, Massachusetts, regarding some land on the River St. John, is in Vol. I of the *New Brunswick Hist. Soc.*, p. 102, and in Vol. III (2nd Ser.), of *Proc. of Mass. Hist. Soc.*, p.67. He had pew No. 21 in King's Chapel, Boston (*Annals of King's Chapel, op. cit.*).

In the Chatham Papers, bundle 225, are various papers concerning his transactions with Captain John Montresor, Chief Engineer of the British Army in America. One surcharge of sundry sums amounting to £5,646 2s. 6d., said to have been paid to McNeill and Charles Whitworth for stores and labour provided by them, was disallowed to Montresor because of his irregular methods of keeping accounts. A similar claim for £199 2s. 5d., alleged to have been on behalf of John Joy (*q.v.*), was disallowed because it was not in Joy's own handwriting and was a suspicious transaction on the part of Montresor. A similar claim for over £591 in the name of George Warden (*q.v.*) was rejected for the same reason. Montresor, from these transactions, would seem to have been suspected of obtaining money by false pretences and by forgery, though his method of keeping accounts was mildly described as " irregular."

Reference : *Ontario Archives, op. cit.*, pp. 918–22.

BENJAMIN MARSTON

was a selectman of Marblehead, whence he escaped to Boston on a dark night in November, 1775, in an open boat accompanied by only one man. He was three times a prisoner during the war. A part of his confiscated property was leased to his nephew, Marston Watson. His wife was Sarah Sweet, sister of Joseph Sweet. There is an inventory of his goods and real estate (A.O. 12/10, ff. 166-177). With his original memorial are lists of valuable personal property (confiscated) and of objects sold in March, 1779, with the prices realised, and details of his real estate (A.O. 13/51). He claimed £1,415 4s., and was allowed £150 (A.O. 12/109).

Benjamin Marston was a refugee in New Brunswick, and was first sheriff for Northumberland County. In March, 1792, he had, however, accepted an appointment as surveyor general to a large company for the settlement of the Island of Bulama on the west coast of Africa, and died there on August 10 following (*Judges of New Brunswick, op. cit.,* pp. 12, 185, 224). He was born at Salem and graduated at Harvard College in 1749; he was a prosperous merchant and one of the most prominent inhabitants in Marblehead (*Stark, op. cit.,* pp. 460-2). An account of this loyalist and some of his letters and poems are printed in the *New England Hist. and Gen. Reg.,* xxvii, 390-403.

Reference : *Ontario Archives, op. cit.,* pp. 605-8.

MICHAEL MARTIN

An appraisement and particulars of the estate of this loyalist and that of his wife, Zilpah, at Northborough, are with the papers of Ebenezer Cutler (*q.v.*) in A.O. 13/50. He is mentioned in A.O. 12/83, f. 2. A loyalist of this name is described in the Banishment Act as a trader, of Brookfield.

COLONEL WILLIAM MARTIN

was for 42 years an officer in the Royal Artillery, and served in America throughout the Revolutionary war. By his marriage to Ann, daughter of James Gordon (merchant, of Boston, and warden of King's Chapel in 1739-40, who died in 1770), he acquired considerable property in Boston and elsewhere in Massachusetts and in New Hampshire. With his petition is a schedule of his property ; an official copy of the order of the Judge of the Probate Court to divide the Gordon property, March 11, 1771 ; an affidavit of John Sparhawk, late of Portsmouth, New Hampshire (formerly Colonel Martin's agent in that province), stating, *inter alia,* that James Gordon died intestate and that two-thirds of his property in New Hampshire was set off by the Probate Court to William Gordon, son of James Gordon, and one-third to Ann Martin ; and affidavits of Abijah Willard and Walter Logan to Colonel Martin's estate (A.O. 13/47). His wife's house and wharf in Boston were rased to the ground by order of General Gage, and the materials used in building a fortification on the same spot in 1775 (A.O. 12/71, ff. 102-8). Claims against the estate are in A.O. 12/81, f. 110.

Some correspondence which passed between him and his father-in-law is in *Proceedings of Mass. Hist. Soc.,* 2nd Ser., xiii, 379-396.

Reference for James Gordon : *Annals of King's Chapel, op. cit.*

JOHN MASCARENE

died of a broken heart, having remained loyal to the last. In 1767 he
was appointed Comptroller of the Customs at Salem. He left a widow,
Margaret (A.O. 12/101, f. 230), who was the daughter of Edward Holyoke,
President of Harvard College. He was the son of General Jean Paul
Mascarene (1684-1760), and was born at Annapolis Royal, Nova Scotia,
in 1722, and died at Boston September 24, 1779. His miniature portrait
is in the possession of Mrs. E. R. Warren, of Boston (Ex inform. Mr.
Paul Mascarene Hamlen).

 Descendants claim that he was not a loyalist, despite his widow's
declaration that he " remained loyal to the last."

SAMUEL MATHER

son of the Rev. Samuel Mather, of Boston, was " descended from some
of the most ancient and respectable settlers " of Massachusetts. In the
war with France he served as an officer in the Provincial forces, and for
some years as a deputy commissary-general. In 1763 this rank was
continued to him in Quebec by General Amherst, as a reward for his
services in the war, but in consequence of the change from military
control to civil government he lost the appointment. He was appointed
a justice of the peace in the province of Quebec and a commissioner of the
Court of King's Bench. His two brothers died on service in the wars
with France—one at the siege of Havana and the other with his regiment
at Halifax, Nova Scotia. Early in 1771 he received the appointment of
chief clerk in the Customs at his native place, Boston, where he had
other employment, worth £200 a year. Samuel Mather says he was
" guilty of disobliging the best of fathers by refusing his advice &
commands to quit the service of His Most Gracious Sovereign & enter
into that of the States of America." He appears to have been an exile
in South Wales during a part of the war. In a letter of October 29,
1782, to Counsellor Price, of Cowbridge, Glamorganshire, he says that
he had " intended removing back to some part of Glamorgan as soon as
the bathing season was over here [at Ilfracombe] and to have taken a
small cot with a bit of land to myself if I had received my allowance
from Government, that I might enjoy the pleasing acquaintance I had
made in that county, but alas! I cannot stir for want thereof." He
called upon the counsellor *in forma pauperis*, having lost the only friend
he could apply for assistance, his maternal uncle, Thomas Hutchinson,
Governor of Massachusetts * (A.O. 13/47).

 Samuel Mather was compensated £200 from his claim of the same
amount and at the rate of £200 for the loss of his official income during
the war. He was also granted a pension of £100 until his death early

---

 * Governor Hutchinson's sister, Hannah, was the wife of the Rev. Samuel
Mather.

John Lovell

PLATE XXXIII

PLATE XXXIV   Rev. William McKinstry

in 1813 (A.O. 12/109; A.O. 459/7; T. 50/8; T. 59/44). Other references to him are in A.O. 13/75 and A.O. 12/99, f. 226).
A loyalist of this name died in Boston in 1813 (Sabine).

SAMUEL MATTHEWS
With his memorial, dated Fort George, Penobscot, March 24, 1784, stating that he had been resident as a yeoman at Penobscot for nearly twenty years, is a schedule of his losses by the Revolution (A.O. 13/91).

EBENEZER MEDBERY
was born at Rehoboth, Massachusetts. In September, 1781, he was in Barbados, and there joined H.M.S. *Berbice* as a volunteer. He served in several ships of the Royal Navy until March 11, 1783, when he was discharged as consumptive (A.O. 13/75).

BENJAMIN MILLIKEN
ship builder and owner of saw mills, of Union River, Penobscot, was employed during the war as a pilot on several British ships, before he was taken prisoner by Colonel Allen and his Indians. Two of his sons-in-law were loyalists. With his memorial, dated from St. Andrews, New Brunswick, March 16, 1786, are certificates to his loyalty from Dr. John Calef (*q.v.*), Captain George Haslam and Thomas Pagan, and a certificate of Jacob Lord, a former tenant of Milliken, regarding his confiscated property, and another from James Lord (A.O. 13/51).

THOMAS MICHELL, or MITCHELL
was born in Devonshire, September 10, 1710, and had lived for 28 years in Boston before the evacuation by the British troops in 1776. He was the owner of considerable property there, including three vessels, and was part owner of five other vessels; he also had a fishery at Point Shirley. His wife remained at Boston. He died, September 8, 1785, at Salcombe Regis, near Sidmouth, in the county of his birth (A.O. 13/75; A.O. 13/91; A.O. 12/105, f. 2; Parish Registers).

WILLIAM MILLER
was Deputy Collector and searcher at the Customs at Newbery, Piscataqua (A.O. 13/71; A.O. 13/75; A.O. 12/106, f. 70). He was allowed compensation at the rate of £100 for the loss of his official salary during the war and was granted a pension of £50 until 1802, when he probably died (A.O. 12/109; A.O. 461/18; T. 50/6). He returned to Boston and was naturalised as a citizen of Massachusetts. By trade he was a wharfinger (A.O. 12/81, f. 44).

NATHANIEL MILLS

was a printer and partner of John Hicks in Boston, where they published a weekly newspaper devoted to the Royal cause, and thereby incurred the displeasure of the republicans, who prevented the news-carriers from circulating their newspaper. Both men left Boston with the British troops in March, 1776, and were at Halifax, Nova Scotia, in 1784. (A.O. 13/96.)

Mills was taken into custody with Joseph Otis, formerly sheriff of Boston, in 1775. (Force, *op. cit.*, Ser. IV, vol. iii, pp. 59-60).

The newspaper was the *Massachusetts Gazette and Post-Boy*.

An account of both men is in Sabine.

MARY MOORE

In evidence, June 10, 1784, she stated that she was a native of New England and lived at Piscataway with her husband. Both left in January, 1775, her husband fearing that he would be compelled to serve with the Americans. He went to the West Indies and was never heard of afterwards. She was entitled to one-third of 600 acres in Casco Bay and one-ninth of 600 acres in Salt Cove. (A.O. 13/75 ; A.O. 12/100, f. 303).

CAPTAIN HENRY MOWAT, R.N.

In 1773, when serving at Portsmouth, New Hampshire, as commanding officer of H.M.S. *Canso* on the general survey of lands in the northern district of America, he applied to Governor Wentworth of that province for a grant of land in accordance with the King's proclamation after the peace of 1763, whereby the officers and men who had served in the British forces in the war with the French in North America were entitled to free grants of land, and he was granted 4,470 acres in New Hampshire (A.O. 13/52). His claim of £2,011 for compensation for the loss of his property in that province was rejected. (A.O. 12/109).

It was this officer who carried out the duty of destroying the town of Falmouth (Portland), Maine, on October, 1775, as is recorded by several loyalists in these pages.

Captain Mowat was born in Scotland in 1734, the son of Captain Patrick Mowat, R.N., and served at sea for six years before receiving a commission as Lieutenant in H.M.S. *Baltimore* in 1756. For twelve years he served in H.M.S. *Canso*, mostly on the North American station, and also in H.M.S. *Albany* during the Revolution. He died off the American coast, near Cape Henry, April 14, 1798, on board H.M.S. *Assistance*, and was buried at Hampton in Virginia. He had written shortly before his death, " A Relation of the Services in which I was engaged in America, from 1759, to the close of the American War in 1783 " ; but it was never published. Three brothers served in the Royal Navy (*Acadiensis*, viii, 306-16 ; *The Frontier Missionary*, *op. cit.*, pp. 160, 274-5 ; *Am. MSS. in Roy. Inst., op. cit.*, i, 16, 381, 393, 436, 441, 459, 461, 462 ; ii, 230).

His commissions were : Lieutenant, January 22, 1759 ; Commander, June 2, 1776 ; and Captain, October 26, 1782.

JAMES RYDER MOWAT

In response to the proclamation of the British Commander-in-chief at Penobscot and the officers of the Royal Navy on that station, inviting all loyalists to join them and assist them against the rebellious subjects and promising them protection, he repaired to Penobscot and there bought a house and land in 1779. Here he had contracted for building a wharf before the cession of this new province to the Americans. He was the commander of an armed cruiser on the coast of Penobscot during the war, and was taken prisoner and eventually exchanged. He was in London in March, 1784. (A.O. 13/91).

THOMAS MULLINS

of Worcester County, is mentioned in A.O. 12/83, f. 2.

MAJOR DANIEL MURRAY

was a lawyer, who, rather than submit to take oaths to and arms for the Americans, relinquished his property at Rutland and, with three brothers,* joined the British forces as volunteers. With " thirty-seven others, young gentlemen of consideration in the country," he joined a company called Wentworth's Volunteers† and he was appointed Captain commandant, June 1, 1777. As these young gentlemen volunteers anticipated a speedy termination of the war, they stipulated that they would serve without pay. The war having been prolonged beyond their expectations they were obliged to borrow considerable sums of money for their subsistence, upon the security of their patron, Governor John Wentworth, of New Hampshire. They served without pay until April, 1778, in the campaigns in Rhode Island and Connecticut, after which the corps was disbanded.

On February 22, 1781, Daniel Murray received a warrant as Major to raise a corps of Light Dragoons, known as the King's American Dragoons,‡ to consist of six troops of sixty each. In August, 1782, the corps was completed, at great expense to himself of £2,032, in subsisting the recruits for nearly eleven months and buying horses. For this sum he was actually arrested after the war. (A.O. 13/47 ; A.O. 13/75 ; A.O. 12/100, f. 195.)

* See p. 217.
† See Appendix.
‡ For this Regiment see Benjamin Thompson.

His farm at Rutland was bought by General Putnam. With his papers are documents concerning his confiscated property (A.O. 13/47), for which he was compensated £1,200 from his claim of £2,493. (A.O. 12/109.)

Major Daniel Murray was born about 1752 and died February 24, 1832 (*Ind.* 5605-6). At the end of the war he went to New Brunswick, and was a Judge of the Court of Common Pleas. From 1793 to 1802 he was Major of the King's New Brunswick Regiment. (Jonas Howe in *Colls. of New Brunswick Hist. Soc.*, i, 13–15). He was married to Abigail Cummings, spinster, at Burlington, Vermont, April 30, 1822. (W.O. 42/M50.)

Daniel Murray was the eldest son of Colonel John Murray (*q.v.*), and served his legal clerkship with, and lived for several years in the family of, James Putnam (*q.v.*). (*Loyalists' Claims, op. cit.*, pp. 178–80 ; *Judges of New Brunswick, op. cit.*, pp. 44, 127.) He graduated at Harvard College in 1771, and died at Portland, Maine. (Stark, *op. cit.*, p. 377.) He was an able and enterprising man, but unfortunate. (*Winslow Papers*, p. 30, n.)

JAMES MURRAY (Plate xxxv)

This loyalist Scotsman was a settler in, and a conspicuous man in the colonial history of North Carolina, as President of the Council. He afterwards settled in Boston and was there extremely active as a magistrate, especially in the " affair of Captain Preston," during the so-called Boston Massacre, when he was burnt in effigy. (A.O. 12/99, f. 319.) Some of these facts are also embodied in the memorial of his widow, Margaret, dated from Edinburgh, March 15, 1784, with the addition that she herself lost £2,000 by the American Revolution. She was granted a pension of £50. (A.O. 13/91.) He died in exile at Halifax, Nova Scotia, in 1781. His brother, Dr. John Murray, of Norwich, England, claimed for his confiscated property in behalf of his (James's) daughters, Dorothy Forbes, widow, and Elizabeth Murray, spinster, and his grandchildren. (A.O. 13/90.).

A full account of this loyalist may be found in *Letters of James Murray, Loyalist*, ed. by N. M. Tiffany and S. I. Lesley, 1901.

His portrait by Copley is in the possession of Frank Lyman, Esq., Brooklyn, New York.

JOHN MURRAY

For over forty years he was a resident in Massachusetts, where, through the smiles of Divine Providence upon his industry, he had acquired a fortune sufficient to educate and support a large family and to settle them in a genteel way of life. In 1751 he was elected by the town of Rutland, his place of residence, as its representative in the General Assembly, and was elected annually until 1774. A year later he was chosen a Justice of the Peace for the county of Worcester, and in 1755 appointed

Colonel of militia and a Judge of the Court of Common Pleas in that county. In 1774 he was appointed a member of the Council by mandamus, and in consequence he was obliged to abandon his home and estate and seek the protection of the British garrison in Boston, where he remained until the evacuation in March, 1776, when he sailed for Nova Scotia, and thence to England in June, 1776. For reasons of economy he was compelled to live in Wales. In 1778 his family consisted of a wife and ten children, including four sons in Wentworth's Volunteers. He appealed for help from Government to support him in his distress and to educate his children. With his memorial is a schedule of his losses. (A.O. 13/75.)

John Murray in evidence stated that his rent roll from his great property amounted to £26,000, and in addition he had £1,000 from his fortune. His estate was four times as large as Hatch's or Lechmere's. He complained with some bitterness that while the three loyalists, David Ingersoll, Bliss, and Benjamin Gridley, were undeservingly granted loyalist pensions of £150 each, John Chandler (q.v.) received only £100. All these three, he added, would have been glad to have eaten a dinner in Chandler's kitchen in New England. Thomas Flucker (q.v.) spoke well of John Murray, as did General Sir William Howe in person. (A.O. 12/105, f. 14.)

A schedule of the notes of hand due to him, a schedule of the title deeds of his estate, with many copies of deeds and papers relating to his land and the confiscation of his property, are in A.O. 13/47.

He claimed £21,832 10s. for the loss of his property, and was allowed £9,774, less £80 for pension. He also claimed £30 for the loss of his professional income (as judge) during the war, and was granted that amount. His loyalist pension was continued until his death. (A.O. 12/109; A.O. 459/7; A.O. 461/16; T. 50/6.)

This loyalist settled in New Brunswick, and was first sheriff of York County. He died at St. John, August 30, 1794, and, according to the inscription on his monument, he was born in Ireland, November 22, 1720. A daughter married Joshua Upham (q.v.). (*Judges of New Brunswick, op. cit.*, pp. 12, 56, 80, 96.)

John Murray's four sons, mentioned above as in Wentworth's Volunteers, were Daniel (q.v.); probably Samuel, a graduate of Harvard College and a loyalist, who is described as Dr. Samuel Murray, of H.M. military hospital at Charlestown, South Carolina, where he died in October, 1781*; and Robert and John, both of whom became captains in the King's American Dragoons.

His portrait, by Copley, is in the possession of his descendant, Hon. Sir Douglas Hazen, K.C.M.G., of New Brunswick.

John Murray emigrated to America in 1735. During the blockade of Boston he served in the Associated Loyalists, in the same patrol as Sir William Pepperell, and was very active. (*Loyalists' Claims, op. cit.*, p. 27; Stark, *op. cit.*, pp. 376–8.)

---

* *S. Carolina Hist. & Gen. Mag.*, xvii, 161.

WILLIAM MURRAY

went from Ireland to Boston and was appointed tidewaiter at the Custom House in 1772 through the influence of his relation, Colonel Murray (? John Murray (*q.v.*)). In 1774 he was transferred to Marblehead. He joined the Royal Irish Volunteers at Boston in 1775 under James Forrest (*q.v.*). In 1777 he was serving with the loyal militia in the city of New York, and in the same year went to England. (A.O. 13/75; A.O. 12/99, f. 186; A.O. 12/100, f. 197). His claim of £151 5s. was disallowed. His claim for £45 for the loss of his office during the war was met by an allowance of £40, and he was granted a pension of £20. (A.O. 12/109.) According to a letter of Joshua Locke (*q.v.*), dated February 17, 1789, Murray was made an Excise watchman at the Port of London, and afterwards at Hull, late in, or after, the war, but in consequence of excessive drinking and neglect of duty he was dismissed and went to the North of Ireland. (A.O. 13/47.)

Reference: *Loyalists Claims, op. cit.*, p. 185.

DANIEL NEAL

was a mast maker in the town of his birth, Boston, and from 1777 served in the loyal militia of New York and of Charlestown, South Carolina, until he was taken prisoner at Yorktown. He was at Shelburne, Nova Scotia, in 1786. (A.O. 13/51; A.O. 12/10, ff. 178–181.) His claim for timber and tools at Boston was disallowed, having been left in possession of his father, "a rebel." (A.O. 12/61, f. 25.) He was a member of the Ancient and Honourable Artillery Company of Massachusetts in 1772. (Roberts, *History of the Company*, ii, 170.)

Reference: *Ontario Archives, op. cit.*, pp. 107–8.

REV. ROBERT BOUCHER NICKOLLS

His father was formerly an officer of Customs at Wilmington, Virginia, but appears to have settled near Boston, where he had a small post under Government, and where he died during the Revolution. His mother and her family were obliged to flee from their home and to take refuge in Quebec, where one of her sons distinguished himself by his bravery in the defence of that place against the Americans.

This loyalist says he was the only person in Massachusetts who had any share in the instruction of youth in principles at all favourable to the union of the Colonies with the Mother Country, all the seminaries of learning in New England having been solely calculated to form republicans and independents in Church. He officiated as a clergyman at Boston,* and afterwards as curate at Salem to the Rev. William McGilchrist, Rector of St. Peter's Church. From the beginning of the Revolution

* As assistant to the Rev. Henry Caner (*q.v.*).

he served successively as chaplain on board H.M.S. *Bristol,* and was present at the attack on Sullivan's Island,* in South Carolina, and later in the army in New York and Rhode Island. His widowed mother and her children were living at Leicester, in England, in October, 1782. (A.O. 13/47 ; A.O. 13/75.)

In addition to his curacy he had a flourishing school at Salem.† Daniel Parker Coke [one of the Commissioners for American Loyalists' Claims] had known him for twenty years, having been at the same Oxford College. (A.O. 12/105, f. 74.) He is mentioned in a letter of Governor Hutchinson, July 24, 1775. (British Museum : Addl. MSS., 35427.) In a letter to Lord Dartmouth he relates his distresses and loyalty, and prays for an appointment in Ireland. (*Earl of Dartmouth, MSS., op. cit.,* ii, 348.)

In the admissions to Queen's College, Oxford, he is described as the son of Isaac Nicholls, of Barbados, gentleman. He matriculated in 1762, aged 18 ; took the degrees of B.A. in 1766 and B.C.L. in 1778.

The date of his appointment as assistant to the Rev. William McGilchrist was 1771. About twenty members of this congregation signed the address to General Gage in 1774. The Rector himself was a staunch loyalist, and refused to read the Declaration of Independence, and continued to read the prayer for the King and Royal family. Continuous disturbances of his Church services by the mob at last compelled him to close the building in February, 1777. Broken in health, he died on April 19, 1780, at the age of 73, after a ministry in Salem of 33 years. (Gavet, *Hist. Sketch of St. Peter's Church*). Of him the Salem loyalist, Samuel Curwen (*q.v.*) wrote on July 13, 1780, that he was a man of undissembled virtue and singular integrity, and of the most friendly heart a man to whose memory he could not fail to pay the tribute of a tear.

In 1786 this loyalist was presented by the Lord Chancellor to the benefice of Middleham, in Yorkshire. He was not only Dean of Middleham, but he also held at the same time the living of Stoney Stanton, in Leicestershire, to which he had been presented in 1779 by the Earl of Huntingdon. He was a man of no ordinary stamp. He was closely associated with Wilberforce and Granville Sharp in the suppression of the slave traffic. During the French Revolution he was among the foremost in exposing what he regarded as its danger. The Press teemed with his writings on this subject and his pulpit echoed with his denunciation of the " evil thing." He published about six sermons and nearly twenty anonymous tracts on slavery, the French Revolution, and on his oppo-

Reference : *Publications of Colonial Hist. of Mass.,* XXIV, 435–8.

* This was the attack on Fort Moultrie, June 28, 1776, which gave to Admiral Lord de Saumarez, then a midshipman on this ship, his first commission for his gallant conduct.

† One of his pupils was John Rowe (nephew of John Rowe, the great Boston merchant), who graduated at Harvard in 1783. (*Proc. of Mass. Hist. Soc.,* 2nd Ser., x, 11.)

sition to Catholic emancipation. He died at Stoney Stanton, October 11, 1814, aged 75, and there is a monument to his memory in the church. (*Gent. Mag.*, 1818, p. 485; *Docs. relating to Collegiate Church of Middleham*, by Rev. W. Atthill. (Camden Soc., 1847.)

JOHN NUTTING

was a native of Massachusetts, resident at Cambridge as a builder, employing fifty men. Soon after the arrival of General Gage as Governor, he served as lieutenant in the militia. By his information the powder and military stores in the magazine at Cambridge (which the rebels wished him to seize for them) were saved and removed to Boston. He now undertook to build barracks for the British troops in Boston, but his work was stopped by the threats and misrepresentations of the revolutionary leaders, which induced some of his men to leave, while he himself was seized and maltreated, and put on a boat under the charge of four men with directions to take him to Cambridge for trial; but by persuasion and a "small consideration" he was set at liberty by these men. The barracks were eventually completed in the face of considerable opposition. In September, 1777, Nutting embarked with Lieutenant-Colonel Small on a private expedition to the New England coast, and on his return sailed for England. Here he was appointed overseer of works at Landguard Fort, in Suffolk, and remained there until August, 1778, when he received orders to go to New York on business regarding the establishment of a post at Penobscot.* On the passage his ship was engaged with an American warship, and he was wounded. Before surrendering he threw overboard the despatches which he was conveying to General Sir Henry Clinton, Commander-in-Chief in America. He was taken to Corunna, in Spain, and detained a prisoner there for six weeks. Once again this loyalist sailed for New York, and thence to Halifax and Penobscot, where he not only suffered a siege of twenty days, but also the obloquy of the officers, who regarded him as the means of their going there and being sold to the rebels. In the spring he was requested by General Francis Maclean, in command of the forces in Nova Scotia and the garrison at Penobscot, to embark for England, and having arrived there during the Gordon riots, was unexpectedly detained. Lord Townsend sent him a peremptory order to proceed to

---

* Governor Hutchinson, in his diary, under date of September 3, 1778, states that Nutting was going to Penobscot to rebuild the fort; and again under date of September 19, 1778, that William Knox (Under-Secretary of State in the American Department) had at last accomplished his desire in persuading the Government to take possession of Penobscot, with a view to establishing a new province as an asylum for the loyalists. Governor Hutchinson denounced it as a preposterous measure, of which few people in England thought well. Thomas Goldthwait (*q.v.*), however, recommended it.

Admiral Sir George Collier asked Nutting what could possibly have induced him to recommend the establishment of a settlement in so infernal a spot. Nutting denied that he had ever recommended it. (*American MSS. in Royal Inst., op. cit.*, ii, 19.)

James Murray

PLATE XXXV

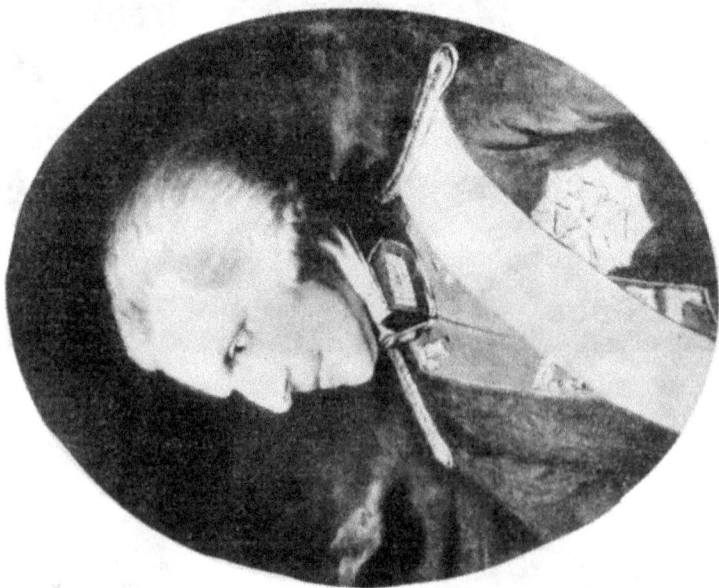

Count Rumford

Andrew Oliver

PLATE XXXVI

Landguard Fort, his lordship declaring that John Nutting could not be spared out of the kingdom. Shortly afterwards, however, he left again for New York, with an appointment as engineer, and was ordered by General Sir Guy Carleton (Clinton's successor) to go to Halifax as overseer of the military works. (A.O. 13/51; A.O. 13/75; A.O. 12/10, ff. 65–74.)

This loyalist was compensated to the amount of £300 from his claim of £2,450. (A.O. 12/109.)

His wife, Mary Nutting, was granted land at Penobscot, June 21, 1781. (A.O. 13/51.) His son, John, was granted a commission as Lieutenant in the Royal Artillery, March 24, 1791, and as Captain-Lieutenant, October 1, 1795. Sophia, daughter of John Nutting, junior, married Michael Berger Grant, eldest son of Captain John Grant, a loyalist Scotsman, formerly of New York, who settled at Loyal Hill, Windsor, Nova Scotia.

Three witnesses to his loyalty, at Halifax, Nova Scotia, were Samuel Pool, Josiah Henny, and Nathaniel Bust, probably loyalists.

A loyalist of this name signed the address to Governor Hutchinson, but apologised for doing so. (*Force, op. cit.*, Ser. IV., vol. ii., p. 852.)

References: *Ontario Archives, op. cit.*, pp. 58–60; *Sabine, op. cit.*; *American MSS. in Royal Inst., op. cit.* iii, 226, 234; iv. 76; *Life and Surprising Adventures of John Nutting*, by S. F. Batchelder, in *Proc. of Cambridge Hist. Soc.*, reprinted 1912.

LIEUTENANT-GOVERNOR ANDREW OLIVER (Plate xxxvii)

member of the Council, Secretary of the Province, and Lieutenant-Governor of Massachusetts, died in 1774, his death having been hastened by his close application to public affairs and by the ill-treatment of the mob in the discharge of his duties. With this memorial of his son, Daniel (*q.v.*), and his son-in-law, Thomas Hutchinson (*q.v.*), as his executors, is a schedule of his real estate and a copy of the record of the Superior Court of Rhode Island relating to the confiscation of his property. His wife was Mary, daughter of William Sanford. The heirs of his estate were his children, Daniel; Elizabeth Lyde, wife of Edward Lyde (*q.v.*); Sarah, wife of the above Thomas Hutchinson; William Sanford Oliver; Peter Oliver (*q.v.*); Brinley Sylvester Oliver (*q.v.*); and Louisa Oliver. (A.O. 13/48; A.O. 13/75.)

According to an anonymous note to the Secretary of the Commissioners of American Claims, dated November 23, 1787, the Lieutenant-Governor is said to have suffered damage in the Stamp Act Riots, as the holder of the Stamp Act, but was handsomely compensated for his losses. (A.O. 13/48.)

This able and conscientious public servant graduated at Harvard College in 1724, and was a liberal benefactor in books and manuscripts to the College. He died at Boston in March, 1774, aged 67, and was succeeded as Lieutenant-Governor by Thomas Oliver (*q.v.*). (*Stark, op. cit.*, pp. 181–3.)

His brother was Peter Oliver (*q.v.*), Chief Justice of Massachusetts.

He resigned the office of Commissioner for the distribution of the Stamps [under the Stamp Act in 1765], and declined to act. (C.O. 5/754.) His letter book, beginning October 20, 1767, is in the British Museum. (*Egerton MSS.* 2670.)

He is frequently mentioned in Adams's *Works*.

His miniature portrait, by Copley, is in the possession of Mrs. Fitch Oliver, of Boston, with a portrait group, by Smibert, of the three brothers, Daniel Oliver (who died young), Chief Justice Peter Oliver (*q.v.*), and the Lieutenant-Governor himself.

Andrew Oliver, son of the Lieutenant-Governor, a graduate of Harvard College (1749), a judge of the Court of Common Pleas in Essex County and a loyalist, was the only member of this loyalist family who remained in Massachusetts, where he died at Salem in 1799. William Sanford Oliver, another son, settled at St. John, New Brunswick, and held several public offices before his death there in 1813. (*Stark, op. cit.*, p. 190; *Judges of New Brunswick, op. cit.*, pp. 4, 12.) Andrew's portrait, by Blackburn, belongs to Mrs. Fitch Oliver. (Plate xxxvi.)

BRINLEY SYLVESTER OLIVER

youngest son of Lieutenant-Governor Andrew Oliver (*q.v.*), served as a purser in the Royal Navy from April 5, 1800, in the *Chameleon*, sloop of 16 guns, until June, 1802, when this ship was paid off and his former loyalist pension of £60 was resumed. This pension was first granted in 1782, and was increased later to £100. He died about July, 1828. (A.O. 13/85; A.O. 12/105, f. 16; T. 50/6; T. 50/28.)

He graduated at Harvard College in 1774.

DANIEL OLIVER

son of Lieutenant-Governor Andrew Oliver (*q.v.*), was bred to the law, and was admitted barrister-at-law in 1767. He settled on a farm at Hardwick, which town he represented in the General Court in 1770–1, and was a Justice of the Peace for the county of Worcester from January 13, 1768. Shortly after his flight to Boston he was appointed a Clerk to the Supreme Court of Justice, and was one of the Associated Loyalists. (See Appendix.) He accompanied the British troops at the evacuation of Boston. His loyalist pension was paid until his death in 1826. (A.O. 13/75; A.O. 12/105, f. 16; A.O. 459/7; A.O. 461/15; T. 50/6; T. 50/27.)

With his memorial are papers relating to his estate and letters of July 10 and August 14, 1788, concerning claims against his estate. (A.O. 13/48.) He was allowed £1,075 from his claim of £1,663, and at the rate of £100 for the loss of his professional income during the war. (A.O. 12/109.)

He graduated at Harvard College in 1762. Daniel Oliver died at Ashted, near Birmingham, May 6, 1826, aged 82. (*Stark, op. cit.*, pp. 189–90.)

LOUISA OLIVER

was a daughter of Lieutenant-Governor Andrew Oliver (*q.v.*) She was in receipt of a loyalist pension until her death in 1801. (A.O. 12/105, f. 16 ; A.O. 461/18 ; T. 50/6.)

PETER OLIVER (Plate xxxvii)

was in the service of the Crown for over thirty years. In 1744 he was appointed a Justice of the Peace, in 1747 a Judge of the Court of Common Pleas, and in 1748 a Justice of the Quorum, all in the county of Plymouth. At the importunity of Governor Shirley he was appointed in 1756 a Judge of the Superior Court, by which appointment he lost a lucrative practice as a lawyer. From 1759 he served in His Majesty's Council and performed the duties of this office until 1766, when he was dismissed by the violent faction which brought on the revolt of the Colonies. In 1761 Peter Oliver was made a Justice of the Peace throughout the province. In 1772 he was appointed Chief Justice of Massachusetts.

His long state of his case, dated March 11, 1784, is an interesting and pathetic revelation of his sufferings and of the great difficulties of his position and the danger to his life if he persisted in exercising the functions of his office as Chief Justice before the Revolution. Nothing now (he says) but the protection of Heaven was left for him to depend upon for the safety of his life until the King's troops arrived. He quitted his country house and repaired to Boston for safety ; but even there, in attempting to hold a court, a large mob of over 1,000 persons assembled to prevent him. General Gage, sensible of the impending danger, offered to aid him ; but, determined as he was to try the force of the civil power, the Chief Justice, happily, succeeded and passed through the mob unmolested. During the blockade of Boston he repeatedly and narrowly escaped assassination. (A.O. 13/48.)

He was determined to exert himself in the support of Government, and did not quit his offices until the evacuation of Boston by the British troops. (C.O. 5/154, f. 198.)

A schedule of his property includes eight family pictures, 300 ounces of silver plate, and a pew in Middleborough Meeting House (*Ib.*).

In a letter, dated Birmingham, April 13, 1787, he gives a long and interesting account of his iron works, the only system of its kind in Massachusetts. His stream of water was supplied from five ponds, the lower one being nine miles round, the next ten miles long, two others each four or five miles round ; and the fifth three miles round. Eight wheels were often going at the same time on one dam and waste water for eight more wheels. The river was of such importance as to be noted on the map of the province. He had been thirty years in forming the system. (*Ib.*)

Peter Oliver was intended to be the Governor of a new province between the Penobscot and St. Croix Rivers. (C.O. 5/175.)

He graduated at Harvard College in 1730 and received the degree of D.C.L. at Oxford in 1776. (Foster, *Alumni Oxon.*)

The last of the Chief Justices under the Crown, "a man of courage, firmness, learning and character, and an able magistrate," he died at Birmingham, October 13, 1791, aged 78, and was buried in St. Philip's Church. (*Publications of Colonial Soc. of Mass.*, vi, 71–4; *Gent. Mag.*, vol. 72, p. 112.)

His miniature portrait, by Copley is in the possession of Mrs. Fitch Oliver, Boston.

There are many references to him in Adams's *Works*.

Compensation, £2,668, was granted to him from his claim of £4,941, less £25 for pension; and at the rate of £200 a year for the loss of his office during the war. (A.O. 12/109; A.O. 459/7; A.O. 459/10; T. 50/6; T. 50/45.)

Chief Justice Oliver's original Journal of his tours in England, 1776–1780, is in the British Museum (Egerton MSS. 2672–3), and comments freely on the people, and the places visited.

His brother was Lieutenant-Governor Andrew Oliver (*q.v.*), and his son was Peter Oliver (*q.v.*).

Other references : A.O. 12/105, f. 41; A.O. 13/75; A.O. 13/137; Stark, *op. cit.* pp. 188–9.

PETER OLIVER

second son of Chief Justice Peter Oliver (*q.v.*), settled in 1764 as a surgeon and physician at Middleborough. In 1768 he was appointed a justice of the peace for the county of Plymouth. In September, 1774, a mob of forty men, armed with clubs and bludgeons, assembled outside his house and compelled him, through fear of his life and to save his family, to sign a paper promising to refuse any commission under General Gage. In February, 1775, another mob assembled, headed by one Conant, which obliged him to flee to Boston, where he served as a common soldier during the blockade. Peter Oliver sailed for England in April, 1776. In 1784 he was living in Birmingham, and declared that but for the benevolence of a few friends both he and his family must have been beggars on the streets. (British Museum : Egerton MSS. 2559; A.O. 13/48.)

This loyalist claimed £4,528, and was allowed £3,200, less £25 for pension. His claim of £100 for the loss of his professional income during the war was allowed, and his pension of £100 was continued until his death. (A.O. 12/109; A.O. 12/105, f. 142; A.O. 459/7; T. 50/6; T. 50/46.)

Peter Oliver graduated at Harvard College in 1761, and married Sarah, daughter of Governor Hutchinson. He died at Shrewsbury, England, July 30, 1822, aged 81 (Stark, *op. cit.*, pp. 188, 189). His youngest son, Peter, matriculated at Queen's College, Oxford, June 6, 1792, aged 17, and was admitted to the Middle Temple, January 28, 1793.*

* E. Alfred Jones, *American Members of the Inns of Court*, 1924.

As a student and collector of antiquities and the owner of a considerable collection of coins, medals and other objects of vertu, he contributed to the *Gentleman's Magazine* (see vol. 61, p. 974 ; vol. 72, p. 112 ; vol. 92, p. 185).

PETER OLIVER

was the son of Lieutenant-Governor Thomas Oliver (*q.v.*), and was a physician and surgeon at Salem. Early in life he was instructed by example and precept in principles of loyalty and good government. For safety he was compelled to flee from Salem to Boston, where he was appointed a surgeon's mate in the General Hospital. At the evacuation of Boston in March, 1776, he accompanied the British troops to Nova Scotia and New York. At New York he was in charge of the sick and wounded prisoners until 1779, when ill-health obliged him to sail to England. On February 25, 1780, he was appointed surgeon to the 1st (or Royal) Regiment of Dragoons. With his memorial is a schedule of his estate. (A.O. 13/48.)

Peter Oliver was placed on half-pay of this regiment. (A.O. 13/83). According to his will, dated April 10, 1783, he left all his real estate in New England to his wife, Love Oliver. In a codicil of April 20, 1793, he is described as a resident at Dorchester, Dorset, and in the document of administration, April 21, 1795, he is described as of the parish of St. Marylebone (London), and as formerly surgeon to the First or Royal Regiment of Dragoons, afterwards surgeon to the 1st Regiment of Dragoon Guards, but late surgeon to the staff of his Majesty's forces on the Continent. He died in London in 1795 (Stark, *op. cit.*, p. 190).

He graduated at Harvard College in 1769, and was presumably the man of this name who took the degree of B.A. there in 1769 and of M.D. at Marischal College, Aberdeen, in 1790.

THOMAS OLIVER

According to his memorial of October 2, 1783, he was appointed Lieutenant-Governor and President of the Council of Massachusetts in 1774 without his knowledge, and from principles of loyalty he accepted this trust, although he foresaw that he would be drawn from a state of tranquillity to a difficult situation. He was driven from his estate in Cambridge to Boston, with his wife and six children. With his memorial is a schedule of his property and an account of the expenses in building his house, from which it appears that the stone came from Connecticut and the glass from England. (A.O. 12/105, f. 143 ; A.O. 13/48 ; A.O. 13/75 ; A.O. 13/87.)

He claimed £5,167 17*s.*, and was allowed £2,320. He was allowed at the rate of £300 a year for the loss of his official income during the war. (A.O. 12/109.) A claim was also made for two horses. (A.O. 13/87.) He received a pension until his death [at Bristol] on November 29, 1815. (A.O. 459/7 ; T. 50/6 ; T. 50/45.)

P

He graduated at Harvard College in 1753, and was the last Lieutenant-Governor under the Crown (Stark, *op. cit.*, pp. 183–8).

He was buried at St. Paul's, Bristol; his wife, Harriet, died July 16, 1808, aged 50. In his will, dated September 8, 1812, and proved January 4, 1816, Thomas Oliver mentions three daughters: Frances Oliver Lucy, widow of Henry Hope Tobin; Harriet Watkins Oliver, and Emily Freeman Oliver; three sons-in-law, Joseph Rogers, John Cave, and Charles Anthony Partridge, husbands respectively of his daughters Elizabeth, Penelope and Mary; his grandson, Thomas Oliver Anderson; his granddaughter, Lucy, wife of Butler Claxton, of Bristol; and three grandsons, James Hughes Anderson, John Lavicount Anderson, and Freeman Anderson, sons of his deceased daughter, Ann, and her husband, John Proctor Anderson (39 Wynne).

EDWARD OXNARD

was a merchant at Falmouth (Portland), Maine, in partnership with John Kent. His loyalist pension of £100 was continued. (A.O. 13/48; A.O. 12/105, f. 145.) He was a churchwarden at Falmouth under the Rev. John Wiswall (*q.v.*). He graduated at Harvard College in 1767.

This loyalist was born in America. After the battle of Lexington he was called upon by the rebels to join them, but he refused, and sailed for England in June, 1775, for reasons of safety. His partner, Kent, was also a loyalist. (*Loyalists' Claims, op. cit.*, pp. 353–4.) He was a member of the New England Loyalists' Club in London (Curwen Diary, *op. cit.*). Edward Oxnard returned to Portland after the war, and died there, July 2, 1803, aged 57 (Sabine, *op. cit.*). His brother was Thomas Oxnard (*q.v.*).

THOMAS OXNARD

was a native of Massachusetts, who resided for many years at Falmouth (Portland), Maine. He claimed for part of the sloop *St. Vincent*, and cargo of lumber. (A.O. 13/87.)

He signed an address to Governor Hutchinson, and recanted (Force, *American Archives*, Series iv, vol. iii, pp. 625–7). His brother was Edward Oxnard (*q.v.*). He died at Portland, May 20, 1799, aged 59. His wife, Martha, who was a sister of Commodore Edward Preble, U.S.N., was permitted by a resolve of the General Court, September 24, 1782, to join her husband at Penobscot. (A.O. 12/82.) His son, Thomas Oxnard, commanded the American privateer *True Blooded Yankee*, in the war of 1812. (Sabine, *op. cit.*)

Reference: Willis, *Hist. of Portland*, pp. 830–3.

ADINO PADDOCK

was a merchant in Boston. From 1763 to 1775 he commanded a corps of 100 men in the Ancient and Honourable Artillery Company of Massachusetts; he was popular and was esteemed a soldier; two of his sergeants became Colonels in the American army during the Revolutionary war. Tempting offers were made to him by the Americans to join their army, in which he might have had command of their artillery. In July, 1775, he was appointed to command a company in the Associated Loyalists of Boston.* (A.O. 13/49 ; A.O. 12/105 ; A.O. 13/75.)

He claimed £3,151, and was allowed £1,336, less £10 10s. for pension. (A.O. 12/109.) Certificates dated March 22, 1784, to the value of his property are in A.O. 13/49. He was one of the first assistant aldermen of St. John, New Brunswick, in 1785 (*Judges of N. Brunswick, op. cit.*, p. 4). His pension was paid until his death. (A.O. 461/19 ; T. 50/6.) A list of claims against his estate is in A.O. 12/81, ff. 114–5. He died in the Island of Jersey, March 25, 1804, aged 76. (Winsor, *Memorial Hist. of Boston*, iii, 62 ; Stark, *op. cit.*, pp. 305–8.)

An account of his career is in Roberts, *Hist. of Ancient and Hon. Artillery Company of Mass.*, ii, 112–4.

ROBERT PAGAN

was a Scotsman who emigrated in 1768 and settled at Falmouth (Portland), Maine, as a partner in the firm of Robert Lee and Joseph Tucker, shipbuilders and lumber merchants, of Greenock, Scotland. His store at Falmouth was tarred and feathered and he himself insulted and his life threatened by an " unruly multitude." Finally, his house and store were destroyed in the burning of Falmouth by Captain Mowat (*q.v.*) in October, 1775. He afterwards retired inland, and there, notwithstanding his misfortunes, his factious neighbours continued their insults to him and insisted upon his joining the American militia as well as contributing money to raise men, all of which demands he resolutely refused. His position having become dangerous, he embarked secretly in the night of February 28, 1776, with his family, on board the brigantine *Falmouth* (John Martin, master), built at Falmouth, belonging to his firm, and bound for Barbados. This vessel, was taken by H.M.S. *Argo*, and condemned under the Prohibitory Act in the Vice-Admiralty Court in Antigua† in April, 1776, and sold by auction. Pagan now went to New York, and was there engaged in business until December, 1780, when he removed to Penobscot, and was appointed a magistrate in June, 1781. In the course of his business career in New York and Penobscot thirty-six vessels were lost, mostly by capture, of which he and his brothers, William and Thomas, were the sole or principal owners. (A.O. 13/93.)

According to a petition, dated Fort George, Penobscot, in April, 1783, and signed by Robert Pagan, Nathaniel Gardener, Jeremiah Pote (*q.v.*) and Thomas Wyer (*q.v.*) numbers of loyalists had fled to Penobscot for safety, in response to the invitations of Government, and built houses and huts on the lots of land granted to them. Over 100 heads of families desired now to remove to Nova Scotia, there to enjoy, as they

* See Appendix.
† A copy of the proceedings is with the Pagan papers in A.O. 13/51.

hoped, the blessings of that government which they still revere and to escape from the resentment and threats of those against whom they have from principle taken up arms in the royal cause. By the unexpected evacuation of Penobscot their situation is most distressing, and they prayed for provision for removing them. The petition is followed by a list of houses and their owners' names. Robert Pagan's own claim, with details, is also included. (A.O. 13/51.) His claim of £864 was met by a grant of £110. (A.O. 12/109.)

This loyalist settled in 1784 in St. Andrews, New Brunswick, and was there active and popular in public affairs, as magistrate, judge of a court, colonel of militia, and member of the first House of Assembly. He died November 23, 1821. His brother, William, was chosen an alderman of the first council of the City of St. John, and also a member of the House of Assembly of New Brunswick, and died at Fredericton in 1819. His other brother, Thomas, removed from that province to Halifax, Nova Scotia, and died in Scotland in 1804. (Stark, *op. cit.*, pp. 464–5 ; *Judges of New Brunswick, op. cit.*, pp. 4, 6.)

References : Sabine, *op. cit. ; Acadiensis*, ii, iii & vii ; *Ontario Archives, op. cit.*, pp. 304–7.

WILLIAM PAILTHORPE

was a hairdresser in Boston, where he was one of the Associated Loyalists in 1775. He died in London, July 4, 1778, leaving a widow, Ann. (A.O. 13/75.)

SAMUEL PAINE

was born in Worcester, and succeeded his father, a mandamus councillor, as Clerk of the Court of Common Pleas and Clerk of the General Sessions of the Peace of Worcester County, in 1774. In consequence of his opposition to the rebels he was obliged to seek the protection of the British army as Boston, where, on October 30, 1775, he was appointed second lieutenant in the Loyal Associated Loyalists. From that year he followed the fortunes of the army, and rendered all the services in his power. He joined the Associated Loyalists formed in Rhode Island to fit out armed vessels, and subscribed £50 to the fund. His father [Timothy Paine], although a loyalist, remained at Worcester during the war. (A.O. 13/51 ; A.O. 13/75 ; A.O. 12/10, ff. 29–33, 421 ; A.O. 12/61, f. 5 ; A.O. 12/109.) He received a pension until his death [at Worcester in 1807]. (A.O. 459/7 ; A.O. 462/21.)

Copies of his two appointments mentioned above and an affidavit of William Campbell (*q.v.*), declaring that Samuel Paine was active at public meetings in opposition to the rebels, are in A.O. 13/51.

This loyalist graduated at Harvard College in 1771, and was a nephew of John Chandler (*q.v.*), His brother was William Paine (*q.v.*).

For his alleged statements that the goods from the house of one Ebenezer Bradish were taken, not by the British army, but by local inhabitants ; and that the American troops quartered in Harvard College

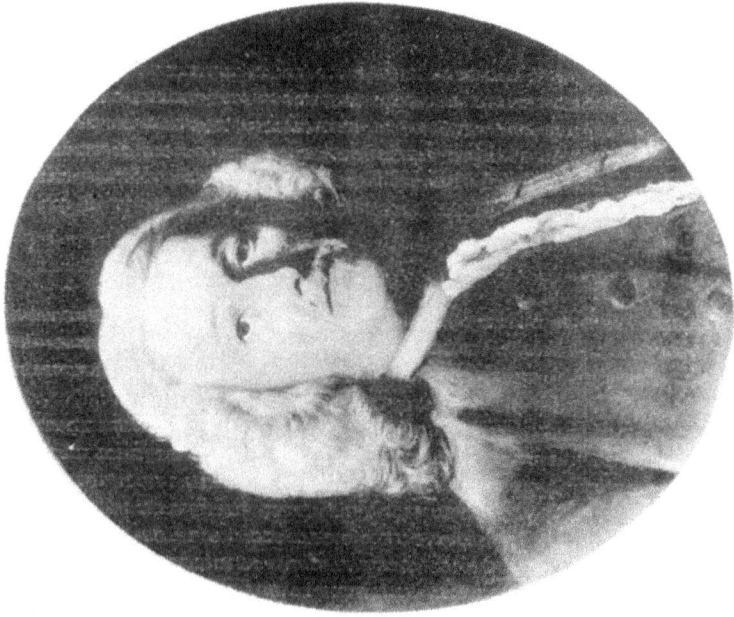

Chief Justice Peter Oliver

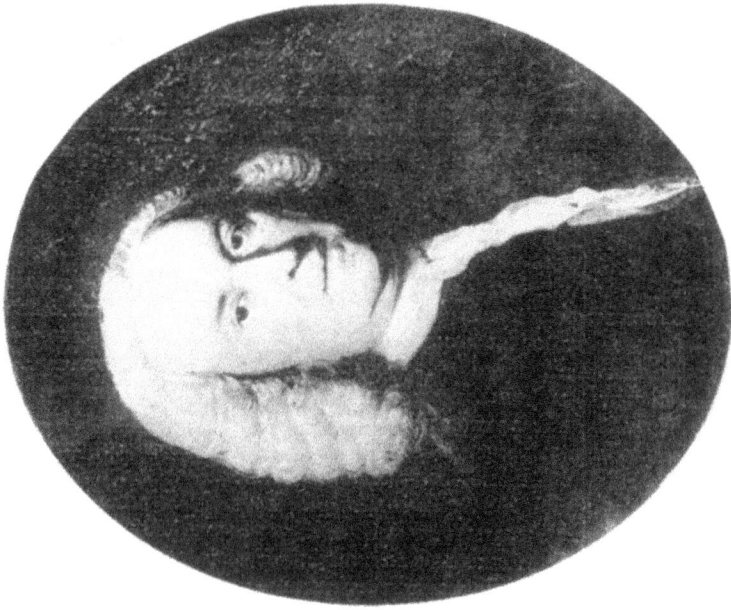

PLATE XXXVII Lieut.-Governor Andrew Oliver

PLATE XXXVIII   William Paine

were " lousy and deserted by hundreds," it was resolved that he should be sent to Watertown or Cambridge, with William Campbell (q.v.), to be dealt with as the Congress or Commander-in-Chief should think proper. (Force, *Amer. Archives*, Ser. iv, vol. ii, pp. 538–9, 798–9.)

Reference : *Ontario Archives, op. cit.*, pp. 32–3.

DR. WILLIAM PAINE (Plate xxxviii)

was a physician and apothecary at Worcester and a partner of Levi Shepherd, apothecary, and Ebenezer Hunt, physician, both of Northampton. He served throughout the war as a physician and apothecary to the British army. With his memorial are a schedule of his losses ; an inventory of his personal estate left at Worcester ; and copies of the appraisement of his estate and orders for the confiscation of it. (A.O. 13/50 ; T. 1/518, f. 150 ; A.O. 12/10, ff. 413–9.) He was allowed £300 from his claim of £1,440. (A.O. 12/109.)

Dr. Paine studied medicine under Dr. Edward Augustus Holyoke, of Salem, after graduating at Harvard College in 1768. The degree of M.D. was granted to him by Marischal College, Aberdeen, in November, 1775. (*Scottish Notes and Queries*, December, 1898, p. 95 ; *Proc. of American Antiquarian Soc.*, New Series, vol. 13, pp. 394–408.) He married in 1773 Lois Orne (1756–1822), of Salem. (Stark, *op. cit.*, pp. 385–7.) In the records at Worcester his name appears in case No. 44823A, and his estate was appraised on January 7, 1779, as real, £300, and personal, £1,938 5s.

At the end of the war he served for a while as physician to the British garrison at Halifax in Nova Scotia, and afterwards settled at St. John, New Brunswick, where he took an active part in public affairs, as an alderman in its first corporation, with two other Massachusetts loyalists, George Leonard (q.v.) and Adino Paddock (q.v.) ; and as one of the representatives of Charlotte County in the first House of Assembly of New Brunswick, of which he was appointed clerk in January, 1786. In the war of 1812 he was called up as an officer on half-pay for service with the British, but declined, and retired to Worcester, Massachusetts, and was naturalized before his death in 1833. (*Judges of New Brunswick, op. cit.*, pp. 4–7.) William Paine was one of the founders of the American Antiquarian Society, and his portrait, as an old man, hangs in the room of the Society at Worcester, Massachusetts. An excellent pastel portrait was executed as a younger man. The portrait of his wife as a child was painted in 1757 by Joseph Badger (1708–65), and is owned by Mr. Robert Saltonstall, of Readville, Mass. His brother was Samuel Paine (q.v.).

References : *American MSS. in Royal Inst., op. cit.*, iii, 171 ; iv, 153.

ROBERT PARKER

He was born in Boston, and in 1770 was appointed Surveyor of Customs there. He served in the Associated Loyalists in Boston in 1775. (A.O.

13/49 ; A.O. 13/75.) For the loss of his income during the war he was allowed at the rate of £160 a year. (A.O. 12/109.)

Early in or shortly before 1783 he was appointed lieutenant in the Berkshire militia in England. (A.O. 12/99, f. 284.) After the war he was appointed to the lucrative offices of Comptroller of Customs and Ordnance Storekeeper at St. John, New Brunswick, where he died in 1823, aged 83. (*Judges of New Brunswick, op. cit.* ; Raymond, *The Winslow Papers*, p. 545 ; *Loyalists' Claims, op. cit.*, p. 9.) His son, Robert, became Chief Justice of New Brunswick.

SAMUEL PARTRIDGE

of Boston, merchant, claimed for goods seized by order of General Howe in 1775. (A.O. 13/93.)

CHARLES PAXTON (Plate xxxix)

On October 12, 1785, and May 6, 1786, he gave evidence regarding his losses, which included mortgages on the property in Connecticut of Godfrey Malbone, late of Newport, Rhode Island, a loyalist, and valuable pictures from Italy, old and valuable furniture, and a large library of books, neatly bound and gilt. (A.O. 13/49 ; A.O. 12/101, f. 332.) He was granted compensation, £800, from his claim of £1,200, and at the rate of £500 a year for the loss during the war of his official income as Commissioner of Customs. (A.O. 12/109.) Papers relating to the confiscation of his property are in A.O. 13/49, and a list of claims against his estate is in A.O. 12/81, f. 116.

During his illness in 1779 he displayed much concern at the prospect of being buried in London, where he feared that his bones might be dug up after a few years and be cast into a common heap, in accordance with what he imagined was a general custom. He told Governor Hutchinson that he would give 100 guineas to be buried by his father and mother under King's Chapel, Boston. (Governor Hutchinson's Diary, ii, 240–1.) He was warden of this chapel in 1760–8.

Charles Paxton died at the English seat of William Burch (*q.v.*) in 1788, aged 84. (Stark, *op. cit.*, pp. 318–9.) In his will, dated September 13, 1786, and proved February 28, 1788, he left legacies to Mrs. Elizabeth Hatch, of Pangbourne, Co. Berks (whose son, Paxton, was named after him), and her three daughters, Jane, Mary and Susan Hatch. (90, Calvert.)

His portrait is in the possession of the Massachusetts Historical Society, and another portrait, by Cornish, 1751, belongs to the American Antiquarian Society, Worcester, Massachusetts.

JEREMIAH PECKER

originally of Haverhill, gentleman, had been settled for several years at Penobscot, and was at Shelburne, Nova Scotia, in November, 1783. (A.O. 13/93.) According to Sabine he graduated at Harvard College in

Charles Paxton

PLATE XXXIX

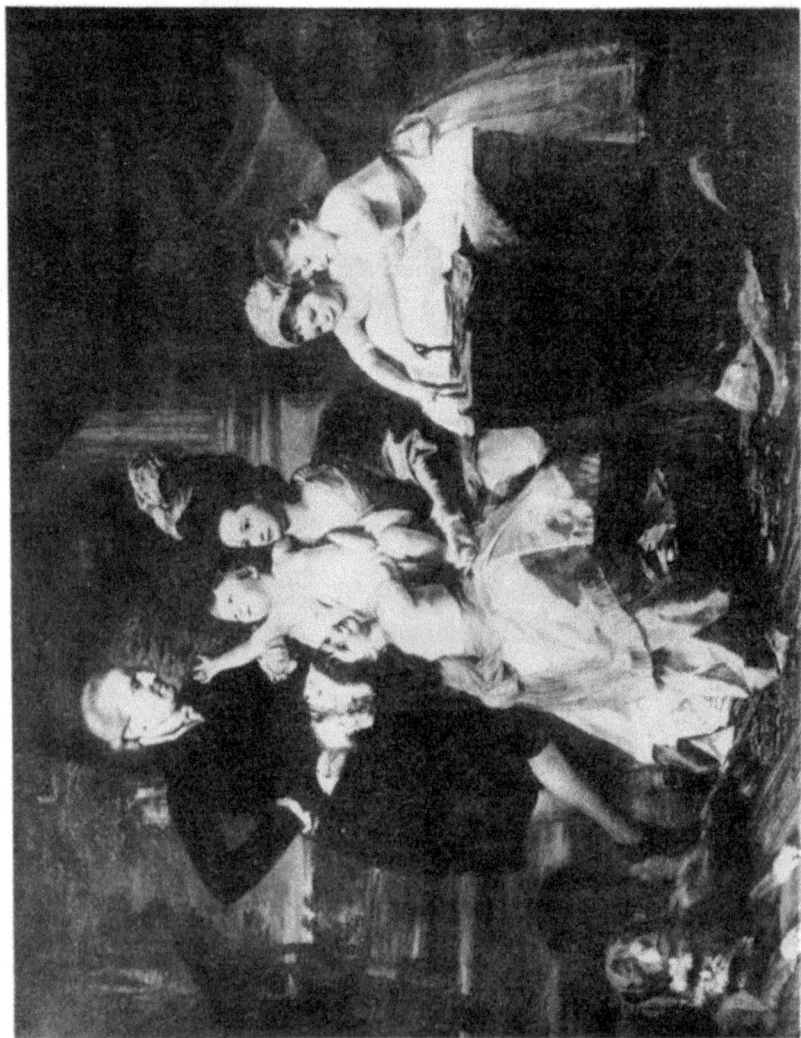

Sir William Pepperell and Family

1757, and was a school teacher at St. John, New Brunswick, where he died in 1809.

HENRY PELHAM

was educated in the art of painting by John Singleton Copley, whom he succeeded " in all the business of a large Country without having a rival." (A.O. 13/49.) His " duty to his most gracious Sovereign and Veneration for the British Government " left him, upon the removal of the army from Boston, no alternative than to quit a country where " the only terms for his Peace and Safety would be renunciation of his Allegiance to his King and an active oppugnation to the laws and authority of Great Britain." He was one of the Associated Volunteers in Boston during the blockade. All his books, furniture and personal property were left behind in Boston. (A.O. 13/75 ; A.O. 12/105, f. 76.) His loyalist pension was continued until his death. (A.O. 462/22 ; T. 50/20.)

This loyalist painter and engraver was the son of Peter Pelham, artist and engraver, of Boston, and half-brother of Copley, the artist, who painted his portrait in 1766 as the " Boy with the Squirrel." Henry Pelham executed a plate of the so-called Boston Massacre in 1770, and allowed Paul Revere, the famous Boston silversmith and engraver, to have the loan of it, with the result that Revere made a copy of it and brought upon himself a bitter reproach in a letter from Pelham for having deprived him of the expected advantages from the sale of engravings as truly as if he had been plundered on the highway. " If you are insensible (Pelham wrote) of the Dishonour you have brought on yourself by this Act, the World will not be so. However, I leave you to reflect upon and consider of one of the most dishonourable Actions you could well be guilty of." (*Letters and Papers of J. S. Copley and Henry Pelham*, 1739–1776 (1914), p. 83.)

Before sailing from Boston with the British troops in March, 1776, Pelham had executed a plan of the " battle of Charlestown," of which he was an eye-witness, and which was embodied in a large map of Boston and its environs, published in London in June, 1777. He became a land surveyor in Ireland, and was employed on a survey of the County of Clare in 1782. His labours were embodied in a large map of twelve sheets, the topographical part of one map being engraved by I. Cheevers, and the writing designed and engraved by T. Harmar. The whole was dedicated to George III, and published in 1787, just in time to escape a fine of £100, threatened by the Grand Jury of Clare if the work were longer delayed. In this same year Pelham was engaged by William, second Earl of Shelburne and first Marquess of Lansdowne, as his agent for the family estates in County Kerry. The large amount of correspondence* which passed between Pelham and his employer clearly reveals him as a hard-working and conscientious agent, ever mindful of his master's interests.

* This correspondence is in the possession of the Marquess of Lansdowne, to whom I am indebted for notes upon it.

After ten or twelve years' service he left Lord Shelburne's employ, in consequence of a disagreement.

Henry Pelham exhibited some of his miniatures at the Royal Academy in 1777-1778, and at the Society of Artists in Dublin in 1780. In Grose's *Antiquities of Ireland* are three plates after drawings by him of views of Quinn, Clare, and Ennis Abbeys. He was drowned by the up-setting of a boat on Kenmare River in 1806. (Strickland, *Dict. of Irish Artists*, 1913, ii, 225.)

A long account of this loyalist is in the *Publications of the Colonial Soc. of Mass.*, v, 193–210.

SIR WILLIAM PEPPERELL, BARONET (Plate xi.)

In July, 1781, he was "in the greatest imaginable want for assistance," and was granted £500 bounty. (A.O. 13/75.) His claim of £32,370 was met by a grant of £8,415, and £16,000 was allowed later to Lady Pepperell, widow of the first baronet. He was also allowed the full claim of £1,800 for his infant daughter, Elizabeth Mary Royall Pepperell, whose estate in Rhode Island, bequeathed to her by her grandfather, Isaac Royall, was confiscated. (A.O. 12/109; A.O. 13/48.) His pension of £420 was paid from 1782 until his death in December, 1816. (T., 50/6; T. 50/25.)

The Commissioners described his case as one of great personal merit. He was a Captain of a company of Massachusetts Loyalists in London, who had associated at Boston for the defence of that town. (A.O. 12/105, f. 48.)

Many papers relating to his great property, and a letter, dated Boston, February 9, 1789, from William Tudor, lawyer, stating that the whole of his real estate in Massachusetts was lost for ever, are in A.O. 13/48, together with an extract from the will of his maternal grandfather, Sir William Pepperell, first baronet.

As the grandson of Sir William Pepperell, he took the name and arms of Pepperell by royal licence. His mother was Elizabeth, wife of Colonel Nathaniel Sparhawk; and his brothers were Samuel Hirst Sparhawk and Nathaniel Sparhawk (*q.v.*); his cousin was Samuel Sparhawk (*q.v*).

In a letter dated March 8, 1790, he mentions the death of his two brothers, and that the natural daughter of one (Samuel Hirst) was being maintained by him. (A.O. 13/49.)

Sir William Pepperell appears in a (lost) picture, by Benjamin West (engraved by Moses), depicting the Reception of the Loyalists in England. A group of Sir William Pepperell, with his wife, Elizabeth, daughter of Isaac Royall (*q.v*), and four children, is in the possession of Lady Augusta Palmer at Wanlip Hall, Leicester.

His wife, Lady Pepperell, died on the voyage to England in 1775. The children were accompanied and cared for by a devoted and heroic nurse, whose portrait in old age, a proud possession of the family, has descended to the Right Rev. Bishop C. T. Abraham, with the small medallion of Sir William Pepperell, by Tassie, and a miniature portrait of young William Pepperell, heir to the baronetcy, who predeceased his father, painted by Peter Paillou, 1793, and a miniature of the latter's sister, Mary.

He was a signatory to the undated petition (early in the war) of representative loyalists from eleven colonies, praying for compensation for the great number of loyalist refugees in Great Britain who were wasting the prime of their lives and dragging out a miserable existence, without prospects of settling in any kind of business. A number of these unhappy exiles had, through despondency, died with broken hearts; others had been arrested, imprisoned, and perished in gaol, for debts contracted, while others had been driven into insanity and from insanity to suicide, leaving their helpless widows and orphans to subsist on the cold charity of strangers. (T. 1/518, f. 51.)

Reference : Stark, *op. cit.*, pp. 205-15.

DR. NATHANIEL PERKINS

He was born at Boston, and practised there as a physician in succession to his father from 1740, and enjoyed a lucrative practice among the opulent families, not only in Massachussetts but also in neighbouring colonies. In 1776 he was obliged to embark with the British troops, the selectmen of the town having refused him permission to remain. (A.O., 13/49; A.O. 12/105, f. 77.) He attended General Howe [Sir William] during a very dangerous fever at Boston, in 1759, on the General's return from the conquest of Canada. (A.O. 13/75.)

He claimed £670, and was granted £500. He received a pension of £240 from 1788 to 1799. (A.O. 459/7; A.O. 461/16; T. 50/6.)

He graduated at Harvard College in 1734. Sir William Pepperell describes him as the most eminent physician in Massachusetts, while Dr. John Jeffries (*q.v.*) declared that he was the first physician in Boston. (*Loyalists' Claims, op. cit.*, p. 258.)

WILLIAM LEE PERKINS

of Boston, was the son of a physician. He served as a surgeon during the war with the French in North America. He married Mrs. Gould, widow of John Gould, of Boston, parents of John, Samuel and Elizabeth Gould, mentioned on page 151. (A.O. 12/105, f. 78.)

He was allowed £387 from his claim of £4,782 and at the rate of £400 a year for the loss of his income during the war. He received a pension until 1799. (A.O. 459/7; A.O. 461/16; T. 50/6; T. 50/8.) A list of claims against his estate is in A.O. 12/81, f. 117. He served in the Associated Loyalists in Boston in 1775.

In A.O. 13/49 are several certificates, from General Gage, Earl Percy, General Burgoyne, and one from John Wentworth, formerly Governor of New Hampshire, stating that Dr. Perkins was an original grantee of land, 350 to 400 acres, in the township of Percy, in New Hampshire.   There is also a schedule with papers relating to his property, which included some inherited by his second wife (see below), together with a long list of his debtors.   He petitioned to be appointed physician to the garrison and inhabitants of Quebec, to fill a vacancy, November 19, 1787, but failed to obtain the appointment.   (A.O. 13/49.)

In 1765 he delivered the first medical lectures in Massachusetts. On March 18, 1767, he was one of 28 gentlemen who had a " very Genteel Dinner " at the Bunch of Grapes tavern in Boston, in celebration of the repeal of the Stamp Act.   He married (i) Sarah Drowne, who died in 1773 ;   and (ii), in 1774, Elizabeth Rogers, daughter of Samuel Wentworth, and widow successively of John Gould, junior (died before 1765), of Boston, and of Nathaniel Rogers, of Boston.   He published in 1787 *An Essay for a Nosological and Comparative View of the Cynanche Maligna* . . . of which a second edition was issued in 1790.   In this work he is described as M.D., and member of the Royal Medical Society of Edinburgh, of which he had been elected a corresponding member, April 23, 1785.   On October 26, 1789, he communicated a paper on a case of angina pectoris cured by white vitriol to the Medical Society of London, which was published in the Memoirs of that Society, 1792, iii, 580–1.   Dr. Perkins was in practice at Kingston-on-Thames in 1786, and in 1789 at Hampton Court, where he died, March 30, 1797.   (Mr. Albert Matthews in *Trans. of Colonial Soc. of Mass.*, xx, 10–18.)

SAMUEL PERRY

lived at Sandwich, and was the owner of a house and 100 acres of land.   He took refuge in Rhode Island in September, 1777, and at the end of the war went to Shelburne, Nova Scotia.   (A.O. 13/93.)

Living at the same time at Sandwich were two other loyalists, Silas and Stephen Perry, who were apparently family connections of this loyalist.   They sought refuge in Rhode Island in March, 1778.   (*Ib.*)

WILLIAM PERRY

He was born in Gloucestershire, and emigrated to Boston at the request of a relation, who intended to make him his heir, and settled as a merchant there.   George Washington offered him a commission in the American army.   (A.O. 12/105, f. 79.)

From the first commotions, not only in Massachusetts but also in the adjoining provinces, he opposed the rebels openly and bore arms during the blockade of Boston.   Having been prevented by illness from leaving Boston with the British troops, he suffered abuse and was imprisoned in the common gaol for 106 days and debarred from many necessities.   He was ultimately exchanged on January 11, 1778, and sailed for England. His losses included one-third share in three schooners, named *Hawk*, *Industry* and *Pink*.   (A.O., 13/49 ; A.O. 13/75.)

He claimed £378 and was allowed £220, less £2 10s. for pension. (A.O. 12/109.)

Colonel Benjamin Pickman

PLATE XLI

PLATE XLII

Mrs. Benjamin Pickman

A list of the debts due to him and copies of the orders for his imprisonment, April 18, 1776, and for his retention as a prisoner at Medfield for four months, July 13, 1776, are in A.O. 13/49.

MAJOR JOHN PHILLIPS

Evidence as to his unimpeachable loyalty was given by Mr. Temple on July 19, 1784. He was then over 70 years of age. (A.O. 12/101, f. 234.) He signed the loyal address to George III. (See Appendix.)

MARTHA PHILLIPS

of Boston was at Halifax, Nova Scotia, in 1785. (A.O. 13/26.)

NATHAN PHILLIPS

is described as a gentleman, of Penobscot, where he was made Captain on the occupation of that territory by the British troops. He was master of the sloop *Beaver*, in which he carried provisions and lumber for the British army in Boston. This sloop was captured on July 25, 1775, by the American, James Cargill and others, whose certificate is with his petition and a schedule of his losses in A.O. 13/51. He claimed £808 18s. and was allowed £200. (A.O. 12/109.)

CAPTAIN DAVID PHIPPS

His claim was £3,258 3s., and his grant £1,882. (A.O. 12/109.) He was on half pay as master and commander in the Royal Navy in 1788 (A.O. 13/83.) and received a pension until his death in October, 1811. (A.O. 459/7 ; T.50/6 ; T.50/8.) A certified copy of the libel against his estate in 1780, signed by John Hancock and John Avery, junior, is in A.O. 12/82.

This loyalist was the son of Spencer Phips, Lieutenant-Governor of Massachusetts, and served at the reduction of Louisburg in 1745 and as Commander of a vessel on Lake Ontario in 1760. He lived at Cambridge, a Lieutenant in the Royal Navy, on half-pay, and was High Sheriff of Middlesex County from 1764, the execution of which office made him very obnoxious. In 1774 when distributing writs under a new Act of Parliament, a mob attacked him and extracted a promise from him that he would issue no more of these writs. He removed the 260 casks of gunpowder and two field pieces to Boston from the magazine at Cambridge. On July 20, 1775, he was appointed marshal of the Vice-Admiralty Court at Boston, in succession to Charles Howard, absent, and as such it was part of his duty to arrest and take possession of vessels libelled as prizes or forfeited under the Acts of Parliament and condemned. In 1779 he was appointed master and commander at New York under Admiral Collier, and commanded the *Allegiance* sloop, in which he served until that vessel was captured by the French fleet in August, 1782, when he was taken prisoner to Boston and later exchanged. (A.O. 13/48; A.O. 12/105, f. 146.) His [Mary] sister married Richard Lechmere (*q.v.*).

With his memorial in A.O. 13/48 are many documents relating to the seizure of the schooner *Peggy*, owned by Elisha Thatcher and George Welch, condemned by him; and a schedule of his property, including the estate at Woolwich, Massachusetts [now in Maine], the birthplace of Sir William Phipps.

This loyalist graduated at Harvard College in 1741. He died at Bath, in England, aged 87. (Stark, *op. cit.*, pp. 420–1.)

Reference : *Loyalists' Claims, op. cit.*, p. 230.

BENJAMIN PICKMAN (Plates xli and xlii)

was a merchant at Salem, Colonel of militia, and a Justice of the Peace, and in 1775 fled to England. (A.O. 12/105, f. 80.)

Thomas Flucker (*q.v.*), stated in evidence that Colonel Pickman had not lost a shilling by the war, but on the contrary had " gained by it." The Commissioners themselves reported that as he had lost nothing in consequence of the war and was in good business in England, his allowance of £100 should be discontinued. (*Ib.*)

He was a member of the New England Club of loyalist refugees (mentioned in Curwen's Journal) who met at dinner once a week in the Adelphi, in London.

He was the son of Colonel Benjamin Pickman, a prominent figure in the life of Salem and in the history of Massachusetts, and graduated at Harvard College in 1759. In 1762 he married Mary Barton, daughter of Dr. Bezaleel Toppan, of Salem, and died at Salem, May 12, 1819, aged 79. His sister, Abigail, married (i) William Eppes; and (ii) Dr. Sylvester Gardiner (*q.v.*).

His portrait, and that of his wife, by Copley, are in the possession of Mrs. George Peabody Wetmore, of New York.

Some of his letters written during his exile in England have been deposited with the Massachusetts Historical Society.

Reference : *Hist. Colls. of Essex Inst.*, xxxix, No. 2.

BENJAMIN POLLARD (Plate xliii)

was a flourishing merchant and native of Boston, born about 1749, who declined considerable appointments in the American military forces in the Revolution, in which his brother, Jonathan, was appointed Quartermaster-General to the American army at Boston and aide-de-camp to General Heath from October 2, 1776, to September, 1778. But he preferred a commission in the army of the King to the first place in the gift of the rebels. His younger brother was an officer [in 1780] in the Royal Navy, in Rodney's fleet.* (A.O. 13/49; A.O. 13/75.)

* This brother was doubtless George Pollard, Lieutenant in the Royal Navy, May 7, 1762, and again in 1780.

Benjamin Pollard

PLATE XLIII

William Dummer Powell

Benjamin Pollard became an ensign in the 2nd battalion of De Lancey's Brigade,* which he accompanied to Georgia in November, 1778, and participated in the capture of Savannah in December. He was killed in the defence of Savannah on October 4, 1779.

In a schedule of Benjamin Pollard's property, the names of his parents, Benjamin and Margaret Pollard, are mentioned, and in a copy of evidence mention is made of his brothers and sisters : Jonathan, mentioned above ; Margaret ; Joshua, a loyalist, who died in 1783 or 1784 ; and Peter, who commanded an American privateer in the Revolution.† (A.O. 13/49.) He left a widow, Hannah, a native of Boston, who went to live at Carmarthen in South Wales. (A.O. 12/81, f. 46 ; A.O. 12/105, f. 108.) She claimed compensation, £1,572, and was allowed £200. (A.O. 12/109.) and was granted a pension of £30 until 1818, when she is presumed to have died. (T.50/8 ; T.50/25.)

A portrait of Benjamin Pollard is in the possession of the Massachusetts Historical Society.

Reference : Sabine, *op. cit.*

SAMUEL PORTER

was born in New England and settled as a barrister and attorney at Salem, where he lived as peaceably as he could early in the Revolution, on ready money saved, despite insults. A demand was made on him to join the American forces, but rather than submit to this violation of his loyalty he tried to escape, but was captured on April 19, 1775, and was afterwards subjected to great abuse. On May 25, following, he succeeded in escaping from Salem, leaving all that was dear to him, and wandered over 500 miles in the wilderness, eventually reaching New York and England. Two boys, to whom he was guardian, died soon after his flight. Their sister, also a minor, was induced in the confusion at Salem to accompany a stranger from Ireland into New Hampshire, where she married him. Having secured all her personal and other procurable property he abandoned her. Another stranger then married her and also soon deserted her. Samuel Porter could not state whether these marriages of his ward were legal. He had a valuable library and was the owner of 1,000 acres of uncultivated land. (A.O. 13/75.) There is another memorial, dated February 23, 1776, in T. 1/520.

His claim was £112 10s. and his compensation £10. He was granted compensation at the rate of £160 a year for the loss of his professional income during the war and a pension of £80. (A.O. 12/105, f. 147 ; A.O. 12/109.)

* A regiment of Loyalists raised by Brigadier-General Oliver de Lancey, of New York, in 1776.

† Commissioned Commander of the privateer sloop *Independence*, December 31, 1777 ; prize master on brigantine *Tyrannicide*, 1778 ; 2nd Lieut., brigantine *Active*, on the Penobscot expedition, 1779. (*Mass. Soldiers and Sailors of the Revolutionary War.*)

This loyalist, who graduated at Harvard College in 1763, is described as a school-mate of the Rev. William Clark (*q.v.*).

Samuel Porter was a member of the New England Club which held a weekly dinner at the Adelphi during the early stages of the war (*Journal of Samuel Curwen, op. cit.*). Jonathan Sewall (*q.v.*), in a letter of September 10, 1783, states that Porter was in a low state of health and was determined to leave " this accursed Sodom, as he very piously calls England," for Oporto and lay his bones there, but he returned later. (*Proc. of Mass. Hist. Soc.*, 2nd Ser., x, 422–3.)

Reference : *Loyalists' Claims, op. cit.*, p. 235.

JEREMIAH POTE

was of Falmouth (Portland), Maine, and the father-in-law of Robert Pagan (*q.v.*) and Thomas Wyer (*q.v.*), and escaped from that place in a small boat to Nova Scotia. He removed to New York and thence to Penobscot, where he had been settled for two years before the evacuation. With his memorial are papers on his losses ; a copy of a permit allowing his wife, Betty, to leave Massachusetts, April 12, 1779 ; and a copy of the certificate of the confiscation and sale of his sloop, June 20, 1779. (A.O. 13/51.) He was allowed £374 from his claim of £898. (A.O. 12/109.) He died at St. Andrews, New Brunswick, in 1796. (Sabine, *op. cit.* ; Stark, *op. cit.*, p. 467 ; *Ontario Archives, op. cit.*, pp. 904–6 ; *Acadiensis*, vii.)

JOHN POWELL (Plates xlv and xlvi)

He was born at Boston, where he lived for over thirty years as a merchant and for twenty years as victualler to the Royal Navy. (A.O. 13/75.) His age alone prevented him from taking an active part on the side of the Crown in the Revolution, though he declared upon all occasions his attachment to the British cause. (A.O. 12/101, f. 142.) He had built a spacious house in 1764, which he enlarged in 1771, so as to consist of a drawing room, two parlours and eight bedchambers. He was the owner of those signs of prosperity, a chariot and a chaise. In 1784 he was residing at Ludlow, England. (A.O. 13/93.)

This loyalist was the son of John and Anne (Dummer) Powell, of Boston, and was born about 1715. He married Jane, daughter of Sweton and Temperance (Talmage) Grant, of Newport, Rhode Island. His second son, William Dummer Powell, was a loyalist and a member of the Middle Temple, and became Chief Justice of Upper Canada. (E.M. Chadwick, *Ontarian Families*, 1894, i, 30–2 ; *Letters of James Murray, Loyalist*, pp. 136, 183, 220–3, 234, 263, 276 ; E. Alfred Jones, *American Members of the Inns of Court*, 1924). The portraits of himself and his wife by Copley, and a portrait of his son, William Dummer Powell, by Gilbert Charles Stuart, are in the possession of Mr. Æmilius Jarvis, of Toronto, Canada, great-great-grandson of John Powell. (Plate xliv.)

John Powell   PLATE XLV

PLATE XLVI

Mrs. John Powell

THOMAS POYNTON

was a mariner, of Salem. (A.O. 13/75.) He married at Salem Hannah Bray, who remained there after his departure for England in 1775, and who died there in 1811, without seeing him again. His house in Salem, built about 1745, was still standing in 1917. (Ex inform. Mr. Robert H. Bancroft, a kinsman, who has a quantity of silver bearing the initials of Thomas and Hannah Poynton.) He died on July 13, 1781, aged 70, and was buried at Fitz, near Shrewsbury, in England, where a mural tablet in the Church gives the place of his birth as Ortford in Cheshire and states that he had been a merchant in America for 45 years.

NEWTON PRINCE

a pastry cook in Boston, gave evidence in the trial of Captain Preston. (A.O. 12/99, f. 289; A.O. 13/75.) He received a pension of £10 until 1819. (T. 50/11; T. 50/25.)

BENJAMIN PROCTER

He was born at Boston and in 1774 was an officer in the Customs at Nantucket. His loyalty resulted in imprisonment and he was obliged to leave in 1777. In 1781 he sought refuge at Penobscot, where he acted with great zeal and spirit. A ship, *Black Queen*, with a cargo of masts, which he sent from New England to the West Indies, under licence of Admiral Arbuthnot, was condemned under the Prohibitory Act and he lost his half-share, £1,500. (A.O. 12/101, f. 88; A.O. 13/48; A.O. 13/75.)

The Commissioners reported that in their opinion he told a very incredible story about a ship which he admitted in evidence was freighted and sent as the property of Whigs and was probably with great propriety taken under the Prohibitory Act. A suspicious circumstance in his case was that he stayed in the "rebel country," passing his time between Nantucket and Boston, for two or three years in the midst of rebellion. They doubted uniform loyalty on his part in such circumstances and refused to grant him a loyalist allowance. (A.O. 12/101, f. 88.) The Commissioners seem to have changed their adverse opinion of his loyalty, for they not only allowed him £60 from his claim of £1,120 and his claim at the rate of £120 a year for the loss of his official income during the war, but also granted him a pension of £60. (A.O. 12/109.)

Benjamin Procter was in Newgate gaol in 1787 for debt. (A.O. 13/48.)

THOMAS PROCTER

appears to have lived at Halifax, Nova Scotia, but had a house in, and a plantation near, Boston, bequeathed to him by his paternal uncle. In June, 1778, he was appointed Lieutenant in Lord Rawdon's Volunteers of Ireland, recruited from Irishmen in America for service in the Revolutionary War, and served until the reduction of the corps. He was in Dublin, Ireland, in 1784. (A.O. 13/93.)

DAVID PROPERT

emigrated from South Wales to Boston, where he was a prosperous musician and organist (from 1770) of Trinity Church at the outbreak of the Revolution. One of his patrons was John Rowe, merchant, who mentions him in his Diary.* For example, under date of March 15, 1771, Rowe notes : ". . . when I came home I found Mr. J. Lane and Mr. Propert, who supped and diverted us all the evening by playing on Suckey's† Spinnet and Joyned by Mr. J. Lane in singing—Propert is a fine hand." Two other references in the Diary are : February 3, 1773, " I went to the Concert at the Coffee House‡ of Mr. Propert's—very fine Musick and good performers." February 17, 1773 : "Spent the Evening at the Coffee House with a great number of Gentlemen and Ladies being Mr. Propert's concert."

From Boston he returned home to Swansea in South Wales and there resumed his former position as organist of St. Mary's Church, a position which he filled from 1776 until his death on retirement on March 25, 1784. (A.O. 12/99, f. 327.)

References : Sonneck's *Early Concert Life in America ; Loyalists' Claims, op. cit.,* p. 322.

JAMES PUTNAM

lawyer, of Worcester, was appointed Lieutenant-Colonel in the army, September 24, 1756, and a Justice of the Peace, January 11, 1758. In 1768 he was offered the appointment of Attorney-General of Massachusetts, but declined it. In June, 1774, after unceasing endeavours in and out of public meetings to oppose the unlawful measures and proceedings of the rebellious, he got up the " Worcester Protest " (see Appendix), which was printed in the newspapers and recorded in the town records. Such was the madness and violence of the people in August, 1774, that he found it unsafe to remain in Worcester and he retired to Boston. On July 5, 1775, James Putnam was commissioned to command a company of Loyal Associators in Boston, a duty which he continued in New York from October, 1776, until his departure for England in December, 1779. His eldest and youngest sons§ also did military duty. He was obliged to sell his silver plate in New York for the support of his family. With this memorial is a schedule of his property ; a long official copy of the inventories of his real estate ; a copy of an order for the confiscation of

---

* Edited by E. L. Pierce, 1895.

† Susannah Inman, niece of John Rowe's wife, Hannah ; she married Captain John Linzee, R.N., in 1772. Hannah Rowe presented a silver chalice to Trinity Church in 1790.

‡ The British Coffee House (see page 101).

§ His eldest son, James, graduated at Harvard in 1774, and was an officer in the Associated Loyalists of Boston (see Appendix).

Samuel Quincy

PLATE XLVII

PLATE XLVIII

Isaac Royall and Family

that estate, which is described; copies of the list of confiscated lands sold, with the names of the buyers and the prices realised; lists of property purchased by James Putnam; a list of bonds with the debtors' names and amounts; and an affidavit of Abijah Willard (*q.v.*) as to the property and loyalty of James Putnam, who wrote the above " Worcester Protest." (A.O. 13/49.)

Governor Hutchinson, in a letter to Lord North, September 25, 1776, states that he persuaded Putnam to accept the office of Attorney-General at a time when he could find nobody willing to accept it and who was fit for it; and that he was the most noted lawyer in Worcester County. (A.O. 13/46.)

The Commissioners described him as a man of distinguished situation in his profession who took an active part on the side of the Crown in the Revolution. Furthermore, they recommended him as a very proper person for any vacant Crown appointment in the British Colonies. (A.O. 12/105, f. 17.)

In his letter of October 22, 1782, on the cost of living, Putnam stated that at that moment it was three or four times greater in England than in New England before the Revolution. (A.O. 13/75.) In 1787 he informed Samuel Rogers (*q.v.*) that he could live better in London for £150 than in St. John, New Brunswick, for £600 a year. (A.O. 13/49.)

This eminent loyalist was allowed £4,725 from his claim of £18,246 12s: and at the rate of £700 a year for the loss of his professional and official income during the war. (A.O. 13/85; A.O. 12/109.)

Timothy Ruggles (*q.v.*) recommended by letter, dated April 18, 1775, the appointment of James Putnam to one of the vacancies in the Council of Massachusetts. (C.O. 5/154, f. 63a.)

James Putnam, the last Attorney-General of Massachusetts under the Crown (appointed August 28, 1775), was born in 1726, and graduated at Harvard College in 1746. His wife, Elizabeth, was the daughter of John Chandler (*q.v.*) His most notable pupil in the law was John Adams, second President of the United States. An account of his career as Judge of the Supreme Court of New Brunswick before his death in 1789 is published with some of his correspondence in *The Judges of New Brunswick, op. cit.*

References: A.O. 13/137; Stark, *op. cit.*, pp. 378–82; *Loyalists' Claims, op. cit.*, pp. 175–6.

SAMUEL QUINCY (Plate xlvii)

During the blockade of Boston his house was given up to General Burgoyne. (A.O. 13/93.)

In March or April, 1779, he embarked in England for Antigua, as Comptroller at the Port of Parham in that Island. (A.O. 13/75.)

A list of claims against his estate is in A.O. 12/81, ff. 118–120.

The oil portrait of this loyalist and Solicitor General of Massachusetts, with a number of original letters, is in the possession of Miss Grace W. Treadwell, of Boston.

John Adams, in his reply of April 14, 1776, to a letter from his wife, Abigail (who states that Samuel Quincy's house and furniture had fallen a prey to the merciless Tory party), states that he wishes he could be clear in his mind that it is no moral evil to pity him (Quincy) and his lady, and suggests that love of pomp and gaiety and other social extravagancies had led this loyalist to sacrifice his principles. (Letters of Abigail Adams). John Adams says of Governor Hutchinson that he seduced from his (Adams's) bosom three of the most intimate friends he ever had in his life—Jonathan Sewall, Samuel Quincy and Daniel Leonard—his brother barristers, his cordial, confidential and bosom friends, every one of whom had been as ardent and explicit a patriot as Adams himself, or ever pretended to be. (Adams, *Works*, x, 194, 231.)

Samuel Quincy was born in 1735, the son of Colonel Josiah Quincy, and graduated at Harvard College in 1754. He was admitted to the bar of Massachusetts on the same day as John Adams in 1758. As Solicitor General, he appeared for the Crown in the memorable trial of Captain Preston. He died on the voyage from Tortola to England in 1789 and was buried at Bristol. (Stark, *op. cit.*, pp. 364–76.)

Reference : *Journal of Samuel Curwen, op. cit.*, pp. 630–46.

WILLIAM RANDALL

He lived for many years at Boston as a merchant and had acquired a competent support for himself and his family. In 1760 he was appointed Surveyor and Comptroller of Customs at Charlestown, South Carolina, and in the Bahamas, and on December 6, 1764, he was appointed Surveyor-General of the Southern District of North America, with Jamaica and the Bahamas. This appointment was terminated by the inauguration of a Board of Commissioners of Customs for America in 1767. (A.O. 13/48 ; A.O. 13/75.)

Not having been in America during the war, he was not entitled to a loyalist allowance. (A.O. 12/99, f.227.) His claim of £1,045 was disallowed. (A.O. 12/109.)

William Randall was elected a member of Morden College on March 20, 1778, and died there, February 6, 1789, aged 78. He was a contemporary there of John Bryant (*q.v.*).

According to a copy of the will of Philip Viscount, mariner, of Boston, William Randall's wife, Mary, was his daughter. (A.O. 13/48.)

RICHARD REEVE

was Secretary to the Board of Customs at Boston from 1767, having previously been in the Customs in England. He had been Secretary to Field-Marshal Sir George Howard. (A.O. 13/75 ; A.O. 12/105, f. 42.)

OWEN RICHARDS

emigrated from Wales to Boston about 1750. He was in his Majesty's service by sea and land for nearly 30 years, mostly as a tidesman in the Customs at Boston. By his seizure of a cargo of sugar, etc., illegally imported in 1770, the disaffected inhabitants of Boston were so incensed that on the same night a tumultuous mob of nearly 2,000 assembled outside his house and destroyed his furniture. He was dragged by the heels along the streets to the Custom House, and, after tearing off all his clothes, he was rolled in the channel and put in a cart, tarred and feathered, the feathers set on fire and a rope put around his neck. In this condition he was exposed round the town. (A.O. 13/48; A.O. 13/75; A.O. 13/83; A.O. 12/105, f. 43.)

He received compensation, £120, and a pension until 1800, when he probably died. (A.O. 12/109; T. 50/6; T. 50/8; A.O. 459/7; A.O. 461/16.)

References : *Ontario Archives, op. cit.,* p. 1160 ; *Loyalists' Claims, op. cit.,* p. 80.

ANDREW RITCHIE

This Scotsman lived at Boston for 23 years as a merchant. In 1775 he served in the Loyal North British Volunteers at Boston.

He married Margaret NcNeish in Scotland before emigrating to America. His daughter, Ann, married William Cross (*q.v.*).

On the evening of the " affair " at Lexington he was one of the number who went to the Council Chamber of Boston and declared their allegiance to the King in writing. On November 3, 1775, he was captured by Asa Beech with an armed boat, in his own vessel, the *North Britain,* commanded by his son, John Ritchie, carrying provisions from Nova Scotia, and he and his son were committed to gaol at Salem until June 23, 1776. A witness to his claim at Halifax, Nova Scotia, was Isaac Mansfield, late of Boston, who was presumably a loyalist. (A.O. 13/51 ; A.O. 13/92 ; A.O. 12/10 ; ff. 157–64.)

A copy of the order for his committal to gaol at Salem, November 9, 1775, is in A.O. 13/92, with an affidavit of Andrew Ritchie, junior. He was allowed £100 from his claim for £817 2s. (A.O. 12/109.)

THOMAS ROBIE

was a native of Massachusetts and a resident of Marblehead, where he was uniformly loyal throughout the political disturbances, in opposition to the Non-Importation agreement, and was, perhaps, the only man in Marblehead who withheld assent to the opposition to the Stamp Act. Papers concerning the confiscation and sale of his property are with his memorial in A.O. 13/51. He was allowed £50 from his claim of £2,500. (A.O. 12/109.) Other references to him are in A.O. 13/92 ; A.O. 12/10, ff. 322–8 ; *Acadiensis*, i, 74–81, 143–50 ; *Ontario Archives, op. cit.,* pp. 725–7.

Thomas Robie, a prosperous merchant, married a daughter of the Rev. Simon Bradstreet, great-grandson of Simon Bradstreet, last Charter Governor of Massachusetts. He died at Salem, Massachusetts, about 1812. His son, Simon Bradstreet Robie, was Speaker of the Assembly, Master of the Rolls and President of the Legislative Council in Nova Scotia. (Stark, *op. cit.,* pp. 457–9.)

ANN ROBINSON

This daughter of James Boutineau (*q.v.*) was the widow of John Robinson, a Commissoner of Customs at Boston, whom she married in 1769, and who made the famous assault on James Otis in the British Coffee House (see page 101).

An original letter to William Pitt, Earl of Chatham, signed by James Bowdoin, Samuel Pemberton and Joseph Warren, prays that the British troops be removed from Boston. John Robinson had set sail for England [March 16, 1770] and three other Commissioners had retired or were contemplating retiring from the town. It was apprehended that they would misrepresent conditions so as to lead the Government to believe that their persons were unsafe in Boston without troops. (Chatham Papers, 97.)

References : A.O. 12/99, f. 161 ; A.O. 13/75.

BENJAMIN ROBINSON

He was a native of Massachusetts, who settled at Baltimore, Maryland, and lived there until the political disturbances compelled him in 1775 to sail for London, rather than be disloyal. (A.O. 12/8, ff. 326–7 ; A.O. 12/109 ; A.O. 13/92.)

JACOB ROGERS

This loyalist was for 32 years an officer (19 as lieutenant) in the Royal Navy, and served as Lieutenant in the flagship of Admiral Saunders at the reduction of Quebec ; was tried by court martial in 1773, and dismissed the service. He married an Amercan lady, " used to a superior line of life," and lived at Charlestown, where he and his father-in-law were owners of property, which was lost in the destruction of that place by the British. His schedule of property includes 3,000 acres of land near Stewart Town, New Hampshire, and five acres on Bunker Hill, owned by Captain William Barber (? his father-in-law). On October 7, 1775, the House of Representatives refused him leave to go into Boston to embark for England, on the ground that he had, on April 19 previous, given such assistance and relief in refreshing the King's troops, and in procuring surgeons for the wounded, on returning from Lexington, as to render him "unfriendly to America." This resolute loyalist had been obliged to flee in the dead of night to save his life to the towns of Stoneham and Reading, not daring to return until the fury of the populace had subsided. He refused many temptations to emoluments from the rebels, including a naval command equal to the rank of post captain in the Royal Navy.

On the morning of April 19, 1775, he was alarmed by the inhabitants assembling at the Town House in great consternation and many arming themselves to oppose the British troops returning from Lexington. He immediately, in the strongest terms, represented the impropriety of such measures, as it would involve the ruin of the town by the naval vessels lying before it. Heed was paid to his observation, and the people disarmed themselves, and he had good reason to suppose that his man-œuvre prevented the slaughter of many of the British troops on their retreat and of saving the life of Engineer Montresor, whom he helped to escape to Boston.

Among his services to the British were (a) giving intelligence of the intended occupation of Bunker Hill; and (b) at great risk to his life, point-ing out to the gunners of H.M.S. *Lively* the exact spot of the dismounted ordnance at Charlestown. If the Admiral had attended to his information, the slaughter on the "memorable excursion" to Lexington and Concord might have been prevented. He was for long an object of vengeance to the rebels. Jacob Rogers eventually reached New York, and presented himself to Governor Tryon, to whom he was known, and later set sail for England. Unwilling to be a cipher in the community, he obtained leave in January 1779 to accept a Lieutenancy in the *Queen Charlotte* private ship of war, belonging to the Reprisal Association of the City of London, but having no success in repairing his losses, he was given the command of the privateer *Cæsar*, of 32 guns and 200 men, fitted out at a cost of £17,600 by Sir Francis Bassett and other gentlemen in 1780. (A.O. 13/48; A.O. 13/75; A.O. 12/105, f. 18.) On his cruise in the *Cæsar*, he met several neutral vessels, which had been plundered by British privateers, and he caught a Guernsey privateer, the *Lottery*, commanded by William Mesurier, in the act of plundering a Portuguese vessel. Feeling the stigma of this act, he brought the offenders to justice and thereby revealed to the European powers the abhorrence of Great Britain for such practices, and her determination to punish offenders. For this service he received the public approbation* of the Admiralty.

He was awarded £22 from his claim of £2,752, (A.O. 12/109), and received a pension until 1799, when he probably died. (A.O. 461/19; T. 50/6; T. 50/11; T. 50/28.)

---

* The letter from the Admiralty approving of his conduct, dated June 1, 1781, is in A.O. 13/48.

JEREMIAH DUMMER ROGERS

was a native and inhabitant of Littleton and a barrister-at-law and justice of the peace, who was ever loyal and was compelled by the outrages of the populace to flee from his home in 1775 to Boston. He died at Halifax, Nova Scotia, where by painful industry as a wine merchant (a business in which he had no training or knowledge) he maintained his large family until his death, January 12, 1784, leaving his widow, Bathsheba, with seven young children, the eldest being aged 13. (A.O. 13/48; A.O. 13/75.)

With this memorial of his widow is her pathetic letter, dated January 22, 1784, to her brother-in-law, Samuel Rogers (*q.v.*) in London, announcing the death of her husband, whom she had nursed for some time before his death in her weak condition, having given birth to a son on December 9, previously. This child died a week after his father. She says that she ought, perhaps, to return to New England, but the only person there from whom she might expect kindness had shown no sympathy with her in her banishment.

There are also two letters from Sampson Salter Blowers (*q.v.*) to Samuel Rogers stating that no one had sustained a fairer character or was more respected or esteemed than his brother, the deceased Jeremiah Dummer Rogers. (A.O. 13/48.)

A certificate of Robert Auchmuty (*q.v.*), dated January 24, 1787, states that Jeremiah Dummer Rogers had been a clerk and student of law in his office. (A.O. 13/48.)

Particulars of his confiscated property are with these papers in A.O. 13/48.

Seven children are mentioned, namely, John, Jeremiah Dummer Elizabeth, Samuel, Margaret, Daniel and Sarah. The second was probably the son born in 1771 who was with his uncle, Samuel Rogers, in London and was granted £12 a year for his education, and a pension of £12 from 1784. (T. 50/8; T. 50/28; A.O. 12/101, f. 161.) The children were granted compensation of £700 from their claim of £850. (A.O. 12/109.)

There is a certified copy of the libel against this loyalist's estate, November 28, 1780, signed by John Hancock and John Avery, junior, showing that his estate was forfeited. (A.O. 12/82.)

Jeremiah Dummer Rogers, who graduated at Harvard College in 1762, was a Second Lieutenant in the second company of the Associated Loyalists of Boston in 1775. His wife, Bathsheba, was a sister of the Rev. Peter Thacher, of Brattle Street Church, Boston.

His son of the same name was Byron's tutor for a short time, and his house stood on the Hen Cross, now the Poultry, in the town of Nottingham. He visited his relatives in Massachusetts in 1824, and received the honorary degree of A.M. from Harvard College, where his father, and so many of his name were educated (Sabine). Jeremiah Dummer Rogers, the younger, is, however, mentioned only in one letter in the *Letters and Journals of Lord Byron*, edited by R. E. Prothero.

JOHN ROGERS

was born at Boston, the son of a carpenter, and was established there as a haberdasher. (A.O. 12/105, f.81 ; A.O. 13/48.)

SAMUEL ROGERS

was born in Massachusetts and in 1772 became a partner in the firm of Amory, Joseph Taylor (*q.v.*) and Rogers, merchants of Boston. He was strongly opposed to the separation of the colonies from the mother country, and was a member of the Associated Loyalists and a fireward. He left Boston at the evacuation by the British troops and from December, 1776 to May 1777, he was deputy commissary in New Jersey, until ill-health compelled him to resign. There is a schedule of his property. (A.O. 13/48.)

His brother, Daniel, of Littleton, Massachusetts, appears to have remained there (*Ibid.*). His brother was Jeremiah Dummer Rogers (*q.v.*).

His arms on a document are : . . . a chevron . . . between three stags . . . Crest–A stag . . .

PETER ROSE

was a Swedish shoemaker, settled at Boston, where he was one of the Associated Loyalists in 1775. (A.O. 12/99, f. 119 ; A.O. 12/109 ; A.O. 13/48 ; A.O. 13/75 ; A.O. 13/79 ; F.O. 4/1.)

He was allowed £15 from his claim of £65 2s. (A.O. 12/109), and was awarded a pension of £20 until 1801. (A.O. 461/17 ; T. 50/11.)

References : *Archives of Ontario, op. cit.*, p. 1154 ; *Loyalists' Claims, op. cit.*, pp. 72–3.

ELIZABETH ROSS

was the widow of Alexander Ross, mariner, of Falmouth (Portland), Maine. In answer to her petition, she was allowed to remain in Falmouth, but being a loyalist she was deprived of her houses, which were plundered and afterwards "converted into barracks for the rebels." With her petition is a copy of her husband's will, wherein only she and her daughter, Elizabeth Ross, are mentioned. (A.O. 13/51.) Her claim of £900 was rejected because she remained in the United States throughout the war, outside the British lines. (A.O. 12/61, f. 58.)

Her daughter, Elizabeth, married William Tyng (*q.v.*).

Reference : *Ontario Archives, op. cit.*, pp. 275–6.

THOMAS ROSS

was a mariner, of Falmouth (Portland), Maine, and was part owner of the vessel, *St. Vincent*, with George Lyde (*q.v.*) and Thomas Oxnard (*q.v.*). (A.O. 13/92.) He settled on the Island of Grand Manan in the Bay of Fundy as a master mariner and died in 1804 on the passage home from the West Indies (Sabine).

FRANCIS ROTCH (Plate xxxi)

of Boston was part owner of the ship, *Dartmouth*, which carried to Boston, in November, 1773, 84 whole and 34 half chests of tea, consigned to Richard Clarke and Sons, Thomas and Elisha Hutchinson, Benjamin Faneuil, junior, and Joshua Winslow.   After discharging all the other merchandise, Rotch waited on the consignees of the tea at Castle William, and tendered it to them, but they declined to accept it in face of the popular disturbances.   The tea consequently lay in the ship until the evening of December 16, when a great multitude of disguised people forcibly entered the vessel and threw the whole of the tea overboard. (Treasury Papers, In Letters, 505, No. 16.)

With this memorial is a petition to Lord North, dated January 7, 1776, signed by Francis Rotch, late of Boston, but then of London, and Aaron Lopez, formerly of Rhode Island, but then on his way to London from Jamaica, stating that they had fitted out a number of whaling vessels for the southern latitudes, to be stationed at the Falkland Islands.   Rotch and Lopez had left America at a sacrifice of some thousand pounds. In proof of their opposition to America in the Rebellion, they ordered a large quantity of goods in Great Britain [in defiance of the Non-Importation Agreement].   Moreover, by their uniform conduct they had ever given proof of their loyalty during the disorders and therefore did hope and expect to meet such countenance from Government as would enable them to encounter every danger.   They pray that their ships, in this lucrative whaling industry, may be exempt from the provisions of the Prohibitory Act.   The names of thirteen vessels, with the names of the commanders, are included.

Rotch, despairing of assistance from England, removed to Dunkirk with twelve whaling ships in 1790 (Chatham Papers, 220).

Francis Rotch was the son of Joseph and Love Rotch, of Salem, Massachusetts, and died in New Bedford in 1822.   His silhouette portrait is in Drake's *Tea Leaves*.   A silver spout cup, made by Benjamin Hiller (1687–1739) of Boston, and engraved with the initials of his parents, is in the collection of Francis P. Garvan, Esq., of New York.

Reference : L. Vernon Briggs, *Shipbuilding on the North River, etc.*, 1889, pp. 167, 169.

RICHARD ROUTH

At the age of 17 he emigrated from Bristol, England, to Salem, Massachusetts, and there kept a store for English goods. For seven years he acted as deputy collector of Customs at Salem and Marblehead. On returning from a business voyage to England and the West Indies he found Boston invested by the rebels. At the evacuation, he went to Halifax, and thence to New York, where he joined the Associated Loyalists of Massachusetts for the defence of the city. In October, 1778, he set sail for England with his wife and four children. (A.O. 13/75 ; A.O. 13/92.) In a letter dated from Poole in Dorset, March 22, 1784, he announces his pending departure for Newfoundland, having been appointed Collector of Customs there. (A.O. 13/137 ; A.O. 12/105, f. 44.)

This loyalist married Abigail, daughter of William Eppes, of Salem, July 3, 1771. (*Holyoke Diaries.* 1709–1856, ed. by G. F. Dow, 1911.) He died in 1801 and his wife died in 1835. (Sabine, *op. cit.*) Her mother, Abigail Eppes, married Dr. Sylvester Gardiner (*q.v.*) as his second wife. Her brother was William Isham Eppes (*q.v.*) and her sister, Love, married Sir John Lester, of Poole, in Dorset.

ISAAC ROYALL (Plate XLVIII)

In his memorial he says that he was obliged to flee from home, leaving a large landed estate worth £30,000, besides debts, at the mercy of the rebels. For 25 successive years he was chosen member of His Majesty's Council and on a change of constitution in 1774 he was nominated a Mandamus Councillor, but ill-health (which had compelled him to resign from the Provincial Council in 1773) forced him to decline this office. His daughter married Sir William Pepperell, baronet (*q.v.*). He ends his plea for an allowance as a distressed loyalist, heavily in debt, by praying God that the measures pursued by the King may be the means of opening the eyes of the deluded colonists to see that their true interests as subjects of Great Britain are far above independency. He was granted a temporary allowance of £150 in August, 1777, in response to this petition. (A.O. 13/75.)

Isaac Royall had written anonymously to Lord Dartmouth on January 18, 1774, assuring him of the loyalty of the people, though they were zealous for their constitutional rights, and expressing the opinion that if the Revenue Act were repealed, harmony would return between America and England. On February 22, 1775, he wrote from his home at Medford to Lord Dartmouth, enclosing a copy of the foregoing letter and requesting him to use his influence and interest in behalf of the distressed colonies, which were contending for the restoration of their charter and constitutional rights. He feared that the hostile preparations made by General Gage throughout the provinces would produce fatal consequences. (*Earl of Dartmouth MSS., op. cit.*, p. 273.)

This conspicuous loyalist and member of the Ancient and Honourable

Artillery Company of Massachusetts, died in exile in England in 1781, leaving considerable property, including the estates called "Royalls-borough" and "Royallston." To Harvard College he left land as the foundation for the first Professorship of Law. An English silver cup of the year 1714-5, engraved with his arms, which he presented to the First Parish in Medford, is preserved in that Church, with a silver baptismal basin, by Benjamin Burt, of Boston, bought with his legacy. A silver baptismal basin, engraved with his arms, made by Thomas Edwards, of Boston, was presented by him to St. Michael's Church, Bristol, Rhode Island. All these are described and illustrated in the present author's book on the Old Silver of the American Churches. The Royall House at Medford, a notable specimen of Colonial architecture, where this loyalist dispensed a gracious hospitality before the Revolution, is happily still standing and has been preserved by the Massachusetts Society of Colonial Dames.

A family portrait by Robert Feke, 1741, showing Isaac Royall himself, his wife, his child, Elizabeth, who married Sir William Pepperell (*q.v.*), his sister, Penelope Royall* (afterwards the wife of Colonel Henry Vassall), and his wife's sister, Mrs. Mary Palmer, is at Harvard College. His small medallion portrait by Tassie is in the possession of the Right Rev. Bishop C. T. Abraham.

EVAN ROYS

was a native of Connecticut and settled as a farmer at New Ashford in Berkshire County. He was drafted into the American militia and marched against General Burgoyne's army, but escaped with his two sons, who with him joined the 1st battalion, King's Royal Regiment of New York. (A.O. 12/33, ff. 85-7.) He was allowed £120 from his claim of £205. (A.O. 12/109.)

Reference : *Ontario Archives, op. cit.,* pp. 444-5.

JOHN RUGGLES

fled from his home at Hardwick (where he had twelve deer in the park on his father's property) to Boston, in April, 1775, and was appointed a lieutenant in one of the companies of the Loyal Associated Volunteers until the evacuation of the town by the British. Subsequently he served as a volunteer in Edward Winslow's corps in Rhode Island. Mentioned in his memorial as witnesses at Annapolis, Nova Scotia, are his wife, Hannah Ruggles [daughter of Dr. Thomas Sackett, of New York] and Phebe Sackett [doubtless his niece]. Joseph Ruggles, formerly of Hardwick, and Israel Conkey, of Dartmouth, Nova Scotia, are also men-

* Her portrait with that of Colonel Henry Vassall, by Copley, has been presented by Mr. Robert H. Dana to the Cambridge Historical Society, and held in trust by the Massachusetts Historical Society.

tioned. His claim is endorsed rejected, March 6, 1786. (A.O. 13/51 ;
A.O. 12/10, ff. 345–9.)   He was the son of Timothy Ruggles (*q.v.*) and
died in Nova Scotia, in 1795. (Stark, *op. cit.*, p. 229.)

BRIGADIER GENERAL TIMOTHY RUGGLES (Plate xxii)

was Colonel of the first Provincial Regiment of two battalions and commander-in-chief of all the troops of Massachusetts throughout the. war
with France in North America from 1755 to 1763, and took the French
General, Dieskau, prisoner.   For his services he was granted 1,500 acres
of land by the General Court, a gift which was only to be confiscated by
the State of Massachusetts at the Revolution.*   At the end of this war
he was chosen Speaker of the House of Representatives.   General Sir
Jeffrey Amherst wrote of him to Governor Pownall from Crown Point,
November 19, 1759, that he had on every occasion during the campaign
done everything that he could for the good of the service and that he was
" a zealous, diligent, good man, and I should not do him justice if I
did not mention him to you as such."
     Ruggles was appointed with Otis and two others a representative
of Massachusetts at the Stamp Act Congress at New York and distinguished himself by his zeal and fidelity in supporting the dignity of the
Crown and the just rights of Parliament.   On returning home he was
reprimanded by the House of Representatives for his unfaithful discharge
of his duty at this Congress, and in reply he requested leave to publish
his reasons for his conduct, a leave which was at first granted but was
afterwards refused.   The worthy Ruggles, however, published his reasons
at his own expense and risk and he maintains that the publication quieted
people in general, though many of the more violent people remained his
political enemies, and visited him with their resentment and persecution.
Yet his popularity was still so great that he was re-elected to the House
of Assembly.   As a reward for his fidelity to the Crown at the Stamp
Act Congress he was appointed an Inspector of unclaimed lands in New
Hampshire.   (A.O. 13/75 ; A.O. 12/10, ff. 76–84, 330–5.)
     Sir John Wentworth, formerly Governor of New Hampshire, after-
wards Governor of Nova Scotia, in evidence in support of the claim of
General Ruggles, stated that he was appointed Deputy Surveyor of Woods
in 1771 and that his acceptance of the nomination of a Mandamus Councillor rendered him obnoxious.   He was the means of more persons
remaining loyal in Massachusetts than any other man.   The King's
American Dragoons were raised principally by his influence, though the
command was given to Benjamin Thompson (*q.v.*).   (A.O. 12/10, ff. 76–84,
330–5.)
     Colonel Thomas Gilbert (*q.v.*), who had known him for about forty
years, stated in an affidavit that this loyalist was noted in the province

* An account of the potash farm given to Ruggles in 1764 is in Mr. Blake's
History of Princeton, Mass., pp. 46–59.

for his particular attention to improving his stock of horses, sparing neither pains nor expense in procuring the best sires, both English and foreign, and English mares, by which means his stock had justly acquired the highest reputation of any stud in Massachusetts. He left more than 30 horses and choice mares. One of his best stallions was poisoned by the rebels. (A.O. 13/75.)

With his memorial and a schedule of his losses is a copy of Thomas's *Massachusetts Spy, Or, American Oracle of Liberty*, containing a notice of the sale of Timothy Ruggles's fine horses (about 20), 30 head of cattle and sheep and swine, by public vendue, by order of the selectmen and Committee of Correspondence of Hardwick, at the house of Colonel Jonathan Warner,* innholder, Hardwick, on January 16, 1776. (A.O. 13/75.)

General Ruggles, in a letter, dated from Boston, April 18, 1775, to a friend in England (perhaps Israel Mauduit), relating to his proposal to raise a regiment of 1,500 men to quell the rebellion, says "my heart leaps for joy to find the reception given by their Lordships to my proposals, and if those made to the Governor [Gage] are not acceptable, I hope he will alter them to his mind, as I have the most cordial inclination to contribute every thing in my power to convince these rebellious wretches of their folly and wickedness in despising the best Government both in Theory and administration that ever yet blest the earth we inhabit, and if it causes me as many wearisome days and Sleepness nights as five Campaigns did in the last War, I pray God my constitution may endure it, and my Country will be happy if Success attends his Majesty's Arms, if not many of us will lose our lives and be put out of our present miserable situation I am happy in finding all my best Officers now living, and that servd with me last War, are zealously affected for this service ; by which means I expect soon to recruit the Regiment after the General's proclamation is Issued for severing the Loyalists from the Rebels."

" As there are several Vacancys in the Council here I could most heartily wish that in the filling them, Smugglers might be avoided ; as I am strongly apprehensive that many of our troubles have heretofore arisen from that source." (C.O. 5/154, f. 63ᵃ.)

A copy of his proposals for raising a regiment of Light Dragoons is in the Carleton Correspondence, folio 455.

This loyalist was allowed compensation, £4,994, from his claim of £19,501 14s. and a pension of £150 until his death. (A.O. 12/109 ; T. 50/8 ; A.O. 461/15.)

In one of his memorials he declares that he was driven at the age of 75 into his fourth banishment, this time from New York to Nova Scotia in 1783. (A.O. 13/75.)

A long inventory of his property includes a quantity of silver plate and a silver-mounted sword, his " old friend," and three of the best pews in the Meeting House at Hardwick.

* Colonel on the alarm of April 19, 1775. Commissioned Brigadier, February 13, 1776. (*Massachusetts Soldiers and Sailors of the Revolutionary War*.)

He was one of the " rescinders " (see page 58).

Timothy Ruggles was born in 1711 and graduated at Harvard College in 1732. He commenced practice as a lawyer, first at Rochester, and at Sandwich in 1740, finally settling at Hardwick in 1753. He died in 1795 at Wilmot, Nova Scotia, where he was buried in the Church which he helped to erect by his contributions. His wife died in 1787 at the home of her eldest son at Hardwick.

His eldest son, Timothy, was also a loyalist, but was allowed by the General Court to remain on a part of the Ruggles estate at Hardwick. After his father's death he settled in Nova Scotia. His sons, John and Richard, were loyalists, and died in Nova Scotia.

He was selected as Captain in command of a company of volunteers for an expedition to the Spanish West Indies ; their services not being required, the company was dismissed. (Muster Rolls Series.)

References : A.O. 12/99, f. 328 ; *Ontario Archives op. cit.*, pp. 738-41, 790 ; Sabine, *op. cit.* ; A Pamphlet on General Ruggles, by Henry Stoddard Ruggles, 1897 ; Stark, *op. cit.*, pp. 225-9 ; *Proc. of Mass. Hist. Soc.*, 2nd Ser., iv, 261.

CHARLES RUSSELL

physician, Lincoln, had a large estate and a considerable practice and was a justice of the peace and Registrar of the Vice-Admiralty Court. Aa a loyalist he always opposed with perseverance the principles and practices which culminated in the Revolutionary war and consequently he became an object of popular resentment and of indignities and was shot by a musket ball. After the battle of Bunker Hill he attended the wounded without reward. He was unable to return to Lincoln and set sail with his family for Antigua in 1775 and there practised as a physician until his death in June 1780, when he left a widow, Elizabeth, and five young children. (A.O. 13/75.)

He was the son of James Russell (1715-98), of Charlestown, Massachusetts, a loyalist. He married in 1768, Elizabeth, only daughter of Colonel Henry Vassall, of Cambridge. His brother, James, also a loyalist, married in 1780, Mary, daughter of Richard Lechmere (*q.v.*). (Stark *op. cit.*, p. 453.)

Charles Russell graduated at Harvard College in 1757, and in 1765 received the degree of M.D. at Marischal College (now the University), Aberdeen. (*Scottish Notes and Queries*, December, 1898, p. 95.)

COLONEL RICHARD SALTONSTALL

The following autobiography of this son of Massachusetts is taken from his original memorials in A.O. 13/49 and A.O. 13/83 and from A.O. 12/105, f. 19.

In 1756 he was Major in the Regiment of Brigadier-General Timothy Ruggles (*q.v.*) and served at Lake George under Lord Loudoun. In 1757 he was second in command of the Massachusetts troops at Fort William

Henry at the surrender of that fort, " when he was stript of everything and greatly abused, the only compensation for which was one months pay allowed by the province." In 1759 he was Lieutenant-Colonel in the first battalion of the regiment of General Timothy Ruggles (*q.v.*) in the expedition against Ticonderoga and Crown Point, under Amherst, and in the following year he served in the same rank in General Haviland's expedition. During 1761 and 1762 he commanded a regiment at Crown Point. Meanwhile, in 1761, he was elected a member for the town of Haverhill and continued as such until the dissolution of the General Court in 1768. Having been one of the rescinders he was not re-elected. When the Stamp Papers arrived, he received orders from Governor Bernard to enlist sixty men to defend Castle William, Boston, where these papers were lodged, an act of duty which rendered him so obnoxious as to render his house and person under a threat of violence by the mob. In 1766 he was appointed Sheriff of Essex County, an office worth £200 a year, and performed the duties of this office until September, 1774, when the violence of the mob obliged him to seek safety in Boston. Here he commanded a company of fifty Loyal Associators. At the evacuation of Boston by the British he embarked for England, with only seven guineas in his pocket.

Colonel Saltonstall declares that he was " not conscious of having in any one instance during the contest between Great Britain and America, or his whole life, ever betray'd the strictest loyalty, or omitted his best efforts and endeavours for the British cause and interest, sacrificing thereto his private enjoyments, and exposing himself to abuse, insults and continued hardships."

In a petition, June 5, 1776, he prays to be appointed Inspector of Lands in Canada, in place of Adolphus Benzell, deceased. (A.O. 13/49.)

This distinguished loyalist, who graduated at Harvard College in 1751, died in London in October, 1785, aged 52, and was buried at St. Mary Abbots, Kensington, where his tombstone is inscribed :—

" . . . He was an *American Loyalist*, from Havershill in Massachusetts, where he was descended from a first family, both for the principal share it had in the early erecting as well as in rank and authority in governing that province, and wherein he himself sustained, with unshaken loyalty and universal applause, various important trusts and commands under the Crown both civil and military, from his youth till its revolt ; and throughout life maintained such an amiable private character, as engaged him the esteem and regard of many friends. As a memorial of his merits this stone is erected."

He voted for the rescinding resolution (see page 58).

His brother, Leverett Saltonstall, was also a loyalist and an officer in the 23rd Foot (Royal Welch Fusiliers).

References : *Journal of Samuel Curwen, op. cit.*, pp. 652-4 ; Stark, *op. cit.*, pp. 273-5.

AARON SAMSON

farmer, of Harvard, Worcester County, was driven from home and imprisoned in Worcester gaol, whence he escaped and joined the Loyal Rangers in Canada on October 28, 1781. After the war he settled at New Carlisle, Chaleur Bay, Canada. (A.O. 13/81.)

GRIZZEL SANFORD

was the spinster sister-in-law of Governor Hutchinson, in whose family she had lived for over twenty years. In her memorial of August 16, 1788, she prayed for the continuation of her pension as a loyalist. (A.O. 13/49 ; A.O. 13/135 ; A.O. 12/99, f. 38.)

She was the daughter of William and Grizzel Sanford, of Newport, Rhode Island, and sister of Margaret, wife of Governor Hutchinson.

JOHN SARGENT

was a West India merchant, of Salem. He was obliged to flee in February, 1775, to Boston, having been suspected of helping to discover rebel artillery there. (A.O. 12/105, f. 82 ; A.O. 13/49.)

One John Sergeant was appointed First Lieutenant in the Associated Loyalists of Boston (see Appendix).

He was probably the New England loyalist who was a member of the House of Assembly of Nova Scotia, where he died, January 23, 1824. (Murdoch, *Hist. of N. Scotia*, iii, 524.)

JOSEPH SARGENT

was in the iron business in Boston. (A.O. 12/105, f. 82.)

ABRAHAM SAVAGE

was the owner of an iron forge in Boston and collector of taxes. During the blockade of Boston he was a Lieutenant in the Associated Loyalists (see Appendix) and joined a ship of the Royal Navy to fetch coal from Cape Breton for the British garrison. At the evacuation of Boston he sailed for Halifax and New York, where he was appointed an assistant barrackmaster. He settled at Shelburne, Nova Scotia, and was there June 22, 1786, the date of his petition. (A/O. 13/87.)

ARTHUR SAVAGE

was a merchant in Boston until April 27, 1765, when he was appointed Comptroller of Customs at Falmouth (Portland), Maine. He held this office until November, 1771, when his vigorous suppression of illegal trade (*i.e.*, smuggling) aroused resentment, and he was obliged by ill-treatment from the inhabitants to leave the place. He was taken out of his house in the night by a large number of armed men and treated in the most cruel manner. On July 5, 1772, he was appointed deputy surveyor and searcher of Customs at Boston. (A.O. 13/49 ; C.O. 5/116.)

This loyalist and man of excellent character, as he is described by the Commissioners, arrived in England in August, 1776, with his wife and two children. (A.O. 12/105, f. 45.)

With his memorial are a schedule of his property and letters regarding his sad case, one of which announces the death of his wife in 1781. Thomas Fayerweather, of Cambridge, Massachusetts, in a letter of condolence, states that Mrs. Savage was his niece. One letter is sealed with Arthur Savage's crest, a lion's gamb in a ducal coronet, with his initials and the appropriate motto for an exile, Malo mori quam fædari. (A.O. 13/48.)

He claimed £300 and was allowed £100. His claim of £200 for the loss of his official income during the war was allowed. (A.O. 12/109.) He received a pension until his death in 1801. (A.O. 459/7-461/17 ; T. 50/6.) A list of claims against his estate is in A.O. 12/81, f. 120.

A medallion portrait of Arthur Savage by Tassie is in the possession of Mrs. Louise Appleton Bradbury.

This loyalist, who died in London, March 21, 1801, aged 70, was the son of Arthur Savage (1680–1735), of Boston, donor of a silver baptismal basin, engraved with his arms, in Christ Church, Boston. His brother, Samuel Phillips Savage, supported the American cause in the Revolution. (Sabine, *op. cit.* ; *Ontario Archives, op. cit.*, pp. 1303–4 ; E. Alfred Jones, *The Old Silver of the American Churches*, p. 76 ; *Loyalists' Claims, op. cit.*, pp. 7–8.)

THOMAS SCAMMELL

was inspector and surveyor of the King's white pine-trees in Massachusetts. (A.O. 13/49.)

JOSEPH SCOTT

was a merchant and ironmaster in Boston [where he had property in Scott's Court]. For supplying the British troops in Boston with military stores, " a banditti of ruffians being determined to deprive him of his life, beset his house in the night," but he escaped through the back. His father, Joseph Scott, was a brazier in Boston. A list of debts due to him is with this petition. (A.O. 13/48 ; A.O. 13/49.)

His allowance of £100 was continued. (A.O. 12/105, f. 83.) His claim of £4,644 was disallowed. (A.O. 12/109.) A list of claims against his estate is in A.O. 12/81, ff. 123–5.

Jonathan Simpson, Senior

PLATE XLIX

PLATE L

Robert Traill

JOHN SELBY

appears to have been from Boston, and held a public appointment at
Halifax, Nova Scotia, in 1784. (A.O. 13/49.)   He was Grand Secretary of
Nova Scotia Freemasons, and died at Halifax in 1804, aged 63 (Sabine).

ALEXANDER SELKRIG

He and his brother, James (*q.v.*), were merchants in Boston, trading
as James Selkrig and Company. He was residing at Shelburne, Nova
Scotia, in 1787. (A.O. 13/48 ; A.O. 13/49.)

JAMES SELKRIG

was a brother and partner of Alexander Selkrig (*q.v.*) in the merchant
firm of James Selkrig and Company, of Boston. He joined the First
Company of Loyal North British Volunteers in Boston.   (A.O. 13/48.)
A list of the debts due to the firm, with the names of the debtors, is in
A.O. 13/49.

REV. WINWOOD SERJEANT

It would appear from his own memorial, dated Bristol, England,
July 31, 1779, that after being driven from Cambridge, Massachusetts,
he officiated in King's Chapel, Boston, until July, 1776, when he was
forbidden to pray for the King. Considering this as a prohibition levelled
at the principles of the Established Church of England, he shut up the
Chapel and intended to leave Boston, but a paralytic stroke, which deprived him of speech, detained him there until April, 1779, when he
set sail for England. (A.O. 13/49.)

He died at Bath, September 23, 1780. In a letter from his widow,
Mary Serjeant, dated from Bath, December 1, 1782, she states that she
was the widow, daughter and sister of three clergymen of the Church of
England in New England, all of whom were loyalists. Her husband was
minister of the Church at Cambridge, and might have remained there
and avoided the afflictions which hastened his death by consenting to pray
for the Congress and leave out the King from his prayers. In her valuation
of his property she adds that he was born in England and educated at
Oxford.* Her father was the Rev. Arthur Browne,† first cousin of the
Archbishop of Tuam. Her daughter, Mary, was born June 11, 1770, and
her daughter, Jane E., was born October 24, 1763. (*Ib.*)

In her memorial, dated Bath, March 1, 1784, some of the above
statements are repeated, with the additional information that her late

* The only matriculation under this name was at Merton College in 1690 (Foster,
Alumni Oxon.).

† He was Rector of St. John's, Portsmouth, New Hampshire, and died in the
house of the Rev. Winwood Serjeant, June 10, 1773.

R

husband was minister of Queen's Chapel [Christ Church], Cambridge, and for his loyalty to the King and attachment to the British constitution was seized and imprisoned in 1775, whereby he lost the use of his limbs. With this memorial is a letter from the Rev. Robert Boucher Nickolls (*q.v.*), dated Bath, March 29, 1787, stating that Mrs. Serjeant let lodgings to support herself; and also a schedule of her husband's property at Cambridge, which included 1,000 volumes of books. (A.O. 13/48.)

She claimed £1,410, and was allowed £296 10s. (A.O. 12/109; A.O. 12/99, f. 47.)

This clergyman was probably a native of Bristol, England, and was born about 1739. He was ordained priest in 1756 and licensed on the same day as a missionary for South Carolina, where, early in 1759, he was appointed Assistant Minister of St. Philip's Church, Charlestown. From 1759 to 1767 he was missionary at St. George's Parish, Dorchester, South Carolina. In 1767 he was appointed to Christ Church, Cambridge. His son, Marmaduke, died about 1780. Mary Browne, whom he married in 1765, was his second wife, and died at Bath in 1808. (Sprague, *Annals of the American Pulpit*, v, 81.)

References : Sabine, *op. cit.* ; *Christ Church*, by S. F. Batchelder, 1893, pp. 32–8 ; Ex inform. Mrs. Silvio de Gozzaldi.

JONATHAN SEWALL

On September 1, 1774, the people of Massachusetts first rose up in arms for the purpose of compelling all the Crown officers to resign their respective offices. He resigned his office as Attorney-General with the sanction of General Gage, on August 20, 1775, and embarked with his family for England.

From November 18, 1767, until his departure, was the most turbulent period that the province of Massachusetts had ever experienced and during this time he faithfully discharged his arduous duties and endeavoured to stem the torrent of faction which was gradually rising to open and violent opposition to the established Government.

The following is a list of the commissions of Jonathan Sewall :—

November 20, 1761, a justice of the peace for the county of Middlesex ; March 25, 1767, special Attorney-General ; May 28, 1767, Advocate-General of the Vice-Admiralty Court of Massachusetts ; June 24, 1767, Solicitor-General ; November 18, 1767, Attorney-General ; June 15, 1768, a justice of the peace throughout the province ; and October 17, 1768, Judge Commissary, Deputy and Surrogate of the Vice-Admiralty Court for the colonies of Quebec, Newfoundland and Nova Scotia.

With the above memorial and list are documents relating to his property. (A.O. 13/48.)

Two letters from Sewall to General Gage, dated November 1 and 16, 1782, relate to his salary as Judge of the Vice-Admiralty Court in the above colonies, which if lost to him (as he had been informed) he and his family are beggars, his property in Massachussets having been confiscated. (A.O. 13/49.)

He claimed £5,793, and was allowed £1,600 (A.O. 12/109) and was granted a pension of £150 from 1788 until his death. (A.O. 459/7; A.O. 461/16.)

In a letter, dated St. John, 8 December, 1789, he refers to the claims against him in Massachusetts, most of which were unjust. (A.O. 13/137.)

This distinguished loyalist was born at Boston in 1728 and graduated at Harvard College in 1748. In the judgment of his contemporaries, friend and political foe alike, no member of the bar of Massachusetts excelled or indeed equalled him in intellectual eminence as a lawyer, pleader, and in lively wit and brilliant imagination. He was an intimate friend of John Adams, who said of Governor Hutchinson that he seduced from his (Adams's) bosom three of his most intimate friends, Jonathan Sewall, Samuel Quincy (q.v.) and Daniel Leonard (q.v.), his brother barristers and his cordial, confidential and bosom friends, every one of whom had been as ardent and explicit a patriot as Adams himself, or ever pretended to be. (Adams, *Works*, x, 194, 231.)

In a long letter to General Haldimand, dated Boston, May 30, 1775, Sewall attributes the alarming state of public affairs in America, and the hidden spring of the wonderful movement of rebellion, to the ancient republican spirit brought by the first emigrants, which the form of government in New England has cherished and kept alive. He considers that the calamities might have been prevented by a seasonable application to the cure, and may even now be stopped by a speedy exertion of British vigour and Parliamentary wisdom to the radical cause. (*Earl of Dartmouth MSS.*, *op. cit.*, ii, 305.)

Sewall died, September 27, 1796, at St. John, New Brunswick, where he had resided since 1788 as Judge of Admiralty for that province and Nova Scotia. (*Judges of New Brunswick*, *op. cit.*, pp. 23, 81, 96–7, 171–2, 174, 181, 191, 221.)

Some of his letters are published in the *Winslow Papers* (ed. by W. O. Raymond, 1901).

Several of his letters, written in exile in England, have been published. (*Proc. of Mass. Hist. Soc.*, 2nd Ser., x, 408–427.)

His sons, Jonathan and Stephen, both law pupils of Ward Chipman (q.v.), rose to eminence in the legal annals of Canada, the first as Chief Justice and the second as Solicitor-General of Quebec.

References : Stark, *op. cit.*, pp. 454–7 ; *Loyalists' Claims*, *op. cit.*, p. 233.

SAMUEL SEWALL

He was a signatory to the petition of 29 distressed loyalists from Massachusetts in England, praying for relief. (A.O. 13/46.) In his letter of November 12, 1788, is an abstract from the Massachusetts Act of 1692 for the distribution of the property of intestates. (A.O. 13/137.)

His grandfather, Samuel White, of Brookline, Massachusetts, left him (Sewall) the house in which he lived and died. (A.O. 13/48.)

In his undated memorial (1783) he says he fled to England in July, 1775. With this memorial are many documents relating to his property, including his petition to the General Assembly of Rhode Island for the restoration of his estate there; a list of unjust and fraudulent claims against his estate; and a copy of the will of his father, Henry Sewall, which mentions this loyalist and two other sons, Hull Sewall and Henry Sewall, and a daughter, Hannah. According to a copy of records with this memorial, Hull Sewall died November 27, 1767, aged 24, and Henry Sewall died October 17, 1772, at the same age. (A.O. 13/48.)

A list of claims against his estate is in A.O. 12/81, ff. 121–2. He claimed £27,140, and was allowed £9,462. (A.O. 12/109.)

This loyalist was a member of the same distinguished Massachusetts family as Jonathan Sewall (q.v.), and was born in 1745; graduated at Harvard College in 1761; and died in London, May 6, 1811, aged 56, unmarried. (Stark, op. cit., pp. 456–7.) Administration of his estate was granted to his only sister and next of kin, Hannah Wolcott, wife of Edward Kitchin Wolcott, of Brooklyn, North America. (P.C.C.)

References: A.O. 12/105, f. 148; A.O. 13/49; Loyalists' Claims, op. cit., pp. 205–6.

JANE SIDNEY

In her memorial, dated May 26, 1788, she says that she was born at Boston and was well known to Sir William Pepperell. Her husband, an Englishman, died in 1780 at New York, where he had been a resident for many years. After the occupation of that city by the British troops, she and her husband kept a Boarding School for British officers. Their furniture was destroyed in the great fire in New York in 1776. All her savings had been expended before the date of her memorial, and she was granted a bounty of £30. (A.O. 12/102, f. 136.) In response to her later petition of February 23, 1789, where she complains of failing eyesight preventing her from supporting herself by her needle, she was granted a pension of £16, which was paid until her death in May, 1816. (Ibid., f. 165; T. 50/25.)

DANIEL SILSBY

was a native of Boston and was compelled to flee in June, 1775. Governor Hutchinson, in a certificate on his behalf, states that Silsby was an active loyalist and that during the tumult in the affair of Captain Preston he attended upon the Governor and endeavoured to appease the rage and fury of the people and afterwards secured one or more of the justices of the peace from insult in the course of their duty. He was granted a pension of £100. (A.O. 12/105, f. 84; A.O. 13/49.) He claimed £686 and was allowed £335. (A.O. 12/109.)

Daniel Silsby is mentioned in Curwen's Journal as one of the Massachusetts loyalist refugees who arranged a weekly dinner in the Adelphi in London. He died in Flanders in 1791. (Sabine.)

RICHARD SILVESTER

landwaiter and gauger in the Customs at Boston, was, for his loyalty, imprisoned three times. (A.O. 12/105, f. 46.)

He had served in the Royal Navy for 23 years, including about six years as clerk and secretary to Admiral Lord Edgecumbe. His age in 1779 was 73. (A.O. 13/49.)

ABRAHAM SIMMONS

of Freetown, Bristol County, claimed, as master and part owner (with Peleg Gardner, senior and junior) of the sloop, *Lydia*. (A.O. 13/24)

JOHN SIMPSON

son of John Simpson and brother of Jonathan Simpson, the younger (*q.v.*), died in New York during the Revolution. A list of claims against his estate is in A.O. 12/81, f. 126. His uncle, Jonathan Simpson, left a legacy for his son and daughter.

JONATHAN SIMPSON, THE ELDER (Plate XLIX)

He was a partner with his brother, John Simpson,* as a merchant in Boston, and quitted that place in 1775. He was appointed by the King a councillor of the province by writ of mandamus [but did not take the oath of office]. His brother, John, at his death, left, among other children, two sons, John and Jonathan (*q.v.*), who succeeded to the business upon his (Jonathan's) retirement in 1770. Both were loyalists and left Boston at the evacuation by the British troops. John died at New York during the war. The other children of John Simpson mentioned are : Mary Winslow, widow of John Winslow (*q.v.*) ; Margaret, deceased ; and William. With this loyalist's memorials are lists of his debts and property and copies of documents relating to his confiscated property. (A.O. 13/48 ; A.O. 13/49.) He claimed £1,111 2s., and was allowed £550, less £6 10s. for pension. (A.O. 12/109.)

This loyalist was born in Boston in 1711 or 1712, and in 1754 married Margaret Lechmere, daughter of Richard Lechmere (*q.v.*). He died at Bristol, England, September 19, 1795. His portrait, with that of his wife (both painted by Blackburn), was presented in 1923 by the children of Mr. and Mrs. Robert C. Winthrop, junr., to the Museum of Fine Arts, Boston.

By his long will, dated July 5, 1793 (with a codicil of March 15, 1794) and proved October 23, 1795, he mentions his brothers-in-law,

* A silver flagon in the South Church, Boston, made by Samuel Minott, of Boston, was bought with a bequest of John Simpson, and is engraved with his arms. According to the inscription, he died at sea, July 12, 1764, in returning to his native land. (E. Alfred Jones, *The Old Silver of the American Churches*, 1913, p. 56, Plate XXIII.)

Richard Lechmere and Nicholas Lechmere, and leaves legacies to his niece, Mary Holyoke, wife of Dr. Edward Augustus Holyoke, of Salem, Massachusetts, and his nephew, Nathaniel Glover, late of Boston, merchant, who died between the date of this will and the codicil. He also left a legacy to the son and daughter (not mentioned by name) of his nephew, John Simpson, deceased. To his two nephews, Jonathan (*q.v.*) and William Simpson, he left his property in America. (P.C.C. 612 Newcastle.)

References: *Loyalists' Claims, op. cit.*, pp. 235–6.

JONATHAN SIMPSON, THE YOUNGER

son of John Simpson* and nephew of Jonathan Simpson (*q.v.*), was born at Boston [in 1752], and left there with the British troops in March, 1776, for Halifax, Nova Scotia, thence for England. Having seen no probability of a speedy issue to the war, he accepted an engagement from a London merchant, upon the reduction of Georgia by the British, to sail with a quantity of goods to Savannah, where he remained until the capitulation of Charlestown to the British in May, 1780, when he sailed thither and conducted business until ordered to quit that state as a loyalist before March 1, 1784. He retained throughout the war his unshaken loyalty to the King and his Government. In consequence of his loyalty he was proscribed by an Act of the Assembly of Massachusetts and lost by bonds and notes in that state and in Connecticut £3,784 5s. in lawful money, equal to £2,838 3s. 9d. sterling. He also lost the inheritance of a part of the estate of John Borland,† in right of his wife, a daughter of Borland. The names of his debtors and the amounts are given (A.O. 13/83). Another memorial is in A.O. 13/49. There is a list of claims against his estate (A.O. 12/81, f. 127).

His uncle, the above Jonathan Simpson, left him part of his American estate.

He graduated at Harvard College in 1772, the same year as his brother-in-law, John Lindall Borland (*q.v.*).

Jonathan Simpson, the younger, was warden of Christ Church, Cambridge, Massachusetts, and died in 1834.

JOSEPH SKINNER

This loyalist of Stowe, Massachusetts, had just finished his apprenticeship as a physician in 1775. (A.O. 12/100, f. 312.) He joined the British Army in Canada in 1776, and was taken prisoner with Burgoyne at Saratoga. Upon his release he served with the British Legion and the Light Infantry as assistant surgeon in the southern colonies under Lord Cornwallis, with whom he was taken prisoner at Yorktown. After his

* See page 261.
† See page 41.

exchange he served as surgeon's mate in the General Hospital at New York, and as surgeon to the 71st Foot, with which regiment he embarked at the evacuation of New York in 1783. For his loyalty he was excluded from returning to his comfortable landed estate in New England. (*American MSS. in Royal Inst., op cit.*, iv, 421, 422.) He claimed £2,130 and was allowed £200. (A.O. 12/109.)

Eleazer Wheelock, son of the first President of Dartmouth College, New Hampshire, stated in an affidavit that Joseph Skinner was his class mate at that college. (A.O., 13/49.)

According to an affidavit of Phineas Atherton (*q.v.*), dated February 18, 1789, Joseph Skinner's father, Joseph, was a prosperous farmer at Stowe, and that upon his (Atherton's) visit there in 1778 he was told by Mrs. Skinner that her son, this loyalist, should never be allowed to benefit from his father's estate for taking part against America in the war. (A.O. 13/48.) Between 1787 and 1789 he was in practice as a physician at Fordingbridge in Hampshire, England. (*Ib.*)

REV. ISAAC SMITH

A letter on public affairs written to Isaac Smith, of Salem, Massachusetts, dated from Enfield, near London, December 4, 1775, is in C.O. 5/40.

This loyalist was born May 18, 1749, and graduated B.A. at Harvard College in 1767, and M.A. in 1770. He was tutor and librarian there. He left Massachusetts in 1775 for England, and is frequently mentioned in the Journal of Samuel Curwen (*q.v.*) as Congregational minister at Sidmouth, Devon. His death occurred in 1829 (Harvard Alumni Directory.)

JOSHUA SMITH

of Townshend, settled at Annapolis, Nova Scotia. His declaration of loyalty, with a list of his losses by the Revolution, dated from Annapolis in 1786, is in A.O. 13/25.

SOLOMON SMITH

of Taunton, mariner, served in the Associated Loyalists of Boston. (A.O. 13/97.)

WILLIAM SMITH

was a general trader in Boston, and served in the war as a volunteer in Jessup's Loyal Rangers. In 1786 he was living in the Third Township, above Cataraqui, in Canada. (A.O. 13/51.) His claim was disallowed because he returned to Boston after the evacuation of the town by the British, and engaged in trade. (A.O., 12/61, f. 82.)

JONATHAN SNELLING

was a merchant at Boston, whose father was a decided loyalist and held a commission in the life guard of the Governor of Massachusetts and died before 1786. (A.O. 13/24.)

According to Sabine, Jonathan Snelling, the elder, was Colonel and commanding officer of the Governor's guard and died at Halifax, Nova Scotia, in 1782. His eldest son, the above loyalist, married a daughter of Judge Foster Hutchinson, and died at Halifax in 1809, aged 51. One Jonathan Snelling was commander of the private ship of war, *Molineux*, in 1750. (*Proc. of Mass. Hist. Soc.*, 2nd Ser., v, 93.)

NATHANIEL SPARHAWK

In his memorial, dated from Kittery, Maine, December 26, 1789, he says that he was branded by the rebels as an enemy to his country, and was exposed to every abuse and persecution which a violent and outrageous mob could inflict upon him, and was driven from home. His merchandise and goods were sold by the Americans for two-thirds less than their value, and were paid for in depreciated currency. His merchant ships were captured by the British [under the Prohibitory Act], and shared the same fate as if he had been the most zealous rebel, and thus between Scylla and Charybdis shipwreck was made of his property. He prays for a Government annuity to relieve him of his distress. With this memorial is a letter from his brother, Sir William Pepperell, confirming his distress, and mentioning the death of two other brothers. There is also a certificate to his loyalty from Daniel Rindge and George Jaffrey, formerly of the Council of New Hampshire, both loyalists, and James Sheafe, a member of the New Hampshire Legislature, dated December 26, 1789. (A.O. 13/49.)

Sir William Pepperell in evidence on March 16, 1790, corroborated most of the above statements, adding that the vessels were seized by the British on a voyage from Salem to Surinam in 1777 or 1778, and that the goods were taken from his stores in Boston. His brother was living with his wife and six children at Kittery. A pension of £80 was granted to him until his death. (A.O. 12/102, f. 232.)

Nathaniel Sparhawk graduated at Harvard College in 1765, and settled at Salem. He was appointed to the Council in 1773, but declined. He was one of the twelve men of Salem who in 1775 expressed contrition for signing the address to Governor Hutchinson, and were declared to be worthy of being received and treated as real friends to America. He died in 1814. (Force, *op. cit.*, Ser. IV, vol. ii, p. 852 ; Sabine, *op. cit.* ; Stark, *op. cit.*, pp. 127, 215.)

SAMUEL SPARHAWK

was a merchant and Customs officer in Boston, and joined the Associated Loyalists there in 1775. (A.O. 13/48.)

During his exile in London he earned a precarious living by his pen, probably as a mercantile clerk. He married in England Susannah, daughter of one Crampton, a coal merchant, whom he joined in partnership. (A.O. 12/105, f. 85.)

According to his letter of February 26, 1783, the coal business was not successful, and his wife, far from having a fortune, was possessed of only £200. (A.O. 13/49.)

In his letter of February 22, 1790, he speaks of his distressed condition and of the terrors of prison being constantly before him for debt, without sufficient money to pay his passage to America, whither he was due to depart at the end of that month. (A.O. 13/137.)

He claimed at the rate of £50 a year for the loss of his official income during the war and was allowed his claim. (A.O. 12/109.) He received a pension until 1800. (A.O. 461/15–16; T. 50/6; T. 50/8.)

Sir William Pepperell (*q.v.*) was his cousin.

Reference : *Loyalists' Claims, op. cit.*, pp. 21-2.

SAMUEL HIRST SPARHAWK

This brother of Sir William Pepperell was granted a loyalist pension until he got a commission in the British Army or Marines. (A.O. 12/105, f. 21.) His claim of £900 was disallowed. (A.O. 12/109.)

As a loyalist he was foremost in signing addresses to Governor Hutchinson and General Gage, and served with the Associated Loyalists in Boston in 1775, when he volunteered with a particular corps of loyalists to go outside the British lines on any emergency. With this memorial of March 17, 1784, is an affidavit of John Sparhawk, late of Portsmouth, New Hampshire, regarding this loyalist's property ; and a certificate from General Gage. There is also an extract from the will of his grandfather, Sir William Pepperell, first baronet, leaving him property. (A.O. 13/48.)

He graduated at Harvard College in 1771.

MAURICE SPILLARD

According to his letter of November 24, 1783, he had been an assistant commissary to the Army of the Convention. (A.O. 13/49.)

ANDREW SPOONER

was the son of [John] Spooner, merchant, of Boston (died 1768), and of his wife (died 1772). His uncle, George Spooner (*q.v.*), being unable to support him at New York during the war, sent him to England in the brigantine, *Margaret and Mary*, which was captured by an American

privateer off the English coast and was taken to France, where a stranger
provided him with money to go to England.   Here he went to school
near London.   Having failed to get employment in England, he was
granted one year's allowance of £50 and passage money, £50, to enable
him to return to America.   His estate in Boston was restored to him.
(A.O. 13/49; A.O. 12/105, f. 117.)

He married Anne, daughter of Chief Justice Martin Howard (*q.v.*),
and died January 23, 1802, aged 38.

GEORGE SPOONER

was a native and a merchant of Boston, and left this place with the British
forces in March, 1776, for Halifax, Nova Scotia, where he offered his services as a volunteer in any British regiment during his exile there from
1776 to 1778.   He resided in New York for the remainder of the war, and
then returned to Boston to obtain papers concerning his property.   Here
he remained from 1784 to 1787, but was unsuccessful in business.   He
removed to Worcester in 1787, and there kept a small store.   Meanwhile,
he took the oath of allegiance to the State of Massachusetts.   With his
memorial of February 17, 1790, wherein he says that he was reduced by
the Revolution from affluence to beggary, is a copy of the licence of the
Commonwealth, dated November 2, 1784, allowing him and the following
loyalists to reside in Massachusetts : John Amory, Thomas Oxnard (*q.v.*),
Nathaniel Chandler, Thomas Brattle, David Green * and Isaac Winslow
(*q.v.*).   (A.O. 13/49.)   His list of losses includes the furniture given to his
wife, Phœbe Spooner, by her father, John Borland, husband of Anna
Borland (*q.v.*).   (A.O. 13/49; A.O. 13/95 ; A.O. 12/102, f. 208 ; *Am.
MSS. in Royal Inst., op. cit.*, iv, pp. 221, 239, 255, 256.)

A miniature portrait attributed to Copley, was painted of his wife,
Phœbe.   (Mr. F. W. Bayley's book on Copley.)   His nephew was Andrew
Spooner (*q.v.*).

SAMUEL STARBUCK
See Timothy Folger.

DR. SAMUEL STEARNS   (Plate xxiii)

For over twenty years he had made and published " Astronomical
Calculations, fitted to the Latitude and Longitude of the town of Boston
. . . Massachusetts ; and as they were highly applauded, both by the
Learned and Vulgar, he continued his Publications Annually."

He settled in the town of Paxton and there and in the adjacent towns
followed the practice of physic and surgery.   As a loyalist from infancy
he attempted at the commencement of the unhappy dissensions to serve

* A member of the New England Club of Loyalists in London, mentioned in
the Journal of Samuel Curwen (*q.v.*).

his King by opening the eyes of the deluded in the hope of preventing the effusion of blood and making way for the re-establishment of British Government and the "continuence of Peace, Liberty and happiness in the Colonies." In consequence of his actions he was represented by the malcontents as a very dangerous person, and the sale of his astronomical publications was destroyed and his practice impeded.

From 1775 to 1780 he was greatly persecuted for his loyalty, and not only was he deprived of the benefit of his profession and denied the liberty of the Press, but was also frequently fined for not taking up arms against the King and was cruelly oppressed with heavy taxes. Often was he defamed by his adversaries, who took much pains to destroy his reputation and diminish his influence among the people, and sometimes brought him before a "lawless set of men, called a Committee of Correspondence."

In September, 1780, Dr. Stearns was made a prisoner by virtue of a State warrant, on an accusation of holding a traitorous correspondence with, and affording aid and comfort to, the enemy, and was obliged to find two sureties for £100,000. Having been warned of a design to confine him in gaol and possibly to take his life, he fled for protection to the British Army in New York, with the officer holding the said warrant in hot pursuit. He remained in New York until the peace and succoured the sick and distressed loyalists, without compensation. Meanwhile, judgment was recovered against his sureties, in consequence of his absence from court, and his estate was seized for the Commonwealth.

In 1784 Dr. Stearns attempted to pass through Massachusetts to move his family to Nova Scotia. He found his wife turned out of home and obliged to labour hard to stave off starvation. He was seized and cast into prison in Worcester County, within 48 hours, in violation of the definitive treaty of peace and without a trial. He was kept in that loathsome prison for 35 months, until July 28, 1787. Although his estate had been taken by his sureties for the Commonwealth, and executions issued against them for the payment of the money, yet the sum demanded was not satisfied until 1785, when his sureties were committed to prison and there remained until payment was made of the £100,000, which was afterwards reduced by depreciation to about £1,400 in hard money.

Dr. Stearns declares that in one year not less than 126,000 of his calendars had been sold in America, to his gain of nearly £300. His professional income as a physician was over £70 sterling a month. He kept apprentices. (A.O. 13/48; A.O. 13/49.)

Two certificates of James Earl, portrait painter,* dated London, February 17, and September 26, 1789, state that he was a near neighbour of Dr. Stearns at Paxton and had known him for many years. (A.O. 13/48.)

With a schedule of his property and losses mention is made of the depositions of Daniel Steward, John Houghton and Joshua Sawyer, loyalists and neighbours, and John Rose and Joseph Prescott, probably

---

* James Earl did a portrait of Dr. Stearns as a frontispiece for the *Tour from London to Paris*, by Samuel Stearns, London, 1790.

loyalists, all of whom fled from Massachusetts to Vermont for safety.
(A.O. 13/48.) The three first were at Brattleboro, Vermont, in 1788,
and the others at New York at the same date (*vide* certificates in
A.O. 13/48.)

A certificate of Samuel Paine states that Zaccheus Gates, Timothy
Ruggles, junior, Edward Selfridge, Oliver Witt, senior, and Oliver Witt,
junior, were all loyalists who had signed certificates in favour of Dr.
Stearns. (*Ibid.*) Certificates, dated August 20, 1787, attest the loyalty
of Dr. Stearns from Zaccheus Gates, of Rutland, Timothy Ruggles, junior,
of Hardwick, Edward Selfridge, of Hubbardston, John Houghton, Esq.,
Josiah Arms, gentleman, and of C. Atame or Hame, Lieutenant in the
Queen's Rangers. (A.O. 13/80.) Two petitions, dated London, in 1789,
are similar to his original memorial of September 24, 1789, in A.O. 13/48.
There are letters of no interest in A.O. 13/137.

In evidence on March 8, 1789, he stated that he was kept a close
prisoner for 23 months, and the rest of the time was allowed to walk in
the prison yard. His wife was then keeping a school in Vermont. He
was granted £20 and £25 for his passage to Nova Scotia. (A.O. 12/102,
f. 166.)

Two depositions of Oliver Witt, senior, and Oliver Witt, junior, of
Paxton, dated June 1 and 10, 1786, state that they were taken prisoners
with Dr. Stearns by warrant of James Sullivan in September, 1780, for
holding traitorous correspondence with the enemy.

A deposition, dated October 10, 1788, of John Williams, late of Shrewsbury, Massachusetts, but at that date of New Barbadoes, New Jersey,
declares that he was a loyalist and had been acquainted with Dr. Stearns
for more than 16 years, and that two justices of the peace in Worcester
County, Jonathan Ward and William Dunsmore, had told him that Dr.
Stearns was a man of great learning and influence and had done more
damage to the revolutionary cause than a thousand British soldiers.
While Williams was a prisoner in Worcester, these two justices attempted
to bribe him to turn State's evidence against Dr. Stearns and other Tories,
but he refused to be hired. (A.O. 13/48.) A certificate of Lemuel Rice
gaoler of Worcester, dated May 18, 1787, states that Dr. Stearns was not
kept in prison by his bondsmen, but by order of the Commonwealth, and
that no complaints had been made against him for passing counterfeit
money, for which he was imprisoned. (*Ibid.*) The Rev. Samuel Peters,
in a certificate of March 4, 1789, states that he had received a letter from
General Ethan Allen, testifying to the uniform zeal of Dr. Stearns against
America. (*Ibid.*)

Compensation to the amount of £650 was granted to him from his
claim of £4,119 and £120 per annum for the loss of his professional income
during the war. (A.O. 12/109.) He received a pension until his death
[at Brattleboro, Vermont, in 1809]. (A.O. 459/7 ; T. 50/42.)

During his imprisonment at Worcester he wrote, and in 1786 published, his *Short History of the Treatment that Dr. Samuel Stearns hath met
with in Massachusetts, since the commencement of hostilities between Great*

Britain and her Colonies. Exhibiting The Troubles he has met with, by Reason of his Loyalty, and the Appearance of false Evidence against him. In this account he announces his ardent desire that the inhabitants of every branch of the British Empire may enjoy civil and religious liberty. Although repugnant to the constitution of the Commonwealth of Massachusetts to demand excessive bail or sureties, yet the Judge demanded bail for the excessive sum of £100,000 for his appearance before the Supreme Court. The false witness [Thomas Gleason] against him is said to have been a deserter both from the British and American armies, a man who bore the character of a thief and a liar, and who alleged that he (Dr. Stearns) and Captain Witt and his son had not only kept a correspondence with the enemy, but had also made and passed counterfeit money. This villain is believed to have turned King's evidence to save his own life as a deserter from the American army. Dr. Stearns declares his innocence. Fearing that death, the penalty for the offence of holding correspondence with the enemy, might be his fate, and being satisfied in his conscience that the best men in all ages have fled in a moment of danger to save their lives (*e.g.*, the prophet Elijah from Jezebel when she swore by the Gods that she would kill him), he escaped to New York. This interesting pamphlet is an indictment of the vindictive treatment accorded to him. The Supreme Court, he says, refused to bring him to trial on evidence subsequently proved by the confession of the witness to have been false.

During his residence in New York he published in 1783 a " Universal Kalendar with a Nautical Almanac."

CHARLES STEWART

was appointed Surveyor-General of the Customs in the Eastern Middle District of America in 1762, and upon the suppression of that office and the establishment of the Board of Customs at Boston in 1767 he was transferred there as Cashier and Paymaster. (A.O. 13/48.) He ·was granted a pension of £300 from 1788 to 1800. (A.O. 459/7—461/16.)

Charles Stewart protected Don Pedro Bermudez (with his family), second in command of the Spanish sea service at Havana, in a riot between English and Spaniards in Virginia in November, 1762. (Earl of Dartmouth, *MSS., op. cit.*, ii, 70.)

JAMES STINSON

yeoman, of St. George's, Maine, and later of Penobscot, served on a privateer with William Stuart or Stewart (*q.v.*). He settled at St. Andrews, New Brunswick, and was there in 1787. (A.O. 13/51.) He was allowed £41 from his claim of £218 14s. (A.O. 12/109.)

Reference : *Ontario Archives, op. cit.*, pp. 322-3.

EDWARD STOW

was born in the borough of Southwark [the birthplace of John Harvard], and had served thirteen years in the Royal Navy, including three years between 1734 and 1737, as a midshipman on board H.M.S. *Dreadnought,* before settling in Boston as a master mariner. Ever since the Stamp Act riots he suffered insults, and in 1770 his house was bedaubed with excrement and feathers on two occasions, and with blubber oil and feathers. On July 9, 1770, a mob of nearly 300 persons, headed by John Hambleton, forced open his house at No. 1, Orange Street, and severely maltreated him. On April 3, 1775, his house was again bedaubed with excrement and feathers because he had captured for the King two gun carriages, a pair of swivels and a cow horn. (A.O. 13/51.)

His confiscated house and land in Cambridge, Massachusetts, were sold in 1784 to Ebenezer Brown ; and his house and wharf in Boston were sold at auction in 1784 to Benjamin Thomson. (Certificates, with estimate of losses, in A.O. 13/51.) A certified copy of the libel against his estate is in A.O. 13/82.

He was granted £585 from his claim of £1,454 11s. (A.O. 12/109.)

Edward Stow married Mary Belcher in 1767 and was a refugee at St. John, New Brunswick, in March, 1786, at the age of 76.

Reference : *Ontario Archives, op. cit.,* pp. 851-3.

WILLIAM STUART (STEWART)

yeoman, at St. George's, Maine, afterwards of Penobscot, served on board a privateer with James Stinson (*q.v.*), and captured the American schooner of Abner Blaisdale, of Portsmouth, New Hampshire. He settled at St. Andrews, New Brunswick, after the war. (A.O. 13/51.) He was allowed £85 from his claim of £158 19s. (A.O. 12/109.)

THOMAS SWAN

was a merchant at Groton and was obliged in April, 1777, to flee from home, having refused to abjure his King, and went to New York. There he joined Wentworth's Volunteers, and afterwards served in the Associated Loyalists in Rhode Island, with which corps he made many excursions into Connecticut and elsewhere, burning and destroying many towns and villages. Thomas Swan was ever loyal and was several times imprisoned for his loyalty. With his memorials is a copy of an order by the State of Massachusetts of July 19, 1779, ordering his wife, Sarah Swan, and her two small children, to depart the State. (A.O. 13/49; A.O. 13/51 ; A.O. 12/105, f. 86.) He was granted compensation of £81 from his claim of £2,010 (A.O. 12/109) and a pension of £30 to 1808 (A.O. 463/23). In 1787 he was at Montreal. (A.O. 12/61, f. 81.)

Reference : *Ontario Archives, op. cit.,* pp. 938-9.

JAMES SYMONS

was a native of Somersetshire, and from 1770 to 1779 was settled on Union River, Penobscot, where he suffered continuous insults and the destruction of his crops for his loyalty. Upon the arrival of British troops at Penobscot he joined them and assisted in building a fort there. He was employed in the Engineer's department until the peace. (A.O. 13/51.) His compensation amounted to £45 from his claim of £189. (A.O. 12/109.)

Reference : *Ontario Archives, op. cit.,* pp. 323–4.

SAMUEL TARBELL

of Groton, was from April 17, 1777, until January 10, 1778, a prisoner in Concord. Upon his release he joined Wentworth's Volunteers, and was afterwards [from February 24, 1782] a Lieutentant in the King's American Dragoons. In his memorial and schedule of his property he mentions his farm of 300 acres at Mason, New Hampshire, of which his tenant was William Dodge ; he also mentions Thomas Tarbell, of Mason ; John Fish, his farm bailiff at Groton ; and Aaron Farnsworth, of Groton. At the end of the war he settled in Annapolis County, Nova Scotia. (A.O. 13/51 ; Ind. 5604–5–6.)

This loyalist was born in Groton in 1746 and was the son of Samuel and Lydia (Farnsworth) Tarbell. He died in Groton, March 12, 1796, in poverty. (See *Tarbell Genealogy* by Mrs. Greenlaw.)

References : *Ontario Archives, op. cit.,* pp. 463–5 ; *Trans. of Colonial Soc. of Mass.,* v, 293–7.

SAMUEL TATE

was a mariner, of Falmouth (Portland), Maine, where his father was for many years responsible for procuring masts and other stores for the Royal Navy, while he himself was employed on the ships which conveyed these masts and stores to England. At the outbreak of the war he joined the Royal Navy as master of a transport and served throughout the war. While in port with his ship at Savannah, Georgia, he volunteered for active service and was given the command of a battery during the siege of that place and for his good conduct received the General's thanks. With his memorial is a schedule of his losses. (A.O. 13/75.)

WILLIAM TATE

was a merchant in Falmouth (Portland), Maine, who experienced all the bitter consequences of anarchy and rebellion and as a loyalist was frequently harassed before committees and compelled to take an oath to oppose the British troops. Having refused to supply American troops with clothing, his stock of clothing, to the value of £300 sterling, was forcibly taken from his store. He was an eye-witness of the total destruction of his store in the burning of Falmouth by order of Captain Mowat (*q.v.*) on October 18, 1775. In a letter, dated November 24, 1782, he states that the only person in Bristol (England) who was acquainted with him in America was Captain Thomas Coulson (*q.v.*). (A.O. 13/74; A.O. 13/87.)

He declared his property to be worth £5,000, but this was denied by good testimony. Thomas Flucker (*q.v.*) said that William Tate's father was a rebel. (A.O. 12/105, f. 22.)

JARED TAYLOR

was a native of Connecticut, settled as a farmer at New Ashford, Massachusetts. He was drafted into the American militia, but deserted and joined Jessup's loyalist corps. (A.O. 12/33, ff. 183–5.)

He incurred losses in the loyalist corps of Major Robert Rogers to the amount of £174 18s. He went to Nova Scotia after the war. (A.O. 13/79; *Archives of Ontario, op. cit.*, p. 455.) He claimed £174 and was allowed £75. (A.O. 12/109.)

JOHN TAYLOR.

A list of claims against his estate is in A.O. 12/81, f. 130.

JOSEPH TAYLOR

was born in Boston and was a merchant there from 1772 in partnership with Jonathan Amory, John Amory and Samuel Rogers (*q.v.*). The two latter were loyalists and left Boston with him in 1775, and he engaged in business in New York as partner of Samuel Rogers, of London. In 1779 he was part owner of the privateer, *Spitfire*, supposed to have foundered at sea, and in 1782 of the privateer, *Alert*, blown up by the Americans. On February 1, 1780, he was appointed Captain of the loyal militia in New York. He was at Halifax, Nova Scotia, in 1786. His only surviving brother, John, a loyalist, of Boston, was drowned in 1776. (A.O. 13/24.)

He graduated at Harvard College in 1765 and died at Boston in 1816, aged 71. (Sabine.)

NATHANIEL TAYLOR

was born in Boston and from 1755 to 1775 was deputy Naval Officer for Massachusetts. After the battle of Lexington he was driven to Boston from Salem (whither he had moved with the Customs officials) and there remained until the evacuation by the British. He eventually settled in Quebec and was there in 1787 with his wife and ten children. He lost considerable personal estate in Boston and apparently some real property, to which his wife was entitled. (A.O. 13/51; A.O. 13/75; A.O. 13/137; A.O. 12/10, ff. 422–9, 442–4; *Ontario Archives, op. cit.*, pp. 734–5,

922-5.) He claimed £4,900 for the loss of his property and was awarded £100. For the loss of his salary of £500 a year as Naval Officer he was compensated at the rate of £400 a year during the war, and received a pension until his death, October 10, 1805. (A.O. 12/109; A.O. 459/7; A.O. 462/20; A.O. 462/21.) His letter, dated from Boston, January 16, 1776, to Joseph Taylor* at the New England Coffee House in London, is on affairs in the town of Boston at that time. (C.O. 5/40.)

His wife, Sarah, whom he married in 1768, was a daughter of George and Elizabeth Minot (*Minot Genealogy*, p. 22). Her property in North Carolina was derived apparently through her mother, a daughter of Maurice Moore, of Cape Fear in that colony, and grand-daughter of James Moore, Governor of North Carolina.

Sabine states that Nathaniel Taylor died in Quebec in 1806, at the age of 72.

WILLIAM TAYLOR

was born in Boston and was a merchant there until the evacuation of the town by the British in March, 1776. Later in the war he was in command of a Volunteer Company in New York. His losses (of which there is a schedule) include the schooners, *Elizabeth* and *Pompey* and ¼ part of the *Dolphin*. He was at Halifax in 1786. (A.O. 13/24.) A list of claims against his estate is in A.O. 12/81, f. 129.

A loyalist of this name, formerly of Boston, died at Milton, Massachusetts, in 1789, and another at Shelburne, Nova Scotia, in 1810, aged 73. (Sabine.)

NATHANIEL RAY THOMAS

for several years previous to the war foresaw that the efforts of the leaders of the faction in Massachusetts tended towards a revolution. He therefore opposed them by every means in his power and was generally so successful that the town of Marshfield retained its loyalty long after the evacuation of Boston by the British troops. For his faithful exertions he was appointed in July, 1774, to the new Council by mandamus, which moved him to increased activity in support of his Majesty's government. Threats from the " factious demagogues " were now made against the loyalists of Marshfield and became so violent that he was obliged to ask General Gage for a detachment of troops for their protection. Captain Balfour was sent in command and had the effect of preserving the peace in the large county of Plymouth until the battle of Lexington. His requisition for troops increased the popular resentment against him, but his zeal was in no sense abated. To accommodate 100 soldiers at his house he was obliged to remove his own family in December in a severe winter. In April events had occurred which compelled the recall of the

---

* Joseph Taylor was probably the loyalist, named in the Banishment Act of Massachusetts, who was a member of the New England Club of Loyalists in London, mentioned in the Journal of Samuel Curwen (*q.v.*).

S

troops from Marshfield to Boston. In this dangerous position 100 useful and faithful loyalists at his instigation quitted their farms and joined him (Thomas) at Boston, whither he was forced to seek shelter on September 4, 1774, and where they were employed in useful services. He himself was attached to General Cleaveland's ordnance department and there performed duties which were continued at Halifax and New York until ill-health obliged him to abandon the cause he had embraced and to take passage to England in December, 1777. The loyal town of Marshfield (where his patrimony was the most considerable and his family residence was co-eval with the foundation of that town) was " too distinguished by its zeal and sufferings to need further description." Two painful results of his steadfast loyalty were the loss of his health and the break in the education of his young children. (A.O. 12/10, ff. 56–63.) Marshfield had "through a ten years' political struggle and warfare, never deviated from, but had uniformly and invariably preserved and maintained its Integrity and Loyalty ; a Town, the only one in New England, that in spite of the threats and intimidations of surrounding Towns, counties, and Provinces, dared, publickly and collectively to own and acknowledge their Allegiance, and the Supremacy of the British Legislature." (A.O. 13/74.)

The losses of this loyalist, which are mentioned in detail, included his patrimony of 1,000 to 1,200 acres of land, his new mansion house, 70 to 80 head of black cattle, sheep, hogs, etc., personal property and real estate in the townships of Pembroke (inherited from his ancestors), Londonderry (in right of his wife) and Dorchester (granted by Governor Wentworth in 1771). His wife, who was allowed to remain on one-third part of his property at Marshfield throughout the war, was obliged to sell stock, silver plate and furniture for the maintenance of her family. (A.O. 12/10, ff. 56–63 ; A.O. 12/61, f. 10.)

Daniel White stated in evidence that nearly 200 of the loyal inhabitants left Marshfield with Nathaniel Ray Thomas. (Ib.)

In his memorial of May 10, 1781, he details the sufferings of his wife and states that his estate had been sold in lots in March. (A.O. 13/74.) In another memorial, July 28, 1783, he appeals for a further sum of money to enable him to remove his wife and six children from their intolerable affliction and distressed condition, after a separation from him of nearly nine years, from Massachusetts to Nova Scotia. (Ib.)

In A.O. 13/51 are several papers relating to his property and many letters from him during his exile in Nova Scotia to his friend, Paul Wentworth, in London. In one letter he states that his second son, John Thomas, remained at Marshfield and had obtained part of his estate. There is also a letter from his friend, E. Storer, of Boston, dated September 3, 1783, stating that it was the general opinion that the loyalists who took an early and decided part by accepting commissions from the British Government would be for ever excluded from Massachusetts.

A list of loyalist refugees from Plymouth County includes the names of 73 from Marshfield, with Nathaniel Ray Thomas at their head. (*Proc. of Mass. Hist. Soc.*, 2nd Ser., pp. 234–5.)

Paul Wentworth wrote to the Commissioners on May 7, 1788, stating that this loyalist had died, September 19, 1787, at Windsor, Nova Scotia, leaving his wife and six children, including his daughter, Sarah Deering Thomas, in great distress. (A.O. 13/137.) His wife received a loyalist pension of £80 from 1784 until about 1813–15. (T. 50/24.) Thomas himself was a recipient of a pension. (A.O. 12/105, f. 23.)

Nathaniel Ray Thomas graduated at Harvard College in 1751 and married Sarah Deering. His daughter, Mary, married the Rev. Benjamin Gerrish Gray, D.D. (son of Joseph Gray, loyalist, of Boston), Rector of St. George's Parish, Halifax, Nova Scotia, and afterwards of St. John, New Brunswick.

References : Winsor, *Hist. of Duxbury, Mass. ;* Richardson, *Hist. of Marshfield ; Wentworth Genealogy*, i, 117, 317 ; *Journal of Samuel Curwen, op. cit.*, pp. 660–1 ; L. Vernon Briggs, *Shipbuilding on the North River*, 1889, p. 275.

BENJAMIN THOMPSON (Plate xxxvi)
[COUNT RUMFORD]

At the age of twenty he was appointed Major of a regiment of militia and was later promoted to the command of a regiment of more than 1,000 men, with the rank of Colonel. In December, 1774, he joined the British army in Boston and was soon afterwards named for the command of one of the battalions to be raised by Brigadier Timothy Ruggles (*q.v.*). In May, 1776, he sailed for England with public despatches and in a few days was appointed Secretary of the Province of Georgia. In September, 1780, he accepted the appointment of Under Secretary of State in the American Department, an office which he resigned early in October, 1781, upon his appointment in February as Lieutenant-Colonel Commandant of the King's American Dragoons* (which was raised at a time when other provincial regiments found it almost impossible to recruit). All the officers of this regiment, except the Adjutant [Arthur Nicholson, who was from the 17th Light Dragoons], "were American gentlemen who had been driven from their estates by the rebels on account of their loyalty " and who were loyalists from the commencement of the war. The standards of the regiment were presented by Prince William Henry [afterwards King William IV.] at Flushing, Long Island, New York. Benjamin Thompson (the future Count Rumford) with his loyalist cavalry in a fierce action on February 24, 1782, on the River Santee in South Carolina, supported by a detachment of 100 men from the 30th Foot, the Volunteers of Ireland and 60 Yagers, defeated and nearly destroyed a body of cavalry under Horry, and afterwards defeated and dispersed Marion's force with considerable loss.† (Carleton Correspon-

---

* For other particulars of the Regiment, see H.O. 42/2, and H.O. 42/3.

† The date of this engagement is stated to have been February 25 (*Amer. MSS. in Roy. Inst., op. cit.*, ii, 403–5).

dence, f. 435.) Lieutenant-Governor William Bull, in a letter, gives a version of the defeat of Marion and says that Colonel Thompson, after a march of 36 miles without halting, and with the cavalry only, attacked Marion and totally routed him, taking and killing about 80, without the loss of one man. Among the killed were several youths of good families, who had been forced into the American militia service as privates. (C.O. 5/176, f. 177.) In this affair the New York Volunteers and four troops of the South Carolina Royalists took part and Marion's tent and canteens full of liquor were captured, affording a timely supply to Thompson's troops. (*Amer. MSS. in the Roy. Inst., op. cit.*, ii, 405.) These MSS. contain many papers relating to the King's American Dragoons, including the original rolls of the three troops in June, 1782, commanded by Daniel Murray (*q.v.*), Joshua Upham (*q.v.*) and William Stewart.

By accepting the command of this crack loyalist corps Thompson showed a spirit and zeal for the service in quitting for a time an agreeable and profitable civil situation in the American Department. (*Ib.*, ii, 335.)

A copy of the libel against his estate in 1780, signed by John Hancock, is in A.O. 12/82.

A bundle of his letters is calendared in the Report on the Stopford-Sackville MSS., *op. cit.* His long and interesting observations, dated November 4, 1775, on the condition of the American army, mentions such small details as the marks of distinction worn by American officers and the loud complaints by the Massachusetts forces of the partiality of General George Washington for the Virginians, who on the other hand complain of the enormous proportion of officers from New England, especially Massachusetts, in the army (pp. 13–18).

In an undated petition he prays for permission to proceed to Germany, and in case there should be a war between the great European Powers and Turkey that he may be allowed to offer his services to Germany. (Original Corresp. of Geo. III, H.O. 42/3.)

The subsequent career of this loyalist son of Massachusetts as man of science is well known and need not be recapitulated here.

His birthplace at Woburn is illustrated in Drake's *Hist. Mansions and Highways around Boston*, 1899.

JOSEPH THOMPSON

was a merchant, of Medford, where he was ever an active and loyal subject. In 1774, when supplies for the British forces in Boston were prohibited by the people of the surrounding districts, he, at great personal risk, contracted to furnish materials for building barracks, and purchased twelve hundred thousand bricks at 18s. a thousand, which were ready for despatch on a small vessel bought for the purpose, which was, however, seized and destroyed by the people of Medford. He was now obliged to quit Medford and seek protection in Boston. Early in 1776 this enterprising loyalist undertook to go to Rhode Island for provisions for the British garrison in Boston, but again his efforts were frustrated by his seizure by the rebels in Rhode Island. Upon his release he resided at Swansea, Massachusetts, until July 13, 1777, when he got leave to sail to the West Indies and took passage on the sloop, *Speedwell*, bound for Surinam. Misfortune again overtook him, this vessel having been captured within two days by H.M.S. *Unicorn*. (A.O. 13/49; A.O. 13/74.)

Sir William Pepperell, in his certificate of January 15, 1778, states that Joseph Thompson had been known personally to him for many years and that when fresh provisions were not procurable in Boston he brought in a cargo, which was of great service to the army. (A.O. 13/74.)

His widow, Rebecca Thompson, in her memorials of 1781 and 1784, reiterates his own accounts of his losses, adding that he had died in London, July 22, 1781, and praying for the continuance of his pension of £150, which was the only support of the family. (*Ib.*) She claimed £1,505 as compensation and was awarded £625 (A.O. 12/109), and was granted a pension of £30 from 1782 until her death, July 29, 1818. (T. 50/6; T. 50/25.)

An original letter from Benjamin Thompson (Count Rumford) (*q.v.*), dated August 8, 1781, states that Joseph Thompson was his distant relation. (A.O. 13/74.)

Original certificates to his loyalty and services include those of General Gage, Joseph Goldthwait, barrackmaster, Edward Winslow (*q.v.*), Nathaniel Coffin, junior, William Coffin, junior, Benjamin Davis, James Forrest (*q.v.*), and George Brinley, deputy commissary. (*Ib.*)

He signed the address to George III (see Appendix). His estate was forfeited, November 28, 1780 (A.O. 12/82.) Conveyances of property to him and an order for the confiscation of his property are in A.O. 13/49.

Joseph Thompson was born in 1734 and married Rebecca Gallup, a kinswoman of the wife of Isaac Royall (*q.v.*). (Stark, *op. cit.*, pp. 297-8.)

JOHN THOMSON, OR THOMPSON

was a trader and tin-plate worker in Boston. According to the petition of his widow, Mary, dated August 3, 1777, he had suffered much persecution, guards having been placed at his door to prevent persons from purchasing goods from him or to employ him in his business, or to bring any supplies for his wife and six children. In fear of his life, and anxiety for his family, he languished for many months and at length died. Not content with this barbarity, his forlorn widow was plundered of all her possessions and was threatened with death if she did not quit Massachusetts. By the compassion of General Gage she and her family sailed for England. (A.O. 13/74; A.O. 12/105, f. 109.) An original certificate of Governor Hutchinson, dated August 6, 1777, testifies to the loyalty of John Thomson. (A.O. 13/74.)

SAMUEL THOMSON

In his claim, dated April 28, 1786, for his confiscated property at Boston, he gives his history from 1743, when he served in the Royal Navy in H.M.S. *Winchester*, and from 1744 to 1749 in H.M.S. *Edinburgh*. He was at the taking of the French fleet in 1748. From 1751 to 1752 he commanded a ship in the tobacco trade. In 1754 he served as a volunteer in the 48th Regiment in America, and was wounded in the defeat of Braddock, and with this regiment was at the taking of Louisburg, Quebec and Montreal, and in the reduction of Canada. In 1762 he was present at the taking of Havana, in the 95th Regiment, and accompanied this regiment to England. Once again he joined the Royal Navy, and served in the cutter *Anson* for five years. In 1769 he went to Boston as master of H.M. schooner *Halifax*, and served in other ships.

Shortly afterwards he settled in Boston, where, during the destruction of the tea, he was accused of being an enemy of America and was threatened with tar and feathers. He was obliged to quit and go to England. In 1774 he went over to Boston in H.M.S. *Scarborough*, and served in the Engineers at the destruction of Charlestown. He rejoined the *Scarborough* as pilot for the voyage to Georgia, where he was serving in 1776. From Georgia he went to New York to superintend the forage vessels in the Commissary General's Department. In 1778 he commanded the *Spitfire*, an armed galley, which was burnt at the taking of Rhode Island. He was taken prisoner five times since the evacuation of Rhode Island in October, 1779. After the war Samuel Thomson settled at Digby, Nova Scotia. (A.O. 13/24.)

HENRY TISDALE

blacksmith, of Freetown, Bristol County, was at Newport, Rhode Island, in 1786. (A.O. 13/24.)

ROBERT TRAILL (Plate I.)

was Comptroller of the Customs at the Port of Piscataqua [Portsmouth, New Hampshire]. For his loss of one moiety of the Island of Miquelon, off Newfoundland, which was ceded to France, he was refused pecuniary compensation, but was offered a place under Government in America equal to £550 or £600 a year. After waiting for three years and finding that he could not obtain further redress than a grant of one moiety of six square miles of land [in New Hampshire], he accepted in 1765 the above office in the Customs in a province in which he had resided for fifteen years. He was granted a pension of £50 a year in 1777. (A.O. 13/74.)

He was the son of William Traill, of Westness, in the Orkney Islands, and was born in the Isle of Rousay. He emigrated to America, and was a merchant at Boston and Portsmouth, New Hampshire. In 1748 he married Mary, daughter of William and Mary (Cutts) Whipple, a sister of General W. Whipple, a signatory to the Declaration of Independence. He died in London, February 22, 1785, and his widow died at Portsmouth, New Hampshire, October 3, 1791. His pastel portrait, attributed to Copley, is in the possession of a descendant, Mrs. Heffenger, of Portsmouth, New Hampshire, while the original grant of the above land is the property of another descendant, Mrs. Washburn, of Baltimore. James Russell Lowell was a great-grandson of Robert Traill.

Ex inform. Mrs. Heffenger ; Sabine, *op. cit.*

REV. JOHN TROUTBECK

From several petitions and memorials of his widow, Sarah, the career of this English clergyman at Boston may be traced. He was assistant chaplain, with the Rev. Henry Caner (*q.v.*), of King's Chapel, and married Sarah, daughter of John Gould, distiller, of Boston, who died in 1772. After suffering various insults and persecutions for his steadfast attachment to the English constitution, he was at last under the necessity of leaving Boston, where, as the King's chaplain, he had lived in the greatest friendship with the inhabitants and by preaching and example endeavoured to restore peace and harmony in the revolutionary troubles, which, however, served only to make him obnoxious. The estimate of his estate in 1772 included three dwelling houses in Boston and one in the country, a library worth £266, a chariot costing over £133 in London, two chaises £30 each, and lands in New York, Connecticut, New Hampshire and Massachusetts, as well as debts due to his wife as the sole executrix of her father, £2,000, the whole amounting to £30,293 currency, equal to over £22,719 sterling.

He claimed compensation for property due to four orphans (residing in April, 1777, at Keswick, in Cumberland) as the heirs of William Grave, of Boston.

The Rev. John Troutbeck signed the loyal address to George III (see Appendix). The claims against his estate amounted to £438 12s. 6d.; and the proceeds of the sale to £120. (A.O. 12/81, ff. 131–2.) A copy of the libel against his estate in 1780 is in A.O. 12/82.

He acted as a curate at Cherrington in Warwickshire before his death on August 13, 1779, at Blencowe, his birthplace, in the parish of Dacre, Cumberland. He entered Queen's College, Oxford, in 1737, as the son of George Troutbeck, taking the degree of B.A. in 1741.

In her memorial of May, 1784, Sarah Troutbeck wrote to the Commissioners stating that the whole of her real property in America had been confiscated, but not all sold. She therefore flattered herself that if she were on the spot she would have it in her power to stop further prosecutions against her estate, and begged leave to proceed to America for the term allowed by the Definitive Treaty of Peace, to endeavour to recover all the available part of her property. She wrote from Boston, May 2, 1785, on the difficulties in trying to recover her confiscated estate. She had returned to England before June 5, 1787, the date of her letter stating that her father had left his distilling business in the hands of her husband, the Rev. John Troutbeck, to be carried on for the benefit of his (John Gould's) grandchildren, John and William Gould. (A.O. 13/24; A.O. 13/49; A.O. 13/74; A.O. 13/137; A.O. 12/105, f. 112.)

Sarah Troutbeck claimed £3,043, and was allowed £769. She received a pension of £80 until her death in 1816. (T. 50/11 ; T. 50/23.)

A scurrilous ballad was published in 1774 on this loyalist clergyman's connection with the rum business. (*New Eng. Hist. Gen. & Reg.*, xiii, 132.)

John, Samuel and Elizabeth Gould (*q.v.*) were the nephews and niece of Sarah Troutbeck.

Reference : *Annals of King's Chapel, op. cit.*

REUBEN TUCKER

of Townsend, innkeeper, was a steadfast loyalist who refused to join the American forces, and was imprisoned for fourteen months in Concord gaol from June, 1777. After settling at Shelburne, Nova Scotia, he returned to Massachusetts to endeavour to obtain possession of his property, but was imprisoned. With his memorial is a certificate to his loyalty from Joshua Smith, a loyalist, late of Townsend, dated Digby, Nova Scotia, October 25, 1786. (A.O. 13/51.) Other details are in A.O. 12/10, ff. 383-7.

ROBERT TWYCROSS

Before emigrating to Boston about 1764 he had served over six years in the Royal Navy. He was a trader and planter and for his loyalty he was cruelly persecuted, particularly upon his refusal (after many solicitations) to enter the American Navy as a commander. He made a sacrifice of all he possessed in the world to preserve inviolate his fidelity and attachment to his King and country, and was now (in 1778) reduced to the direst poverty. (A.O. 13/74.)

WILLIAM TYNG

was Sheriff of Cumberland County, and lived at Falmouth (Portland), Maine. According to an affidavit of Dr. Nathaniel Coffin (*q.v.*), Tyng was sheltered in his house from a mob coming into the town from the country to destroy him, and managed to get him safely on board the ship *Canso* in April, 1775. Colonel Samuel Thompson, with a party, plundered Tyng's house of his silver plate and other valuables. With this affidavit is a certificate to the sale of a silver cup, weighing 100 ounces, and a tankard, 37 ounces, to Dr. Joseph Gardner for £46 2s. 3d. ; a certificate of proscription ; and a certificate that James Sutherland, a Scotsman, was overseer of Tyng's business from 1769, and was at Falmouth in 1786. Elizabeth Ross (*q.v.*) was his mother-in-law. (A.O. 13/51.)

He claimed £2,955, and was allowed £569. (A.O. 12/109.) He was a loyalist pensioner for £75 until his death in 1807. (A.O. 459/7; A.O. 462/22; A.O. 12/61, f. 59; *Ontario Archives, op. cit.*, pp. 272–5.)

This loyalist was the son of Commander Edward Tyng, senior commander of the Colonial fleet sent against Louisburg in 1745, and was born in 1737. He represented Falmouth in the General Court in 1772–3. In 1793 he returned from exile and settled at Gorham, Maine, and was buried at St. Paul's Church, Portland, a church erected under his patronage. (Sabine, *op. cit.*; *Proc. of Mass. Hist. Soc.*, 1st Ser., x, 183–6.)

JOSHUA UPHAM.

Joshua Upham was a native of Massachusetts, born in 1741 at Brookfield, the son of Dr. Jabez Upham. After graduating at Harvard College in 1763, in the same class as four other loyalist lawyers, Jonathan Bliss, S. S. Blowers, William Parker and Samuel Porter, he began the study of the law in his native town and practised at the Worcester bar, where as a highly respected and honoured lawyer he enjoyed a considerable practice.

Although a firm and determined loyalist who at the town meeting at Brookfield, the last public meeting attended by him in his native land, spoke strongly against separation from the mother country when independence was contemplated, Joshua Upham had on May 20, 1775, recanted his former Tory views, moderate as they were, and submitted to the resolution of the majority of his neighbours and "to bear an equal share and proportion of such public charge and expense as shall be deemed by such magistracy to be necessary to extricate the country out of its present alarming and critical situation." In this same letter to the Brookfield Committee of Correspondence the Tory lawyer declares his abhorrence of the charge of being an enemy to his country, though not approving of the measures pursued by the colonies to obtain redress of their grievances. (Force, *American Archives*, Ser. IV, vol. ii, pp. 852–3.)

Upham states that by an act of the House of Assembly in 1777 no lawyer was allowed to practise in the law courts of Massachusetts unless he had taken an oath of allegiance to the Americans. By suggesting to Edward Winslow, in 1780, the raising of a Massachusetts brigade of loyalists he incurred the displeasure of the Whigs.

The military services of Upham on the side of Great Britain from 1778 were not insignificant. After serving for some time in command of the Associated Loyalists at Lloyd's Neck, he was appointed by his friend, Lieutenant-Colonel Benjamin Thompson (*q.v.*), Major in his regiment, the King's American Dragoons, in August, 1782, and in the following month aide-de-camp to Sir Guy Carleton, commander-in-chief of the British Army in America. Thompson had a warm regard for Upham, describing him as one of the finest fellows he had ever known.

His original memorial (in F.O. 4/1) to Lord Sydney, dated from London, April 15, 1784, is as follows :—

"Taking it for granted that in the present state of the King's

American Provinces, a Division of one and certain changes & alterations in the government of all, will be found both expedient & necessary, and thinking it highly reasonable and probable that many American Loyalists of fair Pretensions & who have suffered in the late unhappy Contest & particulary such as have nothing to hope from the Treaty, having borne Arms, will find both Employment & Provision in the Regulations & Establishments to be made in that Country, and being myself one of this description of unfortunate Subjects, I take the Liberty to solicit an appointment to the office of a *Puisne Judge* of the Supreme Court in the Province to be erected on the Western Side of the Bay of Fundy. in this application to your Lordship I have Sir Guy Carleton's Permission to make use of his Name.

"In this Situation it becomes necessary and will therefore need little apology, that I state to your Lordship my former Profession & the Offices I held before & during the War.

"I was regularly bred to the *Law* in his Majesty's Province of Massachusetts Bay, was appointed and duly commissioned by the Governor of that Province a *Majestrate* & a *Major* in the Militia.

"Was appointed by Sir Henry Clinton to inspect the Claims of the Loyalists at the Garrison of Rhode Island.

"On the 29th of April, 1779, was appointed by Commission from the King *Advocate* for a Court of Vice Admiralty established at Rhode Island—this appointment was rendered fruitless by the Evacuation of that Place at the very time when I recd. my Commission.

"On the 21st of February, 1781, I recd. a *Warrant* from Sir Henry Clinton *to raise a Regiment.*

"On the 20th of June following Sir Henry Clinton appointed me *Lt. Colonel of Associated Loyalists* & gave me the Command of the *Fort & Post* of *Lloyd's Neck*, being an out post of the Army, for which Service I received no pay, nor was I even allowed the *provincial Rank*, tho honored with Commission of Lt Colonel.

"On the 7th of May 1782, Sir Guy Carleton was pleased to incorporate the Soldiers I had recruited under the Warrant from Sir Henry Clinton into the Corps of Kings American Dragoons and to honor me with a *Majority* in that Corps—the General was also pleased to appoint me one of his *Aide-de-Camp* in which employment I continued until the Evacuation of New York.

"I have uniformly & I hope fairly, tho spiritedly opposed all occasions the Independenc of America & the Severance of the Empire.

"In the fatal struggle I have seen a complete Sacrifice of my little Property and of my Hopes in that Country & have five unfortunate Children from fourteen to seven years of age to partake & of course to encrease my Sufferings.

"For my Character &c prior to the Commencement of Hostilities I venture to refer your Lordship to my Friend Sir William Pepperell with whom I have been long & intimately acquainted. For my Services & consequent Pretensions during the War it is with Confidence & I confess with Pride that I appeal to my worthy Friend Sir Guy Carleton. I therefore entreat your Lordships Patronage & kind Interposition & humbly hope to be appointed to the Office I have ventured to name."

The prayer of Joshua Upham was granted and in due time he was appointed one of the first puisne Judges of the Supreme Court of New Brunswick as well as a member of the Executive and Legislative Council. In 1807 he sailed for England to petition for an increase of salary for the Judges. His mission was successful but he did not live to see the fruits of his labours, having died in London, November 1, 1808, and was buried in Marylebone churchyard.

His claim of £6,221 for the loss of his property was disallowed. He was compensated at the rate of £400 a year for the loss of his professional income during the war and was granted a loyalist pension until his death. (A.O. 12/109.)

The first wife of Joshua Upham was a daughter of Colonel John Murray (*q.v.*) and died in New York in 1782. His second wife was Mary, daughter of the eminent Connecticut lawyer and loyalist, Joshua Chandler. She was granted a loyalist pension after his death, until 1826, the date of her death. (T. 50/28.) His son, the Rev. Charles Wentworth Upham, became President of the Senate of Massachusetts and representative in Congress. Another son, John Murray Upham, of the Volunteers of New England in the Revolution, was appointed Ensign in the King's New Brunswick Regiment in 1793 and on his retirement in 1796 removed to Upper Canada, where he served in the army of defence, 1812–14, and died there. (Howe, *Colls. of New Brunswick, Hist. Soc.*, i, 13–15.)

Some of his letters are published in the *Winslow Papers* (ed. by W. O. Raymond, 1901).

His daughter, Elizabeth (born in 1791), by his first marriage was granted £10 from the Compassionate Fund from 1821. (W.O. 25/3089.) Three daughters by his second marriage, Martha Sophia (born in 1796); Kathron Eliza Putnam (born in 1798); and Frances Chandler (born in 1806), were put on the same Fund in 1822 (W.O. 25/3088.)

Ind.: 5605–6; A.O. 12/100, f. 225; A.O. 13/75; A.O. 13/83; A.O. 13/84; A.O. 13/137.

Judges of New Brunswick and their Times, op. cit., pp. 81–96; *American Loyalists' Claims, op. cit.*, pp. 177–8; *New England Hist.—Gen. Reg.*, X, 127–8; *Journal of Samuel Curwen, op. cit.*, pp. 664–8.

JOHN VASSALL

Upon the refusal of several men to accept the appointment by mandamus to a seat in the Council of Massachusetts, on account of the odium and danger, he accepted it. An accident prevented him from active military service and consequently he removed with his family to Halifax, Nova Scotia, where he chartered at his own risk and expense a vessel to convey provisions and intelligence to Boston. He subsequently removed to England, where his expenses were rendered heavier by his purchase of commissions in the British army for his two sons and providing for another son, a midshipman in the Royal Navy. (A.O. 13/75.)

With his memorial are many copies of deeds of his property. His elegant house at Cambridge * was bought by Nathaniel Tray for £3,600, lawful money. There are also two letters to him from Thomas Russell, of Boston (brother-in-law of John Lowell, the lawyer). One dated August 16, 1783, states that John Vassall had stood well in the estimation of his countrymen as any absentee, until his name appeared in the public prints as a lender of money to the British Government to carry on the war, which hastened the confiscation of his property. This letter was conveyed to England by Nathaniel Gorham, a member of Congress, who had undertaken the voyage by the desire of the distressed inhabitants of Charlestown, Massachusetts, to procure some benefaction for their relief, and Thomas Russell begs Vassall to facilitate Gorham's errand. The second letter, dated April 14, 1784, states that Vassall's affairs were in the hands of Mr. Amory,† "an ingenious young gentleman" connected in business with John Lowell. (A.O. 13/90.)

A letter from Edward Davis, dated Boston, December 31, 1783, states that the house of John Vassall in Boston had been sold to one Doan‡ for £2,400, lawful money. (A.O. 13/90.)

The Commissioners reported that Vassall had a very good house in Boston which cost him £2,000 and other property at Cambridge and elsewhere, worth between £7,000 and £8,000. His valuable property in the Island of Jamaica had produced him £3,000 a year before the partial destruction of it by hurricane. (A.O. 12/99, f. 181.) On the strength of a communication by Lieutenant-Governor Thomas Oliver§ that Vassall's property in Jamaica now (1784) produced £1,000 a year, they refused to grant him the allowance asked for, adding that he ought to be ashamed of himself for making the application. (A.O. 12/101, f. 128.)

The compensation granted to him was £4,571 from his claim of £11,895. (A.O. 12/109.) A copy of the libel against his estate in 1780 is in A.O. 12/82.

John Vassall died at Clifton, Bristol, September 24, 1797. (*Gent. Mag.*, vol. 67, p. 898.) By his will (Walpole, 67) he left much furniture, plate, pictures, etc., at his house in the Royal Crescent, Bath, whither he had removed from Brunswick Place, Bath. He carried his loyalty so far as not to use the family motto, *Saepe pro rege, semper pro republica*.

This loyalist was born in 1738 and graduated at Harvard College in 1757. His son, Spencer Thomas Vassall, was commissioned Ensign

* The headquarters of Washington during the siege of Boston, and later the residence of the poet Longfellow. (*Proc. of the Amer. Antiquarian Soc.*, New Ser. XIII.)

† Rufus Greene Amory, who studied law with John Lowell, and was admitted to the Bar of Massachusetts in 1781.

‡ Isaiah Doane.

§ Oliver's sister, Elizabeth, was the wife of John Vassall.

in the 59th Foot in 1778 and served for 28 years in the army, at Gibraltar, in Flanders, and the Cape of Good Hope, of which he became Governor.

As Lieutenant-Colonel of the 38th Foot, Spencer Thomas Vassall was mortally wounded at the storming of Monte Video in 1807 at the moment of conducting his troops within the walls of the fortress. John Vassall's eldest son, John, rose to the rank of Lieutenant in the 65th Foot. The third son mentioned by John Vassall was probably Thomas Oliver, who died in England in 1807.

WILLIAM VASSALL

The only reference to him is in A.O. 12/81, ff. 136-7, in the list of absentee loyalists, with the amounts of the claims against their estates.

This representative of a conspicuous family in Massachusetts and in Jamaica was born in this West India Island in 1715 and graduated at Harvard College in 1733. He fled to England at the Revolution and died at Battersea in 1800. His will discloses the fact that he bequeathed portraits of himself and his first wife, Ann Davis, of his daughter, Sarah, of his deceased son, William, and of his eldest surviving son, William, all drawn by Smibert, to the latter son, William. All these portraits, with one of himself and his son, Leonard (by his second marriage to Margaret Hubbard), painted in one picture by Copley, had been left behind at Boston on his flight in 1776 in charge of Dr. James Lloyd (q.v.). None of them can now be traced.

William Vassall, the younger, was born in Boston in 1753 and graduated at Harvard in 1771. He was admitted to Lincoln's Inn, November 4, 1773, and matriculated at Magdalen College, Oxford, December 4, 1773. His half-brother, Leonard Vassall, matriculated at Oriel College, Oxford, in 1782, and joined Lincoln's Inn in 1783 and was called to the English bar in 1793. His brother, Nathaniel, was a Captain in the Royal Navy (Stark, op. cit., p. 288; E. Alfred Jones, American Members of the Inns of Court, 1924, pp. 211–12.)

AMBROSE VINCENT

was born in 1715 in England and was land waiter and gauger in the Customs at Boston. His age and infirmities alone prevented him from leaving Boston. He has since got his bread by hiring out horses. This loyalist of irreproachable character was granted a loyalist pension of £30 from 1785. (A.O. 12/101, f. 233.) He was a member of King's Chapel, Boston, and had pew No. 50; he died in 1800. (Annals of King's Chapel, op. cit., ii, 119, 313.)

FRANCIS WALDO

was a man of property and from 1757 Collector of the Customs at Falmouth (Portland), Maine. A statement of his claim to the province of Nova Scotia, in virtue of the purchase thereof by Samuel Waldo for £1,000 in

1730 from John Nelson, nephew and heir of Sir Thomas Temple, who bequeathed his right therein in 1674, is in A.O. 13/53, together with particulars of the Muscongus Patent,* of which Francis Waldo and his brother-in-law, Thomas Flucker (q.v.), were part proprietors.

He served 25 years in his Majesty's service. In 1771 he received £1,300 from Mr. Skynner† (afterwards Lord Chief Baron), Mr. Wedderburn‡ (afterwards Lord Loughborough, Lord Chancellor of England), and one Jackson, for 6,000 acres of land in Lincoln County, Massachusetts. His total losses were £15,000 to £20,000, though part only of his great property was confiscated. He made a claim to the " whole province of Nova Scotia or to the consideration given for it by his ancestor & what it was valued at." (A.O. 12/104, f. 69.)

Waldo craved for an allowance for a lad named William Pitman, a native of Falmouth, born in 1762, whose father's house was burnt in the destruction of that town by Captain Mowat (q.v.) in 1775. This boy was put by Waldo at Mr. Mayhew's boarding school in Kensington at a cost of £25 a year. (A.O. 13/75 ; A.O. 13/87.)

This loyalist was the son of Samuel Waldo, a Brigadier-General at the capture of Louisburg, and graduated at Harvard College in 1747. He was a representative to the General Court from Falmouth in 1762–3. He died in London in 1784, unmarried. (Sabine, op. cit.).

ADAM WALKER

was born at Worcester and was a blacksmith there, having previously served in his Majesty's service. He signed the Worcester Protest (see Appendix) and was imprisoned for his loyalty at Worcester and Boston, at which latter place he served with the Associated Loyalists. With his memorial are papers concerning his confiscated property ; a certificate to his merits from Timothy Ruggles (q.v.) ; and a claim for £17 paid by him to redeem his apprentice, Redura, from Worcester gaol, where he was confined for refusing to serve in the American army. His wife, Marcey, or Nancey, inherited property from her mother at Newport, Rhode Island. (A.O. 13/51 ; A.O. 12/10, ff. 114–123 ; Ontario Archives, op. cit., pp. 586–8.) He claimed £1,003 12s. and was allowed £270. (A.O. 12/109.) Adam Walker was perhaps the private of this name in Captain William Clark's company of New England Loyalists, discharged December 27, 1779 (Muster Roll).

His estate is on the records of Worcester County, Case No. 61202 A.

* See page 60.
† Sir John Skynner, Lord Chief Baron of the Exchequer from 1777.
‡ Alexander Wedderburn, Solicitor-General in 1771, and afterwards Lord Loughborough, Lord Chancellor of England, created Earl of Rosslyn in 1801.

JOHN WALKER

had served in the army since 1744 in all the most material operations in America, more particularly at the sieges of Louisburg, Quebec and Havana, and was a commissioned officer from 1755. In 1763 he was put on half-pay as Captain-Lieutenant and received a grant of 3,000 acres for his services in the war and settled in Worcester, where he had property worth £3,000, and was the owner of property in New York and Maine worth £2,000. At the outbreak of the Revolutionary war he refused a commission of considerable rank in the American army, and consequently was ordered to be confined to the bounds of his farm at Worcester, where his house was afterwards plundered by the mob and burnt. He was wounded twelve times in both wars. He went to England in 1781. (A.O. 13/49; A.O. 12/99, f. 91.)

Colonel Joseph Goreham (*q.v.*), in his certificate, states that this loyalist had served under his command in the French war and was appointed an officer in his regiment (the Royal Fencible American Regiment) in 1775. (A.O. 13/49.) The date of his commission as Lieutenant is November 12, 1775. He resigned his commission, April 28, 1781, on account of ill-health. (*Am. MSS. in the Roy. Inst., op. cit.*, pp. 272, 273, 274.) In A.O. 13/49 is an affidavit of his former neighbour, James Putnam (*q.v.*), to his bravery as an officer and to his loyalty; and a copy of the will* of his father, William Walker, husbandman, Worcester, dated May 26, 1760, bequeathing property to his wife, Mary, to his four sons, Adam, Robert (in the army), John and Joseph, and to his three daughters, Isabella, Mary and Nancy.

There is a copy of a deed for the purchase of property in A.O. 12/83. He claimed £2,230 and was allowed £250. (A.O. 12/109.)

He was probably the John Walker, gentleman, of Shrewsbury, Worcester County, named in the Banishment Act. According to the records of the Probate Court of that county he is described as a British officer and gentleman. The court ordered an inventory to be taken of his property, which amounted to £3,336 18s., and included a farm in Worcester and property on the Great Road to Worcester. His wife, Christian, was allowed a third part of the estate to live on after his flight and a pew in the Meeting House. (Ex inform. Mr. H. H. Atwood, Register.)

PATRICK WALL

was an Irishman who emigrated in 1766 and settled as a merchant tailor in Boston. His estimate of the losses and damages sustained by him in consequence of his imprisonment in Boston gaol for six months and in his own house for twelve months at the commencement of the Revolution was £400. He was permitted in December, 1777, to sail for New York, where he remained until the evacuation by the British, when he went to Shel-

* Confirmed by Mr. L. E. Felton, Probate Court, Worcester.

burne, Nova Scotia. There is a certificate to his loyalty from the Rev. William Walter. (A.O. 13/51.) He claimed £600 and was allowed £562. (A.O. 12/109.)

His wife, Margaret, in her memorial of January 31, 1786, states that previous to her marriage to Patrick Wall she was the widow of Crean Brush,* a loyalist member of the Assembly of New York, who had sought shelter in Boston in 1775 and who left there with the British troops in 1776. On the passage he was taken prisoner and carried back to Boston and confined in gaol for a long period. He died in New York in 1778. Brush's property in the provinces of New Hampshire and New York, value at £6,287, was confiscated. (A.O. 13/51 ; A.O. 12/10, ff. 183–7.)

Reference : *Ontario Archives, op. cit.*, pp. 610–1, 724–5.

REV. WILLIAM WALTER (Plate LIII)

According to his memorial he was the only clergyman in Boston who ventured to condemn in public the un-Christian acts of violence by the mob against Andrew Oliver, Distributor of Stamps, in 1767. As the troubles became more general and more serious, he uniformly declared his sentiments against them, and rather than, by his example in remaining in Boston, give any encouragement to the revolters, he left the town with the British troops in March, 1776. By his marriage in 1767 to [Lydia], daughter of Benjamin Lynde, late Chief Justice of Massachusetts, he became possessed of a farm of 130 acres on Thompson's Island† in Boston

---

* Crean Brush was born in Dublin, Ireland, about 1725, and in 1762 emigrated to America, settling as a lawyer at Westminster, Cumberland County, New York, where he held the offices of Clerk of the Peace and Clerk of the General Sessions of the Peace, and which county he represented in the General Assembly. Here he married the above Margaret, then the widow of Colonel Monte Montesque, and daughter of James Calcraft (or Schoolcraft), soldier and schoolmaster. By this marriage he had a daughter, Frances, who married Captain Buchanan, of the Queen's Rangers, a well-known loyalist regiment, and who is described by Sabine as a dashing, fascinating, accomplished and imperious widow at the time of her second marriage to the celebrated free lance and soldier of fortune, Ethan Allen. She married as her third husband Dr. Penniman, of Colchester. Crean Brush was appointed by the British to superintend the removal of all property and stores at the evacuation of Boston. On the passage to Nova Scotia he was captured by the Americans and taken back to Boston. On November 5, 1777, he escaped from prison, disguised in his wife's clothes, and fled to New York, where he died as stated above. A copy of his will, dated October 18, 1777, made in prison in Boston, is preserved, together with an interesting little map of New Brook, in Gloucester County, New York, done by one Benjamin Smith in 1771 (A.O. 13/116). This loyalist was satirised in Trumbull's *McFingal*. Margaret Brush was still a widow in April, 1780, in New York, when she petitioned for an allowance as a loyalist, her estate being in the hands of the rebels (Force, *American Archives*, Ser. IV, Vol. I, p. 1290 ; Sabine, *op. cit. ; Amer. MSS. in the Roy. Inst., op. cit.*, i, 373 ; ii, 116 ; iii, 210). Her portrait was painted by Copley (Bayley's *Copley*).

† For Thompson's Island see Shurtleff's *Topog. Hist. of Boston.*

harbour. With this memorial are papers relating to his property, some or all of which had been sold by the Commonwealth in 1782. There is also a certificate, signed by John Rowe, Daniel Hubbard and Benjamin Greene, dated November 14, 1783, stating that this clergyman was appointed Rector of Trinity Church, Boston, in 1768. (A.O. 13/49; A.O. 13/75; A.O. 12/100, f. 297.)

Peter Frye (*q.v.*) in evidence referred to a letter written by the Rev. William Walter to Sir William Pepperell, disapproving of the measures of Great Britain in the colonies, which was regarded as "an odd letter to be written by a clergyman of his persuasion." Pepperell, however, did not mention it in his evidence. Samuel Hale stated that doubts as to his loyalty were fabricated by Presbyterian ministers. (*Loyalists' Claims, op. cit.*, pp. 154-5.)

He was appointed Chaplain to the 2nd battalion of De Lancey's Brigade, the well-known loyalist regiment, during the war and at the peace received half-pay as such. He was compensated £293 from his claim of £930 and was allowed at the rate of £180 a year for the loss of his income as Rector. He also received a pension until his death in 1800. (A.O. 12/109.) A list of claims against his estate is in A.O. 12/81, f. 133.

In 1767 he joined the clergy of Massachusetts and Rhode Island in petitioning for the appointment of a Bishop in America. (A. L. Cross, *The Anglican Episcopate and the American Colonies*, No. X, 1902.)

This loyalist was born in 1739 and graduated at Harvard College in 1756. He had been master of the Grammar School at Salem and deputy collector at the Port of Salem before his ordination in 1764. In 1791 he left Shelburne, Nova Scotia (where he had settled at the close of hostilities) for Boston and was appointed Rector of Christ Church in 1792. (Stark, *op. cit.*, pp. 338–42.) In 1784 the degree of D.D. was conferred upon him by the University of Aberdeen on the recommendation of Sir William Pepperell, the Rev. Mather Byles, D.D. (*q.v.*) and Robert Auchmuty (*q.v.*).

At Shelburne he was the counsellor and friend of the distressed loyalist refugees, not only from Massachusetts but also from other colonies, and his name as such appears frequently in the documents. During his exile there, his son, Lynde, married Maria, daughter of Colonel Abraham Van Buskirk,* a loyalist refugee from New Jersey; Lynde married (ii) Anne Minshull, and by this marriage had a son, Lynde Minshull Walter, who was the founder and first editor of the *Boston Evening Transcript*, of which his sister, Cornelia, became second editor.

His portrait by Copley is in the possession of Robert Walcott, Esq., of Boston.

Reference : *Amer. MSS. in Roy. Inst., op. cit.*, iv, 245, 480 ; Ex inform., Miss Helen C. McCleary, a descendant.

---

* E. Alfred Jones, *The Loyalists of New Jersey*, 1927, pp. 225-6.

T

GEORGE WARDEN

was a Scotsman who had served his time as a mason in Edinburgh before emigrating to Boston at the age of 15 in 1774. In 1775 he volunteered to serve as master mason in the Engineer Department of the British army, at a moment when no American would assist in face of the violent threats of committees and " unlawful associations." He served in the battle of Bunker Hill and other engagements, at frequent risk to his life, and continued in military service until October 1782, when he obtained leave on account of ill-health to embark for England.

Having lost no property by the war, the Commissioners reported that he had not the smallest pretence to expect anything from Government. (A.O. 13/75 ; A.O. 12/100, f. 85.)

WILLIAM WARDEN

was born in Boston and was a shopkeeper, grocer and hairdresser. He was a loyalist since the time of the Stamp Act and was one of the Associated Loyalists of Boston in 1775. In this year he was sent by General Gage to Salem and Marblehead to receive intelligence from Dr. Benjamin Church,* but failed to execute his business. He carried despatches for the British army, sometimes in open boats, at great risk. His wife, Sarah Cockburn, or Coburn, was grand-daughter of Samuel Hill. There is an affidavit of Abraham Ellison and Peter Lynch, formerly residents of Boston in 1776, dated Shelburne, Nova Scotia, November 29, 1783, testifying to their knowledge of some of his property (A.O. 13/51 ; A.O. 13/75 ; A.O. 12/10 ; ff. 94–102 ; A.O. 12/102, f. 209). He was allowed compensation, £150, from his claim of £448 10s. (A.O. 12/109). In his petition of March 5, 1790, for further compensation, he states that his family were at Shelburne, Nova Scotia, and that he was about to rejoin them. (A.O. 13/137.)

SAMUEL WATERHOUSE

was an officer in the Custom House at Boston from 1772, and in 1774 was promoted Inspector General Extraordinary of Customs there, as well as acting as Secretary in the absence of Richard Reeve. He acquired a considerable amount of land in Massachusetts. (A.O. 13/75 ; A.O. 12/105, f. 47.) He claimed £5,220 and was allowed £150. (A.O. 12/109.) He was granted a pension from 1782 to 1799. (A.O. 461/16 ; T. 50/6.)

In the inventory of his property left behind at Boston, besides handsome furniture, are two half-length portraits of the father and mother of Mrs. Waterhouse ; three portraits, quarter size, of Archdale Palmer, Henry Palmer and Mrs. Bourn, relatives of Mrs. Waterhouse; and portraits of Mr. and Mrs. Waterhouse themselves. In the schedule of his estate is included his house in Boston, inherited from Eliakim Palmer, of London ;

* See page 86.

and land at Saco [Maine] and elsewhere, inherited by Mrs. Waterhouse from her father, Job Lewis, Esq. For letting a house in Boston for the use of the British troops he was stigmatized at a town meeting in 1770 as an enemy to America. (A.O. 13/49.)

Sabine (*op. cit.*) quotes from an unrecorded source that this loyalist was "the most notorious scribbler, satirist, and libeller in the service of the conspirators against the liberties of America," probably in consequence of two pamphlets, printed in 1760 and 1766 and attributed to Waterhouse, namely: *Proposals for printing . . . the history of . . . Vice-Admiral Sir Thomas Brazen . . . by Thomas Thumb, Esq., Surveyor of the Customs,* a satire apparently on Governor Pownall; and *Proposals for printing . . . the history of Adjutant T. Trowel and J. Bluster,* said to be a lampoon of Thomas Dawes and James Otis, respectively. (See Evans, *Amer. Bibliography,* Nos. 8763, 12519.) (Ex inform. Mr. Lawrence C. Wroth, John Carter Brown Library.)

Mrs. Hannah Waterhouse was the only surviving child of Job Lewis (*Colls. of New York Hist. Soc.,* 1900, printed 1911, p. 4).

REV. JOSHUA WINGATE WEEKS

was missionary of the Society for the Propagation of the Gospel, at St. Michael's, Marblehead, where he had a large congregation, whom he had ever endeavoured to keep on the path of steady loyalty, though most of the members were firmly attached to the British Constitution and many had been arrested for not taking the oath of allegiance to the Congress. He himself was imprisoned three times and brought before a special court. The General Assembly refused him permission to leave the country and he was summoned, with thirty other principal persons of Marblehead, to abjure his Sovereign and swear allegiance to the United States, on pain of being imprisoned. Rather than submit to these humiliating conditions, he escaped with difficulty in July, 1778, by water to Newport, Rhode Island, where he made known his distress to the above Society. In all he suffered persecution for nearly four years. (A.O. 13/49; A.O. 13/75.)

In A.O. 13/49 is a copy of the order to appear at Salem to take the above oath of allegiance to the United States, February 26, 1778; and a copy of the order for his arrest and for the arrest of the following loyalists of Marblehead: Robert Hooper; Woodward Abraham, shopkeeper; John Wormstead; Michael Coombes, a warden of St. Michael's (*q.v.*); Edward Bowen, mariner; and Richard Coombes, shoreman.

He claimed £150 and was allowed £50. He likewise claimed at the rate of £165 a year for the loss of his income during the war and was awarded £160. His half-pay as Chaplain to the King's Orange Rangers, in which he served from 1781, was £59 5s. 7d. and his pension, £21. (A.O. 12/109.) His pension was continued until 1804. (A.O. 459/7–462/20.)

After the war this clergyman became deputy chaplain at Annapolis Royal, Nova Scotia, and curate at St. Paul's Church, Halifax, where in 1788 Bishop Inglis described the Church as in an embarrassed condition because of the personal enmity existing between the Rev. Mather Byles, (*q.v.*) then chaplain to the garrison at Halifax, and the Rev. Joshua Wingate Weeks. (A.O. 13/83 and Bishop Inglis's Journal.)

Two letters in A.O. 13/85 are of no interest.

In W.O. 42/W6 is a certificate of the marriage of his son, Captain Joshua Wingate Weeks, of the Nova Scotia Fencible Infantry, to Mary Ann Schwartz, October 4, 1800, and of the death of this son, June 23, 1824, at Sydney, Cape Breton, aged 53.

According to Governor Hutchinson, he was one of the originators of the " preposterous " scheme in 1778 to establish Penobscot into a separate province as an asylum for the persecuted loyalists. (Hutchinson *Diary*, ii, 290–1.)

This clergyman was born at Hampton, New Hampshire, and graduated at Harvard College in 1758. Before taking Holy Orders he was a Congregationalist minister. In 1793–5 he was a missionary at Preston and from 1795 at Guysborough, Nova Scotia, the place of his death. (Sabine, *op. cit.*)

The first instalment of his Journal appeared in the *Hist. Colls. of Essex Inst.*, Mass., in January, 1916. His name is frequently mentioned in the *Frontier Missionary, op. cit.* ; and will be found in *Loyalists' Claims, op. cit.*, p. 328.

JOSEPH WELSH

of Cambridge, painter and glazier, went to Shelburne, Nova Scotia, in 1783 (A.O. 13/51 ; A.O. 13/97 ; *Ontario Archives, op. cit.*, pp. 658–9.)

One Joseph Welch was clerk and sexton of Christ Church, Cambridge, in 1774.

ELIZABETH WENTWORTH

This lady was the widow of Samuel Wentworth, merchant in Boston, and there supported herself " genteely." She was granted a pension of £100. All her children were loyalists and were forced from her by the events of the war. (A.O. 12/104, f. 83 ; A.O. 13/82.)

She was the daughter of Henry and Elizabeth Deering and was born in 1715. She married in 1732 Samuel Wentworth (Harvard College, 1728), son of Lieutenant Governor John Wentworth. He died in 1766, aged 58, and was buried at King's Chapel, Boston. She died in London, at the house of her son, Benning Wentworth, April 6, 1785, and was buried at St. James's Church, Piccadilly. Her daughter, Frances, a lady of great beauty and accomplishments, married as her second husband, John Wentworth, Governor successively of New Hampshire, and Nova Scotia, first baronet (Plate LI). Her son, Samuel, who matriculated at Worcester College, Oxford, in 1768, fell in love with Miss Lane, and having

Governor John Wentworth   PLATE LI

Lady (Frances) Wentworth

been denied intercourse with her, both committed suicide in 1769. (*Wentworth Genealogy*, I, 316, 318; *Annals of King's Chapel, op. cit.*, ii, 159.)

Portraits of Governor Sir John and Lady Wentworth, by Copley, are in the Public Library, New York (Plates LI and LII).

CALEB WHEATON

was an American by birth, born about 1716, and preventive officer of the Customs and trader at Machias, Maine. He had served in all the wars in America from 1744, when he was Lieutenant and Quartermaster in a corps raised by Governor Shirley for the defence of the garrison at Annapolis Royal, which was besieged by the French and Indians. He was afterwards commander of Fort St. George in Eastern Massachusetts. As a loyalist he was the victim of the vengeance of the leaders of the rebellion and was hunted from place to place. By orders of General Sir William Howe he pulled down the Old North Meeting House at Boston. On the voyage to Halifax with the British troops from Boston in March, 1776, he was taken prisoner in the brig *Elizabeth* with his family, and was detained in prison for three months. From 1777 he was a Lieutenant in the Guides and Pioneers.

Caleb Wheaton had sixteen children. Five sons served in the King's service in the Revolution, one of whom was killed in battle. Two were granted half-pay of Lieutenants, John and Caleb (*q.v.*) at the end of the war. One was a pilot in the Royal Navy in Nova Scotia; and the fifth, Joseph, also a loyalist, was taken prisoner and confined in Concord gaol, where he was successfully induced to join the Americans and was given a commission as ensign.

Colonel Joseph Goreham (*q.v.*), in his certificate, March 10, 1784, states that he was present in the defence of Annapolis Royal in 1744 and confirms Caleb Wheaton's statement above.

The death of this loyalist is announced in a letter from one W. Collins, dated March 26, 1788, who adds that he has two wives living, one at Halifax, Nova Scotia, who had shared all his sufferings and hardships as a loyalist, and the other near Rochester in Kent. Mary Wheaton, his widow, at Halifax, writes a letter, November 11, 1788, regarding the estate of her son-in-law, Captain Thomas Cribbin, presumably a loyalist, husband of her daughter, Lucinda. (A.O. 13/49; A.O. 13/75; A.O. 12/102, f. 67.)

Compensation, £350, was granted for the loss of his property and £50 for the loss of his income as a customs officer during the war. He also received half-pay. (A.O. 12/109.) A schedule of his property is in A.O. 13/49.

The only reference to an officer of this name in the Muster Rolls Series, 1710–1774, of Massachusetts, is as Lieutenant in command of a detachment which served from October 15, 1748, to January 29, 1749.

Reference: *Amer. MSS. in the Royal Inst., op. cit.*, iii, 342.

CALEB WHEATON

son of Caleb Wheaton (*q.v.*) was born about 1757 and was a brother (possibly a twin) of John Wheaton (*q.v.*). He was a Lieutenant in Lieutenant-Colonel Timothy Hierlihy's loyalist regiment, formed in March 1777, having previously been a prisoner for 19 months, and in the Nova Scotia Volunteers from December 25, 1780. He was married to Sally Bryant at Trinity Church, Boston, Massachusetts, November 6, 1792, and died at Gut of Canso, Nova Scotia, July 26, 1825. His widow died at Guysborough, Nova Scotia, June 21, 1837. A son, Edward Cornwallis Wheaton, is mentioned. (W.O. 42/W9; Ind: 5604-5-6; *American MSS. in the Royal Inst., op. cit.*, ii, 192, iii, 337.) One Lieutenant Caleb Wheaton, of the Guides and Pioneers, was put on half-pay in 1792. (W.O. 24/751.)

JOHN WHEATON

This son of Caleb Wheaton, senior (*q.v.*), in his petition states that he and his brother, Caleb, have nothing but their half-pay as Lieutenants to subsist upon. According to a certificate of Joseph Osborn, dated December 15, 1788, these two loyalists were appointed officers in the Provincial Independent Companies in 1778, in which he was Captain. These companies were incorporated in the Nova Scotia Volunteers in 1782. One of these two officers had the honour to receive the thanks of General Maclean for his conduct in capturing in 1780 a party of rebels, which exceeded in number the party under his command. (A.O. 13/49.)

John Wheaton was born in America in 1757 and served throughout the Revolutionary war. The date of his commission as Lieutenant in the Nova Scotia Volunteers is December 5, 1781. He was married to Lydia Cook in Cape Breton, June 1, 1810, and died there, October 22, 1819. His widow died, April 21, 1849, aged 73, at Guysborough, Nova Scotia, where her only brother and heir at law, Edward Cook, was living. (W.O. 42/W10; Ind. 5604-5-6.) One Godfrey Wheaton's burial at the age of 30 is recorded at Christ Church, Guysborough, August 15, 1844.

JOHN WHITE

For many years he sailed from Boston to London and other ports in Europe. The port of Boston having been closed in December, 1774, he sailed as master and super cargo of the ship *Nicholas*, owned by Thomas Boylston, of Salem, bound for South Carolina, where he took on board a cargo of rice, and thence sailed for England, Prussia and Russia, and there shipped commodities. From Europe he went to Halifax, Nova Scotia, where his vessel was seized by the British in 1776, but was eventually restored to him. While the owner was a considerable loser, he himself was enriched by this voyage. Benjamin Hallowell had given White a certificate to his character and loyalty (*vide* letter of February 18, 1788), but since this voyage he instituted enquiries and found that White had gone to Boston from Nova Scotia and went voluntarily into prison (whence he was with difficulty emerged), with the object of strengthening his claim for compensation from the British Government. His wife remained in Boston during the war and if he had incurred any losses it was in consequence of her loans of £1,500 to the State of Massachusetts and £500 to the town of Boston in gold and silver and taking depreciated Congress money as security. (A.O. 13/75; A.O. 13/107.)

John White was born in Great Britain and lived in Boston for 25 years. Thomas Flucker (*q.v.*), in evidence stated that he had been ill-used by old Mr. Boylston. (A.O. 12/105, f. 87.)

A man of this name was admitted to the rights of citizenship in 1791 and died in Boston in 1794, aged 75 (Sabine).

JOHN DEAN WHITWORTH

was born in Boston, the son of Dr. Miles Whitworth, and was in business there until the time of the destruction of the tea, when, in consequence of his own trading in tea, he was obliged to leave the town and seek shelter in England. He was in England in 1776, when he was appointed commissary to the Hessian troops. On the advice of General Sir William Howe he resigned this appointment and in the same year was given a commission as Lieutenant in the Queen's Rangers, commanded by Colonel Robert Rogers. He was wounded at White Plains and taken prisoner and carried to Boston, where he was bound in irons and cast into gaol. There he would have lost his life but for the intervention of his father, who died in 1779 and who himself was a sufferer for his loyalty to Great Britain. His regiment was disbanded in 1777 and he was afterwards appointed Lieutenant in the King's Rangers, raised by Colonel Rogers, but he was prevented by various causes from raising his quota of 16 men. Whitworth was ordered in 1780 on the recruiting service between Quebec and Halifax, Nova Scotia, and made a journey of sixty days on foot in snow shoes through the snow, suffering great hardships and losing the sight of an eye. His afflictions obliged him in 1783 to obtain leave to sail for England. He was granted a pension of £36 from 1784 and a military allowance of £35. (A.O. 13/75; A.O. 12/101, f. 15; Ind. 5606.)

Dr. Miles Whitworth remained in Boston after the evacuation of the town by the British and as a Tory ought to have been transported with Dr. Lloyd (Abigail Adams in a letter to John Adams, April 14, 1776). His son, Miles Whitworth, who graduated at Harvard College in 1772, was a surgeon in the Royal Navy and died in 1778. (Sabine, *op. cit.*)

HENRY HOWELL WILLIAMS

was of deep rooted principles of loyalty and his schedule of his property indicates prosperity. His memorial is dated Noddle's Island (now East Boston), Boston Harbour, March 27, 1786. (A.O. 13/24.)

SETH WILLIAMS

studied law under Daniel Leonard (*q.v.*) and was admitted to the Bar.
He quitted the law, however, for the profession of arms in December,
1774, and in the following year was a volunteer on an expedition to obtain
provisions for the British garrison in Boston, where he served in the
Associated Loyalists. On the voyage from Halifax to New York he was
taken prisoner, but eventually escaped from prison and proceeded to
Rhode Island and there received a commission as Captain in the loyalist
corps of Colonel Edward Cole,* February 14, 1777. This corps having
been disbanded in November 1777, he sailed for England in May 1778
and bought a Lieutenant's commission in the 89th Foot in 1779 and
accompanied this regiment to St. Lucia in the West Indies. According
to one statement he was obliged by ill-health to resign his commission
and by another he lost it for leaving St. Lucia without leave in the Spring of
1781. Upon returning to England he married, and, jointly with his
brother-in-law, fitted out a vessel for the government service. (A.O.
13/75 ; A.O. 13/82 ; A.O. 12/105, f. 88.)

This loyalist was the son of Seth Williams, of Taunton, and graduated
at Harvard College in 1765. He is described as a gentleman in the
Banishment Act of Massachusetts.

JOSHUA WILBOR

lived at Swansea, where he was confined from April 13, 1778, until the
Peace for refusing to take the oath of allegiance to the State. (From his
joint memorial with Peleg Chase, in A.O. 13/24.)

ABEL WILLARD

of Lancaster, counsellor at law and justice of the peace, left an ample
fortune when he fled to Boston in 1775. He sailed from Boston at the
evacuation and died in London, November 8, 1781. (A.O. 13/49 ; A.O.
13/75.)

A claim for £2,139 for the loss of his property was disallowed. (A.O.
12/109.)

He graduated at Harvard College in 1752. His brother was Abijah
Willard (*q.v.*)

Reference : *Loyalists' Claims, op. cit.*, p. 377.

* This loyalist was Lieutenant-Colonel of the Rhode Island Regiment, at the
head of which he distinguished himself in Sir William Johnson's victory over Baron
Dieskau in the expedition against Crown Point in September, 1755. For his losses
in the Indian War of 1763 he received a tract of land on the Ohio. He was a tanner
at Newport, Rhode Island.

ABEL WILLARD, THE YOUNGER

He left Harvard College on April 19, 1775, and put himself under the protection of the British troops at Boston, where he served as a common soldier in the Associated Loyalists until the evacuation of the town by the British troops. He was adopted as the son and heir of his uncle, Abel Willard (*q.v.*). (A.O. 13/49.)

ABIJAH WILLARD

This native of Massachusetts served in the siege of Louisburg in 1745 and afterwards in Nova Scotia under General Monckton and as Colonel Commandant of a regiment in the expedition against Canada under Amherst in 1759. In August 1775, in consequence of his acceptance of office as a member of the Mandamus Council, he was persecuted and taken prisoner, and detained for five days. For a second time he was arrested. He had warned Lord Percy in April 1775 of an ambush laid for the troops. At the request of General Gage he undertook the hazardous task of supplying the British troops in Boston with fresh provisions and was Captain in the Associated Loyalists. He left Boston at the evacuation for Halifax and thence for New York, where he was appointed assistant commissary and commanding officer of the Massachusetts Volunteers recruited from refugees.

His large estate at Lancaster, Massachusetts, valued at £7,500 sterling, was lost to him. With his memorial is an inventory of his real and personal estate and documents relating to his confiscated property. (A.O. 13/49; A.O. 12/100, f. 209.)

The Commissioners spoke warmly of his zeal and loyalty and granted him a pension of £150 from 1784. He claimed compensation, £6,314, and was granted £2,912. (A.O. 12/109.) Certificates to his loyalty and services are in A.O. 13/79.

He is mentioned in a letter of Governor Hutchinson, September 22, 1775, as an enterprising man, who went forth and returned with 100 fat oxen and sheep, for the unhappy besieged people of Boston. (British Museum : Addl. MSS., 35427.)

His two original memorials do not add material information to the above, except that his only surviving son, Samuel, joined him on service in 1777 and that he named his farm in New Brunswick, " Lancaster," after the place of his residence in Massachusetts. (A.O. 13/75.)

Abijah Willard died in New Brunswick [where he was a member of the first Provincial Council] on May 28, 1789, when his three children, Samuel, Elizabeth and Ann, were granted pensions of £20 each. (A.O. 12/102, f. 248.) Samuel's pension was continued until 1831. (T. 50/11 ; T. 50/22 ; T. 50/28.) One daughter, probably Elizabeth, married Joseph Walker, and her pension was paid until July, 1822. (T. 50/11 ; T. 50/23 ; T. 50/26.) The other daughter, Ann, married one Goodhue and received her pension until 1831. (T. 50/11 ; T. 50/22 ; T. 50/28.)

Abijah Willard was born at Lancaster, July 27, 1724, and married (i), Elizabeth Prescott ; (ii) Anna Prentice, in 1752 ; and (iii) Mrs. Mary McKown, in 1772. (Ex inform. Miss Susan B. Willard.)

Thomas Jones, the malevolent author of the *History of New York during the Revolution* (i, 345), describes him as cunning, artful and hypo- critical as the devil himself.

References : *The Winslow Papers,* p. 111, n. ; *The Willard Memoir,* 1858 ; Sabine, *op. cit. ; Amer. MSS. in the Royal Inst., op. cit.,* ii, 239, 290, 291 ; *Acadiensis,* Vol. 5 ; *Archives of Ontario, op. cit.,* p. 1333 ; *Loyalists' Claims, op. cit.,* pp. 137–8.

LEVI WILLARD

son of Levi Willard, of Lancaster, had just finished his education at College* at the outbreak of war. Rather than submit to the demand to join the American Army, or provide a substitute, he fled in August (? 1776) to Rhode Island in a boat. He appears to have died before 1782. (A.O. 13/75.)

His paper is marked " dead." (A.O. 12/105, f. 24.)

GEORGE WILMOT

lived in Boston since 1736 as a master mariner. In 1755 he was appointed to command a body of men employed " on the island navigation towards reduceing the french settlements in Canada," and served as such until the peace of 1763. Governor Shirley, of Massachusetts, appointed him in 1756 to a company of batteau men under General John Bradstreet. (A.O. 13/75 ; A.O. 12/105, f. 149.)

JAMES WIMBLE

In an undated petition, praying for compensation for the loss of his shipping by the depredations of the Spanish, he describes himself as a mariner, of Boston. (C.O. 5/754.)

A Boston mariner of this name was the author of a *Chart of His Majesty's Province of North Carolina* in 1738, and was one of the founders of Wilmington in that province in 1733. He was living in Boston in 1738.

EDWARD WINSLOW, THE ELDER

served in several public stations with applause, as first magistrate in the county of Plymouth, Collector of his Majesty's Customs for the port of Plymouth, Register of the Probate Court, and, jointly with his son, Edward (*q.v.*), Clerk of the Common Pleas and General Sessions of the Peace. In 1775 he was deprived of all these offices by the " usurped authority," having refused to take the oath of allegiance to the " rebel

* He graduated at Harvard in 1775.

government." The indignities and persecutions heaped upon him were almost as incredible as they were severe. For his loyalty to the Crown of England he experienced a transition from the most comfortable situation to a state of poverty and distress. From being as much respected for his personal character and family connections as any man in Massachusetts, he was for nine years "the butt of the licentious," and the victim of every species of insult and abuse which the utmost rancour and malice could invent to a man at the age of 67, while his property was confiscated and sold for less than half its value. Worn out by inhuman persecution and labouring under many infirmities at his advanced age, he arrived at New York in December, 1781, and was allowed £200 a year by Sir Henry Clinton, Commander-in-Chief. On August 13, 1783, he left that place, with his wife, two daughters and three black servants, and arrived at Halifax, Nova Scotia, a total stranger. The war had terminated very differently from his expectations.

Edward Winslow died at Halifax, June 8, 1784, leaving a widow, Hannah, and two spinster daughters, Sarah and Penelope. (A.O. 13/45 ; A.O. 13/75). They claimed £1,725, and were allowed £1,110. (A.O. 12/109.) His daughters received a pension of £33 6s. 8d. from 1789 to 1807. (A.O. 463/22 ; T. 50/11.) He was buried in the graveyard of St. Paul's Church. His widow died, May 23, 1795, and was buried at Fredericton, New Brunswick.

This veteran loyalist was the great-grandson of Governor Edward Winslow, of the *Mayflower* company, and brother of General John Winslow,* the eminent colonial soldier. He graduated at Harvard College in 1736, and built the Winslow House at Plymouth in 1754,

* In A.O. 13/43 is a copy of the proclamation of George III to the Governors of the American Colonies, dated October 7, 1763, granting certain lands as a reward for the services of the officers and men in the war just concluded in America. John Winslow, of Marshfield, Massachusetts, who was appointed in 1756 Major-General and Commander of the Provincial forces of New England, New York and New Jersey, received 5,060 acres in New Hampshire. Certain conditions were laid down, namely, (i) that a road should be made through the tract, wide enough for carriages, and be completed in one year on penalty of forfeiture ; (ii) that the grantee should settle or cause to be settled eight families in five years, in failure whereof the property to revert to the Crown ; (iii) that all white and other pine trees fit for masting the Royal Navy should be carefully preserved for that purpose, subject to penalties prescribed for neglect of this condition ; (iv) that the grantee should pay before January 1, 1774, one ear of Indian corn only if lawfully demanded ; (v) that the grantee, his heirs and assigns, should pay to the Crown yearly for ever from January 1, 1783, one shilling proclamation money for every 100 acres he so owns, settles or possesses and so in proportion for a greater or less quantity of the said land ; and (vi) that any part of the land which may appear to be adapted to the cultivation of hemp and flax, or either of them, should be cultivated with those useful articles, to the proportion of 10 acres in each and every hundred of these granted premises within ten years of this date and these to be in full of all other rents and services. The grant is signed by Governor John Wentworth, of New Hampshire, October 21, 1773, and bears the seal of that province. There is also a plan and description of the property.

which is still standing, and which was the scene of the marriage of Ralph Waldo Emerson in 1835. (Stark, *op. cit.*, p. 436; *Proc. of Mass. Hist. Soc.*, 2nd Ser., ii, 229–242; iii, 65–93; *Loyalists' Claims, op. cit.*, pp. 311–2.)

EDWARD WINSLOW

son of Edward Winslow (*q.v.*), lived on an estate which had been in the possession of his ancestors, one of whom was Governor of the Plymouth Colony, since 1620. He was Register of Probate and Clerk of the General Sessions of the Peace and Court of Common Pleas in the county of Plymouth and Naval Officer for the port of Plymouth. Upon the first appearance of opposition to the King's authority he went forward and exerted all his interest and influence to enforce the laws, and was appointed by Governor Hutchinson to the command of a Volunteer Company raised to assist the civil magistrates. By an act of the county congress in October, 1774, he was deprived of all his public offices. Unable to stem the torrent of popular rage, he joined General Gage at Danbury. He served as a volunteer at the battle of Lexington, and received the particular acknowledgments of Lord Percy for his services; he also served later as a volunteer. General Sir William Howe appointed him Collector of Customs at Boston and Register of Probate for Suffolk County. He left Boston at the evacuation by the British, and was appointed Muster Master General of the Provincial forces [in 1776] and served in this office until April, 1783, when he was requested by General Sir Guy Carleton to proceed to New Brunswick and select such lands as would accommodate the disbanded officers and men of the loyalist regiments. He was afterwards appointed military secretary to Brigadier General Fox in Nova Scotia, and later to Major General Campbell. (A.O. 13/22.)

This loyalist was born in 1745 and graduated at Harvard in 1765. He was one of the founders of the Old Colony Club* at Plymouth in 1770. After settling in New Brunswick he held several public offices with great credit, including that of a Judge of the Supreme Court. It was he who carried (or caused to be carried) the Royal Arms from the Old State House at Boston and eventually presented them to Trinity Church, St. John, where they have survived many vicissitudes. The Winslow Papers (published in 1901 and edited by the Rev. W. O. Raymond) are a mine of information on the origins of New Brunswick, and a monument to the memory of Edward Winslow. He died at Fredericton, May 13, 1815. (*Judges of New Brunswick, op. cit.*, pp. 4, 61, 119–148; Stark, *op. cit.*, pp. 436–7.)

---

* An account of this Club, with its records, is in *Proc. of Mass. Hist. Soc.*, 2nd Ser., iii, 381–444.

Rev. William Walter

PLATE LIII

Joshua Winslow and Mrs. Hannah Winslow

PLATE LIV

ISAAC WINSLOW

one of the Mandamus Councillors, lost property and debts due to him to the value of about £13,000 sterling. He died at New York in March, 1777, leaving a widow, Jemima, who sought refuge in England in October, 1780. (A.O. 13/49; A.O. 13/75.) She was granted a loyalist allowance of £100. (A.O., 12/105, f. 114.)

According to John Andrews, August 30, 1774, Isaac Winslow declared his entire willingness to resign from the Council and apologised for accepting membership, adding that his acceptance was due to the persuasion of others than to his own inclinations. (*Letters of John Andrews*, 1772–6, ed. by Winthrop Sargent, 1866, p. 36.)

A loyalist of this name was the owner of an island of about 6,000 to 7,000 acres in extent, at the mouth of the Penobscot River. Elisha Hewes, in a letter of June 9, 1775, to the Massachusetts Congress, suggests that after allowing the ten or twelve families from Connecticut, who were hearty in the American cause, to hold " what they have taken in their own right," on this island, the rest should be deemed forfeit. (Force, *American Archives*, Series IV, vol. ii, pp. 943–4.)

Isaac Winslow was born in 1709, and after graduating at Harvard College in 1727, became a considerable merchant in Boston, in partnership with his brother, Joshua. In religious belief he was a Sandemanian. (*See page* 23.) (Stark, *op. cit.*, pp. 437–8.) His first wife was Lucy, daughter of General Samuel Waldo; and his second was Jemima Debuke, who died in London in 1790. (*Publications of Colonial Soc. of Mass.*, vi, 129–130.) His nephew was Isaac Winslow (*q.v.*).

Joshua Winslow (1727–1801), his brother, who had served in the capture of Louisburg in 1745 and in the expedition to Acadia in 1755, was one of the consignees of the famous tea; his portrait, painted by Joseph Blackburn in 1750, is on loan at the Union League Club, New York (Plate LIV).

ISAAC WINSLOW

was born in Boston, and was a merchant and distiller there and a civil magistrate. He evinced his loyalty early in the Revolution by addressing General Gage and accepting a command in the Associated Loyalists of Boston in 1775. He left with the British troops in March, 1776. With his memorial in A.O. 13/51 is (i) a list of his losses, with details; (ii) a certificate from his brother-in-law, John Winniett, of Boston, stating that all the stock of his three distilleries had been taken away by a quartermaster of the American army after the evacuation of Boston by the British; and (iii) a long inventory of the personal property and a copy of the will (1769) of his father, Joshua Winslow, which reveals a prosperous condition in life and bequeaths a silver-gilt cup to his son, Joshua, a gilt salver to his son, John, and two gilt cans to this loyalist son, Isaac. He was part owner of the schooner *Liberty* and the sloop *Betsey*. (A.O.

12/10, ff. 197–202 ;   A.O., 12/105, f. 89.)   He claimed £847 16s., and was allowed £200. (A.O., 12/109.)

Isaac Winslow was the son of Joshua and Elizabeth Winslow, and was born in 1743. He was educated at the Boston Latin School and graduated at Harvard College in 1762. He married (i) Margaret, daughter of the Rev. John Sparhawk, of Salem ; and (ii) Mary, daughter of Benjamin Davis (*q.v.*), of Boston. He died at Boston (whither he had been allowed by the General Court to return), January 23, 1793. His brothers were : the Rev. Edward Winslow, the loyalist Rector of Christ Church, Braintree (now Quincy), who died in New York in 1780 ; John (*q.v.*) ; and Joshua (*q.v.*). His uncle was Isaac Winslow (*q.v.*).

Reference : *Ontario Archives, op. cit.*, pp. 623–5.

JOHN WINSLOW

was deputy commissary of prisoners, and died in 1781 from a fever contracted in attending to prisoners. Mary, his widow, who was a niece of Jonathan Simpson, the elder (*q.v.*) at her marriage to this loyalist brought to him a handsome property and one of the first fortunes in Boston ; this property was confiscated. She lost at New York by death not only her husband and an only son, but also a brother and sister, both of considerable fortunes in Boston. Mary Winslow went to Bristol, England, after her husband's death, and died at Boston, Massachusetts, early in 1787. (A.O. 13/75 ; A.O. 13/48, with the Simpson papers ; A.O. 12/99, f. 316.)

His brother was Isaac Winslow, the younger (*q.v.*). (*Publications of Colonial Soc. of Mass.*, vi, 129–30.)

JOSHUA WINSLOW

a loyalist, died early in the Revolution, leaving a widow, Hannah, the loyalist daughter of Joshua Loring, the elder (*q.v.*). In her undated letter to her friend, John Blackburn, of Scotch Yard, Bush Lane, Cannon Street, London, she (who was marked out by Providence to be particularly unfortunate), contrasted the more ample Government allowance to other loyalists who had lost little property by the Revolution, with her own meagre allowance. Little did she expect that her own countrymen, the Americans, would refuse to let her return home, unless she went without any expectation of receiving a farthing's worth of her property. (A.O. 13/75.)

Her brother, Joshua Loring (*q.v.*), stated on March 22, 1785, that she had died on February 22, previously, leaving six children unprovided for, who were living with their grandmother, Mrs. Loring. An allowance of £64 was granted to them. (A.O. 12/101, f. 176.)

Hannah Winslow's claims of £1,842, and £450 were disallowed for want of satisfactory proof of loss. (A.O. 12/109.) She was granted a pension of £100. (A.O. 12/105, f. 113.) It was probably her daughter,

Elizabeth Winslow, and Mary Loring Paiba (*née* Winslow), who were granted loyalist pensions of £20 from 1797 to 1799 and 1807, respectively. (A.O. 461/16; A.O. 463/22.)

Joshua Winslow was the son of Joshua and Elizabeth (Savage) Winslow, and brother of Isaac Winslow (*q.v.*), and nephew of Isaac Winslow (*q.v.*).

Hannah Winslow's portrait by Copley is in the possession of Hon. William Caleb Loring (Plate LIV).

REV. JOHN WISWALL

was educated at Harvard College, and was for many years a dissenting Minister at Falmouth (Portland), Maine, before conforming, with many of his congregation, to the Church of England, from the conviction that that Church was apostolic and the British Constitution more beneficial to the rights of mankind than the republican system of New England. He was ordained priest by the Bishop of London. In consequence of his regarding it as his duty to persevere in his allegiance to the King he and other loyalists were called Tories and enemies of America, and were insulted and abused by the Whigs. (A.O. 13/82.)

On May 9, 1775, he and Captain Mowat (*q.v.*) were violently assaulted and imprisoned by a body of armed rebels at Falmouth. Four days later, being in danger of their lives, they escaped and got on board Captain Mowat's ship, H.M.S. *Canso*, which took this clergyman to Boston. He had been exposed continually to gross insults by " abandoned men." The greater part of his congregation were warm friends to Government, but were obliged to remove from Falmouth to escape further persecution. He lost all his library, furniture, his family pictures, and a valuable collection of ancient curiosities. His wife and daughter " fell a sacrifice to the cruelties and hardships of the war," in July, 1776. On June 15, 1775, he was appointed Chaplain of the 63rd Regiment in Boston, and served until January 29, 1776. In this year he sailed from Boston for England, and was appointed Chaplain of H.M.S. *Rainbow*, and served on that ship mostly on the American coast and the West Indies, and afterwards on H.M.S. *Boyne* until November, 1781, under Admirals Howe, Rodney and others. In 1783 he was appointed, by the Society for the Propagation of the Gospel, missionary at Cornwallis, Horton and Wilmot, Nova Scotia. (A.O. 13/51; A.O. 12/10, ff. 309–314; A.O. 12/99, f. 42.) He claimed £1,010, and was allowed £205, and his claim of £80 a year for the loss of his income during the war was allowed. (A.O. 12/109.)

Dr. Sylvester Gardiner (*q.v.*), in a letter says that this clergyman had been driven from Falmouth by a " most abandoned set of villains that ever disgraced human nature." (T. 1/520, ff. 225–230.)

This ardent loyalist was the son of John and Elizabeth Wiswall, and was born at Boston in 1731. He was the third of his line, including his father, to be educated at Harvard College. In 1755 he was a Congregational minister at Falmouth, and in 1764 joined the Church of England. He was the virtual founder of the Episcopal Church in that Maine town. Two sons, Peleg and John, by his first marriage to Mercy, daughter of Judge Minot, served as lieutenants in the Royal Navy during the war. Peleg became a lawyer and judge in Digby County, Nova Scotia, and John settled in the same colony, where he married Hesdeliah, daughter of Ebenezer Cutler (*q.v.*), of Annapolis. The Rev. John Wiswall married in 1784, as his second wife, Margaret Hutchinson, widow of John Hutchinson,* a loyalist from Hanover, New Jersey, who was drowned on the passage to England in 1781. He died December 2, 1821, at Wilmot, Nova Scotia, of which place he was the first rector from 1789. A long account of his life and times, largely based upon his own letters, was published by the Rev. Dr. E. M. Saunders in *Colls. of Nova Scotia Hist. Soc.*, vol. xiii.

References : Sabine, *op. cit. ; Archives of Ontario, op. cit.*, pp. 188–9 ; *Memoirs, Journals and Letters of Rev. John Wiswall*, ed. by W. A. Calnck and A. W. Savary ; *Journal of Bishop Inglis ;* Stark, *op. cit.*, pp. 398–9.

CAPTAIN AARON WRIGHT

of Northampton, held a commission before the Revolution, and was living at that place in 1786. He was probably the Aaron Wright, junior, of Northampton, who appointed Justus Wright (*q.v.*) as his attorney in prosecuting his claim for compensation. (A.O. 13/80.)

He was 2nd Lieutenant in Captain Elisha Pomeroy's company from March 13 to November 5, 1758, on an expedition to Canada. (Muster Rolls Series.)

JESSE WRIGHT

a native of Connecticut, settled as a farmer at New Ashford, Berkshire County, Massachusetts. He was drafted into the American militia, but deserted with eight more, and afterwards served in the 1st King's Royal Regiment of New York, and in Burgoyne's army. (A.O. 12/33, ff. 115–7 ; *Ontario Archives, op cit.*, p. 449.) He claimed £79 10s., and was allowed £40. (A.O. 12/109.)

JUSTUS WRIGHT

In his memorial he says that he was a leader of the loyalists at Northampton, and was frequently fined for not taking up arms against Great Britain, his property being confiscated. After the war he returned to Northampton, and was indicted for endeavouring to overthrow the independence of the United States and the alliance with France, but at the trial he was cleared by the terms of the Treaty of Peace. He was afterwards indicted for the same crimes against the state of Massachusetts only, and was kept in prison on extravagant bonds. In August, 1784, he

* E. Alfred Jones, *The Loyalists of New Jersey*, 1927, pp. 101-2.

escaped to Canada. He returned, in February, 1786, to Hampshire County to procure depositions concerning his losses, but was obliged to secret himself while two gentlemen were obtaining a certificate; but they dare not go and get it sworn before a magistrate because of the implacable malice of his enemies. Justus Wright afterwards made a second attempt to get the necessary depositions, but was apprehended on suspicion of being an emissary of Lord Dorchester* to assist in an insurrection† then existing in Massachusetts. He was committed to prison in Northampton, and thence removed to Boston gaol to the tune of the " Rogues March." Here he was put in irons and only obtained his release upon undertaking to appear at the Supreme Court in Hampshire County in September, 1787, but rather than risk another visit, he forfeited his depositions. (A.O. 13/75 ; A.O. 13/80.)

In evidence on March 12, 1790, he repeated the statements in his memorial, adding that he was born in Massachusetts, and joined the British in 1781, but had been persecuted for his loyalty from 1775. (A.O. 12/102, f. 230.)

The following loyalists, living at Northampton in March, 1786, appointed Justus Wright as their attorney to prosecute their claims for compensation from the British Government : Gideon Clark, Aaron Wright, junior, Ebenezer Putney, Selah Wright and Hains Kingsley. (A.O. 13/80.)

In 1791 he was appointed barrackmaster in Upper Canada, and just as he was about to embark to enter upon his duties, he died in London, December 9, in that year. His brother, Daniel, a merchant in Northampton, was also a loyalist, and sought refuge at Shelburne, Nova Scotia ; he returned in 1789 and the rights of citizenship of Massachusetts were restored to him. (Sabine, *op. cit.*)

DAVID WYER

On December 26, 1769, he was appointed tide waiter in the Customs at Falmouth (Portland), Maine, and did duty as such until December, 1775, when he sought refuge at Fort George, Penobscot. (A.O. 13/51 ; A.O. 13/82.) He died before March, 1787. His son was Thomas Wyer (*q.v.*).

THOMAS WYER

was a merchant at Falmouth (Portland), Maine. From the first he was an active loyalist, and spoke in public meetings against the associations formed by the rebels. He remained in the neighbourhood until May, 1777, when repeated fines and imprisonment for refusing to take up arms in the American cause compelled him to escape from his persecutors in an open boat to Annapolis, Nova Scotia, whence he eventually reached New York. After much suffering he removed from New York

---

* Lord Dorchester, Governor of Quebec from 1786.
† " Shay's Rebellion," 1786–7.

with his wife, Joanna, and his family (whom he was allowed to bring away from Falmouth about August, 1779), to Fort George, Penobscot, in May, 1781, and there it " was universally believed that even in the event of Peace his Majesty's Government would be established." There he built a house as a shelter, not only for his own family, but also for his aged father, David Wyer (*q.v.*), and his father-in-law. He was the owner of pew No. 28 in St. Paul's Church at Falmouth, of which the minister was the Rev. John Wiswall (*q.v.*). With his memorial is an inventory of his property destroyed in the destruction of the town on October 18, 1775, by order of Captain Mowat (*q.v.*), and an inventory of the property of his father. He was the owner of the schooner *Miriam* and half-owner of the sloop *Defiance*. There is also a certificate of Captain Mowat to his loyalty, and a copy of a resolution of the House of Representatives, April 12, 1779, granting him permission to remove his wife, with orders that she should not return to the State, and directions for the confiscation of his property. Thomas Wyer settled at St. Andrews, New Brunswick. (A.O. 13/51.)

He claimed £981 7s., and was allowed £255. He also claimed £501 17s. as the administrator of the estate of his father, and was allowed £15. (A.O. 12/61, f. 68 ; A.O. 12/109.)

According to Mr. Stark (*op. cit.*, p. 466), this loyalist was born at Charlestown, Massachusetts, in 1744, and left home in an open boat with his father-in-law, Jeremiah Pote (father of his second wife), and at New York served as captain of the brigantine *British Tar*, of 65 men. At St. Andrews he was the first sheriff of Charlotte County, Judge of the Court of Common Pleas, and deputy colonial treasurer. He died there in 1824.

It was his brother, David Wyer, lawyer (a graduate of Harvard College in 1758), who signed the address to Governor Hutchinson, and recanted. (Force, *American Archives*, Series IV, Vol. III, pp. 625–7.) He died at Stroud Water, in 1776. (Stark, *op. cit.*, p. 466.)

References : *Ontario Archives, op. cit.,* p. 906 ; *Acadiensis,* iii, v, and vii.

APPENDIXES

$$\begin{bmatrix} July \\ 1776 \end{bmatrix}$$

To The King's Most Excellent Majesty

MOST GRACIOUS SOVEREIGN—At this most important period, when your Majesty's Arms are engaged in reclaiming your revolted subjects in America, and in repelling the combined and unprovoked attempts of France and Spain, We your Majesty's Subjects, who from your Colonies have taken refuge in Great Britain, beg leave to approach the Throne with hearts and lives devoted to Your Majesty's Person and Government, and to offer our unfeigned thanks for those unparalleled exertions, which your Majesty has been pleased to make, for the relief and protection of Your faithfull Colonial Subjects :—And notwithstanding Your Majesty's Arms have not been attended with all the effect those exertions promised, and from which, occasion has been taken, to raise an indiscriminate charge of disaffection in the Colonists,—We beg leave, Some of us from our own knowledge, and others from the best information, to assure Your Majesty, That the greater number of your subjects in the Confederated Colonies, notwithstanding every art to seduce, every device to intimidate, and a variety of oppressions to compell them to abjure their Sovereign, entertain the firmest attachment and Allegiance to Your Majesty's sacred Person and Government. In support of these truths, we need not appeal to the evidence of our own sufferings. It is notorious, that we have sacrificed all which the most loyal Subjects coul'd forego, or the happiest coul'd possess—But with confidence we appeal to the struggles made against the Usurpations of the Congress, by counter resolves in very large districts of Country, and to the many unsuccessfull attempts by bodies of the loyal in Arms, which have subjected them to all the rigours of inflamed resentment,—We appeal to the sufferings of multitudes, who for their loyalty have been subjected to insults, fines and imprisonments, patiently enduring all, in the expectation of that period which shall restore to them the blessings of Your Majesty's Government.—We appeal to the thousands now serving in Your Majesty's Armies, and in private ships of War, the former exceeding in number, the troops enlisted to oppose them ; finally we make a melancholy Appeal to the many families who have been banished from their once peacefull habitations ;—to the public forfeiture of a long list of Estates, and to the numerous executions of our fellow citizens who have sealed their Loyalty with their blood—If any Colony or district, when covered or possessed by Your Majesty's Troops, had been called upon to take Arms, and had refused, or if any attempts had been made, to form the loyal as militia or

307

otherwise, and it had been declined,—we shoul'd not on this occasion have presumed thus to address Your Majesty, but if on the contrary no general measure to the above effect was attempted, if petitions from bodies of Your Majesty's Subjects, who wished to rise in Aid of Government have been neglected and the representations of the most respectable loyalists disregarded, We assure ourselves, that the Equity and Wisdom of Your Majesty's mind, will not admit of any impressions injurious to the honour and loyalty of your faithfull subjects in those Colonies——

Revereing and firmly attached to the British Constitution, which it has been the glory of Your Majesty's Family to strengthen, and of Your Reign to improve, we lament the infatuation of such of our fellow Subjects in America who acting upon different principles, or deluded by their leaders, have thrown aside their just Allegiance, and cast themselves on the assistance of the ancient enemies of their Country, liberties and religion; an allegiance which may enslave, but never can establish the happiness of your Colonists——Animated with these sentiments we supplicate the Supreme Disposer of Events, to crown Your Majesty's endeavours with a success proportioned to the righteousness of your cause; to frustrate the ambitious designs of your Enemies and finally to restore to your Majesty's Subjects in America, that mild Government, under which they long enjoyed so much felicity. C.O. 5/7.

Appended to this petition are the original signatures of thirty-one loyalists:

SIR WILLIAM PEPPERELL	JOHN JOY
BENJAMIN HALLOWELL	JAMES BARRICK
SAMUEL FITCH	JAMES BARRICK, JUN.
DANIEL LEONARD	JOHN FLEMING
SAMUEL WATERHOUSE	WARD NICHOLAS BOYLSTON
PETER JOHONNOT	DAVID INGERSOLL
SAMUEL HIRST SPARHAWK	REV. JOHN TROUTBECK
ADINO PADDOCK	JOHN GOULD
SAMUEL SPARHAWK	LEWIS DEBLOIS
SAMUEL GARNETT	GILBERT DEBLOIS
WALTER BARRELL	JOHN LAWLESS
JOSEPH THOMPSON	NATHANIEL COFFIN
JOHN GORE	JONATHAN PERRIE COFFIN
SETH WILLIAMS	JOHN PHILLIPS
JOLLEY ALLEN	ROBERT JARVIS
ROBERT HALLOWELL	

Elisha Hutchinson in his Diary records the meetings at the Crown and Anchor Tavern in London, on July 2 and 6, 1779, to organise the loyal address to the King. At the second meeting there were 50 present. On the 8th, Barrell (presumably Walter) called upon him with the address for his signature, but he declined to sign it on account of the paragraph which so strongly asserted the loyalty of the " present inhabitants of America."

A list of absentee loyalists, with amounts claimed against their estates, is in A.O. 12/81, ff. 136–7, as follows :

Gibbs Atkins.

(There is a copy of the *Massachusetts Centinel* for October 1, 1788, containing an advertisement of the sale by auction of his house, in A.O. 13/46.)

John Amory*	John Gore (*q.v.*)
Nathan Aldis (*q.v.*)	Ezekiel Lewis, junior‖
Thomas Brattle (*q.v.*)	Edward Lyde (*q.v.*)
John Coffin (*q.v.*)	Theophilus Lillie¶
William Coffin†	Christopher Minot**
Wilfred Fisher (*q.v.*)	Agnes Proctor
Joseph Greene‡	John Rogers (*q.v.*)
Joseph Goldthwaite§	Jonathan Snelling (*q.v.*)

An undated memorial of twenty-nine refugee loyalists from Massachusetts in England, declaring that by their loyalty they had sacrificed their homes and fortunes, and praying for relief, is in A.O. 13/46, and bears their original signatures :

NATHANIEL COFFIN	SAMUEL CURWEN
THOMAS BRINLEY	LEWIS DEBLOIS
SAMPSON SALTER BLOWERS	JOSEPH HOOPER
PETER JOHONNOT	JOHN SARGENT
ABEL WILLARD	MATTHEW HUTCHINS
THOMAS DANFORTH	JOHN BERRY
SAMUEL SEWALL	JOHN ROGERS
WARD CHIPMAN	WILLIAM BOWES
EDWARD OXNARD	JONATHAN SIMPSON, Junior
DANIEL SILSBY	JOHN JOY
FRANCIS JOHONNOT	JOHN GORE
JOSEPH TAYLOR	HENRY LAUGHTON
ROBERT JARVIS	THOMAS POYNTON
PETER OLIVER, Junior	HENRY BARNES
LEWIS GRAY	

* John Amory, in a petition to the Legislature of Massachusetts, stated that although he had left Boston for England in May, 1775, on a voyage which he had long intended, and although he was opposed to the Non-Importation agreement, he was a firm friend to American liberty (Meredith, *The Descendants of Hugh Amory*, 1901, p. 239).

† He was the brother of Jonathan Perrie Coffin (*q.v.*).

‡ Joseph Greene, wit and loyalist, died in London, December 11, 1780. (*Curwen's Journal, op. cit.*, pp. 554–5.) He graduated at Harvard College in 1726.

§ He was a brother of Captain Philip Goldthwait (*q.v.*).

‖ A graduate at Harvard College in 1735 (Stark, *op. cit.*, p. 415).

¶ One of the Associated Loyalists, of Boston. See Stark, *op. cit.*, pp. 308–313.

** Land Waiter in the Customs at Boston.

The "Worcester Protest" was drawn up in 1774 by James Putnam (*q.v.*) and clearly reveals the hand of a lawyer. It protests in measured language against the riotous and seditious actions of the evil minded and ill disposed persons who, under the disguise of patriotism, falsely declare themselves the friends of liberty and intend to reduce all things to a state of tumult, disorder and confusion. It demands the suppression of the committees of correspondence. A true copy is in A.O. 13/73, with the names of the following 52 residents of Worcester :

William Elder	Andrew Duncan (see p. 78)
Daniel Ward	James Goodwin
John Walker (*q.v.*)	Clark Chandler*
Nath Adams	Israel Jennison
Adam Walker (*q.v.*)	Nanthan Patch
Jacob Stevens	Samuel Mower, Junr.
Joshua Johnson	Isaac Moore
Israel Stevens	John Chandler (*q.v.*)
Joseph Clark	James Putnam (*q.v.*)
Isaac Barnerd	Gardiner Chandler (*q.v.*)
William Paine (*q.v.*)	Daniel Boyden
Thaddeus Chamberlain	John Curtis
John Chamberlain	Thomas Baird
William Curtis	James Hart
Abel Stowel	Elisha Smith
Daniel Goulding	Tyrus Rice
William Chandler (see p. 83)	Nahum Willard†
William Campbell (*q.v.*)	Rufus Chandler (*q.v.*)
Samuel Moore	Palmer Goulding
John Mower	David Moore
Joseph Blair	James Heart, Junr.
Micah Johnson	Cornelius Stowell
Edmund Heard	John Phillip
Thomas Beard, Jun.	Samuel Brooks
Samuel Mower	Isaac Willard
Jacob Camberlain	
Samuel Bridge	

The agents in London of the American loyalists in a long petition to Parliament recounted the sufferings of these loyalists for their loyalty. "In the early part of the tumults, those who firmly adhered to their allegiance were in most of the Colonies deprived, by the Insurgents, of the liberty of the Press and of the freedom of speech, and soon after disarmed ; and all those who made efforts to check the rising Sedition, were either imprisoned, fined, banished, or put to Death without even the form of law." (F.O. 4/1.)

In an undated petition to Parliament, 106 loyalists declared that,

---

* Son of John Chandler (*q.v.*).

† Dr. Nahum Willard recanted (*Amer. Archives, op. cit.,* Ser. IV, vol. iii, p. 463.

ever firmly attached to the British Constitution, they did in pursuance of his Majesty's proclamation and the resolution of the two Houses of Parliament, take an open and avowed part against the measures of the insurgents. In consequence of many unavoidable accidents and delays they were prevented from submitting their claims for compensation within the time limited by the several Acts of Parliament. They prayed that their cases may be taken into consideration and an Act passed to enquire into their losses, services and sufferings. The only names from Massachusetts are those of William Hill, William Warden, Justus Wright, John Hill, George Spooner, Edward Dougherty and Thomas Courtney, senior. (A.O. 13/98.)

THE ASSOCIATED LOYALISTS, OR THE LOYAL AMERICAN ASSOCIATORS, OF BOSTON

Scattered throughout this book are the names of many loyalists who were members of the above corps—an association proposed to the loyal citizens of Boston, agreeable to the proclamation of General Howe, October 28, 1775, printed in Force's *American Archives* (Ser. IV, vol. ii, p. 1651.) The corps was at first formed into three companies under the command of Timothy Ruggles (*q.v.*) and the members were distinguished by a white sash round their left arms. (*New York Hist. Soc. Colls.*, 1883, p. 252 ; *Colls. of New Brunswick Hist. Soc.*, No. 5, p. 198.)

General Howe's original commission appointing Abijah Willard (*q.v.*) as Captain, Thomas Beaman (*q.v.*) and George Leonard* as first Lieutenants, and Samuel Paine (*q.v.*) and James Putnam† as second Lieutenants, is in A.O. 13/51. Thomas Danforth (*q.v.*) and James Paine are mentioned as second Lieutenants (*Colls. of New Brunswick Hist. Soc.*, No. 5, p. 198).

The officers of the second company were : Captain James Putnam (*q.v.*) ; First Lieutenants, John Sergeant (? Sargent) and Daniel Oliver (*q.v.*) ; Second Lieutenants, Jeremiah Dummer Rogers (*q.v.*), John Ruggles (see p. 250) and Stephen Jones (*q.v.*). (*Ib.* p. 198.)

The officers of the third company are mentioned on p. 153. But there would seem to have been an earlier third company (see below).

Many of these loyalists served later in the Massachusetts Volunteers at New York, recruited from the refugees and commanded by Abijah Willard (*q.v.*)

In A.O. 13/75 is a list of the names of the men in the third company of the Associated Loyalists, commanded by Adino Paddock (*q.v.*) appointed July 5, 1775. Captain, Adino Paddock, Commanding Officer of Artillery in New England, who was offered an appointment of equal rank in the American service ; First Lieutenant, Edwd. Lutwich [Lutwyche];‡

* Probably the loyalist of this name on p. 153.

† See p. 240, *f.n.*

‡ Edward Goldstone Lutwich (Lutwyche) accompanied the British troops to Halifax in March, 1776.

Second Lieutenant, James Anderson*; Sergeants W^m. Campbell,†
Hopestill Capen,‡ Benjn. Davis§ and Samu^l. Fitch (*q.v.*).

Jno. Graham	Geo Inman (*q.v.*)
Geo. Graham	John Inman (*q.v.*)
Petr Grant	Elisha Jones (*q.v.*)
Jno. Gray, Junr. (*q.v.*)	Josiah Jones (*q.v.*)
Mart Gay (*q.v.*)	Step^n. Jones (*q.v.*)
Sam: Gray	Thos. Joselyn¶
Benj. Grinnel	Pat. Kimmey
Jno. Greary	Edward King (Stark, *op. cit.*,
Thos. Geer	pp. 125, 135)
Saml. Greenwood (*q.v.*)	Saml. King (Stark, *op. cit.*,
Benj. Gridley (*q.v.*)	p. 135)
Jno. Handyside	Jno. Knutton (Stark, *op. cit.*,
John Hoban	p. 137)
Joseph Hall	W^m. Knutton
Zep^h. Hodges	Henry Lee
Jno. Heider	W^m. Lamphier
Jon^n. Hicks‖	Edwd. G. Lutwich
R^d. Hirons	Theo : Lillie (Stark, *op. cit.*,
Jno. Houseman	pp. 308–313)
Saml. Hughes (Stark, *op. cit.*,	Joshu Lorring (*q.v.*)
pp. 125, 132, 134)	Saml. Lloyd (*q.v.*)
Elij (or Ely) Hoyl	Eph. Little
Will. Hunter (Stark, *op. cit.*, p. 132)	Jno. Lovel, Junr. (*q.v.*)
Edwd. Hutchinson (Stark,	Geo. Lush
op. cit., p. 132)	W^m. McAlpine (*q.v.*)
Robt Jarvis (*q.v.*)	

A published list of the confiscated estates of Boston loyalists has been
published (*Proc. of Mass. Hist. Soc.*, 2nd Ser., x, 162–185). It includes
several names not printed here and contains descriptions, location of the
property and names of the purchasers.

* James Anderson was probably the man of this name who commanded the
Loyal North British Volunteers (see p. 313.)

† Probably the William Campbell on p. 76.

‡ One of the merchants and others who presented an address to Governor
Hutchinson in 1774.

§ See p. 113.

‖ He escaped from Concord gaol, September 27, 1775, with Josiah Jones and
William Likely (*Amer. Archives*, Ser. IV, vol. iii, p. 1444).

¶ Of Pembroke, an "infamous Tory "—"stubborn, refractory and evasive."
(*Ib.*, p. 1378.)

THE LOYAL IRISH VOLUNTEERS

were formed on December 7, 1775, from Irish merchants in Boston and their adherents and were distinguished by a white cockade. The officers were : Captain, James Forrest (*q.v.*) ; First Lieutenants, William Granville Hoar and John Brandon* ; Second Lieutenants, John Ramage, Jonathan Stearns† and Ralph Cunningham (*New York Hist. Soc. Colls.*, 1883, p. 270). William Granville Hoar was a Philadelphia wine merchant, a spy and an interesting personality (A.O. 13/70). John Ramage was a miniature painter (Dunlap, *Hist. of Arts of Design*). A member of this corps was William Murray (*q.v.*)

THE LOYAL NORTH BRITISH VOLUNTEERS

were formed mainly from Scottish settlers in Boston, commanded by James Anderson, with David Black (*q.v.*) as Lieutenant. Among the members were George Beattie (*q.v.*), William Black (noted by David Black), Archibald Cunningham (*q.v.*), William McAlpine, the printer (*q.v.*), Patrick McMaster (*q.v.*), Andrew Ritchie (*q.v.*), and John Semple.‡ Charles Geddes, a witness to the claim of Andrew Ritchie, was also a member (A.O. 12/10, ff. 157-164). James Anderson was consignee and part owner of the ship *Concord* (Sabine, *op. cit.*).

This is said to have been the first volunteer company raised in America "in defence of the constitution." (See p. 34.)

Reference : *New York Hist. Soc. Colls.*, 1883, p. 254.

WENTWORTH'S VOLUNTEERS

This troop of Light Dragoons was formed in 1776 or 1777 and was composed of young gentlemen of education and of the first families and connections in America, mostly from Massachusetts, under the patronage and support of John Wentworth, Governor of New Hampshire.

A muster roll of October 16, 1777, shows 28 effective men and officers.§ The Captain-commandant was Major Daniel Murray (*q.v.*). Benjamin Whiting‖ was First Lieutenant and Elijah Williams¶ Second Lieutenant

* He went to Halifax with the refugees in March, 1776.

† He went to Halifax, Nova Scotia (see p. 40).

‡ John Semple died at Marlborough, Massachusetts, in 1793, aged 82 (Sabine, *op. cit.*).

§ At first it consisted of three officers and 80 non-commissioned officers and men (*Colls. of New Brunswick Hist. Soc.*, No. 5, p. 244.)

‖ Of Hillsborough County, New Hampshire, named in the Banishment Act of 1778. He died in 1779. (*Colls. of New Brunswick Hist. Soc.*, No. 5, p. 259.) (*Ib.*, p. 260.)

¶ One Elijah Williams was a lawyer of Keene, New Hampshire, and owner of land at Deerfield and Greenfield, Massachusetts, inherited from his uncle, Ebenezer Hensdale. A loyalist of this name was Captain in the King's American Dragoons from March, 1781.

(with Macdonough papers in A.O. 13/52). The distinguishing badge was red (*Scots. Mag.*, vol. 40, p. 91). The corps was disbanded in 1778 and Captain Murray and doubtless others joined the King's American Dragoons. (See p. 215). Eight members of the corps were the three brothers, Simeon, Stephen and Charles Jones (*q.v.*), Thomas Swan (*q.v.*), and Samuel Tarbell (*q.v.*), and three sons of John Murray (*q.v.*), Robert, John and probably Samuel.

LOYALISTS IN HARDWICK

Deacon James Fay, Jonathan Danforth, Abner Conant, Joseph Ruggles, junior, Israel Corkey and Jonathan Nye, all manifested disposition inimical to the rights and privileges of their countrymen and consequently it was resolved by the committee of correspondence to recommend that no commercial connection be had with them, that they be shunned and treated with contempt and neglect, and that they be confined to the town and ordered not to assemble together more than two, except at public worship and funerals (*Am. Archives*, Ser. IV, vol. III, pp. 59–60).

LOYALISTS OF TOWNSEND

David Halden, Seth Johnson, Joshua Smith, Reuben Tucker, Isaac Wallis.

(COPY)

" To Thomas Mayhew, Esq., one of the Justices of the Peace in the County of Plymouth :—

" I, the subscriber, clerk of the committee of correspondence, inspection and safety for the town of Plymouth, truly represent to you as a Justice of the Peace in the county aforesaid, that there is, in the opinion of said committee, sufficient reason to suspect that the following persons, viz., Edward Winslow and George Watson, Esquires, Captain Gideon White, John Watson, Benjamin Churchill, Captain Thomas Davis, Captain Barnabas Hedge, Isaac LeBaron, Samuel Hunt, Ichabod Shaw, John Kempton, John Kempton, Jr., Zaccheus Kempton, Benjamin Ryder, William LeBaron, Enoch Randall, William Cuffee, Jerry Connel, Richard Durfey, Lemuel Cobb, and James Doten, Jr., are inimical to the United States, and you are requested, upon this representation, to proceed immediately against the above-named persons, agreeably to an Act of said State passed the present session of the General Court, entitled, an Act for prescribing and establishing an oath of fidelity and allegiance.

" Per order of the Committee of Correspondence.

"ANDREW CROSWELL, Clerk.

"Plymouth, 11th February, 1778."

The above names appear in two warrants issued by the Committee of Correspondence in 1778.

Among the loyalists who are not represented by original memorials or claims, are Samuel and Robert Foster, of Kingston. The former, an ardent loyalist, was born in Plymouth, Massachusetts, a town which was destined to be his place of imprisonment and of his death in 1778, at the age of 70. Robert, his fourth son, was born in 1737 at Kingston and married in 1766 Elizabeth Bartlett, daughter of Joseph and Dorothy Wadsworth Bartlett and cousin of General Peleg Wadsworth. According to his own memorandum he was put into Plymouth gaol on October 21, 1776, and locked up close. In 1779 he fled to Nova Scotia and settled at Liverpool in that colony until 1791, when he returned to Kingston, in the hope and expectation of recovering his father's estate, only to find that it had been confiscated. Broken in mind and body he died in delirium on June 29 in the same year (Ex inform. Mrs. George B. Kingsbury).

OTHER LOYALISTS

WILLIAM BARRON, of Petersham, formerly an officer in the British army. He died at that place in 1784. His sons, William Amherst and Thomas, were educated at Harvard College, where the former became a tutor in Mathematics and Natural Philosophy.

WILLIAM BOLTWOOD, of Amherst, recanted (*Am. Archives*, Ser. IV, vol. iii, p. 145).

ELEAZAR BRADSHAW, of Waltham, declared inimical to America in October, 1775 (*Am. Archives*, Ser. IV, vol. iii, p. 937).

SETH CATLIN, of Hampshire County. He endeavoured to persuade the people to return to their allegiance to the Crown (*Am. MSS. in Roy. Inst.*, op. cit., iv, 42).

CAPTAIN JOSEPH CLEMENT, of Boston, settled in New Brunswick (Sabine, *op. cit.*).

RICHARD COURTNEY was a witness to the claim of Joseph Welsh, at Shelburne, Nova Scotia, in 1783 (A.O. 13/51).

LEMUEL COX, of Boston, suspected as a spy (*Am. Archives*, Ser. IV, vol. iii, p. 1402).

AMOS DOLE, a suspected Tory, of Shirley, who was disinherited by vote of a town meeting, January 1, 1776 (Diary of James Parker, transcribed by Mrs. E. S. Bolton, in *New Eng. Hist. & Gen. Reg.*, April, 1915, p. 125).

ROBERT LEWIS FOWLES was born in Boston and settled in Portsmouth, New Hampshire, as a printer (*Loyalists' Claims*, op. cit., pp. 312-3).

DR. SAMUEL GELSTON, of Nantucket, a determined loyalist who escaped from the custody of the messenger of the House of Representatives (*Am. Archives*, Ser. IV, vol. iv, pp. 1337-8, 1397-8, 1414, 1432, 1482).

MOSES GERRISH, of Newbury, was one of the Penobscot loyalists and the first permanent settler on Grand Manon, where he forestalled Colonel Jonathan Eddy, a rebel (*Acadiensis*, v., 170). A loyalist of this name graduated at Harvard College in 1762.

RUFUS GREENE (1707-77), silversmith, of Boston.

SOLOMON HOUGHTON, of Lancaster, is mentioned in A.O. 12/83, f. 2.

His real estate was appraised at £526 and personal at £215 15s., December 14, 1778 (Case 31183A, Records of Worcester).

JOHN HOWE, printer, Boston, went to New Brunswick (*Acadiensis*, viii, 250–7; Stark, *op. cit.*).

JOSIAH JONES and WILLIAM LIKELY escaped from Concord gaol, September 27, 1775 (*Am. Archives*, Ser. IV, vol. iii, p. 1444).

CHRISTOPHER LOVELL, cousin of Daniel and Shubel Lovell (below). These three are in *Am. Archives*, Ser. IV, vol. iv, pp. 1337, 1338.

DANIEL LOVELL, brother of Shubel.

SHUBEL LOVELL, of Barnstaple.

JOHN MILLER was a witness to the claim of Joseph Welsh, at Shelburne, Nova Scotia, in 1783 (A.O. 13/51).

SAMUEL MINOTT (1732–1803), silversmith, of Boston.

MOODY, clerk of King's Chapel, Boston, went to Nova Scotia (*Colls. of Nova Scotia Hist. Soc.*, xiii, 30).

JOSEPH MOORE, of Lancaster. His real estate was appraised at £41,280 and personal at £3,436, September 4, 1780 (Case 41440A, Records of Worcester).

DAVID PARKER, of Boston or Dedham, recanted (*Am. Archives*, Ser. IV, vol. iii, p. 1198).

BENJAMIN PHILIPS, member of the Ancient and Honourable Artillery Company of Massachusetts in 1755, died at Lincoln, Massachusetts, in May, 1792, aged 76 (*Roberts's Hist. of the Company*, ii, p. 75).

NATHANIEL PHILIPS, a native of Marshfield, was described as an " infamous Tory." He appears to have recanted (*Am. Archives*, Ser. IV, vol. iii, p. 1378).

MOSES PITCHER was a member of the Ancient and Honourable Artillery Company of Massachusetts from 1760. He died at Halifax, Nova Scotia, in 1817, aged 84 (Sabine, *op. cit.* and *Roberts's Hist. of the Company*, ii, p. 103).

JOHN PRICE, of Salem, a Tory of the first magnitude, whose schooner, *William*, was retained in November, 1775, and who went to Halifax, Nova Scotia (*Am. Archives*, Ser. IV, vol. iii, p. 1513).

WILLIAM PYNCHEON (1723–89), lawyer, of Salem, married a daughter of Mitchell Sewall, of that place (G. F. Dow, *Holyoke Diaries*, p. 78). He graduated at Harvard College in 1743.

ROBERT SEMPLE (Sabine, *op. cit.*). He was probably the brother of John Semple (see p. 313).

MARY TAILER (Taylor), widow, of Boston (*Amer. MSS. in R. Inst.*, *op. cit.*, ii, 329).

EDWARD WHITE, originally Le Blanc, had been taken with his parents from Acadia to Cambridge. At the outbreak of the Revolution he returned to Nova Scotia and settled at Oak Point and died in 1840 (W. F. Ganong, in *Acadiensis*, iii, 282).

JOB WILLIAMS, ringleader of a party which cut down the "liberty tree" in August, 1775 (*Am. Archives*, Ser. IV., vol. iii, p. 472).

JOHN WILLIAMS, of Hampshire County. He endeavoured to persuade the people to return to their allegiance to the Crown (*Am. MSS. in Roy. Inst., op. cit.*, iv, 42).

JOHN WILLIAMS, of Deerfield, who presented to the First Congregational Church at that place, the silver tankard given to him by the Directors of the Banks of the United States, North America and Pennsylvania in 1801 (E. Alfred Jones, *The Old Silver of the American Churches*, 1913, p. 137).

A list of loyalists is in Stark, *op. cit.*, p. 503; and other loyalists are included in the same book.

INDEX

Y

www.ingramcontent.com/pod-product-compliance
Lightning Source LLC
Chambersburg PA
CBHW060132280326
41932CB00012B/1492